Windows Server® 2008 R2
SECRETS

Windows Server® 2008 R2
SECRETS

Orin Thomas

John Wiley & Sons, Inc.

Windows Server® 2008 R2 Secrets

Published by
John Wiley & Sons, Inc.
10475 Crosspoint Boulevard
Indianapolis, IN 46256
www.wiley.com

Copyright © 2011 by Orin Thomas

Published by John Wiley & Sons, Inc., Indianapolis, Indiana

Published simultaneously in Canada

ISBN: 978-0-470-88658-8

978-1-118-19784-4 (ebk)

978-1-118-19785-1 (ebk)

978-1-118-19786-8 (ebk)

Manufactured in the United States of America

10 9 8 7 6 5 4 3 2 1

For general information on our other products and services, please contact our Customer Care Department within the United States at (877) 762-2974, outside the United States at (317) 572-3993 or fax (317) 572-4002.

Wiley also publishes its books in a variety of electronic formats and by print-on-demand. Not all content that is available in standard print versions of this book may appear or be packaged in all book formats. If you have purchased a version of this book that did not include media that is referenced by or accompanies a standard print version, you may request this media by visiting http://booksupport.wiley.com. For more information about Wiley products, visit us at www.wiley.com.

Library of Congress Control Number: 2011927297

About the Author

Orin Thomas is, among other things, a multiple MCITP, an MCT, a Microsoft MVP and a Microsoft vTSP. He has worked in IT for almost 20 years, starting on a university help desk, working his way up to Senior Systems Administrator for one of Australia's biggest companies. He has written more than 20 books on Microsoft products and technologies and regularly writes for *Windows IT Pro* magazine. He is the founder and convener of the Melbourne Security and Infrastructure Group and regularly presents at industry events including TechED and Microsoft Management Summit. His twitter address is @orinthomas.

About the Technical Editor

Don Thoreson has 20 years of experience in the IT field. For the last 13 years he has been a regional IT manager at a high tech company with offices around the globe. He currently leads a team responsible for all facets of IT operations including data center, network, and end user support functions. He created and runs the global IT group's PMO (project management office) executing projects worldwide. He earned a bachelor's degree in business from the University of New Hampshire's Whittermore School of Business and Economics.

Credits

Acknowledgments

This book wouldn't have been possible without the generous dedication and professionalism of all the people that worked behind the scenes. I'd like to thank Don Thoreson, Katherine Burt, Carol Long, Ginny Munroe, Debra Banninger, and Ashley Zurcher for their invaluable assistance in putting this book together.

Contents at a Glance

Contents

Read This First

The aim of this book is to teach you some things about Windows Server 2008 R2 that you don't already know. It isn't that this functionality is a hidden secret. It is just that there are a lot of things about Windows Server 2008 R2 that you won't know unless you obsess over TechNet documentation or product group blog posts. In my time presenting at conferences such as Microsoft Management Summit and TechED, I've often had people come up to me after sessions expressing surprise that a product they regularly use is capable of doing astonishing things they didn't know about. Even after writing several books on Windows Server 2008 and Windows Server 2008 R2, I'm still discovering cool things that the operating system can do.

This book isn't just about obscure or poorly documented features of Windows Server 2008 R2. Obscure features are usually obscure because no one needs to use them! My aim in writing this book is to cover the important roles and functionality of the operating system without spending time on foundational topics that someone who has worked as a system administrator would already know. I also discuss neat features and tricks that might surprise you. In writing this book, I've tried to explain what each important Windows Server 2008 R2 role does and how you can leverage it, assuming you are someone who has hung around server rooms for a couple of years, rather than someone who is new to the game and doesn't know the difference between DNS and DHCP.

Even as an experienced systems administrator, I believe you'll find the book useful, because Windows Server 2008 R2 is such a vast operating system that there are bound to be things that you don't know it can do. The product does so much that keeping abreast of it all is almost impossible. This book doesn't cover everything, but I've tried to include links at the end of the chapter to web pages where you can start drilling down deeper to learn more.

WHO THIS BOOK IS FOR

The type of people that I had in mind as I was writing this book are the types I see in the Windows Server 2008 R2 classes I teach and the TechED sessions that I present. They are systems administrators who have been in the job a couple of years, who know their way around operating systems such as Windows Server 2003, and who want to know what the Windows Server 2008 R2 does without getting bogged down in basic stuff they already know. The coverage is designed for someone who has the introductory theory down pat and wants to know what a specific Windows Server 2008 R2 role or feature does, and how it might be used in a real-world scenario.

With an audience of experienced administrators, there are, of course, topics that will be more familiar to you than others. Every administrator knows a part of the operating system inside out, and in some chapters, what might seem like a secret to some will appear as blindingly obvious to others. My hope is that even in these topics, the experienced administrator will find one or two nuggets of information that he didn't know was useful to solve a problem when working with Windows Server 2008 R2.

It is also fair to say that almost everything you can learn from this book can also be found in scattered TechNet articles and blog posts. Given that, it's reasonable to ask, "Why buy the book in the first place?" The benefit of the book is that all the information is nicely consolidated in one resource, rather than scattered about the Internet, where it would take you weeks, if not months, to track down. You've only got a finite number of hours on this world and the consolidation of knowledge in this book will save you from wasting those hours sifting search engines looking for nuggets of wisdom. It's also hard to come up with a search engine query to tell you about a role or feature you don't know about!

WHAT THIS BOOK COVERS

This book covers the technologies that are included out-of-the box with Windows Server 2008 R2. Although it's often used as the host operating system for more complicated products, such as Microsoft Exchange and SQL Server, Windows Server 2008 R2 can perform a lot of other roles that are equally important for the day-to-day running of your organization. Windows Server 2008 R2 is a workhorse operating system, and, if it is anything like other Microsoft server operating systems, you're still going to find instances of it running in server rooms and datacenters well into the next decade. With that in mind, it is useful to have a guide that covers the built-in roles and features and how they can be leveraged to accomplish your goals as a systems administrator.

HOW THIS BOOK IS STRUCTURED

In writing the book, I've tried to cover all the roles and features in Windows Server 2008 R2 in a comprehensive but not exhaustive way. I've provided links to appropriate documentation at the end of each chapter so that if you do need to drill down, you can quickly find the relevant TechNet articles and whitepapers.

The book is separated into seven parts, each of which contains two or more chapters.

▶ **Part I: Deployment and Administration Secrets:** This part deals with deploying Windows Server 2008 R2 and the toolkit you can use to manage the operating system.

 ▷ Chapter 1 includes choosing an edition of Windows Server 2008 R2, configuring deployment images, making the choice of physical or virtual deployment, and understanding deployment tools.

 ▷ Chapter 2 includes how to choose the right administration tool: Remote Desktop, PowerShell, Windows Remote Shell, Emergency Management Services, and Microsoft Management Consoles.

 ▷ Chapter 3 is about the Server Core installation option and covers common server core tasks such as domain join, IP address configuration, roles and features installation, registry modification, and server core configuration for Windows Update.

 ▷ Chapter 4 examines Active Directory deployment, sites, functional levels, DNS support, Read Only Domain Controllers, Active Directory Recycle Bin, and Flexible Single Master Operations roles.

 ▷ Chapter 5 includes Group Policy management strategies and tools.

 ▷ Chapter 6 explains useful strategies on user accounts, administrative delegation, group deployment strategies, and Fine-Grained Password Policies.

 ▷ Chapter 7 describes Active Directory Certificate Services, key archiving, template customization, certificate autoenrollment, and revocation.

- ▶ **Part II: Network Infrastructure and Security Secrets:** This part of the book deals with IP addressing, firewalls, network access protection, and domain isolation policies.
  - ▷ Chapter 8 explains how to leverage and secure DHCP, as well as IPv6 addressing and transition strategies.
  - ▷ Chapter 9 describes Windows Firewall, connection security rules, network access protection, and domain isolation policies.

- ▶ **Part III: Shared Folder and Data Protection Secrets:** This section deals with one of the most important roles of an IT infrastructure: the storage and protection of data.
  - ▷ Chapter 10 describes how you can use BranchCache, File System Resource Manager and Distributed File System to manage shared folders infrastructure.
  - ▷ Chapter 11 explains how to use encryption technologies, including EFS, BitLocker, and Active Directory Rights Management Services to protect the integrity of organizational data.
  - ▷ Chapter 12 includes data protection and recovery strategies, and how best to leverage Windows Server Backup and Volume Shadow Copies.

- ▶ **Part IV: Infrastructure Services:** This section deals with Windows Server 2008 R2 in its capacity to host infrastructure service roles such as Internet Information Services, Hyper-V, Update Management, and Clustering.
  - ▷ Chapter 13 includes information about the differences in IIS 7.5, including managing sites, application pools, the delegation of administrative privileges, and FTP.
  - ▷ Chapter 14 describes Hyper-V settings, dynamic memory, virtual machine snapshots, virtual hard disks, and technologies that allow you to perform physical to virtual migration.
  - ▷ Chapter 15 explains how to deploy and configure Windows Server Update Services, including how to use WSUS groups to optimize the update deployment process.
  - ▷ Chapter 16 details how to deploy highly available solutions through network load balancing and Windows failover clustering. The chapter also covers configuring Windows Server 2008 R2 to connect to iSCSI LANs and to function as an iSCSI target.

- **Part V: Remote Access Secrets:** This part explains how you can use Windows Server 2008 R2 to allow clients on remote networks, such as the Internet, access to internal network resources.

  - ▷ Chapter 17 describes presentation and application virtualization, which allow you to deploy applications to computers without installing them locally.

  - ▷ Chapter 18 explains how to deploy Remote Desktop Gateway, Virtual Private Networks, and DirectAccess to allow remote clients internal network access.

- **Part VI: Maintenance and Monitoring Secrets:** This section details strategies related to event log management, auditing, and performance monitoring on Windows Server 2008 R2.

  - ▷ Chapter 19 includes information on setting up advanced audit policies, event log forwarding, filtering, and views.

  - ▷ Chapter 20 explains the Windows Server 2008 R2 technologies for performance, reliability, and resource monitoring.

WHAT YOU NEED TO USE THIS BOOK

To get the most out of this book, you should have access to a copy of Windows Server 2008 R2 that you can play around with without your configuration experiments impacting other people. The best option is to set up some virtual machines so that you can try things out. If you completely destroy the installation, you can always roll it back to a previously functional configuration.

You can download an evaluation copy of Windows Server 2008 R2 from Microsoft's website. You can also use a non-activated copy of Windows Server 2008 R2 as the basis for your lab for between 60-120 days, depending on if you are using the original media or an evaluation copy. You can extend this evaluation period by running the `slmgr.vbs -rearm` command to reset the activation clock up to three times, allowing you a total of 240 days to evaluate the operating system before it runs in reduced functionality mode.

FEATURES AND ICONS USED IN THIS BOOK

▶ Watch for margin notes like this one that highlight some key piece of information or that discuss some poorly documented or hard to find technique or approach.

The following features and icons are used in this book to help draw your attention to some of the most important or useful information—some of the most valuable tips, insights, and advice—that can help you unlock the secrets of Windows Server 2008 R2.

NOTE The Note icon points out or expands on items of importance or interest.

CROSSREF Reference icon points to chapters where additional information can be found.

WARNING The Warning icon warns you about possible negative side effects or precautions you should take before making a change.

PART I

DEPLOYMENT AND ADMINISTRATION SECRETS

CHAPTER 1

Windows Server 2008 R2 Deployment Secrets

IN THIS CHAPTER

- ▶ Understanding the differences between Windows Server 2008 R2 editions
- ▶ Creating a deployment image
- ▶ Choosing virtual or physical deployment
- ▶ Minimizing deployment time
- ▶ Going further with System Center

As an experienced administrator, you've installed Windows Server operating systems more times than you can count. You didn't pick up this book of secrets to read a walkthrough telling you how to insert a DVD into an optical drive and then proceed with a screen-by-screen description of how to perform the install. At this stage of your career, you are likely to perform a traditional optical media OS installation only if you haven't had time to set up Windows Deployment Services or configure a custom image on a USB flash drive.

In this chapter, you learn the differences between the various editions of Windows Server 2008 R2, including the answer to the question, "What is the real difference between the Enterprise and Datacenter Editions, beyond the licensing cost?" And, you find out what the Foundation Edition is and the types of situations where it makes sense to deploy Windows Web Server 2008 R2.

Read this chapter and you will also learn how to set up a USB flash drive to deploy Windows Server 2008 R2 to individual servers far more quickly than using a DVD. You learn how to modify the install image to include drivers and updates, so you don't have to install them as part of post-installation configuration, and you find out how to switch on certain features, so you don't have to do it manually after the deployment is complete.

This chapter contains information you can use to get Windows Deployment Services not only broadcasting images in WIM format, but also how to add VHD images to the deployment server. You also learn about the types of situations where you'll save your organization time and money by using answer files and products like System Center Configuration Manager.

CHOOSING AN EDITION OF WINDOWS SERVER 2008 R2

You probably know that Windows Server 2008 R2 comes in a variety of flavors, but do you know the real differences between each edition? Though most systems administrators deal with only one or two editions of Windows Server 2008 R2 on a regular basis, there are a total of seven editions available. Of course the more editions there are, the greater the complexity in choosing the right one for a specific set of needs. When most administrators see the number of editions that are available, they throw up their hands and choose the Enterprise Edition. In general, choosing the Enterprise Edition of any Microsoft product is a reasonable strategy, because with it, you have access to all the available features and won't be caught unable to install some unusual role like Federation Services. The downside of this strategy is that occasionally you'll spend more on a server operating system license than might actually be necessary. In reality, understanding the differences between the editions comes down to the following factors:

▶ How many virtual licenses you want included with your OS so you can run separate instances on the same machine.

▶ Whether you need a specific feature or role, such as wanting to set up an enterprise root certificate authority.

▶ Whether you have a specific amount of RAM or number of processors that you want to be able to support.

NOTE All versions of Windows Server 2008 R2 run on only 64-bit platforms. If you've got a server that has a 32-bit processor, you won't be able to run Windows Server 2008 R2, though you will still be able to run Windows Server 2008.

There are seven editions of Windows Server 2008 R2. The differences between them are as follows:

▶ The Standard Edition comes with only one virtual license, does not support Active Directory Federation Services, and has caveats when it comes to hosting the Certificate Services role. There are connection limits on Network Policy and Access Services and Remote Desktop Services roles, and DFS is limited to one stand-alone DFS root. The Standard Edition supports up to four processor sockets and up to 32 GB of RAM.

▶ Enterprise comes with four virtual licenses, supports all server roles and features, and supports up to eight sockets and 2 TB of RAM. This version of Windows Server 2008 R2 is most commonly deployed in medium- to large-sized organizations.

▶ The Datacenter Edition differs from the Enterprise Edition only in that you get an unlimited number of virtual instances and can use up to 64 processor sockets. The Datacenter Edition is most often deployed in virtualization scenarios, as it allows you to run as many virtual machines as you want on the one bit of hardware.

▶ The Foundation Edition is available only from OEMs on single-socket servers and is limited to 8 GB of RAM. The key to understanding the Foundation Edition is that it is limited to 15 user accounts. You can have it as a Domain Controller (DC) or as a member server, but if there are more than 15 accounts in the domain or on the stand-alone system, the Foundation Edition will automatically shut down after a ten-day grace period. With that 15-account limitation and a few minor exceptions, the Foundation Edition supports the same features as the Standard Edition of Windows Server 2008 R2. You cannot install the Foundation Edition in the Server Core configuration.

▶ The Web Server Edition supports only the Web server and DNS server roles. It is cheaper to license than other editions, and you should deploy it if you need a server running IIS but nothing else. It supports up to 32 GB of RAM and four processor sockets.

▶ Sockets are different from cores, so if you have a collection of quad-core processors that are all the same, you can install four of these quad-core processors on a server that runs the Standard Edition of Windows Server 2008 R2.

> ▸ The HPC Server Edition is used in high-performance computing applications where it is necessary to run complex jobs against thousands of processing cores. The HPC Server version of Windows Server 2008 is often used with special applications for financial analysis. It supports up to 128 GB of RAM and four processor sockets.

> ▸ Windows Server 2008 R2 for Itanium Edition runs on the Itanium platform and supports only Itanium-specific server applications, like SQL Server 2008 R2.

> **NOTE** 2008 R2 will be Microsoft's last server release for the Itanium platform.

In general, it costs less to deploy a server running the Enterprise Edition than it does to deploy five servers running the Standard Edition. Therefore, it makes sense to choose the Enterprise Edition with its four virtual licenses rather than purchasing five servers running the Standard Edition. A lot of organizations don't actually need all the roles present in the Enterprise Edition of Server 2008 R2 and would be fine using the Standard Edition. A need for domain-based DFS is a common reason organizations choose to deploy the Enterprise Edition of Windows Server 2008 R2 over the the Standard Edition.

> **CROSSREF** You learn more about DFS in Chapter 10, "Secrets Behind Shared Folders."

DECIDING BETWEEN TYPES OF INSTALLATION

After you've worked out which edition of Windows Server 2008 R2 you want to deploy, you need to decide what type of installation you are going to perform. This involves figuring out:

> ▸ Do you want to perform a physical deployment or a virtual deployment?

> ▸ Do you want to install the full version or Server Core?

> ▸ Do you want to install to volume or VHD?

One of the big cost-cutting strategies organizations are pursuing today is server consolidation. That is, rather than deploying a collection of servers physically, the collection is deployed virtually. The virtual licensing options available in the Enterprise and Datacenter Editions of Windows Server 2008 R2 are an attempt to address this strategy. Rather than deploying an extra physical server, you might choose to deploy a hosted virtual server instead. It makes sense to take this approach, because, depending on which edition of Windows Server 2008 R2 you have chosen, you've already got virtual licenses available.

For example, you might have a branch office site where there is currently a file server, a domain controller, a Web server and a mail server. All hosts are running Windows Server 2003, and each of these servers are running on hardware that is approaching its end of life. As you know, "end of life" hardware is generally under-powered by present-day standards. If this underpowered hardware is adequate enough to service the requirements of the roles at the branch office site, it is likely that servicing those requirements will consume only a portion of the resources provided by modern hardware.

Rather than replace each server with one running Windows Server 2008 R2 on current hardware, it might make sense to consolidate all of these servers so that they run as virtual machines on one physical computer running the Enterprise Edition of Windows Server 2008 R2. Because you are using Windows Server 2008 R2, which includes four virtual licenses, you are already covered for the licenses of each of these virtual machines.

The main factor that determines whether a host can be deployed virtually is input/output requirements. In most branch office scenarios, computers hosting traditional roles, such as file server, domain controller, and DNS server, are rarely placed under sustained load. This makes them perfect candidates for virtualization.

Of course you can consolidate all these roles onto a single server without virtualizing each machine. For example, you might configure one server to function as a DC, Remote Desktop server, Web server, and file server rather than configuring four separate virtual machines on the same virtual host. Whether you consolidate the roles onto one computer or split them up into virtual machines depends on several administrative considerations, including:

> ▶ Placing each server role inside its own virtual machine simplifies the process of delegating administrative rights. For example, you might want to allow Kasia to manage all the permissions on file shares on a file server and adjust quotas but not give her any rights in Active Directory. While it is possible to do this when you have the file server and Active Directory roles installed on the same computer, the process is simpler when these roles are installed on separate computers. If you've already got the virtual licenses, why not run dedicated virtual machines, so that you lessen the chance that Kasia ends up with permissions that she shouldn't have.

▶ You are not only saving by not having to buy server hardware, but you're saving because you don't have to buy extra server licenses.

▶ The simpler the process, the less likely there is to be mistakes.

▶ Placing each server role inside its own virtual machine makes the process of migrating roles away from the host server easier. For instance, traffic may increase substantially to your virtualized file server. It takes substantially less effort to migrate file shares, quotas and permissions to a new host, if all you have to do is transfer a virtual machine, than it does if the file server role is co-located with the domain controller. You also have the possibility of performing a virtual to physical migration should the input/output requirements of the file server make virtually hosting the role impractical.

If you are in the process of upgrading to Windows Server 2008 R2 from Windows Server 2003, it is likely that you are going from hardware that is at least a couple of years old to hardware that is probably new. New hardware can usually deal with resource pressure that would cause bottlenecks on older hardware.

Deploying Server Core

▶ When you are considering where to deploy a server running Windows Server 2008 R2, take time to think about whether it might be better hosted virtually or whether it needs to be a physical deployment.

If you are like most administrators, you've heard about Server Core versions of Windows Server 2008 R2, but you probably haven't worked with them. If you haven't heard of Server Core, it is perhaps best described as Windows Server 2008 R2 command-line edition. You perform all the primary setup activities from the command line. After you've got the server set up, you can connect remotely using management consoles that are part of the Remote Server Administration Tools (RSAT).

> **CROSSREF** You learn more about Remote Server Administration Tools in Chapter 2, "The Windows Server 2008 R2 Administrator's Toolkit."

The advantage of a Server Core deployment is that computers running Server Core don't have all the extra components that a full version of Windows Server 2008 R2 has, and thus there are fewer components susceptible to vulnerabilities that require patching. For example, although you need to apply whatever updates are released for Internet Explorer to computers that run the full versions of Windows Server 2008 R2, you don't need to apply these updates to computers that run Server Core.

> **NOTE** The advantage of a Server Core deployment is that you spend a lot less time fussing with patches and worrying about downtime caused by reboots.

The disadvantage is that from the outset, you will have to spend more time mucking about in the command line configuring Server Core so that you can use the RSAT tools to manage the installation.

Another advantage of the version of Server Core that comes with Windows Server 2008 R2 is that it fully supports PowerShell. PowerShell wasn't fully supported in the Server Core version of Windows Server 2008 RTM, which meant that you had an operating system managed from the command line without having access to the most powerful command-line tool on the platform.

The main drawback of Server Core installations is that they don't support all the roles available on the full versions. Another drawback is that Server Core installations do not support server applications such as Exchange or SQL Server. The Enterprise Edition of Server Core supports the following roles:

- Active Directory Certificate Services
- Active Directory Domain Services
- Active Directory Lightweight Directory Services
- BranchCache Hosted Cache
- DHCP Server
- DNS Server
- File Services
- Hyper-V
- Media Services
- Print Services
- Web Services (IIS)

A Server Core installation running the Standard Edition of Windows Server 2008 R2 supports all these roles except BranchCache Hosted Cache. As with the full install, a Server Core installation of Windows Server 2008 R2 Standard Edition is also limited to one stand-alone DFS root. Server Core installations are not supported on Itanium or Foundation Editions of Windows Server 2008 R2.

CROSSREF You learn more about how to configure systems running Server Core in Chapter 3, "Server Core Secrets."

Installing to VHD

Usually, when you install an operating system, the installation routine writes a collection of files and folders across volumes on the hard-disk drive. If you booted the server up with Windows Preinstallation Environment (PE) and looked at the hard-disk drive, you'd see a collection of files and folders. Unlike previous versions of Windows Server, Windows Server 2008 R2 gives you the option of performing an installation to VHD file. The *VHD file* is a container that appears to the computer as a separate volume. When you have configured it correctly, you can format the VHD file, write files to it, and treat it exactly as any other volume on the hard disk. Because you can store multiple VHD files on a disk, you can configure Windows Server 2008 R2 to boot into different versions without having to repartition an existing hard-disk drive. If you install to VHD, boot up from Windows PE, and look at the hard disk, you'll see the VHD file and pretty much nothing else.

Installing to VHD makes your deployment of Windows Server 2008 R2 more portable. You are able to move the VHD file to another computer or even configure the VHD file as a differential disk, so that you can roll back any changes that occur if they cause a problem.

> **CROSSREF** You learn more about differential disks in Chapter 14, "Configuring Hyper-V Virtual Machines."

To prepare Windows Server 2008 R2 for an installation to VHD on a computer with an unformatted disk, perform the following steps:

1. Start the Windows Server 2008 R2 installation routine either by booting from DVD, USB, or PXE.

2. Select your language and click Next. Instead of selecting Install Now, click Repair Your Computer.

3. On the System Recovery Options dialog, click Next (you won't have any system to recover). When Windows fails to find a system to recover, click Cancel. Click Cancel again until you can see the System Recovery Options dialog, shown in Figure 1-1. Then click Command Prompt.

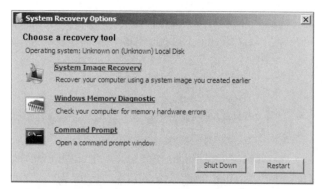

FIGURE 1-1: System Recovery Options

4. From the command prompt, type **diskpart.exe**. From within diskpart.exe, type the following commands:

```
select disk 0
create partition primary
format
assign
create vdisk file="c:\2008r2.vhd" maximum=X
select vdisk file="c:\2008r2.vhd"
attach vdisk
exit
```

> The value you put for the maximum size of the VHD should approximate the size of the volume on which you want to install Windows Server 2008 R2. You set this figure in megabytes. Server 2008 R2 needs about 15–20 GB of space for a normal installation.

5. From the command prompt, ensure that you are still in the X:\sources directory, and then type **Setup.exe**. This will restart the Windows Server 2008 R2 installation routine.

6. In the installation routine, with which you are no doubt familiar, answer the questions until you come to the screen where you are asked, "Where Do You Want to Install Windows?"

7. On the Where Do You Want to Install Windows dialog, select the volume that matches the size of the VHD file that you created.

> Click through the warning that indicates you are unable to install to this drive. The installation will continue from this point as normal.

As backups taken with the built-in Windows Server 2008 R2 backup utility are stored in VHD format, it is also possible to copy a backup across to a new volume, use BCDEDIT to modify the boot configuration, and boot directly to the backup as an alternative boot strategy. This enables you to perform full server recovery on the same hardware without wiping the original operating system.

CROSSREF You will learn how to configure Windows Server 2008 R2 to boot from a VHD file generated from a backup in Chapter 12, "Backup and Recovery."

OPTIMIZING YOUR DEPLOYMENT IMAGE

When you deploy Windows Server 2008 R2 for the first time, you will notice that it comes with no roles or features installed. There is a solid reason for this. When you start with no roles or features installed, it means that the only roles and features that will be installed in the future are the ones that you put there yourself. This all has to do with security. In the past several years, Internet worms propagated because a lot of administrators installed their Internet-facing servers in a default configuration. That default configuration came with a Web server and other roles and features installed and active—something that a lot of administrators didn't realize. The reason that many of these systems admins didn't patch their servers was that they simply didn't know that they were vulnerable. With Windows Server 2008 R2, an administrator has to actually install a feature like Internet Information Services explicitly. In theory, this means that administrators should be aware that any vulnerabilities that impact that feature need to be dealt with as soon as possible.

As good as it is from a security perspective that Windows Server 2008 R2 installs with no features or roles present, this creates a small challenge for administrators who need to regularly and rapidly deploy the operating system. For example, if you wanted to deploy all the pre-requisite software for a Windows Server 2008 R2 system that will function as a mailbox and client access server, you need to install a significant number of roles and features as well as configure several services. As you are aware, manually adding roles and features can take some time. You have to add the roles and then often reboot and log in again before the role is completely installed.

▶ Creating a deployment image where all necessary prerequisite roles and features are preconfigured automatically can save you a lot of time because you don't have to add those roles and features after the server first boots.

Managing Windows Server 2008 Images

In previous versions of Windows Server, such as Windows Server 2003, installation occurred through the extraction of relevant files from compressed archives (called CAB files). Rather than using compressed archives, Windows Server 2008 and Windows Server 2008 R2 use image files that are applied directly to the installation destination.

The Windows Server 2008 R2 image is located in the sources directory of the Windows Server 2008 R2 installation media. The image is stored in WIM format, and the operating system ships with tools that allow you to mount and edit images directly. Of course, before you are able to modify the image, you need to copy the image to a volume that has a read/write file system. You can't write changes back to the original DVD media, but you can write a revised image to a new DVD. The sources directory contains two image files that are of interest to administrators. These are as follows:

▶ **Install.wim:** This file contains the Windows Server 2008 R2 image. You modify a copy of this file when creating a custom image. You install this file on a Windows Deployment Services (WDS) server when you want to perform a network deployment of Windows Server 2008 R2.

▶ **Boot.wim:** This file contains information necessary to boot Windows Server 2008 R2. You install this file on a WDS server as a boot image, allowing the network installation process to prepare a computer for the deployment of Windows Server 2008 R2.

Using DISM to Manage Images

DISM.exe is a command-line tool included with Windows Server 2008 R2. DISM.exe allows you to modify a Windows Server 2008 R2 image whether that image is stored in WIM format or VHD format. You can use DISM.exe to turn on features, add drivers, and add software updates to the image. This process is sometimes referred to as an offline update to the image. Online updates to an image traditionally involve deploying the image, performing the updates on an active system, and then recapturing the updated system to a new image. An advantage of the WIM and VHD image formats is that they allow you to modify an image that you have created without having to go through the rigmarole of performing that modification on a live system.

If you obtain the installation media from Microsoft, TechNet, or MSDN, the install.wim image will allow the following installations:

▶ Windows Server 2008 R2 Standard

▶ Windows Server 2008 R2 Standard (Server Core)

▶ Windows Server 2008 R2 Enterprise

▶ Windows Server 2008 R2 Enterprise (Server Core)

▶ Windows Server 2008 R2 Datacenter

▶ Windows Server 2008 R2 Datacenter (Server Core)

▶ Windows Server 2008 R2 Web

▶ Windows Server 2008 R2 Web (Server Core)

> ▶ You need to have the boot.wim file installed on the WDS server even if you are deploying VHD images rather than WIM images. This file enables the computer to boot up over the network, just as it would if the file was stored locally.

As you'll already know, when you deploy Windows Server 2008 R2, you choose one of these options, and that's the version of the operating system that installs. When you decide to modify the image, you need to select which of these installations you are going to modify, even though they are all stored in the same image file.

To modify an image, you need to specify which installation you want to mount and then mount it in a temporary directory. Each installation image has a corresponding index number that you will need to reference when making modifications. With DISM, you make modifications to one installation at a time. For example, if you add a driver to the Enterprise Edition installation, it does not automatically add the driver to the Standard and Datacenter Editions installation. You can determine the image index number that corresponds to a particular installation by running the command:

```
dism.exe /get-wiminfo /wimfile:c:\images\install.wim
```

For example, on the normal Windows Server 2008 R2 installation media, the index number of the standard version of Enterprise Edition is 3. To mount the Enterprise Edition image so that you can make modifications in a directory called c:\ mount, issue the command:

```
dism.exe /mount-wim /wilmfile:c:\images\install.wim index:3
/mountdir:c:\mount
```

When you finish modifying the image, you will need to commit the image. *Committing the image* writes all the changes back to the install.wim file, which you can then add to your USB flash device, burn to a DVD or add to a WDS server so that you can deploy that image. To commit an image using DISM, issue the command:

```
dism.exe /unmount-wim /mountdir:c:\mount /commit
```

▶ If you don't want to commit the changes you made to the image, substitute the /commit switch for /discard.

▶ After you've committed an image, you'll need to remount it if you want to make any further changes as committed images are read only.

ADDING DRIVERS TO IMAGES

Once the image is mounted, you can use the DISM to add drivers to the image. For example, you could create a directory named c:\drivers and copy all of the driver files into that directory, placing each driver's files in its own separate folder. Once you've placed all the drivers into the directory, you can use DISM to recursively add all of these drivers to the image. To do this, issue the command:

```
Dism.exe /image:c:\mount /Add-Driver /driver:c:\drivers\ /Recurse
```

You may be aware that Windows 7 has better driver detection routines than Windows Server 2008 R2. Rather than attempting to locate each separate driver for a model of computer that you intend to have running Windows Server 2008 R2 and then adding them to the install image for a specific hardware configuration, you can do the following:

▶ Windows Server 2008 R2 can use the same drivers as the 64-bit editions of Windows 7.

1. Install a 64-bit version of Windows 7 on the hardware that you will use to host Windows Server 2008 R2.

2. Allow Windows 7 to connect to the Internet so it can detect and install all the drivers necessary for this hardware configuration.

3. Once all drivers have been installed, copy the contents of the `c:\windows\system32\driverstore` directory to a USB flash drive.

4. Use DISM.exe with the /add-driver and /recurse options to inject all these drivers into the mounted Windows Server 2008 R2 image.

When you use this modified image to install Windows Server 2008 R2, all necessary drivers for this hardware configuration will be present, and you won't have to spend time trying to figure out which unknown hardware device is missing its driver.

ENABLING FEATURES

You can use DISM.exe to enable features such as the DHCP server so you do not have to manually install the role or feature after installation completes. You can see a list of features that you can enable by using the command:

```
dism.exe /image:c:\mount /get-features /format:list
```

To enable a specific feature, use the /Enable-Feature option. For example, to ensure that the DNS server role and management tools are installed on a server during installation, rather than as a post-installation configuration step, issue the commands:

```
Dism.exe /image:c:\mount /Enable-Feature:DNS-Server-Full-Role
Dism.exe /image:c:\mount /Enable-Feature:DNS-Server-Tools
```

Each feature must be enabled separately. This means that if you want to enable the Web server role on a server during installation rather than doing it as a part of the post-installation configuration routine, you need to enable each specific Web server feature.

> **NOTE** All feature names are case sensitive.

ADDING UPDATES TO IMAGES

Every month Microsoft publishes new updates, some of which need to be deployed to computers running Windows Server 2008 R2. Something that you have to take into account when you are thinking about deployment is whether or not you want to include all the currently released updates in the deployment image or whether you want to have the server retrieve all necessary updates after the installation process has completed. Having the server retrieve all those updates and install them can substantially add to your deployment time.

> ▶ In fact, if you don't come up with a way to incorporate updates into your image, you'll eventually find that it takes longer to perform the post-installation update process than it takes to actually install the operating system in the first place!

You can use DISM.exe to add updates to a mounted image. To do this, copy all the updates that have the .MSU extension into the same folder. After all the updates are in the same folder, use DISM.exe with the /Add-Package switch. For example, to add all the updates in the c:\updates directory to the Windows Server 2008 R2 Enterprise Edition image mounted in the directory earlier, issue the command:

```
Dism.exe /image:c:\mount /add-package /packagepath:c:\updates\
```

All of the updates that are added to the image are applied automatically at the end of the installation routine. This is likely to add to the amount of time it takes for the installation routine to complete but uses less time than having each server download the updates from your WSUS server or Microsoft Update server and then install them. As updates are released each month, you can use this simple procedure to perform an offline update of your deployment image.

Unfortunately, you don't apply service packs to images in the same way that you apply updates. Because Windows Server 2008 and 2008 R2 use a different type of image than previous versions of Windows, you can no longer "slipstream" service packs. When the Windows Server 2008 R2 service pack becomes available, you should obtain an updated operating system image from Microsoft that includes the new service pack.

It is, of course, possible to build an updated image and then capture it using a utility such as ImageX.exe, but whether this is worth the effort when the updated image will be available for download is a decision that only you can make.

CROSSREF You learn more about managing updates in Chapter 15, "Patch Management with WSUS."

Applying a WIM to a VHD

You can use the ImageX.exe utility to apply a WIM image that you have prepared to a VHD file and then allow the computer to boot to that VHD file.

To create a VHD file and apply a prepared WIM file to the VHD, perform the following steps:

```
diskpart.exe
create vdisk file=c:\win2k8r2.vhd maximum=30000 type=fixed
select vdisk file=c:\win2k8r2.vhd
attach vdisk
create partition primary
assign letter=v
format quick label=vhd
exit
imagex.exe /apply c:\images\install.wim 3 v:\
diskpart.exe
select vdisk file=c:\win2k8r2.vhd
detach vdisk
exit
```

> ▶ Applying a WIM image to a VHD and then booting off the VHD gives you a quick method of testing whether your WIM image is correctly configured.

You can copy this VHD file across to another computer, as long as the volume on which you put the VHD has enough space. Ensure that the computer to which you are copying already boots and runs either Windows 7 Professional or Ultimate Editions or Windows Server 2008 R2. After the file has been copied, perform the following steps:

1. Run the following command, taking note of the CSLID that is displayed:

   ```
   Bcdedit.exe /copy {current} /d "2K8R2_VHD"
   ```

2. Run the following commands, substitute the CSLID, but keep the square brackets around the drive letter:

   ```
   bcdedit.exe /set {CSLID} device vhd=[c:]\2k8r2.vhd
   bcdedit.exe /set {CSLID} osdevice vhd=[c:]\2k8r2.vhd
   bcdedit.exe /set {CSLID} detecthal on
   ```

When you reboot, 2K8R2.VHD will be present as a boot item. If you want to copy the file across to a computer that does not have an existing boot environment, use diskpart.exe to configure the volume and then the BCDboot tool to create the boot configuration. BCDboot is located on the Windows PE media.

SERVICING VHD FILES WITH DISM.EXE

You can use the DISM.exe utility to service offline VHD files in the same way that you use the tool to service WIM images. Rather than using DISM.exe to mount the VHD file, you use the Diskpart utility to attach the file as a volume.

You can't perform an offline service on a VHD file when you are booted into the operating system that it hosts.

To mount the file c:\2008R2.vhd as a volume associated with the drive letter v, issue the following commands from an elevated command prompt:

```
Diskpart.exe
Select vdisk file=c:\2008r2.vhd
Attach vdisk
Assign letter=v
exit
```

After you've done this, you can use the DISM.exe commands that you learned earlier to service the image. For example, to recursively add drivers stored in the c:\drivers directory to the mounted image, issue the command:

```
Dism.exe /image:v:\ /add-driver /driver:c:\drivers /recurse
```

To add all updates in the c:\updates directory to an image, issue the command:

```
Dism.exe /image:v:\ /add-package /packagepath:c:\updates\
```

To enable a specific role or feature, use the /Enable-Feature option. For example, to enable the DNS server role and to install the DNS management console, issue the commands:

```
Dism.exe /image:V:\ /Enable-Feature:DNS-Server-Full-Role
Dism.exe /image:V:\ /Enable-Feature:DNS-Server-Tools
```

When you are finished servicing the VHD file, you need to detach the VHD to commit your changes. This is done by typing the following from an elevated command prompt:

```
Diskpart.exe
Select vdisk file=c:\2008r2.vhd
Detach vdisk
exit
```

MINIMIZING DEPLOYMENT TIME

Systems administrators are busy people. Although sitting in front of a computer watching a little grey bar go across a screen during the installation process might seem fun the first few times, there are probably better things that you can be doing. In this section, you learn about methods through which you can speed up deployment of Windows Server 2008 R2. These include:

- ▶ Creating a USB device to deploy Windows Server 2008 R2 directly
- ▶ Configuring Windows Deployment Services to deploy Windows Server 2008 R2 to more than one computer at a time

Deploying from a USB Flash Drive

USB flash devices generally have quicker read performance than optical media. This means that performing a direct deployment from a USB flash drive is the quickest method of getting Windows Server 2008 R2 onto a server. With USB 3.0 becoming more prevalent, the speed benefit of deploying operating systems using this method will only increase. As USB flash drives are writable media, you can make modifications to the install.wim image, such as injecting drivers or updates, without having to burn a new installation DVD.

The drawback to using USB flash drives as deployment devices is that you need to muck around with BIOS settings on each server to ensure that it will boot from the USB flash drive. Also, you need to go through the steps of preparing each USB flash drive and ensuring that the answer files and WIM images are kept up-to-date, if you are using more than one. If you are regularly performing bulk deployments of server operating systems, you may prefer to go with Windows Deployment Services (WDS).

To prepare a USB flash drive so that you can use it to deploy Windows Server 2008 R2, perform the following general steps:

1. Open an elevated command prompt on a computer running Windows 7 or Windows Server 2008 R2.

2. Enter the command **Diskpart** and then **list disk**. Determine which of the connected disks represents the USB flash drive.

3. From the Diskpart prompt, issue the command **select disk X**, where X is the number associated with the USB flash drive.

▶ You can also place an unattended installation file on a USB stick and update that as necessary, allowing rapid installation to occur without the necessity of walking through the installation wizard.

4. Issue the following commands:

```
clean
create partition primary
select partition 1
active
format fs=fat32
assign
exit
```

5. After the USB flash drive is prepared, copy the entire contents of the Windows Server 2008 R2 installation DVD across to the device. If you have created a custom WIM image, replace the custom install.wim file with the one in the sources directory on the USB flash drive. If you have an answer file, place it in the root directory of the volume on the USB flash drive.

Configuring Windows Deployment Services

Windows Deployment Services (WDS) is a service included in Windows Server 2008 and 2008 R2 that enables you to perform multicast deployments of operating system images. WDS in 2008 R2 can be configured to not only deploy images in the standard WIM format but also to deploy operating system images in VHD format. You can add only VHD images to WDS using the command-line tools, and you must configure a special unattended installation file for this type of deployment to work.

PREPARING THE WDS SERVER

There are several things that you need to do when preparing a server that is running WDS. These include the following:

▶ WDS requires that Active Directory, DNS, and DHCP be configured and working on your network. These roles don't have to be on the server hosting WDS, but the server hosting WDS should be on a member server in a domain where these role services work.

▶ You shouldn't use the system volume to host your WDS images. As you know, bad things happen when your system volume fills up.

▶ If you've co-located the WDS role and the DHCP role on the same server, ensure that you've configured WDS to listen on another port. You can do this on the DHCP tab of the WDS server's properties as shown in Figure 1-2.

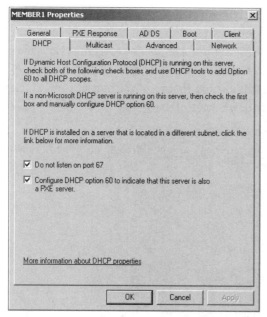

FIGURE 1-2: Configure the DHCP tab if DHCP and WDS are on the same server.

▶ In the PXE Response tab of the WDS server's properties, configure an appropriate response policy. You can configure WDS to respond to any computers that PXE boot, to known computers only, or to both known and unknown computers, but manual administrator approval is required for unknown computers. WDS knows a computer if you have pre-staged an account for that computer in Active Directory and associated that pre-staged account with the GUID of the network adapter. You can pre-stage an account using the WDSUTIL.exe utility from the command prompt. For example, to pre-stage a computer account named SERVER42 with the network card GUID AABBCCDDEE112233445566778899AABB, issue the following command from an elevated command prompt:

```
WDSUTIL.exe /Add-Device /Device:SERVER42 /ID:
AABBCCDDEE112233445566778899AABB
```

▶ On the Boot tab of the WDS server's properties, configure the level of interaction you require from the client. You can choose between having to press the F12 key to continue the PXE boot, always perform the PXE boot, or continue the PXE boot unless interrupted by the ESC key. You can specify the default boot images for each architecture. You can select only from boot images that you've already added to WDS.

▶ In the case of Server 2008 R2, unless you are using IA64, it is almost always going to be x64.

▶ On the Multicast tab of the WDS server's properties, you can configure whether or not you want to allow separate transfer streams. If you don't do this, the transmission will proceed at the speed of the slowest connection. You should select the Separate clients into the three sessions (slow, medium, fast) option as shown in Figure 1-3. This ensures that your transfer occurs as quickly as possible and isn't slowed down if one of the servers has a flakey connection.

▶ Add a boot image by right-clicking on the Boot Images node and then clicking on Add Boot Image. Browse to the boot.wim file that you will add to WDS.

▶ The default location of the boot .wim file is in the sources directory on the Windows Server 2008 R2 installation media.

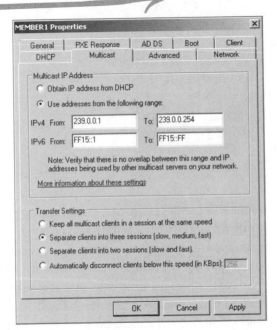

FIGURE 1-3: Configure transfer settings to optimize deployment speed.

DEPLOYING WIM IMAGES USING WDS

After you configure a WIM image so that it meets your requirements, you can add it to the WDS server. Once the WIM image is added to the WDS server, you can deploy that WIM image to clients that PXE boot. If you want to later modify the WIM image, you should remove the version of it that you've added to the WDS server and then re-add the updated WIM to WDS.

To add a Windows Server 2008 R2 image to WDS, perform the following general steps:

1. Open the Windows Deployment Services console.

2. Right-click on the Install Images node, and then click Add Image Group. Provide an appropriate name for the image group.

3. Right-click on the newly created image group, and then click Add Install Image. Navigate to the install.wim file that you have prepared and then click Next. Windows provides you with a list of the installations that are available in the image. Select the installations that you want to add to the WDS server, and then click Next twice. When the image is added, click Finish.

After the image has been added, you can set up a multicast transmission so that clients that perform a PXE boot are able to install the image. To configure WDS to deploy an operating system image in WIM format, perform the following general steps:

1. Open the Windows Deployment Services console.

2. Right-click the Multicast Transmission node, and then click the Create Multicast Transmission item. Provide a transmission name.

3. Select the image group and the image that you wish to deploy, and then click Next.

4. Choose between Auto-Cast and Scheduled-Cast. Choose a Scheduled-Cast if you want to configure WDS to wait for a certain number of clients to request the image or for deployment to start at a particular time.

5. After you've configured the multicast deployment, PXE boot your server hardware and allow the deployment to commence.

▶ An Auto-Cast allows WDS to transmit an image as soon as a client requests it. If another client wants the same image, it is joined to the transmission.

ADDING VHD IMAGES USING WDSUTIL

You can use WDS to deploy VHD images to clients. When you do this, a VHD file is transferred from the WDS server to the target server, and the server is then configured to boot off that VHD image. To configure WDS to deploy an operating system image in VHD format, perform the following general steps:

1. Ensure that the WDS server is configured with at least one boot image. Usually, this is the boot.wim file that you copied across from the Windows Server 2008 R2 installation media.

2. Open an elevated command prompt.

3. Create a separate image group for the WDS images. You can perform this action from the WDSUTIL.exe command-line utility. For example, to create an image group named VHD_Deployment, issue the command:

```
WDSUTIL.exe /Add-ImageGroup /ImageGroup:"VHD_Deployment"
```

4. To add the VHD image to the WDS server, you also use the WDSUTIL.exe utility. For example, to add the VHD image c:\2008R2.vhd to the image group named VHD_Deployment, issue the command:

```
WDSUTIL.exe /verbose /progress /Add-Image /ImageFile:"C:\2008R2.vhd"
/ImageType:Install /ImageGroup:"VHD_Deployment"
```

Once the VHD image is added to the server, you will need to create a special unattend.xml file that will configure the installation procedure to use the VHD file. You then need to associate this unattend.xml file with a pre-staged client. You can find an example unattend.xml file in the TechNet Article "Deploying Virtual Hard Disk Images," the address of which is listed in the Additional Sources section at the end of this chapter.

Using Answer Files

Answer files allow you to automate parts of the installation process, such as performing a domain join, selecting installation features, and partitioning the server. When the installation routine starts, it performs a quick check to locate whether an answer file is present. Although you can put the answer file on the volume on which you are going to install Windows Server 2008 R2, it is generally easier to put it on a USB stick. You can also place answer files on the WDS server, as shown in Figure 1-4. Answer files on the WDS server are done on a per-architecture basis. With WDS, there is also one answer file per architecture ($\times 86$, $\times 64$, IA64). This means that if you want to deploy different server builds that require different answer files, you'll need to come up with some way to swap those answer files on the server level. If you are using System Center Configuration Manager (SCCM), you are able to configure individual deployments and associate them with specific answer files.

Windows Server 2008 R2 answer files are stored in XML format. Although it is possible to create these files in Notepad, you should really use the Windows System Image Manager (SIM), a tool included as part of the Windows Automated Installation Kit (WAIK), to generate these files. To make this even more complicated, the easiest way to obtain the WAIK is to download Microsoft Deployment Toolkit (MDT) 2010 or later.

▶ Just so things are clear, you obtain MDT 2010 to get WAIK, which allows you to build Windows Server 2008 R2 answer files using Windows SIM.

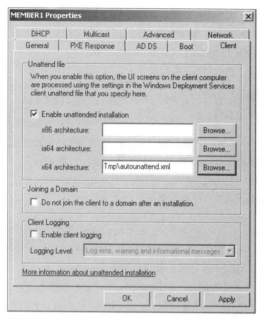

FIGURE 1-4: Configure unattended installation files in WDS.

There are several reasons why you should use Windows SIM rather than Notepad to create your Windows Server 2008 R2 answer files. These include:

▶ The answer file XML syntax is complicated, and you are likely to mess something up if you do it manually. There are better uses of your time than trying to figure out where you made a syntax error in an XML file.

▶ Windows SIM is designed to create these files, and you'll probably find out about automatic configuration options that you weren't aware of when you use the tool.

▶ Windows SIM generates a catalog file based on the image that you are importing. This means that you will only be able to configure settings that are relevant to the image for which you are creating the answer file.

▶ Windows SIM allows you to validate your answer file, which will go some way toward ensuring that the installation file you've created will work.

To create an answer file, perform the following general steps:

1. Open Windows System Image Manager.

2. Click New Answer File. When asked if you want to open a Windows image file, click Yes. Navigate to the install.wim file. Select the image for which you want to create an answer file. Most of the time this will be install.wim.

3. Click Yes when prompted to create a catalog file. This step takes several minutes.

4. Right-click on a component and then click on Add Setting to Pass. Press **F1** to learn more about the settings available for a specific component.

5. When you have finished configuring all necessary components, click on the Validate Answer File to perform a check and then save the answer file as autounattend.xml. This is the file name that the Windows setup routine auto-matically looks for when you perform an installation.

One could write a whole book detailing all the possible settings to configure for an unattended installation file. Finding all the settings is primarily a matter of navigating through each of the items in the Windows Image section and configuring an appropriate setting. Figure 1-5 shows an answer file configuration where the DHCP server and tools will automatically be installed. This unattended installation file must be located under the folder you configured for WDS.

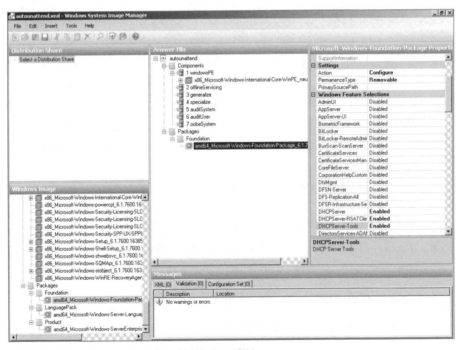

FIGURE 1-5: Configure answer file with Windows SIM.

ACTIVATING WINDOWS

Part of getting deployment right is ensuring that the Windows Product Activation process occurs smoothly. *Product activation* is a process by which a Windows Product Key and a hardware identification are registered with Microsoft. Product activation generally occurs over the Internet, but it is also possible to perform product activation over the phone. The drawback to performing product activation over the phone is that it can take a long time, and, if you make an error, you need to start over again. Systems administrators only perform product activation over the phone if their computers don't directly connect to the Internet. If you have more than one server that isn't connected to the Internet, you should investigate performing activation using the Volume Activation Management Tool, which you will learn about later in this chapter.

Windows product activation must usually occur within 30 days of completing the installation of Windows Server 2008 R2. If activation has not occurred within this 30-day period, Windows Server 2008 R2 enters reduced functionality mode. During reduced functionality mode, the operating system continually prompts you to perform activation. The functionality of services, applications, and remote administration are not impacted in reduced functionality mode. You can manually rearm a computer's activation clock three times to stave off reduced functionality mode. Each reset gives you an additional 30 days of use before you must perform activation.

To rearm a computer's activation clock, issue the command:

```
slmgr.vbs -rearm
```

Even after you've activated a computer, there are certain circumstances where activation must be performed again. Reactivation is usually triggered if you change a substantial number of hardware components on the server, such as changing the server's motherboard and the amount of RAM it supports. When reactivation is triggered in this manner, you have three days for reactivation to complete successfully before the server enters reduced functionality mode.

NOTE You can't rearm a computer after it has been activated.

Purchasing Multiple Activation Keys

▶ You cannot recover a MAK once that activation has been consumed.

A Multiple Activation Key (MAK) is a special key issued by Microsoft that allows you to perform a specific number of activations. For example, you might purchase a MAK from Microsoft that allows you to perform 50 activations. You can use this key to activate 50 different computers, but you will not be able to use this key to activate a 51st computer. For example, you build a new server, install Windows Server 2008 R2 on it, and activate it using a MAK. The MAK allows you 25 activations, and you've already used 24, so the number of activations against the MAK comes to 25. Two days later, that same server mysteriously falls off the roof of your building and lands six floors below in a dumpster. Even if you replaced the server with identical hardware and gave it the same name, you would still need to obtain a new key, because once an activation is consumed, you can't reclaim it.

You can perform activation with a MAK using two different methods. The method you choose depends on whether the servers that you want to activate are connected to the Internet or on an isolated network.

- ▶ **MAK Independent Activation:** MAK independent activation works the same way as activating with a retail key. The server either connects through the Internet to Microsoft's servers, or you perform activation over the phone.

- ▶ **MAK Proxy Activation:** MAK proxy activation allows you to collect activations from multiple computers, performing them all at once. For example, you might have a number of servers and clients on an isolated network but not enough to meet the threshold for using KMS. You could use MAK proxy activation to activate all these computers at once rather than activating them individually. MAK proxy activation requires that you use the Volume Activation Management Tool (VAMT).

Using the Volume Activation Management Tool

You use the *Volume Activation Management Tool (VAMT)* to centralize activation requests from multiple servers and then allow them to be collectively sent to Microsoft. When the VAMT communicates with Microsoft, it collects activation confirmation identifiers, which can then be distributed back to servers seeking to activate. An advantage of using the VAMT is that it stores these confirmation identifiers in a database. This allows clients to reactivate in the event that you need to rebuild them without consuming additional MAK activations.

To perform MAK proxy activation, perform the following general steps:

1. Install the VAMT on a computer on the isolated network.

2. Create a computer group and use the VAMT to discover all computers on the isolated network.

3. Configure VAMT with the MAK. Right-click the computer group and select the MAK Proxy Activate option. Make sure that neither the Get Confirmation ID nor Apply Confirmation ID checkboxes are enabled.

4. Save the collection file.

5. Install the VAMT on a computer that is able to connect to the Internet. Transfer the collection file from the computer on the isolated network to this computer, and then import the collection file.

6. Right-click on the computer group and then select MAK Proxy Activate. Make sure that the Get Confirmation ID from Microsoft option is selected but that Install MAK and Apply Confirmation ID and Activate are not selected.

7. After the VAMT on the connected computer has obtained the Confirmation IDs from Microsoft, export the collection.

8. Save a separate copy of this file, as you can use it to reactivate these computers in the event that you need to rebuild them.

9. Import the file to the computer running VAMT on the isolated network. Right-click the computer group and select MAK Proxy Activate. Ensure that the Apply Confirmation ID and Activate option is selected but that both Get Confirmation ID from Microsoft and Install MAK are not selected.

You can also use the VAMT to automatically determine which computers on your network haven't been activated, install a MAK on those computers, and force activation.

Activating with Key Management Services

Key Management Services (KMS) allows a computer to function as a local activation server. Rather than having each server contact Microsoft's servers on the Internet for activation, each of your servers performs activation against the KMS server. Clients are able to locate the KMS server through DNS, or you can configure clients to use the KMS server using the VAMT. Although you can configure computers that run Windows Vista and Windows 7 to function as KMS servers, these computers cannot function as

▶ Using the VAMT can save you from having to type the same MAK into each computer separately, enabling you to perform the task of populating computers with keys centrally.

KMS servers for computers running Windows Server operating systems. You should keep the following in mind when considering KMS:

▶ You can use KMS only if you have five servers or twenty-five clients.

▶ You configure KMS by adding a specific KMS key to a server and then performing activation. After activation is completed, the computer functions as a KMS server. You should use the telephone method to activate KMS on an isolated network.

▶ You can install the same KMS key on up to six computers, and each KMS server can be reactivated up to nine times, if necessary.

▶ Computers that activate against a local KMS server need to reconnect with that server every 180 days. If the KMS server cannot be contacted within a 180-day period, the computer enters reduced functionality mode.

▶ The KMS server does not need to contact Microsoft's servers unless a change in the hardware configuration of the KMS server itself triggers reactivation. This means that KMS is a good solution for isolated networks.

> **NOTE** Although answer files and WDS can minimize the amount of time it takes to deploy Windows Server 2008 R2, with Microsoft's System Center Configuration Manager, you can go further and fully automate the deployment process. Not only can you configure separate answer files for different deployment types, but you can also incorporate the deployment server applications, such as Exchange Server 2010 or SQL Server 2008 R2. If you want to get to the stage where you can fully automate the deployment of a new Exchange server, you should investigate System Center Configuration Manager. You can also configure the deployment of virtual machines using System Center Virtual Machine Manager. Virtual Machine Manager enables you to optimize the process of deploying to virtual hosts.

SUMMARY

There are seven editions of Windows Server 2008 R2. The Enterprise Edition supports all features and comes with four virtual licenses, and the Datacenter Edition provides unlimited virtual licenses. You can install Windows Server 2008 R2 so that the entire installation is held in a single VHD container. This simplifies the process of multiple boots and also simplifies physical to virtual migrations. Using DISM.exe, you can configure a Windows Server 2008 R2 installation image with extra drivers. You can also use DISM.exe to automatically install Windows Server 2008 R2 roles and features and install software updates during the installation process. You can configure a USB flash drive with the installation files so that you can perform a quicker deployment of a custom image than you could if you were using a DVD or WDS. WDS allows you to deploy Windows Server 2008 R2 to multiple computers at the same time, either by deploying WIM images or by deploying images in VHD format. Unattended installation files are generated by Windows SIM and allow portions of the installation process to be automated. You can use KMS to provide an activation server on your local network rather than having computers activate against Microsoft's servers on the Internet.

Additional Sources

If you are interested in finding out more about the topics covered in this chapter, consult the following online resources:

Windows Server 2008 R2 Editions

`http://www.microsoft.com/windowsserver2008/en/us/editions.aspx`

Creating Virtual Machines from a Template

`http://technet.microsoft.com/en-us/library/cc764306.aspx`

Deploying Virtual Hard Disk Images

`http://technet.microsoft.com/en-us/library/dd363560(WS.10).aspx`

Planning Volume Activation

`http://technet.microsoft.com/en-us/library/dd996589.aspx`

Zero Touch, High-Volume Deployment

`http://technet.microsoft.com/en-us/library/dd919178(WS.10).aspx`

CHAPTER 2

The Windows Server 2008 R2 Administrator's Toolkit

IN THIS CHAPTER

▶ **Using Remote Desktop**

▶ **Administering through Management Consoles**

▶ **Remoting with Windows PowerShell**

▶ **Resorting to Emergency Management Services**

Unless something has gone catastrophically wrong, you probably don't spend much time in the server room. Why would you want to? Server rooms tend to be loud places with bad furniture and worse lighting. It isn't as though you need to go down to the server room each morning to cycle the backup tapes. Backup is increasingly moving to disk-based devices or the SAN. While server rooms can be a nice place to visit on a hot day, as a systems administrator you probably perform most of your daily tasks from a cubicle that isn't on the same floor or even in the same building as the servers you manage. This chapter is about remotely administering Windows Server 2008 R2.

Chances are, many of the servers that you are responsible for managing are hosted as virtual machines and do not have a physical existence other than as data stored on magnetic, hard-disk drives. As you don't directly interface with them, virtual machines are almost entirely managed through remote administration techniques. So, not only is remote administration useful because you don't spend as much time in the server room, but it is important because most of the infrastructure that you are responsible for managing is being transitioned to a virtual environment.

You can use a variety of different remote administration tools to manage Windows Server 2008 R2. You might already be familiar with some of these tools, such as Remote Desktop. Others you might not have heard of, such as Emergency Management Services. The available tools can be useful for some types of tasks and next to useless for others. In this chapter, you learn about the tools that can save you time when you need to perform specific remote administration tasks against computers running Windows Server 2008 R2.

CHOOSING THE RIGHT REMOTE ADMINISTRATION TOOL

An important part of systems administration is picking the right tool for the job. You wouldn't use a hammer to cut a piece of wood and you wouldn't use a screwdriver to drive in a nail. A great systems administrator always tries to use the tool that enables him to complete the job in the simplest, most straightforward, and least time-consuming manner. When it comes to administering Windows Server 2008 R2, the tool you will often use is Remote Desktop. This tool provides a very similar desktop experience to the one that you would get if you were sitting in front of the computer and logged on directly. Although Remote Desktop is the most commonly used tool, there may be other situations where another remote administration tool is more appropriate. Consider the following situations:

- ▶ You want to gracefully shut down a server that has a failed network card and graphics adapter.
- ▶ You want to check the logs of a server that has frozen with a STOP error.
- ▶ You want to run the same Windows PowerShell script on a large number of servers without logging on to each one.
- ▶ You want to check the status of the DNS service on 15 different servers at the same time.

In some cases, you can't perform these tasks using Remote Desktop. In other cases, you can use Remote Desktop, but doing so takes significantly longer than using a different tool, such as a custom management console or Windows PowerShell remoting. In the following pages, you'll learn what you can accomplish with each tool and where each tool has advantages over other tools in your kit.

REMOTE DESKTOP

Remote Desktop is the tool that most administrators use to perform general management tasks on Windows Server 2008 R2. Remote Desktop has two components, the Remote Desktop client that runs on your local computer or management workstation, and the Remote Desktop server that is present on the computer you want to manage running Windows Server 2008 R2. All versions of Windows Vista, Windows 7, Windows Server 2008, and Windows Server 2008 R2 include the Remote Desktop client.

The Remote Desktop server component is also present, though not enabled, on each of these operating systems. Enabling Remote Desktop is a simple operation. You just need to make sure that you've enabled it before you attempt to make a connection to the server. Murphy's Law dictates that you'll only remember that you haven't enabled the Remote Desktop option after you've deployed the server somewhere rather distant from your cubicle. It is even more likely that you'll have forgotten to enable Remote Desktop if your server room is located somewhere that you can only get to by walking through adverse environmental conditions.

As an administrative tool, Remote Desktop has the following advantages:

▶ It gives you the experience of being directly logged on to the server that you are managing. You can run multiple consoles locally and get many different tasks done in the one session.

▶ You don't need to add any services. You just need to enable Remote Desktop on the computer running Windows Server 2008 R2, and you can manage it remotely.

▶ Remote Desktop works through firewalls as long as the appropriate ports are open, or you have configured a Remote Desktop gateway.

▶ It is simple to make Remote Desktop connections to stand-alone servers or servers in untrusted forests, as long as you have appropriate credentials on the target server.

Although Remote Desktop is useful, as an administrative tool it does have some disadvantages. These are as follows:

▶ When you use Remote Desktop, you can only interact with one computer at a time. If you want to interact with two servers, you need two Remote Desktop sessions. If you want to run a command against ten servers, you'll need to run the command in ten separate Remote Desktop sessions.

▶ You can have only two concurrent Remote Desktop administrator connections to a server running Windows Server 2008 R2.

▶ Remote Desktop doesn't work well over intermittent or lagged connections without proper tuning.

Defining Remote Desktop Client Settings

You can launch the Remote Desktop client in a few ways: by running Remote Desktop Connection from the Start menu, by using the Remote Desktops tool, or by using the mstsc.exe command-line utility. The differences between these are as follows:

▶ **Remote Desktop Connection:** Enables you to create and save connections with specific properties. You can configure how many colors to display, set the height and width of the connection window, optimize the amount of information displayed to conserve bandwidth, and connect local devices to the Remote Desktop session. You can also specify a Remote Desktop gateway if necessary. Remote Desktop Connection is shown in Figure 2-1.

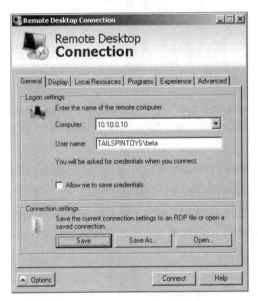

FIGURE 2-1: Remote Desktop Connection

▶ **Remote Desktops:** A remote server administration tool (RSAT) that enables you to configure connection shortcuts to multiple servers. This includes the size of the connection window. The advantage of this tool is that it gives you a single console where you can quickly connect to multiple computers. The disadvantage of the tool is that it doesn't enable you to do much in the way of optimizing performance. The Remote Desktops tool is shown in Figure 2-2.

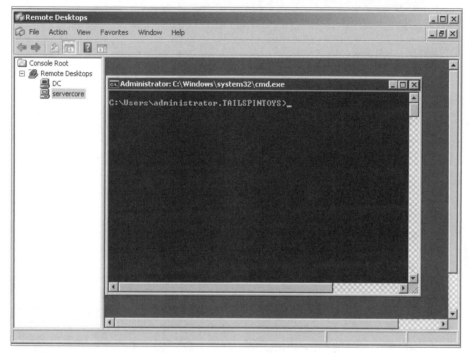

FIGURE 2-2: Remote Desktops RSAT tool

▶ **MSTSC.exe:** This is the command-line version of the Remote Desktop Connection client. Many administrators configure batch files that call mstsc.exe with specific options rather than saving Remote Desktop shortcuts. To force an administrative connection to server SVR1 that is 800 pixels wide and 600 pixels high, use the command:

```
Mstsc.exe /v:svr1 /admin /h:600 /w:800
```

When you connect to a computer running Windows Server 2008 R2, you may encounter the dialog box shown in Figure 2-3. The purpose of this dialog box is to warn you that the identity certificate for the server you are connecting to is not issued by a trusted source. By default, each computer running Windows Server 2008

R2 creates its own identity certificate. You can choose the option to "View and then Install" the certificate or you can choose the option "not to be warned" if you simply want to ignore the warning. A long-term solution is to configure certificate services so that the computer presents a certificate issued by a trusted certificate authority.

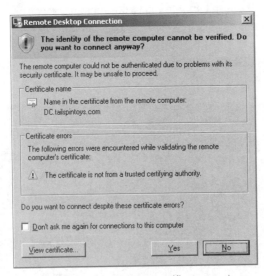

FIGURE 2-3: Remote Desktop certificate warning

NOTE If you want to force an administrator connection from the console, you need to enter the admin switch after the server address. Using this option is useful when you want to make an administrative connection to a server that is also used as a Remote Desktop Services server, and you don't want to consume a Remote Desktop Services Client Access License.

If you connect to the server, and there are already two other administrators connected, you might get the message shown in Figure 2-4. You have the option to trigger the logoff of one of the users. When you try to force the currently logged on user to log off, he or she has 30 seconds to decline your request to connect before being logged off forcibly. Generally, it is a good idea to contact the administrator before forcibly logging him off as he may be attempting to do something important and might not be happy about your interruption.

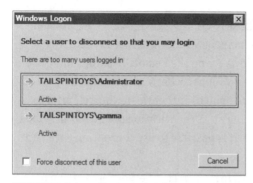

FIGURE 2-4: Logoff other administrator message

Configuring Remote Desktop

The Remote Desktop server component is not enabled automatically on computers running Windows Server 2008 R2. To enable it, you need to view the computer's System Properties windows (open Start Menu, right-click Computer, and choose Properties), and then click Remote Settings. You then choose between requiring clients to use Network Level Authentication or allowing connections from clients running any version of Remote Desktop. This option is set on the Remote tab of the System Properties dialog box (referred to elsewhere as "Advanced system settings") shown in Figure 2-5. When you enable this option, Windows Server 2008 R2 automatically configures firewall rules that allow Remote Desktop connections.

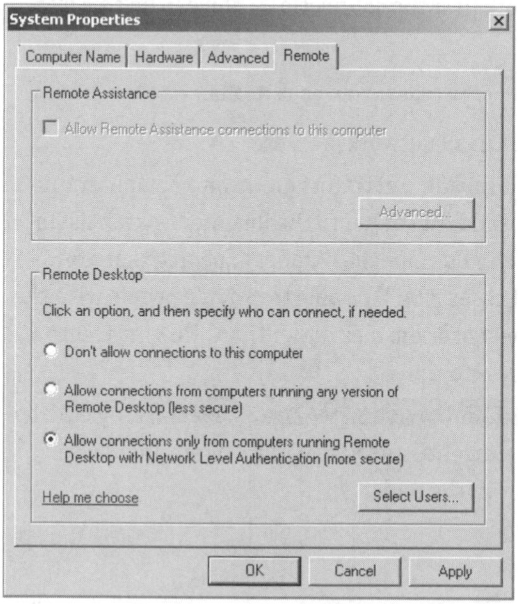

FIGURE 2-5: Enable the Remote Desktop.

▶ You would turn off the Network Level Authentication requirement if you perform administration using Remote Desktop clients that don't support the feature, such as those available for computers running non-Microsoft operating systems.

In most cases, you would probably choose to go with the Network Level Authentication option. Chances are that you will manage Windows Server 2008 R2 from a computer running Windows Vista or Windows 7, and the Remote Desktop Connection client included with these operating systems supports Network Level Authentication. Network Level Authentication requires you to authenticate yourself prior to establishing a connection, rather than using an authentication dialog box provided by the server to which you are connecting. It is possible to use this option with Windows XP Service Pack 3.

To enable Remote Desktop from computers running the Server Core version of Windows Server 2008 R2, issue the following commands:

```
cscript.exe c:\Windows\System32\scregedit.wsf /ar 0
```

```
cscript.exe c:\Windows\System32\
scregedit.wsf /ar /v
```

The default security on Remote Desktop connections to computers running Server Core requires that clients support Network Level Authentication. If you want to connect to a server using a client that doesn't support Network Level Authentication, you need to run the following command:

```
cscript.exe c:\Windows\System32\scregedit.wsf /cs 0
```

Unlike the typical version of Windows Server 2008 R2, where firewall rules are automatically configured, you need to configure the firewall on a computer running Server Core to support incoming Remote Desktop connections. You can do this by running the command:

```
netsh.exe firewall set service remotedesktop enable ALL
```

This particular firewall rule applies in all network profiles.

If a person is not a member of the local administrators group on a computer running Windows Server 2008 R2, you can add him or her to the Remote Desktop users group to grant access. As always, you should limit the number of people that are able to access your server directly. In most cases, you'll be able to provide people with the necessary level of access by letting them use consoles rather than allowing them to log on to the server through Remote Desktop.

▶ There aren't a lot of good reasons why you would want to change the Remote Desktop port number.

Remote Desktop uses TCP port 3389. You can change this, if necessary, by editing the HKEY_LOCAL_MACHINE\System\CurrentControlSet\Control\TerminalServer\WinStations\RDP-tcp\PortNumber key in the registry.

MANAGEMENT CONSOLES

You'll likely be familiar with management consoles as they are the primary method through which you administer computers (local or remote) running Windows Server 2008 R2. If you create a custom console, you can manage both a local and a number of remote computers from the same console. You learn about creating custom consoles later in the chapter.

Consoles have the following advantages:

▶ You can use the same tool to perform remote management against the server that you would if you were logged on to the target server locally or via Remote Desktop.

▶ You can create custom consoles that allow you to create a "one stop" tool to perform your most common administrative tasks.

Consoles have the following drawbacks:

▶ Consoles rarely work across firewalls, because you generally don't want to open remote procedure call (RPC) ports on firewalls.

▶ Most consoles can only be used to manage a remote server where there is an existing security relationship, such as the computer being in the same or a trusted Active Directory forest.

If you want to use consoles to manage servers that run Windows Server 2008 R2 from a management workstation running Windows Vista or Windows 7, you need to install the Remote Server Administration Tools (RSAT). The RSAT are a collection of consoles that can manage any of the roles and features added to a server running Windows Server 2008 R2. A drawback of the RSAT is that you can't install them on computers running Windows XP. Additionally, the Administrative Tools on management computers running Windows XP cannot be used to manage servers running Windows Server 2003 that manage computers running Windows Server 2008 R2. You can only install the RSAT for Windows 7 on computers that run the Enterprise, Professional, or Ultimate editions of the operating system. If you have Windows 7 Home Premium edition, you need to run the Windows Anytime Upgrade to convert to an edition that supports the RSAT for Windows 7.

The RSAT include only consoles for roles and features native to Windows Server 2008 R2. If you want to manage a product such as Exchange Server 2010 or SQL Server 2008 R2 from a computer that runs Windows 7, you need to install that console separately from the product installation files.

▶ If you manage servers that run Windows Server 2008 R2, and you are stuck using Windows XP, you should do your best to convince whoever holds the purse strings at your organization that your management workstations need upgrading.

NOTE You can obtain the RSAT for computers running Windows 7 operating system by navigating to www.microsoft.com/downloads and searching for RSAT.

When you install a role or feature on a computer running Windows Server 2008 R2, the install routine also adds the appropriate console for that tool to the Administrative Tools menu. For example, if you install the Hyper-V role, the Hyper-V Manager console becomes available in the Administrative Tools menu. However, this is not the case if you are installing a role on a computer running the Server Core operating system. Server Core computers don't use consoles locally, but you can manage them remotely using consoles.

If you want to install a particular RSAT console, but haven't installed the relevant role or feature, you can add the console separately from the Add/Remove Features item in the Server Manager console. For example, you might want to remotely manage DNS on a second server from a first server that doesn't have the DNS role installed. When you are using Windows Server 2008 R2, you don't need to download and install the RSAT. You can add them directly as a feature. To add a console without adding a role, perform the following general steps:

1. From the Server Manager console, click the Features node, and then click Add Features.

2. Expand the Remote Server Administration Tools node as shown in Figure 2-6. You can choose to install all consoles or specific consoles. Consoles are separated into Role Administration Tools and Feature Administration Tools, and then into categories. An advantage of adding all categories is that it gives you greater flexibility in building custom consoles, as all tools are available.

When using a normal console, such as the DNS console, you have the option of connecting to a local computer or a remote computer. The general process for connecting to a remote computer is as follows:

1. Open the console that you want to use from the Administrative Tools menu.

2. If the service isn't located locally, you'll get a dialog box asking you whether you want to connect to this computer or a different computer. This dialog box is shown in Figure 2-7.

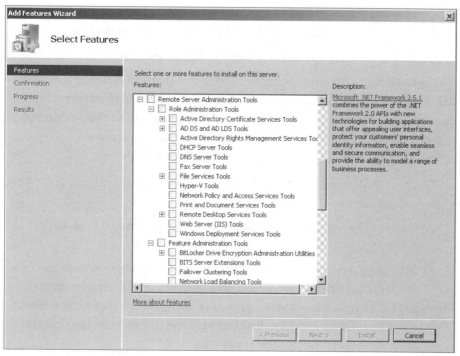

FIGURE 2-6: Install additional consoles.

FIGURE 2-7: Connect to DNS server.

Consoles generally connect using the current user's security context. This means that it can be difficult to directly manage a server with which the computer doesn't have an existing security relationship, such as being a member of the same Active Directory forest or a trusted forest. Some consoles do support using alternate security credentials, but this is the exception rather than the rule.

To configure a Windows Server 2008 R2 computer running Server Core so that you can manage it using management consoles, you need to configure the firewall to accept incoming remote administration connections. You can configure a computer running Server Core to allow these connections by issuing the command:

```
netsh.exe firewall set service remoteadmin enable ALL
```

The key to using Microsoft management consoles as effective remote administration devices is to save useful consoles where you have pre-configured them to connect to target servers. This way you can quickly open up a console that, for example, connects to all DNS servers in your organization, not just the local one.

To create a custom console, perform the following steps:

1. Open the Start menu and type **MMC** in Start Menu Search, then tap Enter. This opens a blank console.

2. From the File menu, click on Add-Remote Snap-in. This opens the Add or Remote Snap-ins dialog box.

3. In this tool, select the consoles that you want to add. When you add a console, you are asked whether you want it to connect to a local or remote computer. You can add additional copies of consoles, each of which connect to different computers. Figure 2-8 shows building a console that provides information about Services on four separate computers.

4. When you are finished adding all the necessary snap-ins, you can then save the console. The next time you open the console, it automatically loads the snap-ins targeted against the servers that you configured when you created the console.

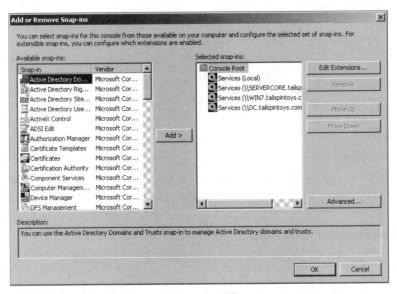

FIGURE 2-8: Add multiple snap-ins targeting different computers.

When creating a custom console, you also have the option to limit the ability of other people to change the console. If you want to allow your subordinates to use a specific tool but don't want them to modify the console, you can save the console in User Mode rather than Author Mode.

You do this by choosing File, Options, and then the appropriate mode in the Console tab of the Options dialog that displays.

REMOTE WINDOWS POWERSHELL

Windows PowerShell is designed as a command-line scripting environment for administrators. This distinction is important because, until Windows PowerShell came along, system administrators tended to avoid using command-line tools—they are cumbersome and the syntax and structure of how each command is used is often unique to that command. This is because many languages were originally designed for other purposes, such as text processing. While they are cleverly repurposed as systems administration languages, administrators find them difficult to pick up. Another good rule about administration tools is that if they require too much effort to pick up, then administrators won't bother using them.

You can run Windows PowerShell scripts against a remote server using a capability called Windows PowerShell Remoting.

This is supported on computers running Windows 7, Windows Vista Service Pack 1 or later, Windows Server 2008 and, of course, Windows Server 2008 R2.

To enable Windows PowerShell Remoting for a computer in the local or trusted domain, perform the following general steps:

1. Launch a Windows PowerShell session with administrative privileges.

2. Verify that you run the WinRM service using the following command:

   ```
   get-service winrm
   ```

3. If the service is not running, issue the following commands:

   ```
   Set-sevice winrm -startuptype automatic
   Start-service winrm
   ```

4. Configure remote Windows PowerShell by issuing the command:

   ```
   Enable-PSRemoting -force
   ```

Once you've configured the remote computer to support Windows PowerShell, you can use the Invoke-Command cmdlet on the local computer to run the command against the remote computer or computers. Specify the list of computers that you want to run the script against using the ComputerName parameter.

If you want to run individual commands, you can put them in curly brackets. For example, to run the Get-Process cmdlet, which lists all the processes on a computer, on computers DC1 and SVR1, issue the following command:

```
Invoke-Command -script {Get-Process} -computername DC1, SVR1
```

If you wanted to check all of the security updates on servers ALPHA, BETA and GAMMA, you could run the command:

```
Invoke-Command -script {get-hotfix -Description Sec*}
  -computername Alpha, Beta, Gamma
```

EMERGENCY MANAGEMENT SERVICES (WHEN ALL ELSE FAILS)

Emergency Management Services (EMS) is a command-line-based administration environment that allows you to connect to a server running Windows Server 2008 R2 through a COM or USB port. You can use EMS when the server is operational but when other methods of connecting to the server have failed. For example, you can use EMS to connect to a server that has suffered a STOP error, also known as a Blue Screen of Death (BSoD). Many administrators don't realize that even when a computer is suffering from a BSoD, you can still perform some administrative functions. You can also use EMS in non-BSoD scenarios. For example, you might find EMS useful when you have a server failure that causes it to lose its network card and graphics adapter, but where the server itself is still running. Rather than just flipping the switch to power down the server, you could use EMS to connect and shut down the server in a more graceful way prior to replacing the failed hardware. Pulling the plug on a server can lead to unexpected data corruption; if there is an alternate method to shut down an unresponsive server, you should take it.

As a remote administration tool, EMS is useful in the following situations:

▸ The server has encountered a STOP error/Blue Screen of Death.

▸ The server is under intense resource pressure, such as being under a Distributed Denial of Service (DDoS) attack, and the network interface is slow or incapable of responding to requests.

▸ The network card, TCP/IP stack, or network card driver has failed.

▸ The boot menu or recovery console is running.

▸ The server has yet to successfully complete booting.

You can also use EMS with a hardware device known as a console server. Console servers are also confusingly known as terminal servers. This confusion may have been one of the reasons that Microsoft renamed Terminal Services to Remote Desktop Services in Windows Server 2008 R2. A console server is a hardware device you connect to multiple servers that you want to manage through EMS either through their COM or USB ports. You connect to the console server through Telnet or SSH, and the console server redirects that traffic down the COM or USB cable to the server. Some console servers are available that have a web-driven interface that allows administrators to interact with EMS through a graphical environment.

Installing EMS

To set up a computer running Windows Server 2008 R2 so that it uses EMS, you need to use the bcdedit.exe command with the /EMS parameter from an elevated command prompt. You can't use bcdedit.exe to enable EMS on a computer that is experiencing a BSoD. The syntax of the command to enable EMS is as follows:

```
Bcdedit.exe /EMS [ON | OFF] /EMSSETTINGS [BIOS] | [[EMSPORT:<port>] |
[EMSBAUDRATE:<baudrate>]]
```

Use the ON option after the /EMS parameter to turn EMS on. Use the OFF option to disable EMS. The /EMSSETTINGS parameter allows you to specify which port is used for EMS communication. If you want to use the USB to communicate with the server, choose the BIOS option. The EMSPORT and EMSBAUDRATE parameters allow you to specify the port and baud rate used for redirection. You don't need to use these parameters if you use the BIOS option for the /EMSSETTINGS parameter.

Using the Special Administration Console (SAC)

The majority of EMS management is performed from the Special Administration Console (SAC). Once you enable EMS and the server is powered on, the SAC is running. If SAC is unable to load properly, the server starts the !SAC console. You learn about the !SAC console later in this chapter. When you are in the SAC console, you are presented with the SAC prompt, which has the following appearance:

```
SAC>
```

You can use the commands listed in Table 2-1 from within the SAC.

▶ You have to have EMS enabled before you hit the problem, rather than enabling it after the problem has occurred.

▶ You connect to EMS using a terminal emulator program. You can download freeware or shareware emulators from the Internet. You use the terminal emulators to connect through a RS-232 serial port cable or USB cable to EMS.

TABLE 2-1: SAC Commands

COMMAND	DESCRIPTION
Ch	Lists SAC channels
Cmd	Creates a Windows command prompt channel, when you create a channel you need to authenticate locally; you can then run command prompt utilities including Windows PowerShell scripts
Crashdump	Forces a BSoD and creates a memory dump file
D	Provides a dump of the current kernel log
T	Lists processes and threads that are currently running
F	Toggles the output of the T command between processes only or processes and threads
I	Enables you to view and set IP address information
Id	Provides server information; useful if you are connecting via a console server as a method of ensuring that you are actually connected to the right computer
K	Enables you to kill a specific process by process ID
L	Enables you to lower the priority of a given process
R	Enables you to raise the priority of a given process
Lock	Enables you to lock off command-prompt channels
M	Enables you to restrict the amount of memory a process can use
Restart	Forces the computer to reboot
S	Enables you to display or set the system time
Shutdown	Powers off the computer
?	Displays a list of SAC commands
Ch -si <n>	Enables you to change to the command prompt channel number ←n→
<ESC><TAB>0	Returns you to the SAC channel

As you might have noticed by reading through the available SAC commands, anyone connected to SAC has significant power over the server. Although any server's security is essentially compromised the moment someone has direct access to it, keep security in mind if you are setting up a console server and ensure that all connections to it are properly authenticated before traffic is passed through to EMS.

Entering !Special Administration Console (!SAC) Mode

When a computer has encountered a STOP error that makes it unresponsive to SAC commands, you can use !SAC mode. EMS automatically puts you into !SAC mode when it is unable to enter SAC mode. You can also enter !SAC mode manually. When !SAC becomes available, you are presented with a prompt that appears as follows:

```
!SAC>
```

You can use the following commands in !SAC mode:

- ▶ **Restart:** Enables you to restart the server immediately
- ▶ **D:** Enables you to view log entries one page at a time
- ▶ **Id:** Enables you to verify the computer's identity
- ▶ **Q:** Quits !SAC
- ▶ **?:** Lists available commands

!SAC is primarily useful in allowing you to view log entries in an attempt to diagnose what error is causing the BSoD. If you are getting a BSoD when a server is in the process of powering up, you may be able to use EMS to diagnose the cause of the error, assuming that you find the STOP error text that accompanies the BSoD less than illuminating.

SUMMARY

The remote administration tool that you choose depends very much on the kind of task that you want to perform. For a variety of configuration tasks, such as adding roles and features, configuring DNS, and modifying the settings of Internet Information Services on a single computer, it makes sense to use Remote Desktop. In that case, you could make one connection and perform all of the necessary tasks .

If, for example, you wanted to make a single modification to the DNS settings of three different DNS servers that are all in your organization's Active Directory forest, you would be better off using an RSAT management console. That way you could make the same modification to each different DNS server from the same console.

If you want to run a script against a large number of computers, you should enable Windows PowerShell Remoting. Once enabled, you can use the Invoke-Command cmdlet to specify the commands that you want to run and the ComputerName parameter to specify the computers you want to run the commands against.

Emergency Management Services is your remote administration tool of last resort. You can use EMS when Windows Server 2008 R2 is suffering from a Blue Screen of Death. When the computer is in this state, you can interrogate the logs and then force a graceful shutdown.

Further Links

Getting Started: Windows Server 2008 R2 Administration with Windows PowerShell

http://technet.microsoft.com/en-us/library/ee308287(WS.10).aspx

Enable PS Remoting

http://technet.microsoft.com/en-us/library/dd819498.aspx

BCDedit

http://technet.microsoft.com/en-us/library/cc731662(WS.10).aspx

Server Core Secrets

It is no secret that Windows Server 2008 R2 computers running the Server Core installation option are not as easy to set up as computers running Windows Server 2008 R2 with a full set of graphical tools. This makes sense because Microsoft put a lot of effort into simplifying the process of graphical user interface (GUI)-based administration so fewer administrators can get more done. As Microsoft provides a substantive set of graphical tools to allow server configuration with a minimum of effort, it follows that performing configuration without these tools requires more time and concentration.

Many administrators pass over the Server Core installation option, because they don't feel they have the time to figure out how to jump through the hoops necessary to configure the server. I've seen a lot of administrators who are initially enthusiastic about Server Core deployments but end up deciding that it isn't worth the effort after they spend some time attempting to configure the operating system from the command line.

Microsoft has simplified the command-line server setup process as much as possible, but in the end, you set up a complex operating system environment from the command line, and this necessitates entering sets of equally complex commands. If you're used to configuring a computer's IP address and DNS server settings using graphical tools, the thought of having to do it from the command line might make you decide not to bother with Server Core.

This begs the question: Why go with the Server Core option when deploying Windows Server 2008 R2 server?

You might have heard a lot about "reduced server hardware footprint" and "reduced attack surface" when people talk about why they need to deploy the Server Core operating system. Hardware footprint is something to consider, but most computers these days, other than a netbook, are going to be able to run Windows Server 2008 R2 with all of its bells and whistles turned on. Similarly, although attack surface is also important, a competent systems administrator should be able to lock down the services and applications on a standard installation of Windows Server 2008 R2 so this isn't the primary excuse for the extra hassle of configuring the server entirely from the command line.

The real reason to go with a Server Core deployment is that you have to update it less frequently. Microsoft releases a lot of updates for computers running Windows Server 2008 R2 that deal with GUI-dependent items, such as Internet Explorer. If you deploy Windows Server 2008 R2 in the Server Core configuration, many updates are no longer relevant. Fewer updates mean that you spend less time planning the application of updates to these servers. Rather than worrying about rebooting for all the domain controllers and DNS servers out at your organization's branch offices, deploying Server Core means that you have to reboot those servers less frequently. When you think about it like that, it might be worth the hassle of figuring out how to configure Server Core to perform a lot of those critical infrastructure tasks, such as functioning as a domain controller, DHCP server, DNS server, or file server.

In this chapter, you learn when to deploy Server Core over a traditional deployment and some tricks for taking the complexity out of managing Windows Server 2008 R2 when it is configured to run with this installation option.

USING SERVER CORE ADMINISTRATION TOOLS

Although you can manage a Windows Server 2008 R2 computer running the Server Core installation option from the command line, once you have the server set up properly, you'll be able to manage it from your workstation using the usual tools like management consoles, Remote Desktop, and remote PowerShell commands. It is important to remember this because many administrators believe that, with Server Core, they'll have to do everything from the command line.

Although we covered the steps to configure Server Core throughout the previous chapter, as a quick reminder, you need to do the following:

1. To enable Remote Desktop, run the following command:

```
cscript.exe c:\Windows\System32\scregedit.wsf /ar 0
```

2. To enable Remote Desktop for clients that do not support Network Level Authentication, run this command also:

```
cscript.exe c:\Windows\System32\scregedit.wsf /cs 0
```

3. To configure the firewall to support incoming Remote Desktop connections, run the command:

```
netsh.exe firewall set service remotedesktop enable ALL
```

▶ *If you set up a computer running Server Core properly, you won't have to touch the command line all that often!*

To allow the roles and features on the computer running Server Core to be managed using Microsoft management consoles on a management workstation in the same or a trusted domain, you need to configure the firewall and Windows Remote Management. You can do this using *sconfig.cmd* tool, which you'll learn about later in this chapter, or, you can issue the commands:

```
netsh.exe firewall set service remoteadmin enable ALL
winrm quickconfig
```

Figure 3-1 shows a Windows Server 2008 R2 computer that was installed using the Server Core configuration option. It is managed remotely using a custom console with the Server Manager snap-in focused to the Server Core computer's address. To accomplish this, remote administration settings are configured using the sconfig .cmd utility.

To enable PowerShell remoting, you'll first have to install the PowerShell feature. You'll learn how to do this later in the chapter. Once you've done that, run the following commands:

```
PowerShell.exe
Set-Service winrm -startuptype automatic
Start-Service winrm
Enable-PSRemoting -force
```

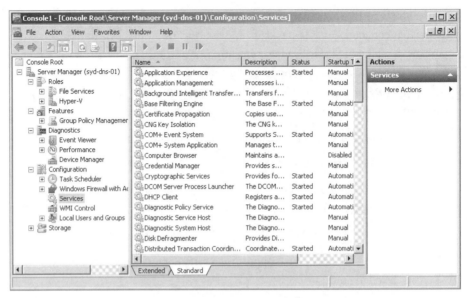

FIGURE 3-1: Remote management with Server Manager console

PERFORMING SERVER CORE POST-DEPLOYMENT TASKS

Before you get to the stage of being able to manage Server Core using tools such as Microsoft Management Console or PowerShell remoting on your administrative work-station, you need to perform a certain amount of post-installation configuration. The most obvious of these tasks is to configure the server with an IP address, but other tasks include configuring a computer name, performing activation, and joining the computer to an Active Directory domain.

Although Server Core has a reputation of being command-line driven only, there are several GUI tools that you can use with a default installation. You don't need to add these tools using ocsetup.exe or dism.exe; they are already included out-of-the-box. These tools are:

> **Regedit:** As you are probably aware, you use Regedit to modify the registry. Server Core computers still use the registry, and editing it from the command line would be an exercise in frustration. Regedit can be launched from the Server Core command line by typing **regedit.exe**.

▶ **Notepad:** Use this tool to modify text files, such as PowerShell or Windows Script Hosts. Notepad can be launched from the Server Core command line by typing **Notepad.exe**.

▶ **Task Manager:** Task Manager functions the same in Server Core as it does in a traditional install. You can use it to view and end processes, view point-in-time performance data, and launch new tasks. You can start Task Manager from the command line by typing **taskmgr.exe** or by pressing <CTRL><ALT><DEL> and selecting Start Task Manager from the menu.

There is another important graphical tool, called *Core Configurator*, of which you should be aware. This tool is a supported add-on for Windows Server 2008 R2 computers running Server Core, but it is something that you have to download from the Internet. You'll learn more about this graphical tool and how to get it later in the chapter. You'll also learn about the sconfig.cmd utility, which you can use to perform a lot of post-installation configuration.

You should remember that typing **Exit** at the Server Core command prompt closes that command prompt. Although this seems obvious, losing the command prompt on a version of Windows Server 2008 R2 that does not come with a Start Menu can leave many administrators flummoxed. Don't feel bad if you do this. We're so used to closing command prompts on servers that it's natural to think "oops" when we encounter the completely blank Server Core desktop.

Another basic trick you need to remember is how to shut down and reboot a server when you don't have access to a Start Menu. To shut down a computer running Server Core, at the command prompt with a five-second delay, type:

```
Shutdown /s /t 5
```

To reboot a computer running Server Core with a five-second shutdown delay, at the command prompt, type:

```
Shutdown /r /t 5
```

Configuring IP Address Information

Unlike workstations, computers that function in a server role generally need static IP addresses. Both the Server Core and traditional installations of Windows Server 2008 R2 use DHCP to configure their network addresses by default. One way to ensure that your Server Core computer has the same IP address each time is to create a DHCP reservation associated with the Server Core computer's MAC address. Although this

▶ Luckily, if you absent-mindedly type Exit while administrating a computer running Server Core, you can easily get a command prompt back by pressing <CTRL><ALT> <DEL>, starting Task Manager, selecting New Task on the File menu, and typing cmd.exe.

is generally a straightforward process, it usually involves logging on to the computer and running the ipconfig.exe command-line utility to figure out the MAC address of the Server Core computer. If you've logged on locally, you might as well set a static IP address rather than go to all the extra trouble of configuring a specific reservation.

> **CROSSREF** You'll learn more about configuring DHCP reservations in Chapter 8, "Network Addressing."

If you want to configure a static IP address, use the following command:

```
Netsh interface IPv4 set address "Local Area Connection" static
x.x.x.x y.y.y.y z.z.z.z
```

▶ All of the commands in this section work on both Server Core and traditional installations of Windows Server 2008 R2.

Where x.x.x.x is the IP address, y.y.y.y is the subnet mask and z.z.z.z is the default gateway. "Local Area Connection" is the name of the network adapter that you want to configure. By default, the first adapter on a computer is "Local Area Connection," the second is "Local Area Connection 2," and so on. To configure the computer to use a specific DNS server, use the command:

```
Netsh interface IPv4 set dnsservers "Local Area Connection" static
x.x.x.x primary
```

Here, x.x.x.x is the IP address of the DNS server. You can check that you got the configuration correct by using the following command:

```
Ipconfig /all
```

Renaming the Computer

Unless you use an answer file or other automatic installation method, every time you install Windows Server 2008 R2, the computer will be assigned a random name. You can figure out what a computer's name is by using the following command:

```
Hostname
```

The problem with random names is that they provide no descriptive context as to the server's role in your organization. You don't want to have to query a spreadsheet to figure out which computer functions as the DNS server at your organization's Sydney site. Instead, you probably want to set the name of the computer to something like "SYD-DNS-01." Server names should reflect the role the server plays within your organization. They should be meaningful at a casual glance. This means that you shouldn't name servers after your favorite science fiction characters! To change the name of a Windows Server 2008 R2 computer (in this case, to SYD-DNS-01), issue the following command:

```
Netdom renamecomputer %computername% /newname:SYD-DNS-01
```

After you issue this command, the computer requires a reboot. You can reboot the computer using the shutdown command you learned about earlier in the chapter.

Joining a Domain

Once you have named the computer, you can use the netdom.exe command to join it to the domain. The trick to remember with domain joins is to ensure that the computer that you want to join to the domain is able to contact a DNS server that hosts domain-related information. Usually this means setting the primary DNS server to the address of a domain controller in the same site as the server, as most organizations place these two roles on the same computer. You learned how to configure the DNS server address settings earlier in this chapter.

To join the computer to a domain, issue the following command:

```
Netdom join %computername% /domain:domainname /UserD:Administrator
/PasswordD:*
```

Here:

▶ Domainname is the NetBIOS name of the domain that you want the computer to join.

▶ Administrator is the name of an account that has the rights to join a computer to the domain.

▶ %computername% is a variable that automatically substitutes the computer's name, so you should enter it as written.

Using the * after the PasswordD parameter means that you will be prompted for the password for the account that has the necessary privileges to join the domain. After the computer has joined the domain, it will be necessary to restart the computer for the domain join operation to complete. You can reboot the computer using the shutdown command you learned earlier in the chapter. When a computer first reboots after a domain join, the logon will remain set to the last user that logged on, which with a Server Core machine, is usually the local administrator account. If you want to then log on with the domain administrator account, you'll need to remember to change the logon user to **domainname\administrator**. If you just type **Administrator**, Windows Server 2008 R2 will default to the computer's local administrator account. Of course, it is best practice not to use the account administrator as a domain administrator account and instead create a separate administrative account associated with each administrator in your organization.

> CROSSREF You'll learn more about creating role specific administrator accounts in Chapter 6, "Managing Users and Computers."

Installing PowerShell

One of the biggest annoyances about the version of Server Core that was available with the first release of Windows Server 2008 was that you couldn't manage the server using PowerShell. In essence, Microsoft released a server operating system that you could manage from the command line and a powerful command-line toolkit, yet they didn't work with each other! Luckily, with Windows Server 2008 R2, this issue has been resolved. You can install PowerShell on computers that are running the Server Core version of Windows Server 2008 R2 and use PowerShell to manage these servers.

To install PowerShell, run the following command:

```
Dism /Online /Enable-Feature /FeatureName:NetFx2-ServerCore
/Enable-Feature /FeatureName:MicrosoftWindowsPowerShell /Enable-
FeatureName:ServerManager-PSH-Cmdlets /FeatureName:BestPractices-
PSH-Cmdlets
```

To get access to PowerShell, type:

```
PowerShell
```

> ▶ Using PowerShell is a far easier way to add and remove features and roles than using Deployment Image Servicing and Management (DISM) or Optional Component Setup (OCSetup).

To get access to the server management cmdlets, run the following command from the PowerShell prompt:

```
Import-Module ServerManager
```

Once you've taken these steps, you can use the Get-WindowsFeature, Add-WindowsFeature, and Remove-WindowsFeature to manage roles and features on the server. This trick also works in the full version of Windows Server 2008 R2. Figure 3-2 shows the output of the Get-WindowsFeature cmdlet. Features that are installed on the server are represented by an [X].

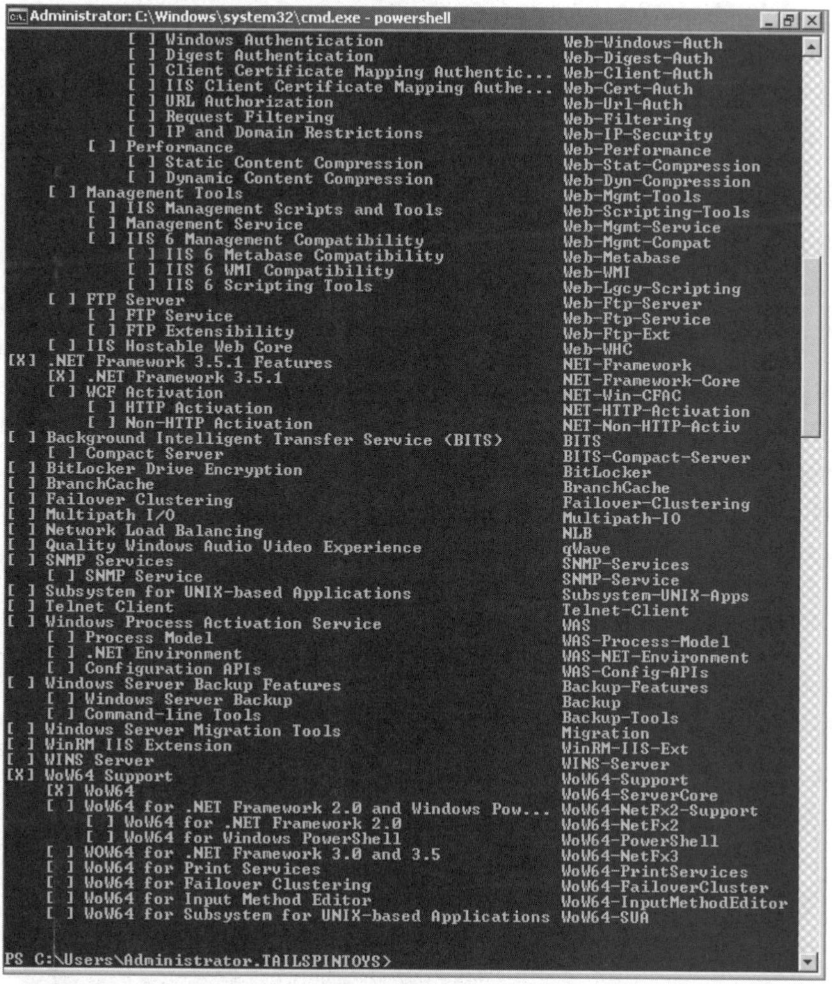

```
Administrator: C:\Windows\system32\cmd.exe - powershell                    _ 8 X
        [ ] Windows Authentication                   Web-Windows-Auth
        [ ] Digest Authentication                    Web-Digest-Auth
        [ ] Client Certificate Mapping Authentic...  Web-Client-Auth
        [ ] IIS Client Certificate Mapping Authe...  Web-Cert-Auth
        [ ] URL Authorization                        Web-Url-Auth
        [ ] Request Filtering                        Web-Filtering
        [ ] IP and Domain Restrictions               Web-IP-Security
     [ ] Performance                                 Web-Performance
        [ ] Static Content Compression               Web-Stat-Compression
        [ ] Dynamic Content Compression              Web-Dyn-Compression
   [ ] Management Tools                              Web-Mgmt-Tools
      [ ] IIS Management Scripts and Tools           Web-Scripting-Tools
      [ ] Management Service                         Web-Mgmt-Service
      [ ] IIS 6 Management Compatibility             Web-Mgmt-Compat
         [ ] IIS 6 Metabase Compatibility            Web-Metabase
         [ ] IIS 6 WMI Compatibility                 Web-WMI
         [ ] IIS 6 Scripting Tools                   Web-Lgcy-Scripting
   [ ] FTP Server                                    Web-Ftp-Server
      [ ] FTP Service                                Web-Ftp-Service
      [ ] FTP Extensibility                          Web-Ftp-Ext
   [ ] IIS Hostable Web Core                         Web-WHC
[X] .NET Framework 3.5.1 Features                    NET-Framework
   [X] .NET Framework 3.5.1                          NET-Framework-Core
   [ ] WCF Activation                                NET-Win-CFAC
      [ ] HTTP Activation                            NET-HTTP-Activation
      [ ] Non-HTTP Activation                        NET-Non-HTTP-Activ
[ ] Background Intelligent Transfer Service (BITS)   BITS
   [ ] Compact Server                                BITS-Compact-Server
[ ] BitLocker Drive Encryption                       BitLocker
[ ] BranchCache                                      BranchCache
[ ] Failover Clustering                              Failover-Clustering
[ ] Multipath I/O                                    Multipath-IO
[ ] Network Load Balancing                           NLB
[ ] Quality Windows Audio Video Experience           qWave
[ ] SNMP Services                                    SNMP-Services
   [ ] SNMP Service                                  SNMP-Service
[ ] Subsystem for UNIX-based Applications             Subsystem-UNIX-Apps
[ ] Telnet Client                                    Telnet-Client
[ ] Windows Process Activation Service               WAS
   [ ] Process Model                                 WAS-Process-Model
   [ ] .NET Environment                              WAS-NET-Environment
   [ ] Configuration APIs                            WAS-Config-APIs
[ ] Windows Server Backup Features                   Backup-Features
   [ ] Windows Server Backup                         Backup
   [ ] Command-line Tools                            Backup-Tools
[ ] Windows Server Migration Tools                   Migration
[ ] WinRM IIS Extension                              WinRM-IIS-Ext
[ ] WINS Server                                      WINS-Server
[X] WoW64 Support                                    WoW64-Support
   [X] WoW64                                         WoW64-ServerCore
   [ ] WoW64 for .NET Framework 2.0 and Windows Pow...  WoW64-NetFx2-Support
      [ ] WoW64 for .NET Framework 2.0               WoW64-NetFx2
      [ ] WoW64 for Windows PowerShell               WoW64-PowerShell
   [ ] WoW64 for .NET Framework 3.0 and 3.5          WoW64-NetFx3
   [ ] WoW64 for Print Services                      WoW64-PrintServices
   [ ] WoW64 for Failover Clustering                 WoW64-FailoverCluster
   [ ] WoW64 for Input Method Editor                 WoW64-InputMethodEditor
   [ ] WoW64 for Subsystem for UNIX-based Applications  WoW64-SUA

PS C:\Users\Administrator.TAILSPINTOYS>
```

FIGURE 3-2: Core Configurator control panel menu

Configuring Software Updates

In most organizations, software update configuration is handled through group policy. This includes configuring how updates will be installed and whether or not the computer will use a WSUS server as a source of updates and approvals.

> *CROSSREF* You'll learn more about configuring software updates in Chapter 15, "Patch Management with WSUS."

If a computer running Server Core is not a member of a domain and hence is not subject to group policy, you can enable or disable automatic updates using the *scregedit.wsf* script. To enable automatic updates, use the command:

```
Cscript.exe c:\windows\system32\scregedit.wsf /AU 4
```

To disable automatic updates, use the command:

```
Cscript.exe c:\windows\system32\scregedit.wsf /AU 1
```

Configuring Licensing and Activation

You use the *slmgr.vbs* script to perform product key and activation related activities for computers running the Server Core operating system. It is not necessary to use slmgr.vbs if your organization has already configured a KMS server. You learned about KMS servers back in Chapter 1.

You can determine the current activation state of the computer by running the command:

```
Slmgr.vbs /xpr
```

If you aren't ready to perform the activation process just yet, you can re-arm Windows Server 2008 R2 to extend the activation period three times using the command:

```
Slmgr.vbs /rearm
```

To configure a computer running Server Core with a product key, you need to use slmgr.vbs with the /ipx option. For example, to install the product key 12345-12345-12345-12345-12345, you would issue the command:

```
Slmgr.vbs /ipk 12345-12345-12345-12345-12345
```

After you have installed the product key, you can commence activation using the following command:

```
Slmgr.vbs /ato
```

Whether or not you'll be able to activate Windows Server 2008 R2 depends on whether your organization uses a proxy with a password to mediate traffic from hosts to the Internet. If your organization does use a proxy with a password, you need to use a tool such as the *Volume Activation Management Tool (VAMT)* to perform indirect activation. You learned about the VAMT in Chapter 1, "Windows Server 2008 R2 Deployment Secrets." If your proxy does not require a password, you can configure Server Core to use it with the following command:

```
Netsh winhttp set proxy proxyaddress.domainname.com:8080
```

To view the current proxy configuration, use the following command:

```
Netsh winhttp show proxy
```

Managing Services

The easiest way to manage services on Windows Server 2008 R2 computers running the Server Core operating system option is to use the service-related PowerShell commands. These commands allow you to configure all aspects of service properties. The service-related PowerShell commands are as follows:

- **Get-Service:** Allows you to view the properties of a service. Run by itself, it will list all services on the local computer and their status.

- **New-Service:** Allows you to create and register new services using existing executables.

- **Restart-Service**: Stops and then starts a specific service. Running this cmdlet is the same as running the Stop-Service cmdlet followed by the Start-Service cmdlet.

- **Suspend-Service:** Allows you to pause a service without stopping that service. Use this when you don't want to shut down a service, but do want to temporarily stop it from functioning.

- **Resume-Service:** Allows you to resume a suspended service.

- **Start-Service:** Starts a stopped service. To have a service automatically start, you need to use the Set-Service cmdlet.

- **Stop-Service:** Stops a running service.

- **Set-Service:** Allows you to configure the properties of a service such as the service startup type. Although you can use this cmdlet to configure a service to start automatically the next time the server boots, you cannot use this cmdlet to start a service directly. To accomplish that goal, use the Start-Service cmdlet.

▶ Remember that starting a service doesn't mean that the service will automatically restart the next time the server boots.

For example, the following command sets the WinRM service to start automatically each time the server boots:

```
Set-Service WinRM -startuptype automatic
```

UNDERSTANDING THE SCONFIG.CMD

Sconfig.cmd is a text menu-based configuration utility that is included with Windows Server 2008 R2 when you install the Server Core installation option. Sconfig.cmd allows you to perform many of the tasks described earlier, though often only with a limited amount of the functionality possible with those tasks. Sconfig.cmd provides the options shown in Figure 3-3.

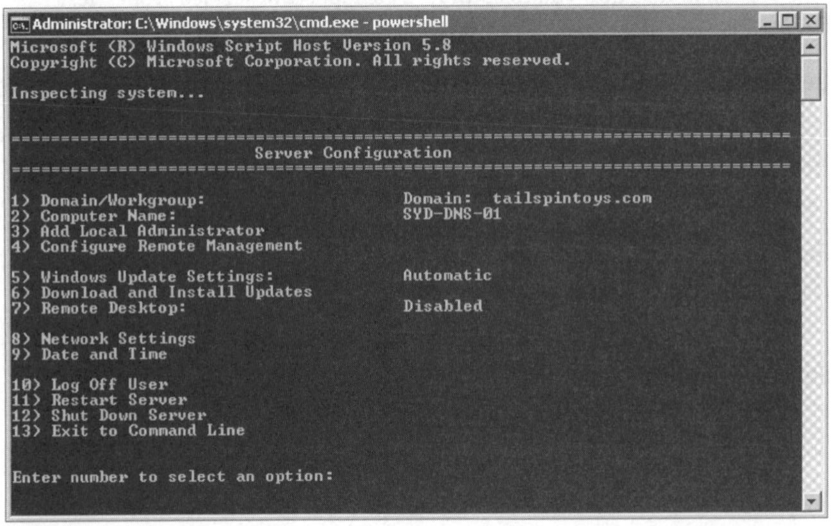

```
Administrator: C:\Windows\system32\cmd.exe - powershell                          _ □ ×
Microsoft (R) Windows Script Host Version 5.8
Copyright (C) Microsoft Corporation. All rights reserved.

Inspecting system...


===============================================================================
                               Server Configuration
===============================================================================

1) Domain/Workgroup:                        Domain:  tailspintoys.com
2) Computer Name:                           SYD-DNS-01
3) Add Local Administrator
4) Configure Remote Management

5) Windows Update Settings:                 Automatic
6) Download and Install Updates
7) Remote Desktop:                          Disabled

8) Network Settings
9) Date and Time

10) Log Off User
11) Restart Server
12) Shut Down Server
13) Exit to Command Line


Enter number to select an option:
```

FIGURE 3-3: Sconfig.cmd

You can use sconfig.cmd to perform the following configuration tasks:

▶ **Domain/Workgroup:** To join the computer to a domain or specific workgroup.

▶ **Computer Name:** To change the computer's name.

▶ **Add Local Administrator:** To add a local administrator to the computer. The user must have an existing domain or local user account.

▶ **Configure Remote Management:** To allow MMC remote management, enable remote management through PowerShell, allow remote management through Server Manager, and display current Windows Firewall settings.

▶ **Windows Update Settings:** To switch between having updates installed manually or automatically. You cannot use this option to specify an alternate source, such as a WSUS server, for Windows updates.

▶ You can only allow Server Manager remote management if you enable PowerShell remote management.

- ▶ **Download and Install Updates:** To trigger an automatic download and installation of updates.

- ▶ **Remote Desktop:** To enable or disable Remote Desktop as well as determine whether clients need to support Network Level Authentication to make a successful connection.

- ▶ **Network Settings:** To set the IPv4 configuration of the computer's network adapters.

- ▶ **Date and Time:** To configure the date and time settings, including changing the time zone to which the computer is assigned.

- ▶ **Log Off User:** To log off the currently logged on user.

- ▶ **Restart Server:** To initiate a server reboot.

- ▶ **Shut Down Server:** To initiate server shutdown.

- ▶ **Exit to command line:** To exit back to the Server Core command prompt.

ADMINISTERING WITH SERVER CORE CONFIGURATOR

Although it is worth learning how to perform Server Core configuration completely using command-line tools, Microsoft indirectly supports a tool through CodePlex called *Core Configurator*. Core Configurator is a set of basic GUI-based administration tools that allow you to configure Server Core. After you've performed the initial configuration, you can remove Core Configurator without impacting the configuration you've created. Core Configurator works as a graphical front end to a collection of PowerShell commands, similar to how Exchange Management Console creates and executes configuration commands based on the input entered into GUI forms.

▶ You can obtain Core Configurator at the following address: http://coreconfig.codeplex.com.

You start Core Configurator by running the Start_CoreConfig.wsf script. This script checks that you have PowerShell and any necessary modules installed. The main screen, shown in Figure 3-4, allows you to navigate to menus for the configuration of Computer Settings, Control Panel items, Network Settings, License Settings and, if the computer running Server Core is configured as a Hyper-V server, Hyper-V settings.

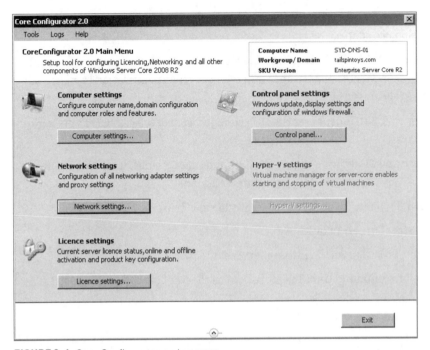

FIGURE 3-4: Core Configurator main screen

The Computer Settings dialog, available from the Core Configurator home screen and shown in Figure 3-5, allows you to access the following dialog boxes:

▶ **Computer and Domain:** To change the computer name, to add or remove the computer from a domain, or to change the workgroup to which the computer belongs.

▶ **Add or Remove Roles:** To add and remove roles and features, similar to the Add-WindowsFeature and Remove-WindowsFeature PowerShell cmdlets.

▶ **Services:** To start, stop, and restart services as well as view the current status of the service. Does not allow you to modify the service startup type.

▶ **Domain Settings:** To configure the Server Core computer as a domain controller. You can use this control panel to add the server as a new domain controller or as a Read Only Domain Controller (RODC) in an existing domain, or to remove the domain controller from the domain. You cannot create a new forest or domain using this control panel.

▶ **Remote Management Settings:** To enable Remote Desktop connections and determine whether Network Level Authentication is required, or to enable or disable Windows Remote Management.

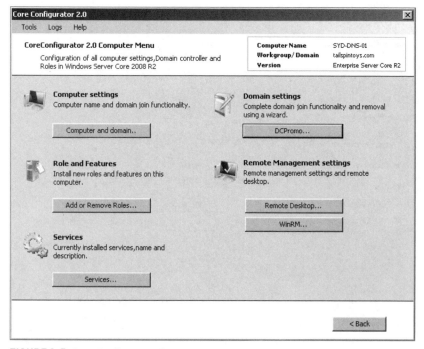

FIGURE 3-5: Core Configurator Computer menu

The Network Menu, shown in Figure 3-6, allows you to perform several network-related tasks, including local group management and SAN configuration. Clicking on the items in this menu allows you to perform the following configuration tasks:

▶ **Manage Network Card Settings:** This includes IPv4 configuration settings and enabling and disabling specific network cards.

▶ **Configure Membership of Local Groups:** To modify the membership of local groups, such as the Administrators and Remote Desktop Users local groups.

▶ **Manage Shared Folders on the Server:** To create new, shared folders. Does not allow you to modify the permissions assigned to shared folders.

▶ **Configure Proxy Settings:** Remember that you can't use a proxy if the proxy requires credentials from the Windows Server 2008 R2 computer running Server Core.

▶ **iSCSI and MPIO Configuration:** To manage how the Windows Server 2008 R2 computer running the Server Core operating system connects to devices on the SAN.

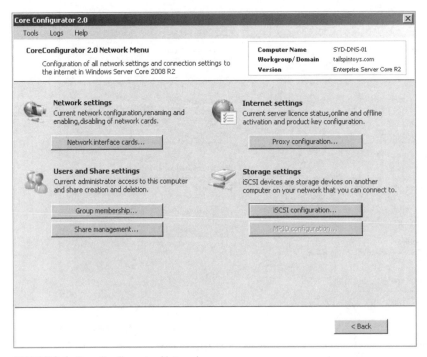

FIGURE 3-6: Core Configurator Network menu

The License Settings Menu allows you to view whether or not the Windows Server 2008 R2 computer running Server Core is currently activated. You can also install, clear, or uninstall a specific product key. This control panel also allows you to configure the address of any KMS server that may be present on your organizational network.

The Control Panel Menu allows you to configure several options that are found in the control panel of a standard installation of Windows Server 2008 R2. Through the control panel you can configure the following items:

▶ **Windows Update Settings:** To configure whether updates are installed automatically and to configure the address of the WSUS server.

▶ **Firewall Settings:** To configure the firewall on a per network location basis, or to enable or disable basic firewall rules, such as those allowing Remote Desktop and ICMP replies. Allowing ICMP allows you to ping the server. You cannot use this control panel to create firewall rules.

▶ **Keyboard:** To configure formats, current location (separate from time zone), welcome screen settings, and system locale. Most of the settings under

▶ This is the easiest way of configuring the address of a WSUS server on a computer running Server Core that is not a member of an Active Directory domain.

this item are more relevant to full installations rather than Server Core installations.

▶ **Date and Time:** To change the system time and the computer's assigned time zone.

▶ **Display Resolution:** To configure the display resolution, color depth, and whether the screen saver is enabled, and the length of time required for the screen saver to activate.

▶ **Add Drivers:** To import hardware drivers, by specifying the location of the driver's INF file.

▶ **Add or Remove Programs:** To add or remove programs from the Windows Server 2008 R2 computer installed in the Server Core configuration. This will only work with programs designed to run on Server Core.

The Hyper-V settings item allows you to manage Hyper-V virtual machines when you have configured a Windows Server 2008 R2 computer running with the Server Core installation option with the Hyper-V role. You can start and stop existing virtual machines, but you cannot use this control panel to create new virtual machines.

UNDERSTANDING SERVER CORE INFRASTRUCTURE ROLES

Windows Server 2008 R2 computers running the Server Core installation option are most commonly deployed in the domain controller, DNS server, and DHCP server roles. This is generally because, once you install these roles, you rarely have to do a significant amount of post-installation configuration. Although each of these roles is covered in greater detail by later chapters, over the following pages you will learn the basics of installing and configuring each of these roles on a Windows Server 2008 R2 computer running the Server Core installation option.

Server Core Domain Controllers

Domain controllers need to be located at branch offices to authenticate domain logons by users at the branch office. Domain controllers are a natural fit for Server Core, as one of the primary benefits of using the Server Core installation option is a reduced requirement for patching and, therefore, a reduced amount of downtime due to rebooting.

You can configure a Windows Server 2008 R2 computer running the Server Core installation option to become a domain controller in an existing domain, including installing the Active Directory integrated DNS service using the following command:

```
Dcpromo /installDNS:Yes /ReplicaOrNewDomain:Replica /ReplicaDomainDNSNa
me:tailspintoys.com /SafeModeAdminPassWord:Pa$$w0rd
```

When you use this command, the necessary Active Directory binaries are also installed on the server. As with any domain controller promotion, it will be necessary to reboot the computer to complete the installation.

After you have installed the Active Directory Domain Services role, you can install the Active Directory specific PowerShell module using the command:

```
Dism /online /Enable-Feature /FeatureName:ActiveDirectory-PowerShell
```

You then import the Active Directory module into a PowerShell session using the command:

```
Import-Module ActiveDirectory
```

▶ All of the commands in this section work on both Server Core and traditional installations of Windows Server 2008 R2.

ADDING AN ORGANIZATIONAL UNIT

You use the *New-ADOrganizationalUnit cmdlet* to create a new organizational unit (OU) when the Active Directory module is loaded into a PowerShell session on a Windows Server 2008 R2 computer running the Server Core installation option. For example, to create a new OU named "Students" in the Tailspintoys.com domain, use the command:

```
New-ADOrganizationalUnit -Name Students -Path "DC=Tailspintoys,DC=COM"
```

ADDING A USER

You use the *New-ADUser cmdlet* to create a new user when the Active Directory module is loaded into a PowerShell session on a Windows Server 2008 R2 computer running the Server Core installation option. To create a new user named "Rooslan" with the password "P@ssw0rd" in the Students OU of the domain TailspinToys.com, use the command:

```
New-ADUser -SamAccountName Rooslan -Name "Rooslan" -AccountPassword
(ConvertTo-SecureString -AsPlainText "P@ssw0rd" -Force) -Enabled
$true -Path 'OU=Students,DC=Tailspintoys,DC=COM'
```

CHANGING A USER'S PASSWORD

You use the *Set-ADAccountPassword cmdlet* to reset a user's account password when the Active Directory module is loaded into a PowerShell session on a Windows Server 2008 R2 computer running the Server Core installation option. For example, to reset the password of a user named "Rooslan" to "P@ssw0rd," use the command:

```
Set-ADAccountPassword -Identity Rooslan -NewPassword (ConvertTo-
SecureString -AsPlainText "P@ssw0rd" -Force)
```

ADDING A GROUP

You use the *New-ADGroup cmdlet* to create a new group when the Active Directory module is loaded into a PowerShell session on a Windows Server 2008 R2 computer running the Server Core installation option. To create a new global security group named "Martians" in the Students OU of the TailspinToys.com domain, use the command:

```
New-ADGroup -Name "Martians" -SamAccountName Martians -GroupCategory
Security -GroupScope Global -DisplayName "Martians" -Path "OU=Students,
DC=Tailspintoys,DC=COM"
```

ADDING A USER TO A GROUP

You use the *Add-AdGroupMember cmdlet* to add a user to a group when the Active Directory module is loaded into a PowerShell session on a Windows Server 2008 R2 computer running the Server Core installation option. For example, to add the user Rooslan to the group Martians, use the command:

```
Add-ADGroupMember -Identity Martians -Member Rooslan
```

> **CROSSREF** You learn about domain controllers in detail in Chapter 4, "Active Directory Domains and Forests."

Configuring Server Core DNS Servers

To install the DNS server service on a Windows Server 2008 R2 computer running the Server Core installation option, perform the following general steps:

1. Start PowerShell.

2. Import the ServerManager PowerShell module.

3. Run the command:

```
Add-WindowsFeature DNS
```

If you have configured the Windows Server 2008 R2 computer running the Server Core installation option to support management by Microsoft Management Console, you can remotely connect from a computer that has a custom console to manage the DNS service. This will provide you with full DNS server functionality.

In the event that you want to manage the DNS server from the command line, you can use the DNSCMD command-line utility to accomplish this goal. For example, to create a primary DNS zone named "Canberra.tailspintoys.com," stored in the file Canberra.dns, issue the command:

```
Dnscmd /zoneadd canberra.tailspintoys.com /primary /file Canberra.dns
```

The Canberra.dns file will be stored, by default, in the c:\windows\system32\dns directory. If you wanted to add an Active Directory Integrated Zone called "Adelaide .tailspintoys.com" to the DNS server, you would use the command:

```
Dnscmd /zoneadd adelaide.tailspintoys.com /dsprimary
```

To add a host record to DNS with DNSCMD, use the RecordAdd parameter. For example, to create the A record for the host whyalla.adelaide.tailspintoys.com that has the IP address 10.10.0.101 in the Adelaide.tailspintoys.com DNS zone, issue the command:

```
Dnscmd /recordadd Adelaide.tailspintoys.com whyalla A 10.10.0.101
```

To remove a host record with DNSCMD, use the RecordDelete parameter. For example, to remove the A record for the host whyalla.adelaide.tailspintoys.com, issue the command:

```
Dnscmd /recorddelete Adelaide.tailspintoys.com whyalla A 10.10.0.101
```

DHCP Server

A common use for Windows Server 2008 R2 computers that have the Server Core version of the operating system installed is as branch office DHCP servers. The DHCP service is generally of minimal impact and, once set up, often requires little in the way of maintenance.

To install the DHCP role, perform the following steps:

1. Start PowerShell.

2. Import the Server Manager module.

3. Run the following command:

```
Add-WindowsFeature DHCP
```

After it is installed, the DHCP service is in a disabled state. To configure the DHCP service to start automatically, and to then start the service, use the following PowerShell commands:

```
Set-Service DHCPServer -Startuptype Automatic
Start-Service DHCPServer
```

After the DHCP server is enabled, you'll need to authorize it in Active Directory. Unless DHCP is authorized, it will not be able to provide addresses to clients. You can view a list of authorized DHCP servers by running the command:

```
Netsh dhcp show server
```

To authorize the DHCP server, you need to specify both its fully qualified domain name and its IP address. To authorize the DHCP server syd-dns-01.tailspintoys.com that has the IP address 10.10.0.102, issue the following command:

```
Netsh dhcp add server syd-dns-01.tailspintoys.com 10.10.0.102
```

Verify that the DNS server has been added correctly by listing all DHCP servers using the netsh dhcp command listed earlier.

CREATING A SCOPE

To create a new scope, use the netsh dhcp server add scope command, specifying the network address and subnet mask. For example, to create a new scope for the network 192.168.15.0 with the subnet mask 255.255.255.0 and to label this scope "Delta," use the command:

```
Netsh dhcp server add scope 192.168.15.0 255.255.255.0 "Delta"
```

SETTING A SCOPE OPTION

You can configure DHCP scope options, such as configuring the DNS server address used for scopes, using the OptionValue parameter. For example, to configure the 192.168.15.0 scope to configure clients with a DNS server address of 192.168.15.101, use the following command:

```
Netsh dhcp server scope 192.168.15.0 set optionvalue 006 IPADDRESS
192.168.15.101
```

CREATING AN ADDRESS RESERVATION

To create an address reservation within an existing scope use the netsh dhcp server scope command with the Add Reserved IP parameter. For example, to configure an address reservation for IP address 192.168.15.10 for a network adapter with the MAC address AA00BBAA00CC, issue the command:

```
Netsh dhcp server scope 192.168.15.0 add reservedip 192.168.15.10
AA00BBAA00CC
```

You'll learn more about the DHCP role in Chapter 8, "Network Addressing Secrets," including how to use the DHCP snap-in of a Microsoft Management Console to perform common administrative tasks.

SUMMARY

The Server Core versions of Windows Server 2008 R2 don't do everything that the full versions do, but they also require a lot less rebooting and patching, which reduces the amount of time you need to spend directly managing them. Only the initial configuration of computers running Server Core needs to occur from the command line. Once you have the server up-and-running, you can download Core Configurator to add and remove roles and perform the initial configuration. You can also perform the initial configuration using the included, but more limited, sconfig.cmd text menu utility. The Get-WindowsFeature, Add-WindowsFeature, and Remove-WindowsFeature cmdlets are part of the Server Manager PowerShell module. These cmdlets significantly reduce the amount of work you have to do to add and remove roles from the computer running Server Core.

Additional Sources

Configuring a Server Core installation of Windows Server 2008 R2 with sconfig.cmd

http://technet.microsoft.com/en-us/library/ee441254(WS.10).aspx

Server Core Configurator

http://coreconfig.codeplex.com

Active Directory Administration with Windows PowerShell

http://technet.microsoft.com/en-us/library/dd378937(WS.10).aspx

DNSCMD Command Line Reference

http://technet.microsoft.com/en-us/library/cc772069(WS.10).aspx

Active Directory Domains and Forests

Active Directory domain controllers are the type of servers that most administrators don't tend to spend a lot of time worrying about. This is because, unlike a lot of other servers, there is a built-in redundancy to Active Directory domain controllers. Once you have more than one domain controller (DC) in a domain, you can generally recover any DC that fails by reinstalling it, allowing it to sync with the other DCs and then by seizing any operations' master roles that were held by the failed DC. In terms of the stresses involved in ensuring that other important infrastructure servers are recoverable, this recovery procedure is relatively straightforward, as it doesn't involve locating backups or performing full server recovery.

▶ Try to have at least two domain controllers in each domain. That way, if one domain controller fails, you can always reinstall the failed server without having to recover the Active Directory database from a backup.

As Active Directory domain controllers are some of the most important servers on your organization's network, this built-in recoverability is a good thing. The only drawback to the design of Active Directory is if you make a mistake, such as accidentally deleting an important organizational unit, that mistake will replicate across all of the other domain controllers and will require substantially more effort to undo. Later in this chapter, you'll learn how to minimize the chance of such a mistake by protecting important objects. By reading this chapter, you'll also learn a few hints about managing Active Directory on Windows Server 2008 R2 networks, including new features such as read-only domain controllers and the Active Directory Recycle Bin, how to configure Windows Server 2008 R2 so you can boot into Directory Services Restore Mode when necessary, and how to reset the Directory Services Restore Mode password.

UNDERSTANDING FORESTS AND DOMAINS

A *forest* is a collection of domains that automatically trust one another and have a common Active Directory schema. Most of the time systems administrators don't need to know what an Active Directory schema is, so it becomes difficult for them to determine whether they need more than one forest. In reality, most small- to medium-sized organizations get by with a single domain forest. Generally speaking, it tends to be the larger organizations (with more than a couple of thousand users) that require more than one domain or forest.

Creating More than One Forest

▶ An example of requiring different schemas is a company that needs completely separate Exchange organizations. There can only be one Exchange organization in a forest, so if you want multiple Exchange organizations, you'll need multiple forests.

Unless your organization has unusual security requirements, you will most likely be fine with a single Active Directory forest. A single forest supports multiple domains, and these domains can have disjointed namespaces, such as wingtiptoys.com and tailspintoys.com. The only time you really need multiple forests is if you need to run separate schemas or if your organization has specific security requirements, such as requiring completely separate systems administration teams.

Your organization might also have more than one forest during an upgrade from a previous version of Active Directory. Although it is possible to upgrade from one version of Active Directory to another while keeping the same infrastructure, some organizations decide to make a fresh start when adopting Windows Server 2008 R2.

They migrate objects from their old forest to the new forest rather than upgrade their old forest. Although this might sound cumbersome, it makes sense if you consider that many organizations have had their Active Directory domain structure for a decade or more. At some point it is easier to start over than to try to adapt design decisions made in 2001 to an Active Directory environment that may still be in production well into the 2020's.

> **NOTE** About 10 years ago I was working in an organization that was being taken over by two different companies and was essentially being split down the middle. As two of the three major players in this particular industry were splitting and consuming the third, the Australian government competition regulator dictated that the split had to be total. There could be no chance that an administrator on one side of the split business would have administrative rights over objects on the other side of the split business; hence the requirement for separate forests.

A more common reason to have separate forests is where you need complete administrative separation; where, for the purposes of regulation, there needs to be absolutely no personnel in one part of the business able to manage the IT infrastructure of the second part of the business. In this case you might establish a second or third forest. When the organizations are separate, there is no chance that an administrator in one forest will end up with rights over objects in another forest.

It is possible to almost completely partition administrative responsibilities from within a single Active Directory domain if you know what you are doing. However, this is a complex procedure. Active Directory is designed around the idea of there being at least one account that has privileges over all objects, such as the first administrator account in the first domain. Of course, it is possible to de-leverage these accounts, but the process of doing so, and then proving that it is done to a team of auditors, is significantly more involved than just creating a second Active Directory forest.

Also, even when you have separate forests, it is possible to create what are known as *forest trusts*. A forest trust is where all of the domains in one forest trust all the domains in another forest. This allows users in one forest to access resources in the other forest without administrators in one forest having any administrative rights over resources in the other forest. The administrators in one forest are able to set permissions on resources, allowing users in the forest that they trust to access specific resources.

> ▶ In my experience people in one side of a split company were able to print on the other side of the split. But, if the printer had a problem, they had to call the other company's IT support team because their own support team could do nothing.

Forest trusts are only possible if the functional levels of both forests are set to Windows Server 2003 or higher. You also need to be able to resolve DNS names for domain controllers in each forest from the other. To create a forest trust, perform the following general steps:

1. Open the Active Directory Domains and Trusts console from the Administrative Tools menu on a domain controller in the forest root domain.

2. Right click on the forest root domain, which is the domain at the top of the forest, and then click Properties.

3. On the Trust tab, click the New Trust button, and then click Next.

4. Enter the DNS name of the root domain of the Active Directory forest with which you wish to establish the trust, and then click Next.

5. On the Direction of Trust page, choose between:

   ▷ **Two-Way:** A trust where users in either forest can access resources in the other forest.

   ▷ **One-Way: Incoming:** Although the terminology can be a little confusing, this allows users in your local forest to access resources in the remote forest. An outgoing trust must also be established in the remote forest to your local forest for this to work.

   ▷ **One-Way: Outgoing:** This allows users in the remote forest to access resources in your local forest. An incoming trust to your local forest also needs to be established in the remote forest for this to work.

Having More than One Domain

Each domain controller in a Windows Server 2008 R2 functional level domain can support the creation of up to 2.15 billion objects, like user accounts and groups, during its lifetime. It is possible to go higher than 2.15 billion objects by adding domain controllers, but 2 billion objects is a nice round number when considering the aggregate of all objects from all partitions. As this number is a little hard to get a handle on, in terms of practical limitations, a single domain should never have more than 1,200 domain controllers. If you have two domain controllers at each site for the purposes of redundancy, that's roughly 600 individual sites supported for an individual domain.

Although replication traffic was a definite reason for separate domains in Windows Server 2003 environments, Windows Server 2008 and 2008 R2 Active Directory replication has been made vastly more efficient than that which was available in previous versions of the operating system. Rather than replicating whole objects to each domain controller in the domain when an attribute on the object is changed, only the attribute is replicated. This reduces the amount of data that needs to be replicated.

It is also likely that your organization has much better WAN bandwidth today than it did back when you designed your Windows Server 2003 infrastructure. So, not only is less replication data being transmitted, it is likely that your infrastructure can cope with a greater amount of replication data on a per kilobit per second basis.

How much data is replicated between domain controllers depends a lot on the way the domain functions, which will be unique to each organization. It is difficult to put a ballpark figure on the number of users and computers needed before it makes sense to create separate domains. I've heard of organizations that have single domain forests and more than 20,000 users, and I've heard of organizations that have five domains with less than 3,000 users.

Another reason why organizations go with separate domains is because they want to enforce different password policies on different parts of the organization. With Windows Server 2008 R2, you can use a feature named *Fine-Grained Password Policies* to enforce separate password policies within the same domain. You should note that Fine-Grained Password Policies are somewhat laborious to implement.

A more common reason for multiple domains is political. Large organizations often have multiple separate subsidiaries. I once worked at a company that included fifteen distinct businesses, each with its own website and management, that ultimately reported to an umbrella company. This organization used a single Active Directory forest, but within that forest there were fifteen separate domain trees. The reason for the large number of domain trees was primarily cultural. Each business was distinct, and management felt that forcing users from one of these businesses to log on to a domain that either had the name of the head office or one of the other businesses would take something intangible away from the uniqueness of that part of the organization.

This is a clear example of how sometimes network design isn't about what is possible (in this case all users in the organization would have fit comfortably within a single Active Directory domain) but instead about meeting the organization's aspirations, which in this case, was that each business have the appearance of independence from the rest of the conglomerate.

It isn't necessary to establish a second forest in the event that you want to have domains that have separate namespaces. One of the often-missed things about an Active Directory forest is that it can contain multiple namespace trees. For example,

▶ If you have a really big domain, you might want to consider multiple domains, because otherwise your WAN links are going to be flooded with Active Directory updates.

▶ It is often just easier to enforce a more rigorous password policy on everyone in the organization than it is to create separate domains or Fine-Grained Password Policies to enable different password policies in the same domain.

you could have a forest root domain named contoso.com that has child domains in the contoso.com tree named northamerica.contoso.com, europe.contoso.com and antarctica.contoso.com, but within the same forest domain you could have a separate fabrikam.com tree that includes Europe.fabrikam.com and Africa.fabrikam.com.

Creating a child domain in an existing forest, whether it is the root of a new domain tree or a child domain in an existing one, is relatively easy. To create a child domain, perform the following general steps:

1. Run DCPROMO on a computer that will function as the first domain controller in the new domain. This computer needs to be configured so that it can perform name resolution against a domain controller in the domain that will function as the parent domain. Ensure that you select the Advanced Mode Installation option if you want to create a new tree in an existing forest.

2. Select the New Domain in an Existing Forest option, shown in Figure 4-1. You only have the option to create the new domain tree root if you select the Advanced Mode Installation option.

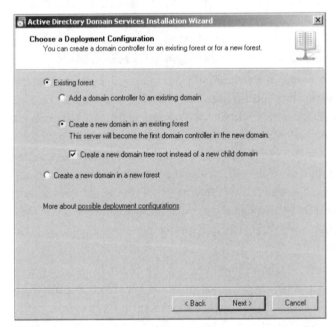

FIGURE 4-1: New domain in existing forest

3. Specify the name of any domain in the forest where the new domain will be installed. You may also need to provide alternate credentials at this point for that domain, depending on existing security relationships.

4. If you are creating a new domain tree, enter the fully qualified domain name (FQDN) of the new domain. If you are creating a child domain, enter the FQDN on the parent domain and the single name of the child domain.

5. Continue the Active Directory Domain Services Installation Wizard as normal, and reboot the newly installed DC when necessary.

SETTING DOMAIN AND FOREST FUNCTIONAL LEVELS

Domain and forest functional levels determine which Active Directory features you can use and are dependent on the domain controllers that your organization is using. For example, if you want to leverage the Windows Server 2008 R2 Active Directory Recycle Bin, you need to be running all domains in the forest at the Windows Server 2008 R2 functional level. In general, the higher your domain and forest functional level, the more advanced features you get. The cost of this is that you need to ensure that all your domain controllers are running Windows Server 2008 R2, which may be a bit of a hassle if some of your existing domain controllers have x86 processors.

It is important to remember that domain and forest functional levels only limit the domain controllers that can be present in the environment and not the member servers that can be present. For example, while setting a Windows Server 2008 R2 functional level means that only Windows Server 2008 R2 domain controllers are supported, the domain itself can still have member servers running Windows Server 2003 and computers running the Windows XP operating systems.

You can see what functional level the domain and forest are set to by using the Active Directory Domains and Trusts console. Domain functional levels support the following domain controllers and features:

▶ **Windows 2000 Native:** This domain functional level supports Windows 2000, Windows Server 2003, Windows Server 2008 and Windows Server 2008 R2 domain controllers. You wouldn't use this functional level unless you are unable to retire your domain controllers running Windows 2000. This functional level supports the fewest features compared to higher functional levels.

▶ **Windows Server 2003:** This domain functional level supports domain controllers running Windows Server 2003, Windows Server 2008 and Windows Server 2008 R2. This is the default functional level when you install a domain controller running Windows Server 2008 R2 as a new DC in a new forest. This functional level supports more features than the Windows 2000 Native functional level does, but doesn't support the new Active Directory features available in Windows Server 2008, such as Fine-Grained Password Policies.

▶ **Windows Server 2008:** This domain functional level supports domain controllers running Windows Server 2008 and Windows Server 2008 R2. This domain functional level supports better replication technologies than the Windows Server 2003 functional level as well as features like Last Interactive Logon information and Fine-Grained Password Policies.

▶ **Windows Server 2008 R2:** This domain functional level only supports domain controllers running the Windows Server 2008 R2 operating system. If you raise the forest functional level to Windows Server 2008 R2, which you can only do if all domains are at that functional level, you can access the Active Directory Recycle Bin feature by configuring the Windows Server 2008 R2 forest functional level.

You set forest functional levels based on the lowest functional level of any domain that is a part of your organization's forest. For example, if your forest has five domains, with four of those domains set to the Windows Server 2008 R2 functional level and one set to the Windows Server 2003 functional level, you'll only be able to use the Windows Server 2003 forest functional level. If you upgraded that final domain to the Windows Server 2008 functional level, rather than the Windows Server 2008 R2 functional level, you'd be able to set the forest to the Windows Server 2008, rather than 2008 R2 functional level.

> **NOTE** Raising a domain or forest functional level is a one-way operation. Once you've raised the functional level, you won't be able to lower it in future. The only exception is that you can roll back from Windows Server 2008 R2 to Windows Server 2008 if the forest functional level is set to Windows Server 2008 or lower.

Before you raise the domain or forest functional level, you must:

▶ Ensure that the account used to raise the domain functional level is a member of the Domain Admins group.

▶ Ensure that the account used to raise the forest functional level is a member of the Enterprise Admins group.

▶ Raise the domain functional level on the computer that hosts the *primary domain controller (PDC)* emulator role. The Active Directory Domains and Trusts tool automatically targets this server, but you're probably safer logging on locally to the PDC emulator to perform a functional level upgrade. You will learn how to locate computers that host operations master roles later in this chapter.

▶ Raise the forest functional level on the computer that hosts the schema master role. The Active Directory Domains and Trusts tool does automatically target this server, but you're probably safer logging on locally to the schema master.

▶ Ensure all domain controllers in the domain are running operating systems supported by that functional level. For example, you can't upgrade to the Windows Server 2008 R2 functional level if you have a domain controller running Windows Server 2003.

You use the Active Directory Domains and Trusts tool to verify the current functional level and, if necessary, to raise it. It is also possible to use the Active Directory Users and Computers console to raise the domain functional level. To raise the domain functional level or verify the current functional level, perform the following general steps:

1. Open the Active Directory Domains and Trusts tool on the computer in the target domain that hosts the PDC emulator role.

2. Right click on the target domain and then click on Raise Domain Functional Level.

3. Select the target functional level.

You should wait for the change to propagate out before attempting to raise the forest functional level. If you try to raise the forest functional level too soon after raising the domain functional level, you may be blocked, as the domain might not have reached the minimum functional level required to update to the new forest functional level. To raise the forest functional level, or verify the current functional level, perform the following general steps:

1. Log on to the computer that hosts the schema master role in the forest and open the Active Directory Domains and Trusts tool.

2. Right click on the Active Directory Domains and Trusts item and then click on Raise Forest Functional Level.

SELECTING THE DNS SERVER

It is an understatement to say that DNS is tightly integrated with Active Directory, as clients use it to locate most resources on the network. Through DHCP and automatic updates, you can configure every client on the network to register itself with DNS. Although it is possible to install the DNS role on a computer that is not a domain controller, you get the smallest administrative burden if you install the DNS role on a DC. When you install the DNS role on a DC, you get the option of storing all DNS zone information in Active Directory. The advantage is that it makes it simple to replicate that zone information to other DNS servers in your organization. As Active Directory uses a multi-master model, you don't have to worry about the old Primary/Secondary DNS model, where only the primary DNS server was able to process updates to the DNS zone. Any Active Directory-integrated DNS server can serve as the master of the DNS zone and process updates.

There are several types of zones, including:

▶ **Forward lookup zones:** Translate hostnames to IP addresses. A forward lookup zone for each domain can be automatically created when you install the first domain controller in that domain. Windows Server 2008 R2 DNS servers support Active Directory-integrated forward lookup zones, primary forward lookup zones, secondary forward lookup zones and stub zones.

▶ **Reverse lookup zones:** Translate IP addresses to hostnames. These zones must be created manually, but once created, can be populated automatically. You can configure DNS so that when a record in a forward lookup zone is updated, the record in the corresponding reverse lookup zone is updated. These zones aren't required on most networks, which is why they aren't automatically created when you install Active Directory.

Generally speaking, if you set up dynamic updates properly, you won't have to create DNS records on a regular basis. For example, every time you add a DNS server to your Active Directory forest, a name server record associated with that DNS server is automatically added to the appropriate DNS zone.

▶ The coverage of DNS in this chapter is primarily from the perspective of it supporting Active Directory and doesn't delve into topics such as replication with non-Microsoft DNS servers or the creation of Mail Exchanger (MX) records.

Using Internal Versus External DNS

Although you can use your organization's external domain name as your organization's internal domain name, most organizations find it easier to go with a custom

DNS suffix, such as .internal, rather than use one of the official domain suffixes, like .com, .net or .org. The advantage of this approach is that it allows you to clearly differentiate your external hosts, which have externally resolvable addresses, from your internal hosts, which have addresses that are only able to be resolved to clients on your internal network. When you create a new domain and specify the fully qualified domain name for that domain, the Active Directory installation routine performs a check to see if the correct DNS delegations have been created. This process is far less finicky if you use a custom DNS suffix, as the installation process will then offer to create a local DNS server to host the zone associated with the domain, rather than try to cajole an external DNS server into performing the same task.

Most small- to medium-sized organizations have their external DNS zone hosted by their ISP. If your organization hosts its own external DNS zone, usually on a DNS server on the perimeter network, you might choose to use a standard, primary DNS zone rather than an Active Directory-integrated zone, as you can configure a stand-alone server that is not a member of a domain to function as a DNS server. If you do host your own DNS zone, you still may have to contact your ISP about configuring appropriate reverse lookup records for the public IP addresses assigned to your organization, as it is unlikely that your organization has been granted enough address space to host the reverse lookup zone yourself. You'll learn more about reverse lookup zones later in this chapter.

▶ Ensure with your ISP that you can configure your organization's SMTP mail gateway reverse lookup zone. If your group's SMTP server's IP address isn't associated with your mail domain name, outgoing e-mail may be dropped by anti-spam heuristics.

Understanding Active Directory-Integrated Zones

Active Directory-integrated zones have several benefits over traditional primary and secondary zones. When you use Active Directory-integrated zones, any DNS server in the organization is able to process updates to the zone. There is also no single point of failure. When you use the traditional primary/secondary model, you can only have one primary server processing updates, and there is a fair amount of configuration involved in switching a secondary server over to function as a primary in the event that the primary server fails.

When you create a new Active Directory-integrated zone, you have the option of determining the replication scope of that zone. The options are: to all DNS servers that are hosted on DCs in the forest, to all DNS servers that are hosted on DCs within the domain, or to all DCs that are enrolled in a specific custom Active Directory partition.

▶ This third option isn't used often because it involves the creation and maintenance of a custom Active Directory partition.

To create an Active Directory-integrated forward lookup zone, perform the following steps:

1. Log on to a domain controller that has the DNS server role installed.

2. Open the DNS Manager console.

3. Right click on the Forward Lookup Zones node and then click on New Zone.

4. On the Zone Type page, choose Primary Zone and ensure that the Store the Zone in Active Directory option is selected. This option will not be present if the DNS server is installed on a computer that is not a writable domain controller.

> **NOTE** Unless you have a good reason not to do so, you should generally replicate Active Directory-integrated forward lookup zones to all DCs in the forest. This way any client in the forest will be able to directly resolve the IP address of any other client in the forest, rather than having its DNS query passed over WAN links to authoritative servers in other domains.

5. Choose the replication scope. As Figure 4-2 shows, you can choose from all DNS servers running on domain controllers in the forest, all domain controllers in the domain, or, if you have created a specific directory partition, all domain controllers that host that specific partition.

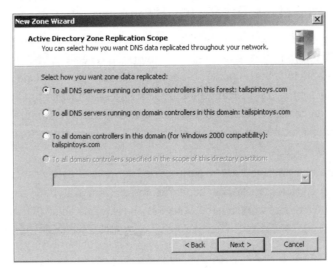

FIGURE 4-2: DNS replication scope

6. Enter the zone name.

> **NOTE** For Windows-only environments, you should choose the Allow Only Secure Dynamic Updates option. If you are running a mixed environment, you might have to allow both non-secure and secure dynamic updates, though this is generally not recommended as attackers could theoretically poison your DNS server with unauthorized, illegitimate updates.

7. Choose to allow only secure, dynamic updates; allow both secure and non-secure updates; or do not allow updates.

When you choose the forest or domain replication scope, the zone will automatically replicate to all DCs that have the DNS role installed within that scope. It will also replicate to any DCs with the DNS role installed that are newly promoted within that scope at any point in the future.

Utilizing Reverse Lookup Zones

> **NOTE** This is the reason why it can be fun tracking down who hosts the reverse lookup zone for the public IP addresses your organization has been allocated. Public IPv4 addresses are sliced and diced so finely these days, that you may need to get in contact with your ISP's ISP to get reverse lookup working properly for your organization's external hosts.

Reverse lookup zones are used to translate IP addresses to fully qualified domain names. Reverse lookup zones generally aren't needed on Active Directory networks but can be necessary if applications need to perform reverse IP address lookups. The trick with reverse lookup zones is specifying the correct network address. This is because reverse lookup zones only support Class C address allocation schemes, and you can only create a reverse lookup zone based on a Class C address block. To create a reverse lookup zone, perform the following general steps:

1. Open the DNS Manager console on a writable DC that has the DNS server role installed.

2. Right click on the Reverse Lookup Zones node, and then click on New Zone. Click Next.

3. Choose Primary Zone and ensure that the Store the Zone in Active Directory option is selected. Click Next.

4. Choose the replication scope. Unless you have good reason to do otherwise, choose the To All DNS Servers Running on Domain Controllers in the Forest option, and then click Next.

5. Choose between an IPv4 and an IPv6 reverse lookup zone. If you choose an IPv4 lookup zone, you will need to specify the first three quads of the Class C network ID as shown in Figure 4-3. If you choose an IPv6 reverse lookup zone, you need to specify the IPv6 address prefix. Click Next.

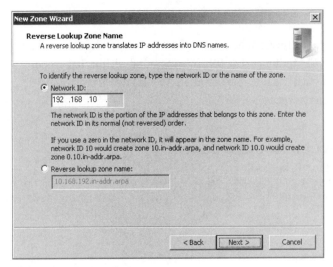

FIGURE 4-3: Reverse lookup zone

6. Choose to accept only secure, dynamic updates; both secure and insecure, dynamic updates; or not to allow dynamic updates. Click Next, then click Finish.

Using Delegations

Delegations are used to redirect clients to child DNS zones from parent zones. As DNS is hierarchical, delegations allow zones at the top of the hierarchy to create a path to zones lower down the hierarchy. For example, if your organization uses the tailspintoys.com domain and you want to add a child DNS zone named tonga .tailspintoys.com that is hosted on a different set of DNS servers, you'd create a delegation from the tailspintoys.com zone pointing to the DNS servers that host the tonga.tailspintoys.com zone. You don't need to manually create a delegation if you are using DCPROMO to add a new child domain or a new domain tree to your organization's forest, as the Active Directory Installation Wizard handles this for you. You generally need to do this when parts of your organization might be in another forest or use non-Windows DNS servers, and they need to use a child zone of a zone that you are hosting on your DNS servers.

To configure a delegation, perform the following general steps:

1. In the DNS Manager console, select the zone from which you want to delegate. For example, if you want to create a delegation to the zone tonga.tailspintoys .com, right click on the tailspintoys.com zone in the DNS Manager console, and then click on New Delegation.

2. Ensure that you have created the target zone as a forward lookup zone on the target DNS server to which you will be performing the delegation. You can only perform a delegation to a server that already hosts the child zone.

3. In the New Delegation Wizard, specify the name of the delegated domain. The name of the parent zone will be included on this page, as shown in Figure 4-4. Click Next.

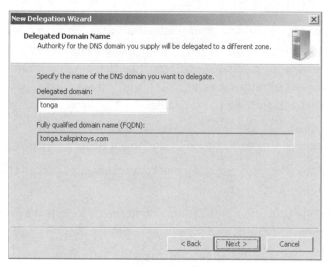

FIGURE 4-4: Zone delegation

4. Specify the address of the DNS server that will host this zone. You need to specify the address of a DNS server that is already authoritative for this zone (see step 2) for this to work. Click Next, and then click Finish.

Creating Conditional Forwarders

Conditional forwarders allow you to specify a target DNS server to resolve queries against a particular DNS zone. For example, if people in your organization need to regularly query hosts in the adatum.com zone, you could create a conditional forwarder to point to a DNS server in the adatum.com zone. This way DNS queries would be more quickly resolved than if they were passed up to the root servers and then back down through the chain of delegation to the servers authoritative for the adatum.com zone.

To configure a conditional forwarder, perform the following general steps:

1. In the DNS Manager console, right click on the Conditional Forwarders item, and then click on New Conditional Forwarder.

2. Specify the DNS domain that the conditional forwarder applies to and the DNS server to which you want queries against this domain forwarded. You can also choose to replicate the forwarder to all DNS servers in the forest.

Configuring Stub Zones

Stub zones differ from conditional forwarders in that the target DNS servers of the stub zones are dynamically updated, whereas conditional forwarders are static. If the DNS server set as the target for the conditional forwarder changes, the conditional forwarder will no longer work. Stub zones are most useful when you have configured forest trusts, as there are likely to be a large number of authoritative DNS servers in the target forest.

To configure a stub zone, perform the following general steps:

1. In the DNS Manager console, right click on Forward Lookup Zones and then click on New Zone. Click Next.

2. On the Zone Type page, click Stub Zone and then choose to Store the Zone in Active Directory. Click Next.

3. Choose to replicate to all DNS servers hosted on DCs in the forest, domain, or enrolled in a specific partition, and then click Next.

4. Specify the zone name. This zone needs to be able to be resolved from the DNS server. Remember to enter the zone name, not the name of any specific DNS server within the zone.

5. Specify the IP address of a DNS server in the zone. This DNS server will be queried to locate other name servers, hence populating the stub zone.

DEFINING ACTIVE DIRECTORY SITES

Sites exist to ensure that clients access resources locally rather than remotely. You don't want a client in Sydney to authenticate against a domain controller in Seattle, and you don't want a person in Canberra opening a file from a Distributed File System (DFS) replica in Copenhagen when there is one located in a room down the hall. Sites are used by an increasing number of Microsoft technologies, from Exchange to the System Center suite, to ensure that clients know where they are in the domain or forest.

A common misconception about sites is that you can only have a site associated with one domain. You define sites at the forest level, and you can have multiple domains within a single site and a single domain that covers multiple sites.

To create a site and associate it with an IPv4 network or IPv6 network, perform the following general steps:

1. Open the Active Directory Sites and Services console.

2. Right click on the Sites node and then click on New Site.

3. Enter the name for the new site. Click on a site link object. You can change this site link later. Click OK.

4. Right click on the Subnets node and then click on New Subnet.

5. On the New Object - Subnet dialog box, shown in Figure 4-5, enter either an IPv4 network in Classless Inter-Domain Routing (CIDR) notation or an IPv6 network prefix. Select a Site Object to associate with this network address and then click OK.

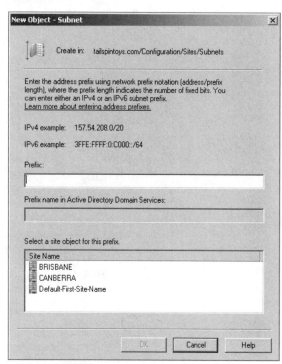

Once you have configured your sites, you can configure site links. Site links allow Active Directory to know how sites connect to each other. You need at least two sites created and associated with subnets before you can create a site link. You can configure the site link cost to get Active Directory to prefer one connection over another. The default site link cost is

FIGURE 4-5: Creating a new site

100, with lower site link costs being preferred for traffic over higher site link costs. You can also configure the replication interval and replication schedule by editing the site link properties. *Replication interval* determines how often replication occurs between sites, with the default being every 180 minutes. The *replication schedule* determines when replication occurs, with the default being all the time. To create a site link, perform the following general steps:

1. Open the Active Directory Sites and Services console.

2. Right click on the Sites\Inter-Site Transports\IP node, and then click on New Site Link.

3. On the New Object - Site Link dialog, add the two sites that you want connected by the site link, and provide the site link with a descriptive name.

4. Right click on the newly created site link, and then click on Properties.

5. On the Properties dialog box, shown in Figure 4-6, configure the site link cost and the replication schedule. If you want the site link to be preferred over other links, give it a lower number than the other links.

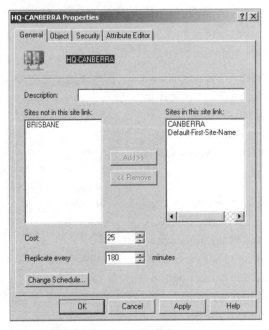

FIGURE 4-6: Configuring a site link

DEFINING FSMO ROLES

Domain controllers aren't entirely interchangeable. There are five special server roles called the *Flexible Single-Master Operations (FSMO)* roles that are present in each Active Directory forest. Three of these roles must be present on domain controllers in each domain in the forest. Many administrators either forget or don't know about the FSMO roles. This is because the FSMO roles are automatically installed on the first domain controller in the forest and on the first domain controller in any new child domain without requiring administrator intervention. This can cause problems when a domain controller that hosts one of these roles fails. Because everyone is used to thinking of DCs as interchangeable, no one realizes that the FSMO role is also down. As the problems caused by the loss of the FSMO role holder may not become immediately apparent, it might be some time between the failure of a DC that hosts specific operations master roles and anyone connecting it to a current set of problems.

Defining the Schema Master Role

The *schema master* is the only server in the organization that can process updates to the schema. Only one domain controller in the forest can hold the schema master role. The schema master is generally the only one of the FSMO roles where you will have a practical need to know its location. This is because you need to perform updates to the Active Directory schema to install products like Exchange Server 2010, and this is best done either on the schema master itself or on a computer that is in the same Active Directory site as the computer hosting the schema master role.

You can determine which computer hosts the schema master role by running the following PowerShell command when the Active Directory administrative module is loaded:

```
Get-ADForest tailspintoys.com | FT SchemaMaster
```

▶ You load the Active Directory PowerShell module using the command Import-Module Active Directory.

Defining the Domain Naming Master Role

The *domain naming master* role manages the addition and removal of domains throughout the forest. Only one computer in the forest hosts the domain naming master role. This role is also responsible for managing references to domains in trusted forests. You can determine which computer hosts the domain naming master role by running the following PowerShell command when the Active Directory administrative module is loaded:

```
Get-ADForest tailspintoys.com | FT DomainNamingMaster
```

Defining the PDC Emulator Role

The *PDC emulator* is responsible for processing changes to passwords for accounts in the domain and is also used for time synchronization in a domain. You should ensure that the PDC emulator in the root domain is able to synchronize regularly against an external time source, as this server will be used as the basis for all time keeping in the forest. There is a PDC emulator in each domain in the forest. You can determine which computer hosts the PDC emulator role by running the following PowerShell command when the Active Directory administrative module is loaded:

```
Get-ADDomain tailspintoys.com | FT PDCEmulator
```

Defining the Infrastructure Master Role

The *infrastructure master* is responsible for keeping track of changes in other domains in the forest as they apply to objects in the local domain. There is an infrastructure master in each domain in the forest. Generally, the infrastructure master should not be hosted on a computer that is also a global catalog server; though in most cases, people never move the FSMO roles from the first DC in a domain, and the first DC is a global catalog server by default. This rule is not important if all DCs in the domain function as global catalog servers. You can determine which computer hosts the infrastructure master role by running the following PowerShell command when the Active Directory administrative module is loaded:

```
Get-ADDomain tailspintoys.com | FT InfrastructureMaster
```

Defining the RID Master Role

The *RID master* processes relative ID requests from domain controllers in a specific domain. Relative IDs and domain Security IDs are combined to create a unique Security ID (SID) for the object. There is a RID master in each domain in the forest. You can determine which computer hosts the RID master role by running the following PowerShell command when the Active Directory administrative module is loaded:

```
Get-ADDomain tailspintoys.com | FT RIDMaster
```

Seizing FSMO Roles

In the event that a DC that hosts one or more of the operations master roles fails, you'll need to seize the role from the computer and transfer it to another DC. You can do this from PowerShell when the Active Directory module is loaded using the

Move-ADDirectoryServerOperationMasterRole cmdlet. For example, to seize the RID master, infrastructure master and domain naming master roles and place them on server DC-III, use the command:

```
Move-ADDirectoryServerOperationMasterRole -Identity DC-III
-OperationMasterRole RIDMaster,InfrastructureMaster,
DomainNamingMaster -Force
```

USING READ-ONLY DOMAIN CONTROLLERS

Domain controllers are the most important infrastructure servers on your network. In the best of all circumstances, you have these servers placed away safely in server rooms that are protected by locks that require two-factor authentication. This sort of security is necessary for domain controllers because, if someone attacks your organization and compromises a domain controller, any of the accounts in the domain may be compromised. At a minimum, you're probably looking at having to reset everyone's passwords. At worst, your entire network infrastructure may be compromised; because, if the attackers get access to a highly privileged account, such as the first administrator account created in the root domain, they could theoretically do anything.

While most organizations might be able to afford this sort of security infrastructure at their head office location, it is a bit more difficult to create at a branch office. The *Read-Only Domain Controller (RODC)* is a DC that is designed around the problem of insecure branch offices where domain controllers may be compromised. The RODC only store a limited number of passwords, so in the event they are compromised or stolen, you can quickly reset those passwords. Active Directory specifically keeps track of which accounts have been used in conjunction with the RODC.

To deploy an RODC, perform the following general steps:

1. Ensure that the forest functional level is set to Windows Server 2003, Windows Server 2008, or Windows Server 2008 R2. You learned how to modify forest functional levels earlier in this chapter.

2. Run adprep/rodcprep from the \sources\adprep folder of the Windows Server 2008 R2 installation media on the computer that hosts the schema master role in the forest.

3. Ensure that at least one domain controller running Windows Server 2008 or Windows Server 2008 R2 is already present in the domain where you want to deploy the RODC.

4. When you run DCPROMO, select the Advanced option. You can only add an RODC to an existing domain. On the Additional Domain Controllers Options page, shown in Figure 4-7, choose the Read-Only Domain Controller (RODC) checkbox.

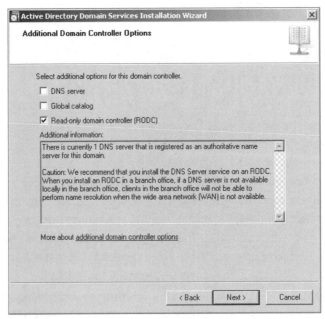

FIGURE 4-7: RODC installation

Securing the RODC

There are several steps to take to secure the RODC. The first is to make some attempt at physical security, although if you've chosen to install the domain controller as an RODC, you've already reached the point where you believe that the physical security of the server is questionable. If a dedicated, locked server room is not possible, at least attempt to place the RODC in a locked cabinet in a locked office. Placing a server in a high-traffic area where anybody can touch it is bound to end in disaster.

RODC PASSWORD REPLICATION

One of the most important steps in configuring an RODC is limiting which passwords can be replicated down to the server from a writable domain controller. The default configuration of an RODC has it store almost everything from Active Directory except for user and computer account passwords. In the event that a user or computer account needs to be authenticated against Active Directory, the RODC acts as a proxy for a writable Windows Server 2008 DC. The authentication occurs but depends on the WAN link to be functional, as if you could host a writable DC locally, you wouldn't need the RODC.

Although you can configure an RODC to not cache any passwords locally, you can configure an RODC to cache the passwords of select staff that work at the branch office to speed their logon. Caching passwords also allows branch office users to log on in the event that the WAN link fails. If the WAN link fails and the user's credentials are not cached, the user will simply be unable to log on to the domain.

To allow user accounts to be cached locally on an RODC, perform the following steps:

1. Open Active Directory Users and Computers on a writable domain controller.

2. Locate the RODC's computer account. This will usually be in the Domain Controllers container.

3. Right click on the RODC's computer account and select Properties.

4. On the Password Replication tab, shown in Figure 4-8, configure the groups for which password replication to the RODC is allowed.

5. If you click on the Advanced button, you can view a list of all accounts that are currently stored on the RODC. You can also pre-populate the RODC with the passwords of all users that you've authorized to log on using the server.

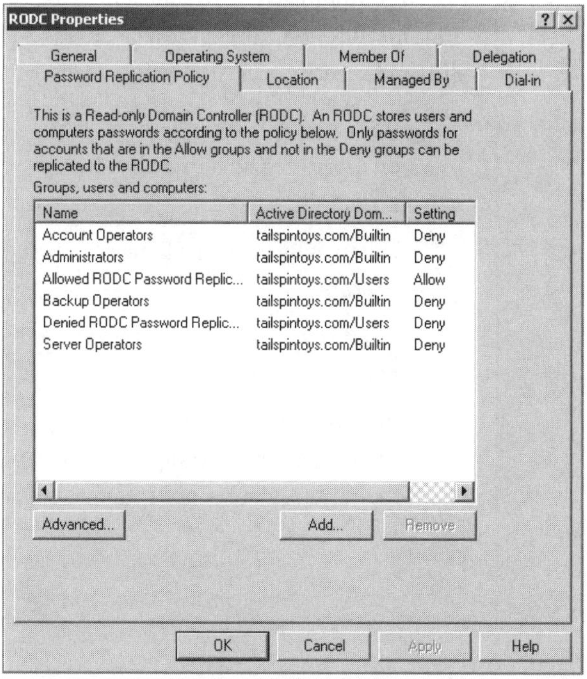

▶ Most computers allow logons using locally cached credentials, so even if the WAN link fails, most of your users can log on using the credentials cached on their local machines. Only computers where they've never logged in will have a problem.

FIGURE 4-8: RODC password replication

RODC LOCAL ADMINISTRATORS

> **NOTE** There is no reason why a computer that functions as an RODC cannot also host other roles. The main caveat with installing other roles is that, in choosing to deploy the server as an RODC, you've admitted to yourself that the physical security of the server is questionable. You probably don't want to be hosting sensitive data on the server if there is a possibility of it being removed or compromised.

Because you deploy them as a security measure, RODCs are almost always placed at branch office sites. As resources at branch office sites are often sparse, it is also likely that you'll co-locate other services on the server hosting the RODC role. For example, a server that functions as an RODC can also function as a file server, DNS server, DHCP server, and local intranet server.

If the computer hosting the RODC role also needs to host other roles, you may need to allow a user who works at the branch office, but who is not a member of your organization's usual IT staff, administrator access in case your normal remote administration techniques don't work. RODCs differ from normal domain controllers in that you can grant local administrator access without having to make the user a member of the Domain Admins group.

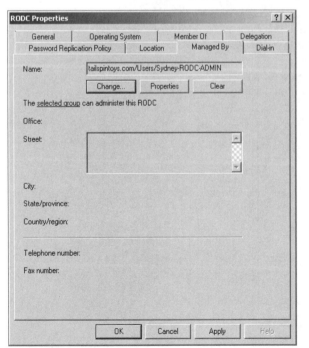

To configure a user to function as a local administrator on the computer that hosts the RODC role, perform the following general steps:

1. Open Active Directory Users and Computers on a writable domain controller.

2. Locate the RODC's computer account. This will usually be in the Domain Controllers container.

3. Right click on the RODC's computer account and select Properties.

4. On the Managed By tab, shown in Figure 4-9, select the user or group to which you want to grant local administrator privileges.

FIGURE 4-9: Local RODC admin

RODC AND BITLOCKER

As you choose to implement the RODC because you believe there is an increased risk of the domain controller being physically compromised, a final step that you should take to protect the server is to implement BitLocker drive encryption. *BitLocker* is a technology that allows you to fully encrypt the hard-disk drive of a laptop computer running Windows 7 or Vista. With BitLocker, if someone loses his laptop computer, the person that found it can't rip out the hard-drive, mount it, and then read all the data that it holds. As you are only likely to deploy an RODC because you have concerns about the physical security of the domain controller, you should take similar steps by encrypting the hard-disk drive.

You have several options when it comes to enabling BitLocker on a computer running Windows Server 2008 R2. The first thing you need to do is add the BitLocker feature. If the computer is running the full version of the operating system, you can enable BitLocker from the Control Panel. If you are running a Server Core version of Windows Server 2008 R2, you can enable BitLocker once the feature is installed by using the following command:

```
Manage-Bde.exe -on
```

> **NOTE** While it is possible to use BitLocker on an RODC that doesn't have a TPM chip, the startup key is likely to be lost. You have to perform the BitLocker recovery process every time someone misplaces the BitLocker startup key; you probably shouldn't bother with the process.

It is possible to enable BitLocker on a computer without a Trusted Platform Module (TPM) chip. When you do this, you'll have to create a startup key out of a USB flash device. This device stores a special digital file that the domain controller will use as a part of the boot process. Without this startup key, the computer will be unable to boot.

Decommissioning an RODC

If you suspect that an RODC has been compromised, you can delete the account of the RODC from the Domain Controllers container in Active Directory Users and Computers. When you do this, you will get the option of resetting all passwords for user and computer accounts that were cached on the RODC as well as exporting a list of all potentially compromised accounts, as shown in Figure 4-10.

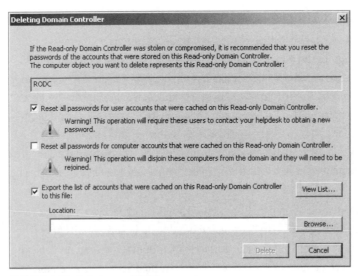

FIGURE 4-10: Deleting an RODC account

SECURING WITH GLOBAL CATALOG SERVERS AND UNIVERSAL GROUP MEMBERSHIP CACHING

Global catalog servers help with user logon requests and searches for objects through-out the forest. Specifically they help determine universal group membership. *Universal groups* are the type of security group that can have members from any domain in the forest, so a query to a global catalog server is necessary so that Active Directory can figure out if the user it is authenticating is a member of any such groups.

In a single domain forest, Microsoft recommends that you configure all domain controllers as global catalog servers. This is because enabling the global catalog server role doesn't require any extra disk space, CPU usage, or replication bandwidth. All of the groups that the user will be a member of will be local to the domain, and there will be no need for the global catalog to store information about other domains.

You have two options for branch office locations. You can enable *Universal Group Membership Caching (UGMC)* or configure a global catalog server. UGMC is sort of like a stripped down version of a global catalog server, as it caches universal group mem-bership information rather than storing it specifically like a global catalog server does. In general you should do the following:

▶   If you have a single domain forest, make every DC a global catalog server.

▶ If the site has more than 100 users and the forest has more than one domain, you should deploy a global catalog server.

▶ If the site hosts Exchange or another application that requires access to the global catalog, you'll need to deploy a global catalog server even if you have less than 100 users.

▶ If the site has less than 100 users, enable Universal Group Membership Caching.

To configure a computer as a global catalog server, perform the following steps:

1. Open the Active Directory Sites and Services console.

2. Locate the domain controller that you want to make a global catalog server.

3. Expand the Domain Controllers node, right click on the NTDS Settings item, and then click on Properties.

4. On the General Tab, shown in Figure 4-11, enable the Global Catalog checkbox.

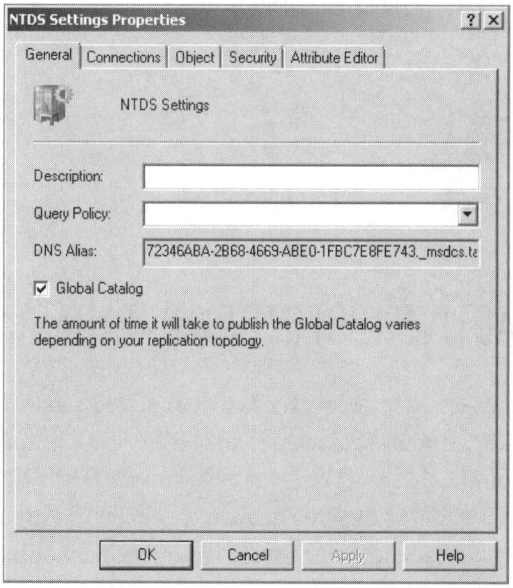

FIGURE 4-11: Enabling global catalog

To enable Universal Group Membership Caching, perform the following steps:

1. Open the Active Directory Sites and Services console.

2. Locate the site for which you want to enable Universal Group Membership Caching.

3. Right click on the NTDS Site Settings item, and then click on Properties.

4. Select the Enable Universal Group Membership Caching checkbox as shown in Figure 4-12.

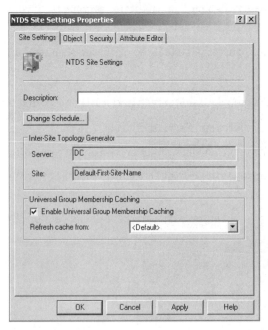

FIGURE 4-12: Enabling Universal Group Membership Caching

MAINTAINING THE ACTIVE DIRECTORY DATABASE

Although you learned earlier that Active Directory tends to look after itself and rarely needs to be recovered from backup, if you've got more than one domain controller, there are several reasons why you should still take regular backups of Active Directory. For one, having a backup makes it easier to deploy a domain controller in a branch office site. For another, if you have a backup, you can recover items that may have been inadvertently deleted through a process known as an authoritative restore.

Performing Advanced Installation of Active Directory

Promoting a computer to function as a domain controller is a fairly straightforward exercise, and something that you, as an experienced administrator, have likely done many times before. The important thing when adding an additional DC to an existing domain is to ensure that it has DNS connectivity to a DNS server that is authoritative for the domain you are attempting to join. The only other part of DCPROMO that tends to trip up administrators is when they receive the warning about the server requiring a static IP address. You'll get this even if you have set a static IPv4 address, but in this case the wizard will be warning you about the static IPv6 address. Unless you have an existing IPv6 address infrastructure, you don't really need to worry about this. You promote and demote a domain controller using the DCPROMO command. As is the case with all server roles and features in Windows Server 2008 R2, you don't need to have the installation media present when you add this role.

When you run the DCPROMO command, you also have the option of selecting the Advanced Mode Installation. You can use Active Directory Advanced Installation to accomplish the following tasks:

▶ To install Active Directory off a backup. This is the Install from Media option and only works if you are adding a domain controller to an existing domain. When you install from media, the newly promoted DC doesn't have to transfer all of the domain information across the network but instead only has to transfer updates done since the backup was taken. The Install from Media option is shown in Figure 4-13.

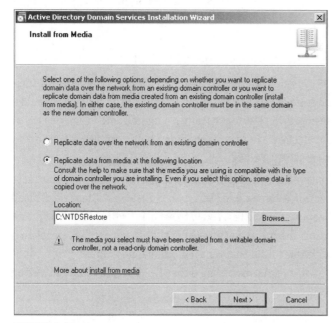

FIGURE 4-13: Install from media.

▸ To replicate data from a specific domain controller rather than the one chosen by the wizard

▸ To install an Active Directory domain controller as a read-only domain controller. You learned about read-only domain controllers earlier in this chapter

▸ To create a new domain tree in an existing forest

Recovering Deleted Items

Once you have a few domain controllers up-and-running, you don't really have a problem in terms of losing information. If one domain controller ends up crashing horribly, you can install another one and have it replicate all of the Active Directory data back across the network.

Having this sort of redundancy doesn't remove the need for backups entirely. Active Directory backups are handy when someone accidentally deletes a whole lot of information from Active Directory that shouldn't have been deleted. When you deliberately delete something from Active Directory, that deletion replicates to all the other domain controllers in the domain. If this is just a single user account, it is generally easier to recreate the account from scratch. If someone gets really creative and deletes a whole OU tree, it is time to go restore from the Active Directory backup or a snapshot.

PROTECTING ITEMS FROM ACCIDENTAL DELETION

▸ Removing the protection involves switching Active Directory Users and Computers over to the Advanced Features view and navigating to the Objects tab, which means that it requires a small amount of effort and makes the chance of an accident remote.

Windows Server 2008 provided administrators with a feature that allowed important items to be protected from accidental deletion. Protecting an item from accidental deletion just means that it won't automatically be deleted when someone tries, or accidentally tries, to remove it. To remove the item that is protected from accidental deletion, you have to remove the protection first.

Once you have removed the protection, they can delete the item as normal. Think of deleted item protection as breakable glass over a fire alarm. Glass was placed over fire alarms so that people would be less likely to set off the fire alarm as a prank. If you really want to set off the fire alarm, breaking the glass won't be a problem for you. The designers of fire alarms found that requiring someone to break glass would stop 99% of people who set off fire alarms because they liked pushing big red buttons to see the result.

In Windows Server 2008 R2, newly created OUs are protected by default, though user accounts are not. In general, you should go through and protect important accounts from deletion. To protect an item using Active Directory Users and Computers, perform the following general steps:

1. Enable the Advanced Features view in the Active Directory Users and Computers console.

2. On the Object tab, check the Protect Object from the Accidental Deletion checkbox as shown in Figure 4-14.

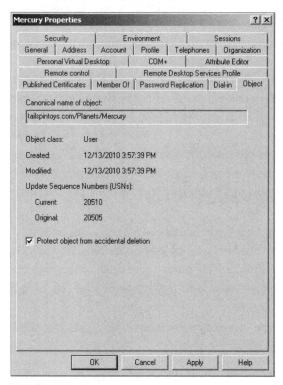

FIGURE 4-14: Protect from accidental deletion.

To protect all OUs in a domain from accidental deletion, issue the following PowerShell command when the Active Directory Administration module is loaded:

```
Get-ADOrganizationalUnit -LDAPFilter '(name=*)' |
Set-ADorganizationalUnit
-ProtectedFromAccidentalDeletion $true
```

In general, you shouldn't protect absolutely every item in your organization from being deleted from Active Directory. If you do, you will always have to go back and unprotect items before you delete them. This will add a substantial amount of time to your Active Directory maintenance routine. On the other hand, if the deliberate deletion of items from Active Directory in your organization is a rare event, configuring item protection will make it increasingly unlikely that you will have to perform an authoritative restore or use Active Directory Recycle Bin, because objects will only be deleted when they should be deleted.

AUTHORITATIVE RESTORE

An *authoritative restore* is performed when you want the items you are recovering to overwrite items that are in the current Active Directory database. If you don't perform an authoritative restore, Active Directory will assume that the restored data is simply out-of-date and will overwrite it when it is synchronized from another domain controller. If you perform a normal restore on an item that was backed up last Tuesday when it was deleted the following Thursday, the item will be deleted the next time the Active Directory database is synchronized. You do not need to perform an authoritative restore if you only have one domain controller in your organization, as there is no other domain controller that can overwrite the changes.

Unlike Windows Server 2003, you can't just press F8 when a domain controller is booting and select the option to enter Directory Services Restore Mode (DSRM). To enter DSRM, you first need to configure the server's boot menu so that the option to enter DSRM is enabled. You can do this from the command line or by using the System Configuration utility.

To use the System Configuration utility to perform this task, perform the following general steps:

1. Open the System Configuration utility from the Administrative Tools menu.

2. Click on the Boot tab. In the Boot options area, select the Safe boot option and then click on Active Directory repair as shown in Figure 4-15. Click OK.

3. When you have finished performing tasks in DSRM, open the System Configuration utility again and, on the General tab, choose the Normal Startup option.

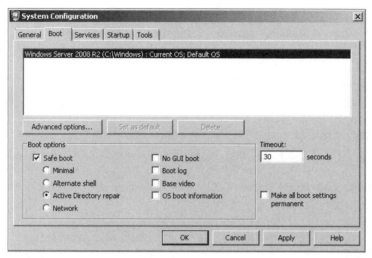

FIGURE 4-15: Configure for DSRM restart.

To configure a server so that you can choose Directory Services Restore Mode as a boot option that is available every time you boot the domain controller, perform the following general steps:

1. Open an administrative command prompt.

2. Run the command:

```
Bcdedit /copy {default} /d "Directory Services Restore Mode"
```

3. At this stage you will be presented with a globally unique identifier (GUID). Use the copy and paste functionality of the command prompt window to store the GUID in the copy/paste buffer. Paste the GUID into the following command:

```
Bcdedit /set {GUID} safeboot dsrepair
```

You will now have the boot option of choosing a normal boot or a boot into Directory Services Restore Mode when the server boots.

To enter Directory Services Restore Mode, you need to enter the Directory Services Restore Mode password. This is a password that you specify when you first set up the domain controller. It is not necessarily the same password as used by the local administrator account, although they can be the same. As the domain controller may have been set up several years ago or by someone else, it is not uncommon for administrators to have forgotten the DSRM password and hence be unable to get into DRSM. Luckily you can reset the DSRM password using the following procedure:

1. Open an administrative command prompt.

2. Enter the command:

   ```
   ntdsutil.exe
   ```

3. At the ntdsutil.exe prompt, enter the command:

   ```
   Reset password on server null
   ```

4. Enter the new DSRM password. When you have done this, type **Q** twice to exit from NTDSUTIL.

To perform an authoritative restore, perform the following general steps:

1. Choose a computer that functions as a global catalog server. This DC will function as your restore server.

2. Locate the most recent system state backup that contains the objects that you wish to restore. You can view Active Directory backup data to verify that the objects are present using the dsamain.exe utility, which you will learn about later in this chapter.

3. Restart the restore server in DSRM mode. Enter the DSRM password.

4. Restore the system state data.

5. Use the following command to restore items:

   ```
   Ntdsutil "authoritative restore"
   "restore object cn=Mercury,ou=Planets,dc=wingtiptoys,dc=com"
   q q
   ```

   Where "Mercury" is the object name, "Planets" is the OU in which it is contained and "Wingtiptoys.com" is the host domain.

6. If an entire OU is deleted, you can use the Restore Subtree option. For example, if you deleted the Planets OU and all the accounts that it held in the Wingtiptoys.com domain, you could use the following command to restore it and all the items it contained:

   ```
   Ntdsutil "authoritative restore" "restore subtree OU=Planets,
   DC=wingtiptoys,DC=com" q q
   ```

ACTIVE DIRECTORY RECYCLE BIN

Active Directory Recycle Bin is one of those features that sounds great on paper but is less than impressive in practice. Active Directory Recycle Bin allows the authoritative restore of items on a domain controller without the hassle of rebooting into Directory Services Restore Mode. While Active Directory Recycle Bin does accomplish this task, it is fair to say that the option as it exists in Windows Server 2008 R2 is only marginally better than rebooting into Directory Services Restore Mode. Given that you need to be running the organizational forest at the Windows Server 2008 R2 forest functional level to use this feature, most organizations won't bother with it anyway.

To enable Active Directory Recycle Bin, perform the following general steps:

▶ Once you enable Active Directory Recycle Bin, you will not be able to disable it.

1. Ensure that the forest functional level is set to Windows Server 2008 R2.

2. Start an Administrative PowerShell session and load the Active Directory module for PowerShell by running the command:

```
Import-Module ActiveDirectory
```

3. Once the Active Directory module is loaded, run the following command, substituting "wingtiptoys" and "com" for the name of the forest root domain:

```
Enable-ADOptionalFeature –Identity 'CN=Recycle Bin
Feature,CN=Optional
Features,CN=Directory Service,
CN=Windows NT, CN=Services,CN=Configuration,
DC=wingtiptoys, DC=com' –Scope ForestOrConfigurationSet –Target
'wingtiptoys.com'
```

4. You will receive a warning informing you that you cannot undo this change. Press Y in PowerShell to enable the Recycle Bin.

To search through deleted items, use the Get-ADObject with the IncludeDeleted-Objects parameter. For example, to view all deleted objects with the display name "Rooslan," from an administrative PowerShell session with the Active Directory module loaded, issue the command:

```
Get-ADObject -Filter {displayname -eq "Rooslan"} -IncludeDeletedObjects
```

Once you've verified that the object exists, you can use that command in conjunction with the Restore-ADObject command. For example, to restore the deleted object with the display name "Rooslan," issue the command:

```
Get-ADObject -Filter {displayname -eq "Rooslan"}
-IncludeDeletedObjects | RestoreADObject
```

You can also use the ldp.exe utility to view and restore deleted items. To view and then restore deleted items using the ldp.exe utility when Active Directory Recycle Bin is enabled, perform the following steps:

1. Open an elevated command prompt, and then run ldp.exe.

2. On the Options menu, click Controls.

3. In the Controls dialog box, select Return Deleted Objects in the Load Predefined dialog as shown in Figure 4-16, and then click OK.

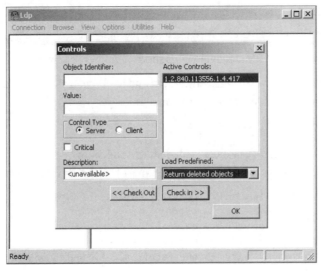

FIGURE 4-16: Return deleted objects.

4. On the Connection menu, click Connect and type **localhost**.

5. On the Connections menu, click Bind, and then click OK.

6. On the View menu, click Tree. Use the drop-down to select your domain, and then click OK. For Wingtiptoys.com, this would be DC=Wingtiptoys,DC=COM.

7. Expand the node and then select the CN=Deleted Object item. This will display a list of all deleted objects.

8. Right click on the Object that you want to restore, and then click Modify.

9. In the Edit Entry Attribute textbox, type **distinguishedName**. Select the Delete radio item, and then click Enter.

10. In the Values textbox, enter the original distinguished name. Select the Replace radio item. Enable the Extended checkbox, and then click Run.

You can also use Active Directory Recycle Bin to modify the *tombstone lifetime* of deleted objects. The tombstone lifetime determines how long a deleted object remains in an undeletable state before being finally purged from the Active Directory database. The default value is 180 days, which means that you can use Active Directory Recycle Bin to restore objects that were deleted in the last 180 days before having to attempt a restore through a backup. Needless to say, modifying this value does not work retroactively and any items that have already been purged due to the expiration of their tombstone lifetime will remain purged. To change this, for example to 400 days, issue the following PowerShell command once you have enabled Active Directory Recycle Bin and loaded the Active Directory module, substituting "wingtiptoys" and "com" for the name of your organization's forest root domain:

```
Set-ADObject -Identity "CN=Directory Service,CN=Windows NT,
CN=Services, CN=Configuration,DC=wingtiptoys,DC=com"
-Partition "CN=Configuration,DC=wingtiptoys,DC=com"
-Replace:@{"tombstonelifetime" = 400}
```

ACTIVE DIRECTORY SNAPSHOTS AND DATABASE MOUNTING TOOL

The Active Directory database mounting tool, dsamain.exe, allows you to view Active Directory data as it exists in snapshots, or backups, of the AD database. The benefit of this tool is that it allows you to view the contents of an Active Directory backup without having to actually restore that backup. For example, you might know that a particular OU was deleted in the last ten days and you might have daily backups of domain controller system states over those last ten days, but you might not know which of those backups contains the OU and its contents in the most recent state. Using the dsamain.exe utility allows you to mount the backups that you've restored in a separate location to determine which of them contains the data that you want to restore.

To create a snapshot of the Active Directory database, run the following command from an elevated command prompt:

```
ntdsutil "Activate Instance NTDS" snapshot create quit quit
```

You can create a scheduled task to create a snapshot using this command on a regular basis. To view a list of current snapshots on the local server, run the following command from an elevated command prompt:

```
Ntdsutil snapshot "list all" quit quit
```

► You don't need to use an Active Directory snapshot; you can use the ntds .dit file that you've restored from a previous backup in a separate location.

Select and mount the desired snapshot. For example, to mount snapshot 1, issue the command:

```
Ntdsutil snapshot "list all" "mount 1" quit quit
```

Although both even and odd numbers are displayed, snapshots only use odd numbers. Take note of the path of the mounted snapshot, as you will need it for the next command. To mount the snapshot so that it is accessible as an LDAP server, use the command:

```
Dsadmin /dbpath c:\$SNAP_201012131929_VOLUMEC$\WINDOWS\NTDS\ntds.dit /
ldapport 51389
```

Here `c:\$SNAP_201012131929_VOLUMEC$\` is the path reported when you created the snapshot. Once you have done this, you will be able to view the contents of the snapshot by performing the following procedure:

1. Open Active Directory Users and Computers.

2. Right click the top node and then click Change Domain Controller.

3. Click on the Type A Directory Server Name:Port here and enter the FQDN of the DC followed by 51389. For example: `dc.wingtiptoys.com:51389`.

4. Verify the contents of the mounted Active Directory snapshot.

SUMMARY

Most small- to medium-sized organizations will be able to meet all their requirements with a single domain forest. Multiple domains in a forest are generally required for political rather than technical reasons. Multiple forests are usually required for regulatory and political reasons, rather than technical reasons. The domain functional level that you set depends on the domain controllers in the domain. If you want to set the Windows Server 2008 R2 functional level, you can only have Windows Server 2008 R2 domain controllers. Forest functional level depends on the lowest domain functional level in the forest. You can locate and seize FSMO roles using cmdlets available in the Active Directory PowerShell module. Read-only domain controllers can be configured to replicate only specific user account passwords as a method of increasing security in the event that the domain controller is stolen. Active Directory Recycle Bin allows you to perform an authoritative restore of Active Directory objects without having to reboot a domain controller into Directory Services Restore Mode.

Further Links

Active Directory Domain Services Database Mounting Tool (Snapshot Viewer or Snapshot Browser) Step-By-Step Guide

`http://technet.microsoft.com/en-us/library/cc753609(WS.10).aspx`

Active Directory Recycle Bin Step By Step Guide

`http://technet.microsoft.com/en-us/library/dd392261(WS.10).aspx`

How Active Directory Replication Topology Works

`http://technet.microsoft.com/en-us/library/cc755994(WS.10).aspx`

How to restore deleted user accounts and their group memberships in Active Directory

`http://support.microsoft.com/kb/840001`

Planning Global Catalog Server Placement

`http://technet.microsoft.com/en-us/library/cc732877(WS.10).aspx`

Planning Operations Master Role Placement

`http://technet.microsoft.com/en-us/library/cc754889(WS.10).aspx`

RODC FAQ

`http://technet.microsoft.com/en-us/library/cc754956(WS.10).aspx`

Understanding Active Directory Domain Services (AD DS) Functional Levels

`http://technet.microsoft.com/en-us/library/`
`understanding-active-directory-functional-levels(WS.10).aspx`

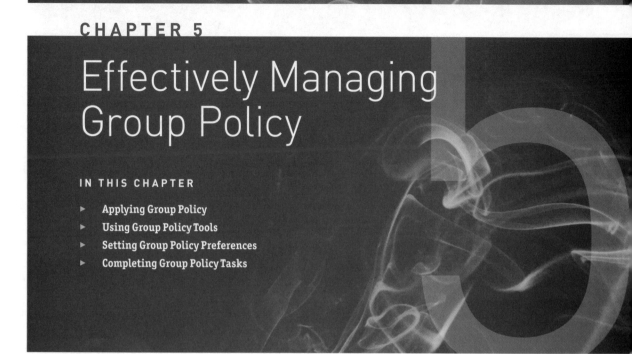

CHAPTER 5

Effectively Managing Group Policy

IN THIS CHAPTER

- ▶ Applying Group Policy
- ▶ Using Group Policy Tools
- ▶ Setting Group Policy Preferences
- ▶ Completing Group Policy Tasks

Group Policy gives you the ability to control almost all settings on a computer. Through the application of Group Policy, you can control the look, feel, and functionality of both the server and client computers in your organization. Group Policy is Windows Server 2008 R2's most powerful network administration tool, and being able to efficiently manage Group Policy is an important skill for experienced systems administrators.

> **NOTE** Most experienced administrators are familiar with the basics of Group Policy, which is why this chapter focuses more on what you can do with newer Group Policy features rather than the basic contents of the User Configuration and Computer Configuration nodes of a Group Policy Object (GPO). Specific policies of interest are covered in appropriate chapters of this book.

Windows Server 2008 introduced Group Policy Preferences, an extension to Group Policy that allows you to simplify the task of assigning shared folders as network drives and applying registry settings at logon and startup, something that was originally done through the use of startup scripts. As startup scripts are the bane of many an administrator, the ability to reduce or eliminate them through Group Policy Preferences comes as a welcome relief.

In this chapter, you learn how to effectively apply Group Policy to reduce logon times. You also learn about tools, such as the Advanced Group Policy Management console, that allow you to adopt a workflow approach to editing and updating the Group Policy in your organization.

APPLYING GROUP POLICY

The key to effectively applying Group Policy is to ensure that you design your organization's Group Policy strategy in such a way as to minimize the number of GPOs that you apply and the places where you apply them. Doing this minimizes the delay caused by Group Policy processing, which occurs when someone switches a computer on, but also occurs when someone logs on to the computer. The more convoluted your Group Policy application, the longer computers take to start up and the longer it takes for users to log on.

Having a simple Group Policy design reduces the complexity of maintaining policy. Organizations that have many policies should analyze their deployment to determine whether there is any method they can use to rationalize policy application. New features, such as Group Policy Preferences, might allow that to happen.

Understanding Group Policy Inheritance

▶ If you don't know how GPO inheritance works, you'll be completely befuddled when it comes to working out policy conflicts.

Unless you're someone who has taken a lot of certification exams, there is probably no reason why you'd have bothered to memorize exactly how GPO inheritance works when GPOs are applied at multiple levels in your organizational environment. *Group Policy inheritance* determines how Group Policy acts when the policy settings in one applied GPO conflict with the policy settings in another applied GPO.

Group Policy inheritance works as follows:

▶ Local policies apply first, from least specific to most specific. If you are using the machine policy and user or admin/non admin policies, the machine policy applies first, the admin/non admin overrides that and applies next with per-user policies overriding those and applying last.

▶ Site policies apply next. In a conflict between a site policy and a local policy, the site policy overrides the local policy.

▶ Domain policies apply next. Domain policies override site policies and local policies.

▶ Organizational Unit policies apply last. If there is an OU tree with multiple levels and policies applied at each level, the policy applied closest to the computer or user account overrides other policies.

▶ Policies configured as Enforced are not overridden as per the standard rules of policy inheritance. You cannot enforce a filtered GPO.

▶ Domain or OU containers configured to Block Inheritance block all policy settings inherited upstream except those configured as Enforced at a higher level. Specific GPOs cannot be blocked, Block Inheritance works in an all or nothing way.

▶ Enforced trumps Block Inheritance.

Note that often multiple GPOs will apply to an object, but there won't be any policy conflicts, hence no need to apply the rules of inheritance. The rules of inheritance apply only when policy settings at one level differ from policy settings at another level. For example, you might have a service configured to start automatically in a GPO applied at one level and the same service configured to be disabled at another. In that case, inheritance matters. If the service is configured only in a GPO applied at the domain level, and there are other GPOs at the OU and site level that don't have policies relating to the service, then you don't have to worry about the rules of inheritance, as the OU-level policies won't interfere with the setting configured at the domain level.

▶ Remember that a single GPO can be linked in multiple places, but can't be linked to the default Users or Computers container.

Using Local Group Policy Objects

Local GPOs are primarily useful in allowing you to apply Group Policy settings to computers that are not members of the domain. The drawback of local GPOs is that they can be cumbersome to configure, as you almost always have to configure them on a per-machine basis, although there are some settings, such as security policies, that you can use templates for to apply them to multiple machines.

With the release of Windows Server 2008, you are able to have differentiated local policies depending on which user is logged on to the computer. You can also differentiate based on whether a user is a member of the local Administrators group or not. This is useful in situations where you have a stand-alone kiosk computer, which generally runs client operating systems rather than server operating systems. Other than configuring specific settings for stand-alone servers, user differentiation of local policies isn't as useful for computers running Windows Server 2008 R2, as you rarely have anyone other than trusted administrators logging on directly to these machines.

Configuring Site-Level Policies

Applying policies at the Active Directory site level allows you to apply a consistent set of settings for a specific geographic location. In multi-domain forests, site-linked GPOs are stored in the forest root domain. This can cause issues with the speed of Group Policy processing, if there isn't a forest root domain controller in a site primarily associated with a child domain. In general, you should try to avoid linking GPOs at the site level and use location-specific, item-level targeting in Group Policy Preferences to accomplish site-specific configuration goals.

Configuring Domain-Level Policies

Domain-level GPOs allow you to apply settings to all computers in a domain. Several specific policies, such as password policies, have an effect only when configured at the domain level. Any general setting that you need across the entire organization should be applied at the domain level. While you can apply multiple GPOs at the domain level, most organizations apply domain-wide policies using the Default Domain Policy. If you choose to take this route, remember to take backups of the Default Domain Policy prior to making modifications.

It is usually a good idea to test policies against a subset of computers in your environment prior to applying policies to all computers. As a way of doing this, you might instead create GPOs and link them to test OUs to check the results prior to linking the GPO at the domain level.

▶ It is possible to use a technology called Fine-Grained Password Policies to apply differentiated password policies in a domain. However, if you need differentiated password policies, it is simpler to have multiple domains.

Managing Organizational Units

Although the name Organizational Unit suggests a structure that reflects the organizational makeup of a company, only in limited cases does the organizational makeup reflect the way that Group Policy should be applied in that company. Organizational Units are containers that hold Active Directory objects, most commonly user and computer accounts as well as security groups and other OUs.

Organizational Unit design should reflect two separate needs:

▶ Efficient application of Group Policy

▶ Delegation of administrative privileges

As Group Policy application can be filtered on the basis of things such as security group membership, delegation of administrative privileges should be paramount in an OU design. Organizing OUs in this manner allows you to assign one group of users administrative permissions over another group of users and computers without giving those users the same administrative permissions over everyone else in the organization. For example, you might want to allow three members of staff permission to manage the user accounts of members of the Research OU, but not allow those members of staff permission over anyone else in the organization. However, having said that, most organizations don't bother with a distributed delegation model when it comes to Active Directory and generally grant anyone with permissions over user accounts the ability to manage those accounts throughout the domain rather than for a specific OU. If that describes your organization, use OUs in a way that makes sense for Group Policy application rather than worrying about administrative delegation.

USING GROUP POLICY MANAGEMENT CONSOLE

The Group Policy Management console is the primary method through which Group Policy is managed in a standard Windows Server 2008 R2 environment. This tool, shown in Figure 5-1, allows administrators to view Group Policy items from the forest level on down. It provides information on which GPOs are linked at the domain, site, and OU level. You can see a list of all GPOs in a domain under the Group Policy Objects node. There is also a WMI Filters node that contains all WMI filters configured for the domain, a Starter GPOs node that contains all starter GPOs, a Group Policy Modeling node and a Group Policy Results node. By right-clicking on a GPO and selecting Edit, you can edit a GPO in the Group Policy Management Editor.

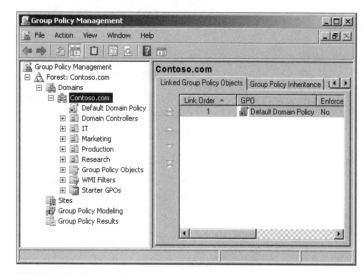

FIGURE 5-1: Group Policy Management console

Using Resultant Set of Policy

The *Resultant Set of Policy* tool allows you to generate a model of Group Policy application, allowing you to figure out which policies will apply to particular objects within the domain. Resultant Set of Policy allows you to figure out why Group Policy application isn't behaving in the way that you are expecting and allows you to resolve Group Policy conflicts.

There are two ways in which you can calculate Resultant Set of Policy. The first is to use Group Policy Modeling. The second is to use Group Policy Results. The difference between these is as follows:

▶ Group Policy Modeling allows you to view the impact of altering site membership, security group membership, filtering, slow links, loopback processing and the movement of accounts to new OU on the application of policy.

▶ Group Policy Results allows you to troubleshoot the application of policy by telling you which settings apply to a specific user or computer account.

By default, members of the Domain Admins and Enterprise Admins can generate Group Policy Modeling or Group Policy Results information. You can delegate permissions so that users can perform on these at the OU or domain level. To use Group Policy Results to troubleshoot the application of policy to a specific computer, perform the following steps.

1. Open the Group Policy Management Console, right-click on the Group Policy Results node, and then click on Group Policy Results Wizard.

2. On the first page of the Group Policy Results Wizard, click Next.

3. On the Computer Selection page, determine whether you want to model policy results for when a user is logged onto a specific computer or whether you want to generate user-specific settings and click Next.

4. On the User Selection page, shown in Figure 5-2, choose a specific user account to model the results for, or choose to display only the results of policy applied to a specific computer account.

5. On the Summary page, click Next, and on the Completion page, click Finish. A new node is generated under the Group Policy Results node showing the report for that particular user and that particular computer, as shown in Figure 5-3.

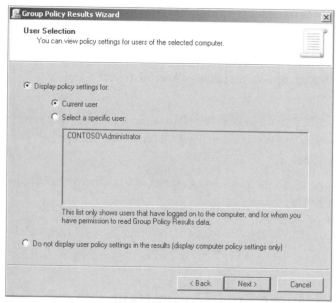

FIGURE 5-2: Group Policy Results Wizard

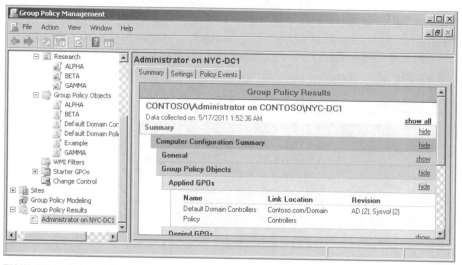

FIGURE 5-3: Group Policy Results report

Using Starter GPOs

A *Starter GPO* is a collection of Administrative Template policy items. Starter GPOs are new to Windows Server 2008. It is important to remember that Starter GPOs do not hold other policy items, just Administrative Template settings. The benefit of using

Starter GPOs is that any new GPO created from a starter GPO will automatically have all the Administrative Template settings that are configured in the GPO.

Starter GPOs allow you to do the following:

▶ Standardize the creation of GPOs that involve Administrative Template settings.

▶ Import and export GPO Administrative Template settings between domains. When you export a Starter GPO, it is stored in CAB file format and can be imported in other domains.

▶ When you create a new GPO, you can select a Starter GPO to inherit the Administrative Template settings from.

Starter GPOs are stored in the Starter GPOs node of the Group Policy Management console.

Understanding Advanced Group Policy Management

Advanced Group Policy Management (AGPM) is a part of the Microsoft Desktop Optimization Pack and is available to Microsoft's Volume License customers. AGPM integrates with the existing Group Policy Management console, extending its functionality as shown in Figure 5-4. AGPM has several benefits over the standard Group Policy Management console that ships with Windows Server 2008 R2.

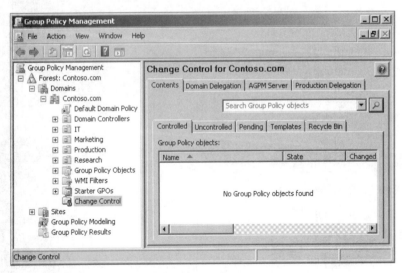

FIGURE 5-4: Advanced Group Policy Management

The biggest advantage of AGPM is that it enables you to apply a workflow to the management of GPOs, allowing you to use versioning and offline editing. This is an advantage over the standard Group Policy Management console where any changes made to an active Group Policy are automatically propagated to clients that are influenced by that policy. Having offline functionality for editing GPOs allows for GPOs that are already active to be more extensively tested during the revision process than might be the case in a traditional GPO deployment.

AGPM offers a more advanced model for editing GPOs, as it allows administrators to track precisely which person in an organization made a specific change to a GPO. In a traditional Windows Server 2008 R2 deployment, even though it is possible to control who has the permissions required to edit and apply a GPO, if multiple people have these permissions, it can be almost impossible to determine who made a specific change to an existing GPO. Being able to track the changes made to a GPO is very important in a high-security environment.

AGPM uses the following roles in its delegation architecture:

▶ **AGPM Administrator:** Users assigned this role are able to perform all tasks in AGPM. This includes configuring domain-wide options as well as delegating permissions.

▶ **Approver:** Users assigned this role are able to deploy GPOs into the domain. Approvers are also able to approve or reject requests from users assigned the Editor role. Users assigned this role are also able to created and delete GPOs, but cannot edit GPOs unless assigned the Editor role.

▶ **Reviewer:** Users assigned the Reviewer role are able to view the contents of GPOs and compare the contents of GPOs, but they do not have the ability to modify or deploy GPOs. The Reviewer role is designed to review and audit GPO management.

▶ **Editor:** Users assigned this role are able to view and compare GPOs as Reviewers can. They are also able to check GPOs out of the archive, edit them offline, and then check those GPOs back into the archive. They are unable to deploy GPOs but can request GPO deployment.

▶ In small environments, GPO security is less of a concern as usually only one person has the ability to manage Group Policy. The ability to do offline editing of policies, however, still makes AGPM a valuable tool.

USING IMPORTANT GROUP POLICY FEATURES

Although this chapter has shied away from describing specific areas of GPOs, there are two areas that are worthy of special mention. Administrative Templates, which allow you to add further policies to a GPO, and Group Policy Preferences, a new feature of Group Policy that debuted with Windows Server 2008.

Using Administrative Templates

Group Policy Administrative Templates allow for Group Policy to be extended beyond the basic settings available on basic GPOs. Administrative Templates are imported to extend a Group Policy. Common software packages, such as Microsoft Office, often include Administrative Templates that can be imported to manage software-specific settings. Until the release of Windows Vista, Administrative Templates were available as files in ADM format. With the release of Windows Vista, Administrative Templates were migrated to a standards-based XML file format called ADMX. You can use both ADM and ADMX files with Windows Server 2008 R2 GPOs, but more modern software is likely to have templates in ADMX format.

▶ Many administrators find startup and logon scripts to be a chore. They don't always work and can be problematic to maintain.

To be able to use an Administrative Template, you can either import it directly into a GPO using the Add/Remove Templates option when you right-click on the Administrative Templates node, or you can copy the Administrative Template files to the Central Store, located in the c:\Windows\Sysvol\sysvol\<domainname>\Policies\PolicyDefinitions folder on any domain controller. You may need to create this folder if it does not already exist. As this folder will then be replicated to all domain controllers, you'll be able to access the Administrative Templates through the Administrative Templates node.

▶ You need to download and update the Group Policy Preferences client-side extensions to computers running Windows XP SP2, Windows Vista RTM, or Windows Server 2003 SP1. These extensions are included, however, if later service packs are applied.

Setting Group Policy Preferences

Group Policy Preferences work around the idea of eliminating, or at least substantially reducing, the need for traditional startup and logon scripts. Logon scripts have a way of becoming convoluted over time. Group Policy Preferences allow simplification of common logon and startup script tasks such as drive mappings and setting environment variables. Group Policy Preferences are automatically supported on computers running Windows Server 2008, Windows Server 2008 R2, and Windows 7.

By reducing or eliminating some of the complexity of logon scripts, you can use Group Policy Preferences to reduce configuration errors. You can also use Group

Policy Preferences as a way of updating deployment images, using appropriate preferences to update newly deployed operating systems.

Group Policy Preferences can be used to configure the following:

- ▶ Applications
- ▶ Drive mappings
- ▶ Environment variables
- ▶ File updates
- ▶ Folders
- ▶ Ini files
- ▶ Registry settings
- ▶ Shortcuts
- ▶ Data sources
- ▶ Devices
- ▶ Folder options
- ▶ Internet settings
- ▶ Local users and groups
- ▶ Network options
- ▶ Power options
- ▶ Printer settings
- ▶ Regional options
- ▶ Scheduled tasks
- ▶ Start menu settings

Some of these items can also be configured using traditional Group Policy. In the event that an item is configured in the same GPO using both, then the traditional setting takes precedence. The difference between a Group Policy Preference and a normal Group Policy setting is that a user is able to change a Group Policy Preference if he has the appropriate permissions. For example, he could un-map a network drive. The drive would remain unmapped until the user logged in again, at which point it would be remapped as shown in Figure 5-5. If you want to enforce a setting, use a standard Group Policy; if you want to apply the setting and allow users to change it, use a Group Policy Preference.

▶ You can enforce a Group Policy Preference by disabling the Apply Once and Do Not Reapply setting in the policy item's configuration.

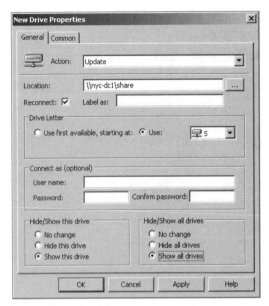

FIGURE 5-5: Map drive

Group Policy Preferences can be targeted so that different preferences can apply to the same item types within a single GPO. You can use the following items to restrict how a Group Policy Preference applies:

▶ The computer has a battery.

▶ The computer has a specific name.

▶ The computer has a specific CPU speed.

▶ Date

▶ The computer has a certain amount of disk space.

▶ The computer is a member of a domain.

▶ The computer has a particular environment variable set.

▶ A certain file is present on the computer.

▶ The computer is within a particular IP address range.

▶ The computer uses specific language settings.

▶ Meets the requirements of an LDAP query

▶ The computer has a MAC address within a specific range.

▶ Meets the requirements of an MSI query

- ▶ The computer uses a specific type of network connection.
- ▶ The computer is running a specific operating system.
- ▶ The computer is a member of a specific OU.
- ▶ The computer has PCMCIA present.
- ▶ The computer is portable.
- ▶ The computer uses a specific processing mode.
- ▶ The computer has a certain amount of RAM.
- ▶ The computer has a certain registry entry.
- ▶ User or computer is a member of a specific security group.
- ▶ The computer is in a specific Active Directory site.
- ▶ Remote Desktop Setting
- ▶ Within a specific time range
- ▶ The user has a specific name.
- ▶ Meets the requirements of a WMI query

To configure a drive mapping to a share named \\fs1\sharedfiles to drive S: for the Research group using Group Policy Preferences, perform the following steps:

1. Edit the GPO that applies using the Group Policy Management Editor.

2. Under User Configuration, expand the Preferences\ Windows Settings node.

3. Right-click on Drive Maps, and then click on New, Mapped Drive.

4. In the New Drive Properties dialog, set the location to \\fs1\sharedfiles and set the Drive letter to S.

5. Click on the Common tab, and then select Item-Level Targeting, as shown in Figure 5-6.

6. Click the Targeting button, and then click New Item. Select Security Group, and then enter the group name Research. Click OK twice.

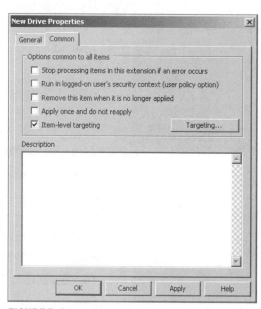

FIGURE 5-6: Item-level targeting

COMPLETING COMMON GROUP POLICY TASKS

Beyond the editing of GPOs, administrators of Group Policy Objects have certain tasks that must be completed on a regular basis. Some of these tasks, such as regularly backing up GPOs before modifying them, are ignored in many organizations. Other administrators find the basics of Group Policy so mystifying that they don't ever manage it beyond basic modifications of the default domain policy. In this section, you learn more about common tasks such as software deployment, linking GPOs, backing up and restoring GPOs, filtering GPO applications, and delegating GPO permissions.

Deploying Software

Although larger organizations are likely to use a solution like System Center Configuration Manager 2012 for software deployment, a substantial number of organizations still deploy applications to computers using Group Policy. When configuring software deployment using Group Policy, keep the following in mind:

- ▶ If you want to add an application shortcut to a computer's Start menu, assign the application to the computer.

- ▶ If you want to add an application shortcut to a specific user's Start menu, assign the application to the user.

- ▶ Assigning an application to a computer installs that application on the computer.

- ▶ Assigning an application to a user means that the application is installed the first time the user attempts to use the application.

- ▶ To ensure that applications required to view a document are installed, enable document activation for published applications.

- ▶ Place the installers for applications that you install using Group Policy on DFS shares. This simplifies the process of deploying applications in organizations with multiple sites.

- ▶ Read permission is the only one required for users and computers for the software installation files.

- ▶ Forced removal allows you to remove applications. Optional removal prevents new software installation but will not remove software from those computers where it is already installed.

Linking Group Policy

When you link a GPO to an object, you apply the GPO to that object and all its children in Active Directory. GPOs exist independently of where you link them. You can link a single GPO to multiple locations in an Active Directory domain. For example, you can link one GPO to as many different OUs as you like. The same GPO can be linked at the domain level or even at the site level. You can even link to GPOs in other domains in the forest, though this is generally a bad idea, as it can make Group Policy processing take substantially longer. By clicking the Scope tab when you have the GPO selected in the Group Policy Management console, you can determine exactly where a GPO is linked and whether the GPO link is set to Enforced. Figure 5-7 shows that the ALPHA GPO is linked to both the IT and Production OUs.

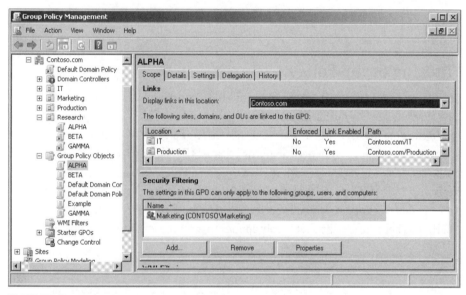

FIGURE 5-7: GPO links

When you link multiple GPOs at the same level, you configure a priority level for each GPO. For example, in Figure 5-8, GPOs ALPHA, BETA, and GAMMA are linked to the Research OU. As GPO BETA is assigned link order 1, conflicting settings in GPO BETA will override those in ALPHA, which will in turn override those in GPO GAMMA.

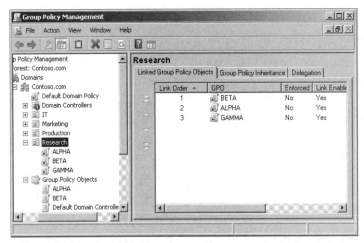

FIGURE 5-8: GPO link order

Filtering Group Policy

GPO filters allow you to restrict the scope of a GPO. The default settings for a GPO filter have it applied to the Authenticated Users group, which means that it applies to everyone in the domain. If, instead, you want the GPO to apply to a specific group of users and computers, you can remove the Authenticated Users group from the Security Filtering settings and replace it with that group. You do this by selecting the GPO under the Group Policy Objects node of the Group Policy Management console and using the Add and Remove buttons in the Security Filtering pane. Figure 5-9 shows that GPO ALPHA has been filtered so that it only applies to members of the Marketing group.

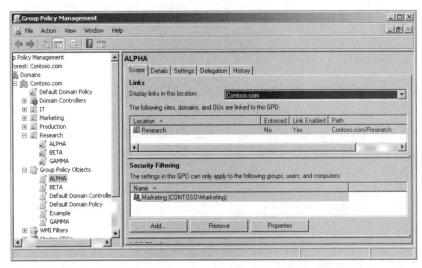

FIGURE 5-9: GPO security filtering

You can also use **WMI** queries to filter Group Policy. To do this, you create a WMI filter first in the **WMI Filters** node of the Group Policy Management console and then select that filter in the **WMI Filtering** node. While WMI filtering is a powerful way of filtering Group Policy, as you can make any possible query, such as who the computer manufacturer is or how much hard-disk space is left, using WMI filters requires that you have an administrator who can actually write them. WMI filter utility is only matched by the complexity of actually implementing them.

A GPO filter applies to all links to that GPO. This means that if you create a WMI filter that applies to a GPO linked to 15 different OUs, the WMI filter will apply to all of the objects in that scope. If you want to selectively filter GPOs, you'll need to create duplicate GPOs and configure separate filters for each.

Backing Up, Importing, and Restoring GPOs

Even if you have the **AGPM**, it is a good idea to regularly back up Group Policy Objects. While GPOs are backed up when you perform a system state backup, they can be troublesome to restore if you delete or modify them in an unintended way. Using a tool like AGPM can reduce the chance that you can't roll back to a previous configuration, but if you don't have AGPM, you should make a backup of a GPO prior to making substantial, or even insubstantial, policy modifications.

Backing up a GPO is straightforward. In the Group Policy Management console, right-click on the policy and then click on Back Up. On the Back Up Group Policy Object dialog box, shown in Figure 5-10, enter the folder that you will back the GPO up to and provide a description. You can back up all GPOs in your organization by right-clicking on the Group Policy Objects node within the Group Policy Management console and clicking on Back Up All.

▶ Given the time and costs involved in getting most administrators up to speed on WMI, you're better off using System Center Configuration Manager to target specific subsets of computers in your organization.

▶ The targeting functionality of Group Policy Preferences reduces the need for GPO filtering.

▶ Should you have a system state or full backup and want to restore a GPO, consider restoring to a virtual machine and then exporting the GPO. Otherwise, the restored GPO will be overwritten by the new GPO upon the next AD replication.

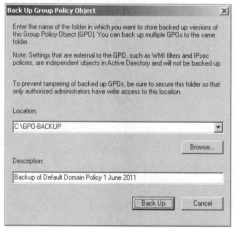

FIGURE 5-10: Back up GPO.

NOTE The BackupAllGPOs.wsf script, located in the C:\Program Files\GPMC\ Scripts directory allows you to configure GPO backup as a scheduled task.

You can manage the backups that you have taken of Group Policy Objects by right-clicking on the Group Policy Objects node and then clicking Manage Backups. This will open the Manage Backups dialog box, shown in Figure 5-11. Using this console, you can restore a backed up GPO, verify what settings are applied in a backup GPO, view where the GPO was linked and how it was filtered, the delegation settings on the GPO, and, if necessary, you can delete a specific GPO backup. You can also restore an individual GPO by right-clicking on that GPO and then clicking on Restore from Backup. When you do this, you have the option of restoring from any backup you've taken of that GPO. Note that restoring a GPO does not restore where the GPO was linked. However, you can configure that prior to restoring the GPO by viewing information about the backed up GPO.

▶ Given how simple the process is, it makes sense to always back up a GPO before you make any modifications to it.

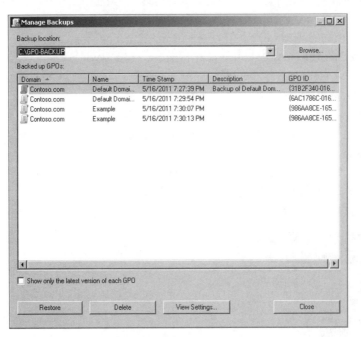

FIGURE 5-11: Manage GPO backups.

You can use the Import Settings Wizard to import settings from a backed up GPO into an existing GPO. You can use this technique to quickly duplicate GPOs, backing one up, creating a new "blank" GPO, and then importing the settings into the new GPO. To run the Import Settings Wizard, right-click on a GPO under the Group Policy Objects of the Group Policy Management console and then click Import Settings. Importing settings into a GPO will overwrite all current settings in the GPO, effectively replacing the current GPO with the backed up GPO. As Figure 5-12 shows, you get the option to back up the GPO that you are going to overwrite when running the wizard, and, even if you are completely sure of what you are doing, this is a good option to take.

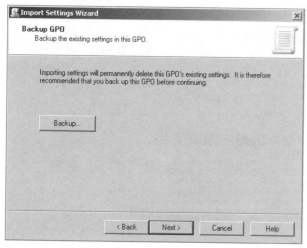

FIGURE 5-12: Back up before import.

Delegating Permissions Related to Group Policy

By default, members of the Domain Admins and the Group Policy Creator Owners group are able to create GPOs. Using the Group Policy Creator Owners group allows you to have users create GPOs without making them full Domain Admins. You can also grant this right to additional groups when the Delegation tab is selected and Group Policy Objects is highlighted in the Group Policy Management console, as shown in Figure 5-13.

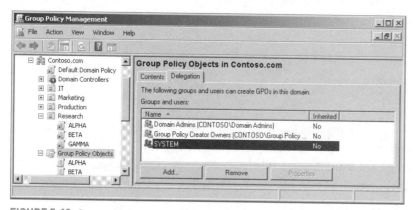

FIGURE 5-13: Create GPO permission.

The default Active Directory settings only allow members of the Domain Admins and Enterprise Admins groups to link GPOs to the domain or OU. You can delegate the ability to link GPOs to a particular OU using the Delegation of Control Wizard. You can also allow linking of GPOs by configuring the Link GPOs permission on the Delegation tab when the domain or a specific OU is selected. Figure 5-14 shows the Link GPOs delegation on the Research OU.

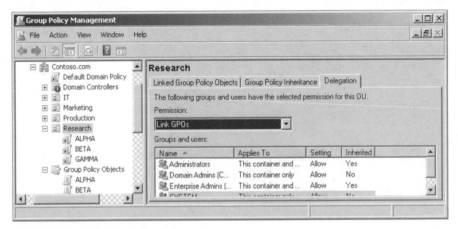

FIGURE 5-14: Link GPO permission

GPO permissions are configured on the Delegation tab of the GPO's properties in the Group Policy Management console. Permissions include:

> ► **Read:** This setting applies to any group that is configured as subject to the policy in the Security Filtering area.

> ► **Edit Settings:** This setting allows modification of the policy.

> ► **Edit Settings, Delete, Modify Security:** This setting allows complete modification of GPOs and gives users assigned this permission the ability to delete those GPOs and modify security settings.

SUMMARY

In general you should organize the OUs in your organization around delegation of administrative privileges and policy application. When there is a policy conflict, GPO settings applied at the OU closest to the user or computer account override those that are applied at higher-level OUs, which override GPO settings applied at the domain, which override GPO settings applied at the site level, which override GPO settings applied in local GPOs. You can use the Group Policy Management console to back up, restore, link, delegate permissions on, model, and manage GPOs. Group Policy Preferences allow you to replicate most of the functionality of logon scripts. Administrative Templates allow you to extend the functionality of Group Policy.

Additional Sources

Advanced Group Policy Management

www.microsoft.com/windows/enterprise/products/mdop/agpm.aspx

Back Up, Restore, Import, and Copy Group Policy Objects

http://technet.microsoft.com/en-us/library/cc754760.aspx

Delegate Permissions for Group Policy

http://technet.microsoft.com/en-us/library/cc732984.aspx

Fun with WMI Filters in Group Policy

http://blogs.technet.com/b/askds/archive/2008/09/11/
fun-with-wmi-filters-in-group-policy.aspx

Use Resultant Set of Policy to Manage Group Policy

http://technet.microsoft.com/en-us/library/cc754269.aspx

Working with Starter GPOs

http://technet.microsoft.com/en-us/library/cc753200.aspx

Managing Users and Computers

A week after I started work as a system administrator, at what was then a prominent Australian company, one of the desktop support guys came into my cubicle and asked if I'd be willing to reset the password on his user account. I was about to do it when I got a phone call from my manager. I waved my new colleague off and indicated that I'd reset his password in a few minutes time. After my phone call, my new colleague returned and told me not to worry about it. I asked him if he'd remembered his password, and he said that he hadn't, but that he had remembered the password of the person who held the systems administrator position before me and had logged on with that guy's account, reset his password, and everything was good. I indicated that I had better disable the account of the guy who had left, as it presented a security risk. My co-worker argued that this was a bad idea, because that would mean that we didn't have a failsafe way to get into the system should we forget our own passwords. Rather than explain all the reasons why this approach to security was dubious, I simply deleted the previous administrator's account.

In this chapter, you learn some techniques to manage user and computer accounts. You also learn about the new Active Directory Administrative Center, some of the new Active Directory-related PowerShell cmdlets, how to apply Fine-Grained Password Policies and use Restricted Groups to manage group membership. You also pick up some of the secrets to effective organizational unit design and managed service accounts.

USING ORGANIZATIONAL UNIT STRUCTURES

It shouldn't surprise you that in most small- to medium-sized organizations, the Users container is about as far as people go with user account organization. Though most administrators have heard of organizational units and have a basic idea what they are and what you can use them for, a good percentage of them simply ignore organizational units, because they don't run their network in a way that necessitates their use. For example, if you are on a network where there are only one or two people responsible for managing user accounts, and everyone runs the same desktop software, a complex organizational unit structure is most likely a waste of time. This is because you won't need different OUs for the purposes of administrative delegation, and you won't need separate OUs for the application of Group Policy.

> **NOTE** It is frustrating to come into a new company and see an organizational unit structure that seems to have no resemblance to the current company organizational chart. OU structures need to be maintained and updated on a regular basis; if they get so out of alignment with the organizational structure, they become useless.

Those companies that do bother with an organizational unit structure often have trouble keeping it up-to-date. In all likelihood, the company's OU structure was set up when Active Directory was first deployed and mirrored the organizational structure of the company at that point in time. Given how often companies are reorganized, with departments being merged, created, deprecated, lost, found, reinvigorated, and reformed, any organizational unit structure based on department structure when

Active Directory was first deployed is unlikely to reflect the current true organizational structure of the business. Only organizations that take the proactive step of regularly assessing their OU structure are likely to have one that is up-to-date.

So, if your company regularly changes its organizational structure anyway, why should you bother going further than dumping all user accounts in the Users container?

The first thing to remember is that the structure of Active Directory doesn't have to mirror the structure of the organization, but it does have to mirror the needs of the IT department in terms of its mission in supporting the infrastructure of the organization. With this in mind, you should have two goals when it comes to OU design:

- ▶ Make it easier to apply Group Policy.
- ▶ Make it easier to delegate control over accounts.

Making It Easier to Apply Group Policy

The main trick to remember is that when you create a nested OU structure, a Group Policy applied higher up the tree applies to all of the nodes under it, unless you get even more complicated and block policy inheritance or apply filters.

Designing an OU structure based on the application of policy very much depends on how many different policies need to be applied. It can be instructive to perform an analysis of your own environment to figure out whether a different organizational unit structure might lead to a more efficient Group Policy application process. In this approach, you work out how many different policies you might need and then work backwards to figure out what OU structure best supports that goal.

When people think of needing different Group Policy Objects (GPOs), they often think of software deployment—as in, department A needs one suite of applications, and department B needs another suite of applications. They solve this problem by putting the users and computers for these departments in different OUs.

> **NOTE** As you learned in Chapter 5, although Active Directory does allow for software deployment, the lack of reporting infrastructure and the difficulty in precisely targeting software deployment means that many organizations use more advanced technologies like System Center for centralized application deployment rather than Group Policy.

Although this approach is a good place to start when it comes to OU design, the justification for the design process becomes more complicated if you are using a product such as System Center Essentials or System Center Configuration Manager. These products will allow you to perform software deployment independently of an OU structure, allowing you to target computers and users based on account properties and software configuration rather than just OU membership.

Making It Easier to Delegate Control

One of the best justifications for a specific OU design is creating an OU structure to precisely meet your organization's administrative privilege delegation requirements. Delegation of control allows you to assign limited administrative rights over a specific set of objects. For example, rather than giving a member of the help desk staff who works out of the Sydney office the ability to reset the passwords of everyone in the country, you could use delegation to ensure that the member can only reset the passwords of people in the Sydney office. In the future, it is likely that systems administration will continue to move toward a more delegated model. From a certain perspective, it makes sense to allow your manager to be able to reset your password, rather than having to put a call into the central IT help desk. The manager is likely to be able to directly verify your identity—something that a help desk located in another city or state might be unable to accomplish.

When planning delegation, you should always delegate rights to groups rather than individual users. When you take this approach, you can assign the delegated rights to people by adding them to the global security group. This approach also allows you to remove rights simply by removing the user account from the global security group.

You use the Delegation of Control Wizard, shown in Figure 6-1, to delegate rights. The Delegation of Control Wizard allows you to delegate common or custom-created tasks. The common tasks that you can delegate using the Delegation of Control Wizard include:

▶ Removing delegated rights by editing the security properties of the Active Directory object is about as much fun as a visit to the dentist. You should never delegate rights to users but always delegate rights to security groups.

- ▶ Create, delete, and manager user accounts.
- ▶ Reset user passwords and force password change at next logon.
- ▶ Read all user information.
- ▶ Create, delete and manage groups.
- ▶ Modify the membership of a group.
- ▶ Manage Group Policy links.

- Generate Resultant Set of Policy (Planning).

- Generate Resultant Set of Policy (Logging).

- Create, delete, and manage inetOrgPerson accounts.

- Reset inetOrgPerson passwords and force password change at next logon.

- Read all inetOrgPerson information.

▶ InetOrgPerson is part of the Active Directory Schema that helps in migrating user accounts from other directory services. Most administrators need not worry about this class.

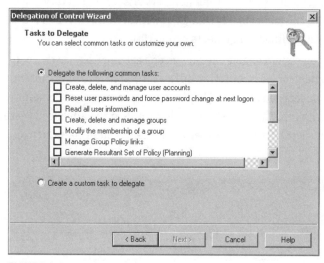

FIGURE 6-1: Delegation of Control Wizard

To perform a delegation so that a specific group of users can reset user passwords on all user accounts within a specific OU, complete the following general steps:

1. Create a global group to which you will delegate the rights.

2. Open Active Directory Users and Computers console (ADUC), and right-click on the OU against which you will delegate rights, and then click on Delegate Control. This will launch the Delegation of Control Wizard.

3. On the Users or Groups page, click Add, and then add the name of the global group that you created in step 1. Click Next.

4. On the Tasks to Delegate page, enable the Reset User Passwords and Force Password Change at Next Logon item, then click Next, and then click Finish.

MANAGING USER ACCOUNTS

Since the release of Windows 2000, most administrators have performed user account management tasks in the *Active Directory Users and Computers console (ADUC)*. Though this tool is functional, it is starting to get a little long in the tooth. Where it works well for organizations with relatively small numbers of user and computer accounts, it works less well for organizations with larger numbers of Active Directory objects. This is primarily because the more objects that exist within Active Directory, the more difficult it is to quickly find those objects using ADUC.

When using ADUC you should enable the Advanced Features view, as this will give you access to extended object properties, such as the ability to protect items from deletion, which you learned about in Chapter 4, "Active Directory Domains and Forests," and the Security tab. The easiest way to determine if the Advanced Features view is enabled is to check whether you can see the LostAndFound container, as shown in Figure 6-2.

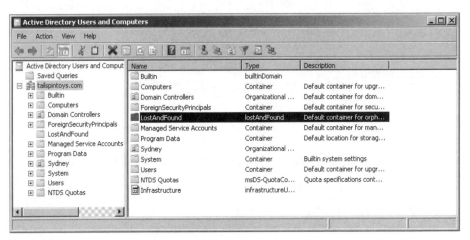

FIGURE 6-2: ADUC advanced features

As an experienced systems administrator, you are most likely already aware of the capabilities of the ADUC console, which is why the coverage in this chapter concentrates on Active Directory Administrative Center and the Active Directory PowerShell module.

Using Active Directory Administrative Center

From the perspective of day-to-day user administration, one of the least noticed differences between Windows Server 2008 and Windows Server 2008 R2 is the inclusion of *Active Directory Administrative Center (ADAC)*. ADAC leverages the PowerShell functionality available in the Active Directory module in a similar way to how Exchange Management Console in Exchange Server 2010 leverages the Exchange Management Shell. Essentially, ADAC provides an interface for building and executing PowerShell commands. Active Directory Administrative Center is available on computers running Windows Server 2008 R2 Standard, Enterprise, and Ultimate editions. You can also install it on computers running Windows 7 Professional, Enterprise, and Ultimate editions if you download and install the Remote Server Administration Tools (RSAT).

The ADAC welcome screen, shown in Figure 6-3, contains three tiles: the Reset Password tile, Global Search tile, and Getting Started tile. Microsoft intends to add more tiles in future service packs and releases of the Windows Server operating system. There are also plans to give administrators the ability to create their own tiles for common tasks.

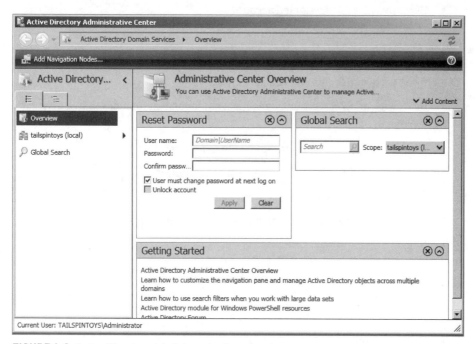

FIGURE 6-3: Active Directory Administrative Center welcome screen

Part of the idea behind ADAC is to simplify the location of important objects, something that can be difficult to do in ADUC. For example, if you wanted to find a specific user account, you could open ADAC and type the name of the account into the Global Search tile. ADAC will then list all objects that meet the search terms. Trying to find the same object from ADUC is a far more involved process. ADAC is designed around quickly finding objects that you want to work on, rather than having to navigate through a forest of user objects trying to find one specific account. It was designed with this functionality, because a big pain point for administrators is finding objects within the ADUC.

USING ADAC QUERIES TO QUICKLY LOCATE ACCOUNTS

After you choose a specific node in ADAC, you can use queries to display the objects that you are interested in. Again, the idea here is that when you are managing user and group accounts, you want to quickly locate an object and get down to modifying its properties, rather than spend time digging through OUs to locate the object in the first place. ADAC allows you to use the following criteria in building queries:

- Users with disabled/enabled accounts
- Users with an expired password
- Users whose password has an expiration date/no expiration date
- Users with enabled but locked accounts
- Users with enabled accounts who have not logged on for more than a given number of days
- Users with a password expiring in a given number of days
- Computers running as a given domain controller type
- Last modified between given dates
- Object time is user/inetorgperson/computer/group/organizational unit
- Name
- Type
- Description
- City
- Country/region

You can use multiple criteria in a single query, and once you create a useful query, you can save it so that it is quickly accessible should you want to use it again. For example, *derelict accounts* are user accounts that persist within Active Directory after the user who was associated with the account has left the organization. Derelict user accounts present a security risk to an organization, because they mean that someone who is no longer associated with the organization still has access to organizational resources.

To use ADUC to find such accounts, create and save a query that looks for users that have not logged on to the domain for a certain amount of time. To use Active Directory Administrative Center to find accounts where users have not logged on for the last 30 days, perform the following general steps:

1. Open Active Directory Administrative Center.

2. Click the Global Search node.

3. Click the Add Criteria drop-down, select the Users with Enabled Accounts Who Have Not Logged On for More than a Given Number of Days item, and then click Add.

4. Click the Number 15. In the drop-down menu, click 30 to reset the value to 30 days.

5. Click the Save icon to save the query. Give the query a descriptive name, such as "More than 30 days without logon" and click OK.

6. Click Search, as shown in Figure 6-4, to execute the query.

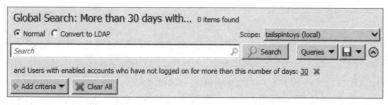

FIGURE 6-4: 30 days no logon

> Unless your organization has a procedure by which the IT department is notified when people have ended their employment, it is likely that there will be derelict accounts stored in Active Directory.

USING ADAC TO MAKE EDITING USER PROPERTIES EASIER

One of the big differences between ADUC and ADAC is the method through which they display user account properties. When using ADAC, you need to navigate through a set of tabs to configure specific settings, such as account expiration, protection from account deletion, username, and unified principle name. Figure 6-5 shows the 19 tabs that are available on a user account's properties page when using ADUC.

▶ Searching through all those tabs for a specific property can take some time, as you'll probably have to check a few to find what you want!

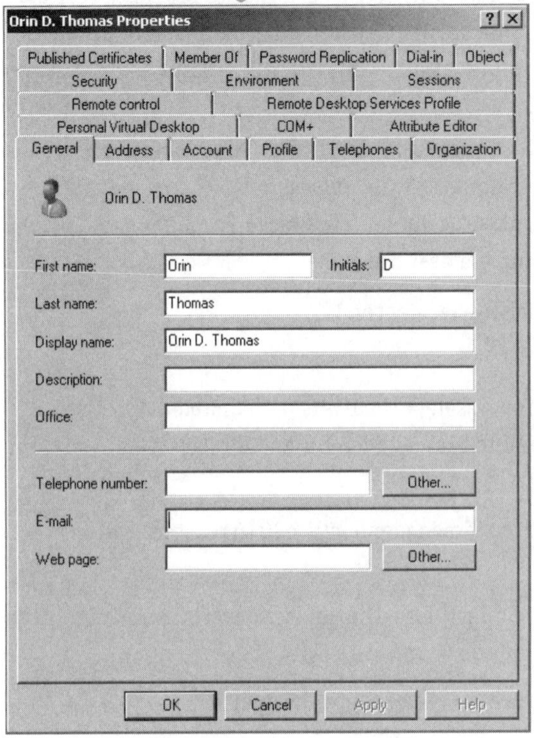

FIGURE 6-5: ADUC user properties

When you view user properties in ADAC, almost all of those properties are laid out on a single page that can be navigated using a scroll bar. The ADAC user properties page includes the display of advanced properties, such as Protect from Accidental Deletion, an item that is only visible within an Active Directory user account's properties if the Advanced Features view is enabled. You can also adjust which properties are visible using the Add Sections menu, removing the Account, Organization, Member Of, and Profile sections as necessary. The ADAC user properties page is shown in Figure 6-6.

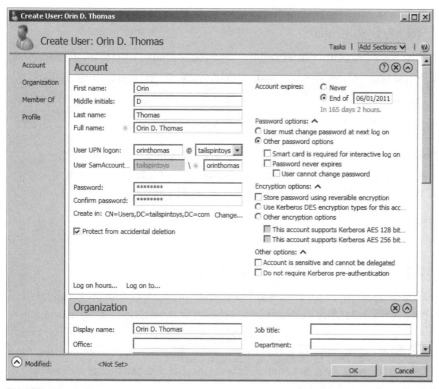

FIGURE 6-6: User properties in ADAC

Using Active Directory PowerShell Module

The Active Directory PowerShell module allows you to perform the vast majority of user, computer, and group account management tasks from the PowerShell scripting environment. The advantage of using the scripting environment is that you can use a cmdlet like Get-ADUser to get a list of Active Directory user accounts and then pipe it to the Set-ADUser cmdlet to configure a specific property for all those user accounts. You can use the following cmdlets when the Active Directory module is loaded in your PowerShell session:

▶ **New-ADUser:** This cmdlet enables you to create a new Active Directory user.

▶ **Get-ADUser:** This cmdlet enables you to query Active Directory users. For example, with the right parameters, you can use this command to get a list of all users who haven't logged on in the last 28 days.

▶ **Set-ADUser:** This cmdlet enables you to configure the properties of an existing Active Directory user account.

> ▶ **Remove-ADUser:** This cmdlet enables you to remove an existing user account from Active Directory.

> ▶ **Enable-ADAccount:** This cmdlet allows you to enable a disabled user account.

> ▶ **Disable-ADAccount:** This cmdlet allows you to disable an enabled user account.

> ▶ **Unlock-ADAccount:** This cmdlet allows you to unlock a locked user account.

For more information on the specifics of each command, use the get-help command-name -detailed command. For example, to get information on how to use all the options of the New-ADUser cmdlet, issue the command:

```
Get-help New-ADUser -Detailed | more
```

Saving Time with Account Templates

▶ *Templates are a great timesaving device.*

An *account template* is an account that has been set up with a set of pre-configured properties that are used by a common class of user. Rather than setting these properties each time you create a new user account, when you want to create a user of that class, you just copy the template user account. Of course, not all properties, for example the user password, are copied. Properties that you can consider configuring in a template account include:

> ▶ **Log On Hours:** This specifies the hours that the account can be used to log on to the network. Although some users may work late, there will be few users who need to be logged on to the network at 4am. This setting can be useful for organizations where employees are only allowed to access network resources at specific times.

> ▶ **Log On To:** This specifies the computers onto which the account can log on. This setting can increase the security of sensitive accounts, like those used by administrators, by limiting the scope of where those accounts can be used.

> ▶ **Account Expires:** You should always set account expiration dates on the accounts used by contractors.

> ▶ **Group Membership:** It is likely that certain types of accounts in your organization, such as those used by specific departments, have common group memberships.

▶ *You can create a template account for these departments as a way of speeding up the user provisioning process.*

Examine which properties are common to the accounts in your organization and then use templates as the basis for creating new accounts with these properties.

CONFIGURING ACCOUNT POLICIES

Account policies are a set of Active Directory Group Policy items that can be used to increase account security. Account policies are found under the Computer Configuration\Policies\Windows Settings\Security Settings node of the default domain policy. Although it is possible to use a different GPO linked at this level to apply policy, best practice is to configure account policies in this GPO. This ensures that other administrators are easily able to figure out which policies are in use.

▶ *If you have different policies applied in different GPOs at the domain level, things can get a little confusing!*

Setting Password Policies

Password policies determine how complicated users' passwords need to be as well as how often users are forced to change their passwords. You configure password complexity in an attempt to prevent unauthorized users from guessing someone's password and then gaining access to the account. Hackers have found that the majority of people use very simple passwords, and that if they try to log on to a user account using random dictionary words, they will be successful on a fairly regular basis.

> **NOTE** There is rigorous debate in the security community about the cost and benefit of forcing users to regularly change their passwords. Some argue that forcing users to regularly change their passwords increases costs, because users tend to forget new passwords and have to make calls to the help desk to get them reset. They would argue that a user with a sufficiently complicated password is protected from most forms of attack, and that there is no need to regularly change complicated passwords, as users are smart enough not to enter their password when someone is watching them closely.

Enforcing password changes attempts to deal with a different problem. Specifically, by enforcing a regular password change, you limit the access an unauthorized person has. For example, if Steve learns Nyree's password, that information will only be useful to him until Nyree is forced to change her password.

Password policies are set at the domain level and are located within the Computer Configuration\Policies\Windows Settings\Security Settings\Account Policies\ Password Policies node of a Group Policy object. The policies that are available and their functions are as follows:

▶ **Enforce Password History:** The default is that the last 24 passwords are remembered. This means that users cannot use any of their last 24 passwords when setting a new password. 24 is the maximum number of passwords that can be remembered when configured through a normal GPO.

▶ **Maximum Password Age:** The default value is 42 days. This policy specifies the maximum amount of time that can expire before a password must be changed. If a user has the Password Never Expires option enabled on his account, then the maximum password age policy is ignored.

▶ **Minimum Password Age:** This is the minimum amount of time that must pass after a password change before another password change can occur. The reason for a minimum password age is that clever users worked out that they could keep changing their password to exhaust the password history. Then, they could change their password back to what it was before they were forced to make the change.

▶ **Minimum Password Length:** The default value is 7. You can raise this to 14 characters, with longer passwords being more secure than shorter passwords.

▶ **Password Must Meet Complexity Requirements:** Enabling this setting means that three of the following four elements must be used in a password: upper case, lower case, numbers, and symbols. As Password1 would meet that requirement, yet is not terribly complex, ensure that you also set a long minimum password length.

▶ **Store Passwords Using Reversible Encryption:** This one tricks a lot of administrators because they see the word "encryption" and think, "ooh, must be more secure." This policy is there to support legacy products, and applying this policy reduces the password protection. Only turn this policy on if you need to support a specific older product.

Although account lockout policy has a separate node within Group Policy, the account lockout policies can be thought of as an extension to the basic password policy. *Account lockout policies* determine how computers will react when a person enters an incorrect password a specific number of times over a specific period of time. Account lockout policies are designed to protect against iterative dictionary attacks, where the attacker fires a list of common passwords against the server, hoping that one of those common passwords is used by an account. These attacks work, because a surprising number of people still use very simple passwords. By using a lockout policy, you can lock an account out for a specific amount of time if there are a certain number of incorrect password entries. Account lockout policies also assist when someone looks over someone else's shoulder as he enters a password and catches most but not all of it.

▶ You should regularly run a query using ADAC to determine which users have the Password Never Expires option enabled and remediate where necessary.

▶ You should also consider that most password cracking software assumes a password length of 8 characters, so requiring longer passwords reduces the possibility of a successful attack.

The drawback to account lockout policies is that enabling them will result in an increased number of calls to the help desk. This is because people forgetting their passwords is a far more common occurrence than someone attacking your network. You can configure the following account lockout policies:

- **Account Lockout Duration:** The default is 30 minutes. You can set this value to 0 minutes, in which case the account remains locked until manually unlocked. Locking the account out for 5 minutes will usually be enough to block iterative dictionary attacks.

- **Account Lockout Threshold:** The default is 5 invalid logon attempts. These attempts are recorded over the Reset Account Lockout After period. This can be set to 999 attempts, though generally people are going to ring the help desk complaining that they have forgotten their password before they make their 20th attempt.

- **Reset Account Lockout After:** The default is 30 minutes. This is the period in which the number of invalid attempts must be made. When the default value is set, and someone enters the wrong password 5 times over a 29-minute period, his account will be locked out for 30 minutes. If, however, the 5 incorrect passwords are entered over a period of 31 minutes, no lockout will occur.

▶ The only way to mitigate the forgotten password problem is to provide a larger account lockout threshold. If someone can't type the right password in ten tries, he or she would probably have called the help desk anyway.

Applying Fine-Grained Password Policies

Normally, you only have one password policy per Active Directory domain. Everyone, from systems administrators to accountants, has to change his or her password according to the same schedule. The idea behind Fine-Grained Password Policies is that it allows you to have separate password policies in the same domain. In theory, it means that you can give people who have accounts that are sensitive, such as systems administrators, a requirement to change their password on a more frequent basis than people who do not have sensitive passwords, such as people in the accounting department.

Password policies are applied through group membership, rather than through Group Policy. Fine-Grained Password Policies are only supported at the Windows Server 2008 and Windows Server 2008 R2 domain functional levels. Only members of the Domain Admins group can create Password Settings Objects (PSO). Fine-Grained Password Policies only apply to user objects and global security groups. You cannot apply Fine-Grained Password Policies to computer objects.

▶ The main problem with Fine-Grained Password Policies is the complexity involved in setting them up. You have to muck around in ADSI Edit and configure complicated settings to get Fine-Grained Password Policies to work.

To create a Fine-Grained Password Policy, perform the following general steps:

1. Log on to a domain controller with a user account that is a member of the Domain Admins group. In the Run dialog box, type **adsiedit.msc**.

2. Right-click the ADSI Edit item and then click Connect To. In the name, type the name of the domain to which you wish to connect, and then click OK.

3. Expand the DC=domainname,DC=Com\CN=System node. Right-click on the CN=Password Settings Container node, and then click New, and then Object.

4. This opens the Create Object dialog box. Ensure that msDS-PasswordSettings is selected, and then click Next.

5. On the Common-Name page, enter a name for the PSO.

6. On the Password Settings Precedence page, enter a precedence with a value greater than 0. This is useful if you are implementing multiple PSOs, and a specific user account might be the target of multiple Fine-Grained Password Policies. A good value is 10.

7. On the Password Reversible Encryption Status for User Accounts page, enter the value FALSE. You only allow reversible encryption in the event that it is necessary for backwards compatibility with older applications. This is unlikely if your organization has adopted Windows Server 2008 R2.

8. On the Password History Length for User Accounts dialog, enter a value for the number of passwords remembered. The maximum value is 1024.

9. On the Password Complexity Status for User Accounts page, enter TRUE to enforce password complexity.

10. On the Minimum Password Length for User Accounts page, enter a value. Maximum value is 255.

11. On the Minimum Password Age for User Accounts page, enter a value between 00:00:00:00 through to the value that you will set for maximum password age, such as 30 days (30:00:00:00).

12. On the Maximum Password Age for User Accounts page, set a maximum age. In general, if you are creating a stricter password policy, this value will be less than that used throughout the rest of your domain. Enter 14 days as 14:00:00:00.

13. On the Lockout Threshold for Lockout of User Accounts page, enter the number of invalid attempts that will trigger a lockout. On sensitive accounts, this should be less than that used throughout the rest of your domain.

14. On the Observation Window for Lockout of User Accounts page, enter the duration in which the threshold number of invalid logon attempts must occur before lockout is triggered. For example, for 10 minutes, enter 0:00:10:00.

15. On the Lockout Duration for Locked Out User Accounts page, enter how long the lockout should occur. For example, for a 15-minute lockout, enter 0:00:15:00.

16. On the Completion page, click on the More Attributes button. On the Select a Property to View drop-down, select msDS-PSOAppliesTo, and then enter the distinguished name of the global security group that will be the target of the PSO, and then click Add. Figure 6-7 shows the PSO applying to the SecureAdmins group. Click OK, and then click Finish.

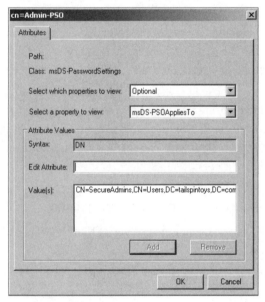

FIGURE 6-7: Create PSO.

Creating Managed Service Accounts

Service accounts are special accounts created by administrators for services when they don't want to associate the standard Local Service, Local System, or Network Service accounts. Best security practice is to use custom service accounts for important services, such as those used by Exchange Server 2010 and SQL Server 2008 R2. Service accounts are generally created as normal user accounts with some rights removed, such as the log on locally right, and other rights, such as the log on as a service right, granted.

The main problem that administrators have with these custom accounts is the management of passwords. It is best practice to ensure that all passwords for all accounts in your organization are changed regularly. Yet, when you change a service account's password, you need to go and find all the services associated with that account and update the password associated with those services. As this can be time-consuming and could cause service outages, a lot of administrators who use custom service accounts set a very long service account password and then configure the account so that the service password does not expire. Or, as an alternative, they go and purchase an expensive solution that manages service accounts completely, so they don't have to worry about them.

Managed service accounts are a new feature of Windows Server 2008 R2 that automate the password management of custom service accounts. The benefit of these accounts is that once they are configured, the administrator doesn't need to worry about them, yet the password and the password on associated services will be updated automatically in compliance with the organization's password policy.

Managed service accounts can be used only on computers running Windows Server 2008 R2 or Windows 7, and only one managed service account can be used for the services on that computer. Managed service accounts cannot be shared between computers and cannot be used in server clusters. Managed service accounts require that the .NET Framework 3.5 SP1 or later and the Active Directory module for PowerShell be installed on the target computer.

To create a managed service account, perform the following steps:

▶ In Windows Server 2008 R2, you can create managed service accounts only from PowerShell. You should use only PowerShell to manage these accounts rather than tools like ADUC or ADAC.

1. Open Active Directory Users and Computers and verify that the Managed Service Account container is present.

2. Open PowerShell and import the Active Directory module by running the following command:

```
Import-Module ActiveDirectory
```

3. From the PowerShell prompt, enter the following command where AccountName is the name of the managed service account:

```
New-ADServiceAccount -SamAccountName AccountName -Name
AccountName
```

4. You can verify the creation of the account by viewing the contents of the Managed Service Accounts container within ADUC.

Once the managed service account is created, it can be installed on the local computer. Once this occurs, the managed service account has the same appearance as the

Local System, Local Service, and Network Service accounts. You need to have the Active Directory module loaded on the local computer to accomplish this. To install the managed service account on the local computer, use the following PowerShell command where AccountName is the name of the managed service account, and you are running PowerShell as a member of the local Administrators group on the computer:

```
Install-ADServiceAccount -Identity AccountName
```

Once the account is installed, you can configure a service to use the account by editing the service properties in the Services console. You must append a dollar sign ($) to the managed service account name, as shown in Figure 6-8. Ensure that the password field is cleared completely and then click OK. You will need to restart the service to complete the configuration of the managed service account.

▶ If your computer isn't a domain controller, you can add these modules by installing the RSAT feature.

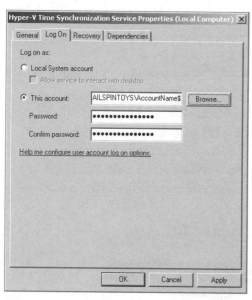

FIGURE 6-8: Managed account

Setting Account Policies for Sensitive Accounts

Administrator accounts are the most sensitive accounts in the organization. They are sensitive because, if these accounts are compromised, the attacker can do far more damage than he could do if a less important account is compromised. With this in mind, you should consider the following organizational policies, rather than Active Directory policies, with respect to administrative accounts:

▶ This type of policy is something you have to put in writing rather than something that you can implement through Active Directory.

▶ Administrators should have separate standard and administrative accounts. Administrators should never log on to their workstation computers using accounts that have administrative privileges. They should log onto their workstations with unprivileged accounts and use separate administrator accounts when they log onto the servers that they manage. You can enforce this policy by editing the properties of the administrator accounts, as shown in Figure 6-9, and limiting the Log On To settings to the computers that the administrator is responsible for managing.

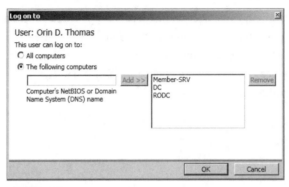

FIGURE 6-9: Log on to

▶ Depending on the role of the administrator, you might want to limit the hours that the account can be used to log on, as shown in Figure 6-10. This ensures that the administrator account isn't used after hours for nefarious purposes; as if someone is going to use an account for something illicit, he is less likely to try to do so when everyone else is around the office and potentially monitoring the situation.

▶ Configure administrator accounts with expiration dates.

▶ Of course, if you do this, ensure that you don't configure all administrator accounts in your organization with the same expiration date.

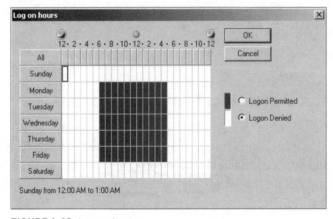

FIGURE 6-10: Log on hours

IT administrators must ensure that the user accounts of IT staff are disabled when those people leave the organization. While people in the IT department may not know that Marge from Accounting left the organization, they ought to know when Erdal, the systems administrator, moves on to greener pastures. As soon as Erdal walks out the door, someone should ensure that his account is disabled and scheduled for deletion. The only reason you wouldn't delete the account is if you decide instead to rename the account and assign it to the person who is replacing the staff member in that role.

When a member of the IT department tenders his resignation or is terminated, you should take the following steps:

► Set the expiration date on all of the member's logon accounts to the day after his final date of employment.

► The day after his final date of employment, do the following:

▷ Manually disable the account.

▷ Change the logon hours for the account so that logon is not allowed at any time.

▷ Reset the account password to a random password. This ensures that logon is impossible.

▷ Rename the account with a prefix such as Disabled. This helps you remember to delete the account when you are sure that it is no longer necessary.

MANAGING GROUPS

The primary purpose of groups is to simplify the application of permissions and rights. This could be as simple as assigning rights to a printer or a file share, or as complex as delegating administrative responsibility over an organizational unit. Rather than assigning permissions and rights directly to users, you assign the permissions and rights to a group. You then add the users to which you want to grant those permissions and rights to the group. Using groups in this manner vastly simplifies the process of determining what permissions and rights have been granted, especially if you add information about this in the group description. Using groups also simplifies the process of removing rights and permissions from users, as all you need to do is remove them from the group rather than editing the security properties of the object.

► Some of the greatest damage done to IT infrastructure has occurred at the hands of systems administrators who log back in to the network after they are fired and trash servers in an act of revenge.

► This often works better than disabling the account, as a lot of administrators forget that you can functionally disable an account by restricting logon hours.

► You can also create an OU named disabled accounts and move the account there, though this may cause problems if you want to enable the account at a later stage and forgot its original location!

When you create a group, you're given the option of configuring a group type and a group scope. The group types are as follows:

▶ **Security group:** This is what you traditionally think of when you think about a group. You assign permissions to security groups.

▶ **Distribution group:** This is a collection of addresses used for messaging.

▶ These are used far less often than traditional security groups. If you're using a product like Exchange, you'll let Exchange manage distribution groups.

A big point of confusion for many administrators is the choice between domain local, global, and universal. Rather than worry about it too much, most administrators just go with the default global security group type, which is fine, because most of the time the global group does what you need it to do. The differences between group types are as follows:

▶ **Machine local:** This group only exists on the machine and includes groups like the local Remote Desktop Users group or the local Administrators group. You should add groups from the domain rather than individual user accounts to these machine local groups. Machine local groups can have universal and global groups from any domain as members, and domain local groups from the same domain as members. For example, you can make members of the domain 1stLevelSupport group also members of the machine local Administrators group. In a large network environment, you should manage the memberships of these groups using Group Policy preferences. You'll learn how to do that later in this chapter.

▶ **Domain local:** Domain local groups can be used only within the domain in which they were created but can have the following as members: groups with global and universal scope from any domain, accounts from any domain, and domain local groups from the same domain. You can convert this group type to universal as long as the group has no domain local groups as members. Microsoft strongly recommends using global groups rather than domain local groups.

▶ **Global:** This is the default group scope when you create a new group. Global groups can contain accounts from the same domain as the global group, as well as other global groups from the same domain as the global group. While it can only contain members from its home domain, the global group can be assigned permissions in any domain. You can convert these to universal as long as the group has no global groups as members.

▶ **Universal:** These groups can contain accounts from any domain in the forest, global groups from any domain in the forest, and universal groups from any domain in the forest. You can assign universal groups permissions to any object in the forest.

The benefit to creating groups with ADAC rather than ADUC is that you can enter all necessary group properties on one page, rather than entering them separately over the course of multiple pages in a wizard and then having to go back and edit the group properties to configure items such as the Managed By attribute. The Managed By attribute allows you to delegate who can manage the group. For example, the Sydney Sales group, shown in Figure 6-11, is managed by the SydneySalesManagers group.

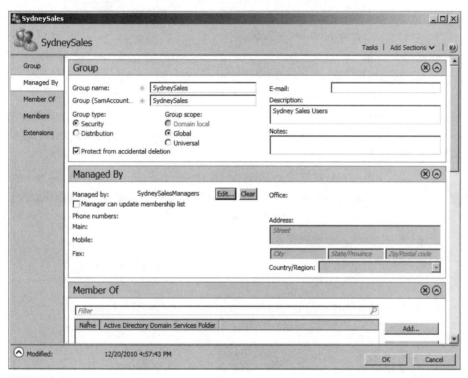

FIGURE 6-11: New group

> **NOTE** A common strategy is to create global groups at the domain level and then to add those global groups to universal groups at the forest level. For example, in a five-domain forest, each domain has a Sales global group. You could collect those five Sales global groups into an All_Sales universal group. The drawback of adding users directly to universal groups is that every time you change group membership, that information needs to replicate throughout the forest. If you are adding and removing user accounts from the universal group all the time, that traffic can add up. If your universal group consists solely of global groups, changes to global group membership, which occur on the domain level, will not have an impact on forest-wide replication traffic.

Managing Membership through Restricted Groups Policy

There are certain sensitive groups, such as the Domain Admins and Enterprise Admins groups, where you want to keep tight control over group membership. One of the easiest methods of doing this is through Restricted Groups policy. Restricted Groups policy uses Group Policy to populate the memberships of specially configured groups. Every time a Group Policy refresh occurs, the group membership is updated. Any accounts that were added to the group through ADAC or ADUC are removed, and any accounts that were removed are added.

As with account policies, the best place to manage group membership through policy is through the default domain policy. Although you can apply Restricted Groups policy at any level, keeping it all within the default domain policy simplifies the process of tracking down and making modifications to the policies as necessary.

To manage the membership of a group using Restricted Groups policy, perform the following general steps:

1. Use the Group Policy Management Editor to edit the properties of the default domain policy. Navigate to the Computer Configuration\Windows Settings\ Security Settings\Restricted Groups node.

2. Right-click the Restricted Groups node and then click Add Group.

3. In the Add Group dialog box, click Browse. In the Select Groups dialog box, enter the name of the group. Click OK twice.

4. Add members to the group, as shown in Figure 6-12. You can also use Group Policy to specify the groups to which this group belongs. Click OK.

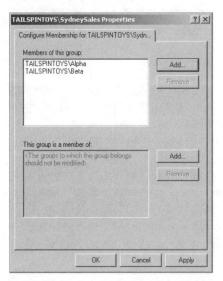

FIGURE 6-12: Restricted Group membership

In large environments, it can be challenging to manage the membership of machine local groups. Most administrators would need to sit for a second to consider how, precisely, they would add a new domain group to the local Administrators group on 2000 desktop computers. Group Policy preferences, introduced with Windows Server 2008, allows for central control over local groups.

To configure the membership of a machine local group with Group Policy preferences, perform the following steps:

1. Use the Group Policy Management Editor to edit the properties of the default domain policy. Navigate to the Computer Configuration\Preferences\ Control Panel Settings Local Users and Groups node, as shown in Figure 6-13.

▶ You should use Restricted Groups policy to manage the membership of domain local, global, and universal groups; and Group Policy preferences to manage the membership of machine local groups.

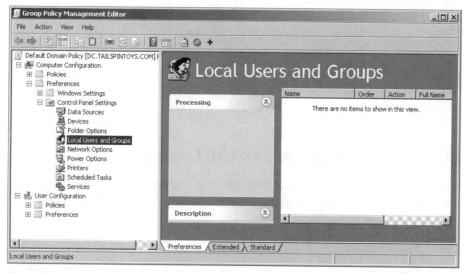

FIGURE 6-13: Group Policy preferences

2. Right-click the Local Users and Groups node, click New, and then click on Local Group.

3. From the Group Name drop-down menu, select the group for which you want to configure membership. For example, to configure the membership of the Administrators machine local group, select Administrators (built-in).

4. Click Add, and then add members to the group. Ensure that you add the Domain Admins group and any other groups that you deem necessary. Ensure that you enable both the Delete All Member Users and Delete All Member Groups options, as shown in Figure 6-14. Click OK.

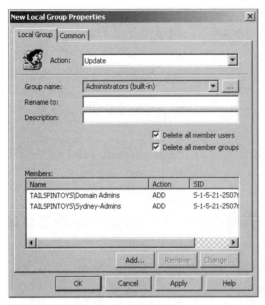

FIGURE 6-14: Manage local Administrators group.

Using Group-Related PowerShell Cmdlets

As is the case with user and computer accounts, you can manage Active Directory groups when you have the Active Directory PowerShell module installed. The module comes with the following group-related cmdlets:

▶ **New-ADGroup:** Use this cmdlet to create a new Active Directory group.

▶ **Get-ADGroup:** Use this cmdlet to get a list of groups that share specific properties or to view the properties of a specific group.

▶ **Remove-ADGroup:** Use this cmdlet to remove an existing group from Active Directory.

▶ **Set-ADGroup:** Use this cmdlet to configure the properties of an existing Active Directory group.

▶ **Add-ADGroupMember:** Use this cmdlet to add a user, group, service account, or computer to a specific Active Directory group.

▶ **Get-ADGroupMember:** Use this cmdlet to view the membership of a specific Active Directory group.

▶ **Remove-ADGroupMember:** Use this cmdlet to remove a user, group, service account, or computer account from a specific Active Directory group.

For more information on the specifics of each command, use the get-help command-name -detailed command. For example, to get information on how to use all the options of the New-ADComputer cmdlet, issue the command:

```
Get-help New-ADComputer -Detailed | more
```

CREATING COMPUTER ACCOUNTS

When you join a computer to the domain manually and the computer does not have an existing account, the computer account is placed into the Computers container. Although it is possible to move accounts manually later, if you are performing a deployment where you know ahead of time the names of the computers that you are deploying, you might choose to create the computer accounts and place them in the appropriate OU ahead of time.

You can create computer accounts using ADAC. When you do this, you can specify the computer name, NetBIOS name, the organizational unit into which the computer account will be placed, and the groups to which the computer belongs as shown in Figure 6-15. This differs from the New Computer dialog in ADUC, where you can only specify the name of the computer and the user or group who can manage the computer account.

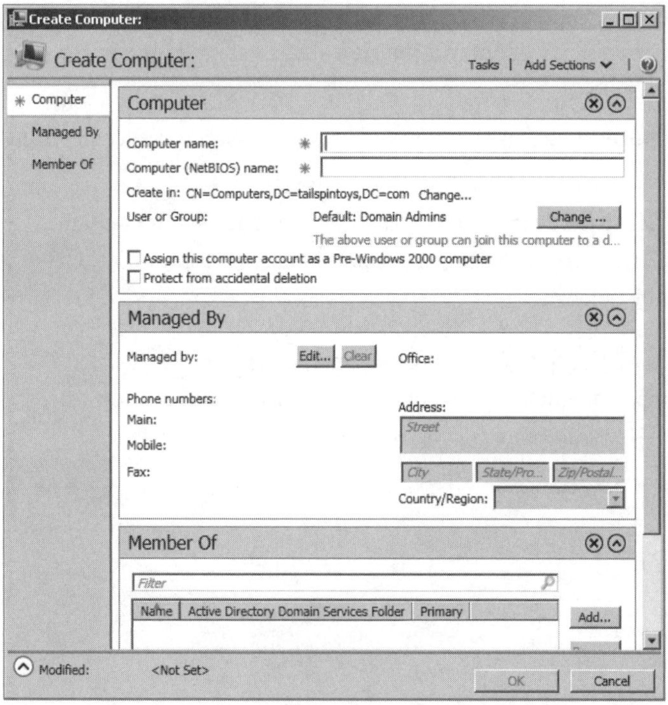

FIGURE 6-15: Create computer

When you join a computer to the domain, a check is performed to see if there is an account name within Active Directory that matches the name assigned to the computer. You can assign a name to a computer using the following command:

```
Netdom renamecomputer %computername% /newname:NAME
```

The most common problem related to computer accounts is that the computer account password becomes desynchronized from the domain. This usually happens when a computer has been powered off for a long time. A common symptom is that users aren't able to log on from that specific computer but have no problems logging on from other computers. The problem can flummox first-level support staff, as when they log on locally, the computer has full network capability, is able to ping local domain controllers, and can resolve DNS addresses, but the user is unable to log on locally. You can fix this problem by resetting the computer account and then joining the computer back to the domain.

The following PowerShell cmdlets can be used to manage computer accounts when the Active Directory module is loaded:

▶ **New-ADComputer:** Use this command to create a new computer account.

▶ **Set-ADComputer:** Use this command to reconfigure the properties of an existing computer account.

▶ **Get-ADComputer:** Use this command to generate a list of computer accounts based on a specific property or get information about a specific computer account.

▶ **Remove-ADComputer:** Use this command to remove a computer account from the domain.

▶ **Reset-ComputerMachinePassword:** Use this command to reset a computer account password in the event that the computer account becomes desynchronized from the domain.

For more information on the specifics of each command, use the get-help command-name -detailed command. For example, to get information on how to use all the options of the New-ADComputer cmdlet, issue the command:

```
Get-help New-ADComputer -Detailed | more
```

SUMMARY

Your company's organizational unit structure should meet your Group Policy application and administrative privilege delegation needs first and reflect the structure of the organization second. Windows Server 2008 R2 introduces the Active Directory Administrative Center, a new console that simplifies the process of finding and managing Active Directory objects. There are a number of new cmdlets available in the Active Directory PowerShell module that are useful for managing user, computer, and group accounts. Fine-Grained Password Policies allow you to apply different password policies across the domain based on group membership. Managed service accounts are special accounts that can be associated with system services, but where the password management for the account is handled completely by Active Directory. You can restrict the membership of sensitive groups either through Restricted Groups policy or through Group Policy preferences.

Further Links

Active Directory Administrative Center

`http://technet.microsoft.com/en-us/library/dd560651(WS.10).aspx`

Active Directory Cmdlets in Windows PowerShell

`http://technet.microsoft.com/en-us/library/ee617195.aspx`

AD DS Fine-Grained Password and Account Lockout Policy Step-By-Step Guide

`http://technet.microsoft.com/en-us/library/cc770842(WS.10).aspx`

Service Accounts Step-By-Step Guide

`http://technet.microsoft.com/en-us/library/dd548356(WS.10).aspx`

Understanding Group Accounts

`http://msdn.microsoft.com/en-us/library/cc733001.aspx`

CHAPTER 7

Managing Active Directory Certificate Services

Active Directory Certificate Services (AD CS) is an increasingly important component of the modern organization's network infrastructure. Ten years ago, an administrator might only have had to install an occasional SSL certificate on an Internet-facing Web server, and, even then, this was only done if the Web server was responsible for serving up secure content. Today, AD CS is becoming as important as network services such as DNS and DHCP. AD CS is a vital component in Windows Server 2008 roles and features, such as IPsec, Network Access Protection, Encrypting File System, BitLocker, DirectAccess, Active Directory Rights Management Services, VPNs, and Smart Cards.

In this chapter, you will learn about the different types of Certification Authority and when you should deploy each type. You will learn about certificate templates and how you can modify them. You will learn how to configure key archiving and recovery to ensure that private encrypted data isn't lost if a user loses his private key, and you will learn about configuring Online Certificate Status Protocol (OCSP) responders, which provide a method of making certificate revocation checks far more efficient.

UNDERSTANDING CERTIFICATION AUTHORITY TYPES

> **NOTE** For the most part, systems administrators don't need to know the minute details of how public and private keys work other than that private keys, which allow access to encrypted data, sometimes can be lost, and if you don't have a backup plan for recovering encrypted data or keys, that data may be lost as well.

A *certificate* is a special type of file created by a certification authority (CA). These files are generated using cryptographic techniques that make them essentially impossible to forge. Certificates are used for the purposes of identification and encryption. On Windows Server 2008 R2 networks, this often takes the form of computer certificates, which can be used for the authentication and then encryption of network traffic and user certificates. Encrypting File System certificates, for example, are used to encrypt and decrypt data.

Understanding CA Hierarchies

CA hierarchies work on the principle that if you trust a CA at the top of the hierarchy, you trust all the certificates issued by CAs that are part of the hierarchy. So, when you configure a client computer to trust an enterprise root or stand-alone root CA, that client will automatically trust all certificates that are issued by subordinates of that CA, even if the subordinate CA is several layers deep in the hierarchy. To create a subordinate CA, the root CA must issue a signing certificate. It is possible to create subordinate CAs under a subordinate CA, in which case the parent subordinate CA creates and issues a signing certificate to the child subordinate CA.

When clients check the validity of a particular certificate, they also check the validity of the CA that issued the certificate. Clients can check the validity of a subordinate CA that issued a certificate by checking the certificate revocation list of the

CA further up in the hierarchy to see if the subordinate CA's signing certificate has been revoked.

You can configure a client to trust a CA by importing its signing certificate into the Trusted Root Certification Authority store. You can configure all clients in an organization to trust a root CA's certificate by publishing that certificate to Active Directory. To publish the root certificate of a CA that is saved as a CRT file named ROOT-CA.crt, issue the following command on a domain controller with a user account that has Domain Admin privileges:

```
Certutil -dspublish -f ROOT-CA.crt
```

Deploying an Enterprise Root CA

An *enterprise root CA* is a special type of root CA that is fully integrated with Active Directory. The certificate of an enterprise root CA is automatically published to Active Directory, and clients in a forest automatically trust certificates issued from this CA. Although it is possible to have more than one enterprise root CA in an organization, this configuration generally causes more trouble than it is worth.

Enterprise root CAs:

▶ Must be installed on computers that are members of a domain

▶ Can issue certificates from the customizable certificate templates that are stored in Active Directory

▶ Can issue certificates to computers, users, or devices that are and are not members of the domain

▶ Can be configured to automatically issue certificates to a security principal in the domain

Root CAs must be online at all times and are recommended for organizations that have less than 300 users or for larger organizations that do not have extensive security requirements. This is because an enterprise root CA is a security risk. Online CAs are far more likely to be compromised by malware than offline CAs, and enterprise root CAs cannot be offline. When an enterprise root CA is compromised, the status of every certificate issued in the organization becomes problematic, as you can't be sure which ones were legitimately issued and which ones were issued by a malicious third party.

Deploying an Enterprise Subordinate CA

> **NOTE**   Organizations that deploy multiple CAs should use an enterprise sub-
> ordinate CA to issue certificates for daily use and an offline stand-alone root
> CA as the apex of the CA hierarchy. This allows you to revoke CA certificates as
> necessary while minimizing risk to the root CA.

Enterprise subordinate CAs are integrated into Active Directory. Every certificate
issued by an enterprise subordinate CA is trusted by every member of the Active
Directory environment. Enterprise subordinate CAs must be installed on computers that are members of an Active Directory domain. An enterprise subordinate CA's
signing certificate can be issued by either an enterprise or a stand-alone CA. Enterprise subordinate CAs must be online at all times, which presents a security risk in
as much as any computer that is always online is more likely to be compromised by an
attacker than a computer that spends most of its time offline. Enterprise subordinate
CAs can issue certificates based on the customizable certificate templates that are
stored in Active Directory.

> **NOTE**   While it is possible to have an enterprise CA's signing certificate issued
> by a trusted third party CA, signing certificates for CAs are often quite expen-
> sive, and you should only do this when all certificates used in the organization
> need to be trusted by clients that are external to the organization.

Enterprise subordinate CAs generally function as issuing CAs. An issuing CA is
responsible for issuing certificates, usually through autoenrollment, to security
principals in the Active Directory environment. Enterprise subordinate CAs can
issue signing certificates to child CAs. When a three-tier CA hierarchy is in use, the
second-tier CAs often function as policy CAs. A *policy CA* is deployed when an organization wants to leverage specific certificate policies. A *certificate policy* is a collection
of written organizational policies and configuration settings that represent a practical implementation of those policies. Policy CAs are generally deployed when an organization needs to conform to a set of regulatory requirements, such as there being a
clear separation between the administrators that manage the server that hosts the
CA and the people who are responsible for approving the issuance of certificates.

Deploying a Stand-alone Root CA

Stand-alone root CAs can be installed on computers that are members of an Active
Directory domain or on computers that are not members of a domain. Stand-alone

root CAs cannot issue certificates based on the customizable certificate templates that are stored within Active Directory. The properties of a certificate issued by a stand-alone root CA depend on the contents of the certificate request file used to request the certificate.

Stand-alone root CAs are recommended for organizations that have more than 300 users when used in conjunction with an enterprise subordinate CA. In this configuration, the stand-alone root CA issues the subordinate CA's signing certificate, and the enterprise subordinate is responsible for issuing all the certificates needed on a daily basis.

This configuration is recommended, because a stand-alone root CA can be configured as an offline root CA. An *offline root CA* is a CA that allows organizations to maximize security by keeping the CA that issues the apex signing certificate almost constantly offline. You only bring an offline root CA online when you need to issue a new signing certificate, revoke an existing signing certificate, or reissue a signing certificate.

Offline root CAs are often configured as virtual machines. For extra security, it is possible to use removable hard disks and BitLocker or BitLocker To Go to store the virtual machine files. When you do this, you place the removable hard disk in a secure location, such as a safe, and the virtual machine is only powered on when it is necessary to perform tasks related to the signing certificates of subordinate CAs.

Offline CAs have the following configuration requirements:

- **Must be a stand-alone root CA:** You can't configure an enterprise root or subordinate CA to be an offline CA.

- **The server hosting the CA cannot be a member of a domain:** This is because the server will be offline most of the time and its computer account password is likely to become desynchronized.

- **Modify CRL and AIA to accessible locations:** The Certificate Revocation List (CRL) and Authority Information Access (AIA) points must be configured for publication to an online location that is accessible to clients of subordinate CAs. Do this on the Extensions tab of the CA properties, shown in Figure 7-1. You will learn about CRLs later in this chapter.

- **Export CRL and CA certificate:** It is necessary to export the CRL and the CA certificate to a location that is online after reconfiguring the CRL and AIA points and ensuring that the new CA certificate uses these points. If external clients need to be able to use or trust these certificates, this publication point needs to be available to those external clients.

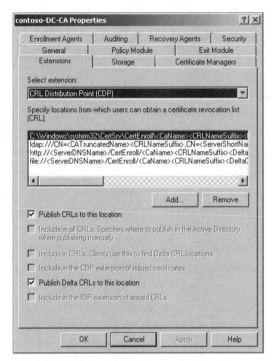

FIGURE 7-1: CA properties Extensions tab

▶ **Ensure clients trust certificate:** Publish the offline root CA certificate to Active Directory in the domain that will host enterprise subordinate CAs.

▶ **Issue signing certificates for subordinate CAs:** Submit and approve signing certificate requests on subordinate CAs.

▶ **Take root CA offline:** Shut down the root CA and store it in a safe location. CA is safest when disconnected from the network entirely.

▶ *If you are going to keep the offline CA on the network when it is brought online, come up with a way of ensuring that patches and updates are applied.*

> **NOTE** Although you can have both an enterprise root and a stand-alone root CA, this configuration is likely to cause more trouble than it is worth. It is better to go with an offline stand-alone root and enterprise subordinate CAs.

Deploying a Stand-alone Subordinate CA

Stand-alone subordinate CAs, like stand-alone root CAs, are limited in the types of certificates they can issue. These CAs can't directly issue certificates based on the certificate templates that are published in Active Directory but can issue certificates based on the properties of a certificate request that is directly issued to the CA. All certificate requests to the stand-alone CA are set to pending by default, and those requests require an administrator to manually approve them. You will learn more about CA administrator settings later in this chapter.

Stand-alone subordinate CAs can be installed on computers that are members of the domain or that have no domain membership. It is more common to deploy on computers that are not domain members. Stand-alone subordinate CAs are often deployed on perimeter networks as a way of making certificates from the internal CA hierarchy available to third party clients.

▶ This is because, if you are going to install on a domain member anyway, you might as well deploy all the extra features available in an enterprise CA.

Opting for Public CAs

Rather than deploying their own CA, some organizations choose instead to purchase certificates from a public CA. Other organizations take a hybrid approach, purchasing certificates for some hosts, such as publicly available Web servers, while setting up enterprise CAs for the deployment of certificates that are only used internally, such as Encrypting File System (EFS) and Active Directory Rights Management Services (AD RMS) certificates.

It is also possible to obtain a signing certificate for a CA from a trusted third party CA. This is only necessary when you need to issue a large number of certificates that must be trusted by clients that are external to your organization. Most organizations don't have this requirement and only need to deal with a public CA when it comes to a small number of certificates required for public servers such as e-commerce sites.

> **NOTE** Typically, a CA can support a large number of people. If your group has multiple sites, you may want to consider deploying a CA to each site, especially if you are using autoenrollment, because there are a large number of certificates being deployed.

MANAGING CERTIFICATION AUTHORITIES

A big problem for any organization is determining how much trust to give an administrator. This is especially true when considering sensitive files that administrators should not be able to view under any circumstances. If an organization uses EFS certificates, it is possible for an unscrupulous administrator to configure his account or a certificate issued to him as a *Data Recovery Agent (DRA)*. A DRA is a special certificate that is used to recover encrypted data. In essence, when configured properly, all encrypted data in the organization is encrypted to a specific user's certificate but is also encrypted in such a way that it can be decrypted by the DRA certificate. DRAs can be very handy when used properly, such as in the recovery of encrypted files in the event that an employee leaves the organization. Needless to say, this makes the DRA something that should be used in a monitored and limited fashion, as any person that has a DRA certificate can read all encrypted data in the organization.

Windows Server 2008 R2 certification authorities can be configured on the basis of *Role Based Access Control (RBAC)* methods so that the user who is responsible for managing the CA doesn't actually have the ability to issue certificates to himself. Similarly, the people who are able to issue the certificates aren't able to manage the CA. This approach is somewhat similar to the concept used by nuclear missile keys, where two different people have to turn a key at the same time so that one single person is unable to launch a missile.

Certification authorities on Windows Server 2008 R2 support the following roles:

- ▶ CA Administrator
- ▶ Certificate Manager

These roles are configured by assigning the appropriate permission on the Security tab of the CA's properties, as shown in Figure 7-2.

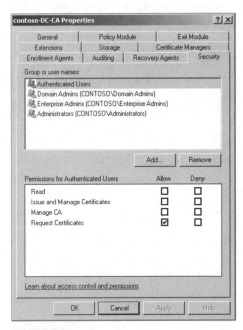

FIGURE 7-2: CA Security tab

Understanding the CA Administrator Role

The CA Administrator role is assigned to the person or people that have local administrative privileges on the server that hosts the CA role. The CA Administrator is responsible for CA configuration and ensuring that the CA certificate is renewed. When you use separate permissions, this person should not be responsible for actually approving the issuance of certificates.

To give a user or group the CA Administrator role, select the Manage CA privilege on the Security tab of the CA's properties. Each CA uses its own security settings, which means, if you have multiple CAs in your organization, you will need to configure this correctly on each of them.

> NOTE It is important to note that this split configuration is not enforceable through software and instead must be maintained through other policies such as rigorous auditing of CA permissions.

Understanding the Certificate Manager Role

The CA Manager is responsible for issuing and revoking certificates. In sensitive environments, this allows a specific user who is not the administrator to issue a certificate to be used as a DRA. This DRA certificate can then be exported and stored in a secure location until it becomes necessary to recover encrypted files. Taking this approach ensures that a nefarious systems administrator won't be able to issue a DRA certificate that no one knows about so that he or she has access to the encrypted files of everyone in the organization.

To assign the Certificate Manager role, a user that holds the Certificate Administrator role must assign the Issue and Manage Certificates permission on the Security tab of the CA's properties. Once a group has this right, it is then possible to set the Restrict certificate managers setting on the Certificate Managers tab of the CA. Figure 7-3 shows this configuration where members of the Alpha user group are able to issue certificates based on the EFS Recovery Agent template.

The default settings allow members of the Domain Admins, Enterprise Admins, and Local Admins groups to issue certificates based on any templates. In organizations that have rigorous security standards, you would configure this tab so that only members of specific user groups would have the right to issue certificates based on specific security templates. You would then control the membership of these groups through restricted Group Policy and audit permissions changes on the CA to ensure that those permissions remain unaltered.

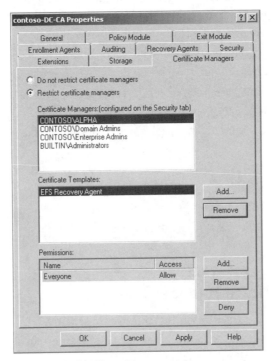

FIGURE 7-3: Certificate Managers tab

As is the case with the CA Administrator permission, CA Managers need to be assigned on a per-CA basis. Just because a particular group is configured with the right to issue certificates for one template on one enterprise CA doesn't mean that the same group has any rights to issue certificate templates on any other CAs. This rule also applies to CAs that are subordinate to that CA, as CA Manager and CA Administrator permissions are not inherited by child CAs from parent CAs.

Assigning CA Permissions

One thing that trips up new systems administrators when they approach the task of separating administrative privileges on CAs is that while the documentation talks about the CA Administrator and CA Manager roles, there is no actual CA Administrator or CA Manager group. These roles exist only through the assignment of specific permissions and will only exist on a server where an administrator has previously configured the server so that there is a domain group with these names. To assign a security principal these roles, you need to assign one of the following permissions:

▶ **Issue and Manage Certificates:** Granting this permission is the same as assigning a hypothetical CA Manager role. This means that the user is able to issue and revoke certificates. With extra configuration it is possible to limit this to issuing certificates based on a specific template. The default settings of a CA which is a member of a domain grant the Domain Admins, Enterprise Admins, and Local Administrators groups this permission.

▶ **Manage CA:** When a security principal is given the Manage CA permission, he has the CA Administrator role, which means that he can edit the properties of the CA, including assigning permissions, such as Issue and Manage Certificates. A user with this permission is not blocked from assigning himself the Issue and Manage Certificates permission, so the only way you can enforce this is through regular auditing. The Manage CA permission is assigned to the Enterprise Admins, Domain Admins, and Local Administrators groups on a CA that is a member of a domain.

▶ **Request Certificates:** This permission allows a security principal to request certificates from the CA. The default settings on an enterprise CA grant this permission to the Authenticated Users group.

USING CERTIFICATE TEMPLATES

Certificate templates define the properties of certificates. There are certificate templates for common certificate types, such as encryption or server identification certificates. Certificate templates are stored within Active Directory and are only available to enterprise CAs.

As certificate templates are stored in Active Directory, when a modification is made to a certificate template on an enterprise root or enterprise subordinate CA, that modification propagates across all other enterprise CAs in the organization. You can modify certificate templates by opening the Certificate Templates console. Once you've modified a template or created a new template, you need to configure the CA to actually issue the template. To configure a CA to issue a template, perform the following general steps:

1. Right-click on the Certificate Templates node of the Certification Authority console, click on New, and then click on Certificate Template to Issue.

2. On the Enable Certificate Templates dialog box, shown in Figure 7-4, select the certificate template that you want to issue and then click OK.

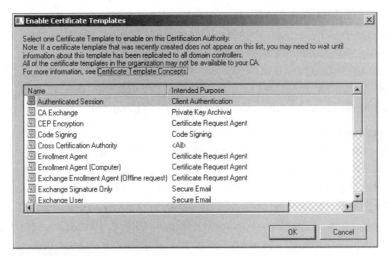

FIGURE 7-4: Enable certificate templates

Understanding Certificate Template Levels

Certificate templates come in three levels that define which CAs the certificate can be issued from and the properties that the CA template can leverage. Certificate template levels have the following properties:

▶ **Level 1:** Level 1 templates can be issued from enterprise CAs running on all currently supported Windows Server operating systems. The only aspect of a level 1 certificate template that can be modified is the permissions. Level 1 templates do not support auto-enrollment.

▶ **Level 2:** Level 2 templates can be fully customized. They do not support Cryptography Next Generation, which is an advanced security solution that supports encryption algorithms, such as those that leverage Elliptic Curve Cryptography techniques. Level 2 templates can be issued from enterprise CAs on computers running the Enterprise and Datacenter editions of Windows Server 2003, Windows Server 2003 R2, Windows Server 2008, and Windows Server 2008 R2.

▶ **Level 3:** Level 3 templates can be fully customized and support Cryptography Next Generation functionality. The drawback of these templates is that they can only be issued from enterprise CAs on computers running the Enterprise and Datacenter editions of Windows Server 2008 and Windows Server 2008 R2. If your organization has a mixture of CAs running the Windows Server 2003 or 2003 R2 operating system, you should not deploy level 3 certificate templates.

Duplicating and Modifying Templates

When you edit a certificate template, you have the option of creating a new template by duplicating an existing template or by editing the current template. In most cases you will duplicate an existing template. You will do this because most of the certificate templates that are initially available for a Windows Server 2008 R2 CA are actually level 1 templates, which means that they don't support enhanced functionality such as auto-enrollment and key recovery.

When you duplicate a template, you are prompted to choose between creating a Windows Server 2003 Enterprise or Windows Server 2008 Enterprise template, as shown in Figure 7-5.

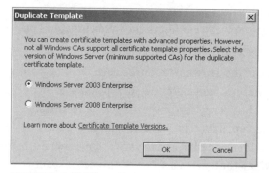

FIGURE 7-5: Duplicate Template

> You might also want to keep the originals around as a base for additional templates as required.

> If your organization has CAs running the Windows Server 2003 or Windows Server 2003 R2 operating system, choose Windows Server 2003 Enterprise, otherwise choose Windows Server 2008 Enterprise.

Modifying Certificate Template Properties

You configure a template by modifying its properties on a set of tabs. There is a slight variation in the layout of these tabs depending on whether you are editing a level 2 or level 3 template. As this book deals with Windows Server 2008 R2, it addresses the layout of a level 3 template.

You can configure the following properties on each tab:

> **General:** This tab relates to general properties such as certificate name, validity period, and availability in Active Directory. You can configure the following items on the General tab:

▷ **Template Display Name:** This field specifies the name the template has in the Certificate Templates and the Certification Authority console.

▷ **Validity Period:** This field allows you to specify the length of time the certificate will remain valid.

▷ **Renewal Period:** Using this field, you can configure the length of time before automatic renewal is attempted.

▷ **Publish Certificate in Active Directory:** Configuring this option allows you to specify whether the public key is published in Active Directory so that it can be accessed by other users or applications.

▶ *This can be useful to deploy when you want to enable users to encrypt files for other users or check digital signatures.*

▷ **For Automatic Renewal of Smart Card Certificates, Use Existing Key if a New Key Cannot Be Created:** Allows renewal to use the existing key pair rather than generating a new one. This is useful if space on the smart card is limited.

▶ **Request Handling:** The Request Handling tab relates to issues such as the purpose of the certificate and whether the private key will be archived in the certificate services database. You can configure the following items on this tab:

▷ **Purpose:** Defines what the certificate template can be used for. The options are Encryption, Signature, Signature and Encryption, and Signature and Smart Card Logon. The Encryption purpose allows a certificate to be used to encrypt and decrypt data. The Signature purpose allows the certificate to be used for identification and to verify that a signature has been applied to data. When the Smart Card Logon purpose is specified, the certificate must be stored in a device that supports two-factor authentication.

▶ *This option is useful if you need to support devices such as smart cards, which have limited storage capacity.*

▷ **Delete Revoked or Expired Certificates:** Configuring this option ensures that expired certificates are removed.

▷ **Include Symmetric Algorithms Allowed by the Subject:** Setting this option allows symmetric algorithms to be used with the certificate by applications such as Outlook.

▷ **Archive Subject's Encryption Private Key:** Configuring this allows the key to be archived if key archiving is enabled on the CA. This allows a user's private key to be recovered in the event that he loses it, misplaces it, or it is lost when the user leaves the organization.

▷ **Allow Private Key To Be Exported:** Determines whether the user can manually export his private key. If this option is not enabled, the user is unable to back up his private key.

▷ **Do the Following When the Subject Is Enrolled and When the Private Key Associated With This Certificate Is Used:** This setting allows you to configure whether enrollment occurs silently, whether the user will be prompted to automatically enroll in the certificate, and whether the user has to enter a password whenever he uses the private key. Most of the time you'll configure autoenrollment to occur silently.

▶ **Cryptography:** This tab allows you to configure which algorithm is used to generate the certificate. You can also specify whether any encryption provider is used or a specific encryption provider is used for certificate requests. If you choose to use a specific provider, you can specify which hash algorithm is used to protect the request.

▶ **Subject Name:** This tab allows you to specify how the certificate subject name is generated. You have the option of having this information supplied in the certificate request or having the certificate server query Active Directory for this information.

▶ **Server:** The settings on this tab allow you to ensure that certain certificates cannot be revoked, even if a user has the appropriate revocation permissions. On this tab you can specify the following settings:

▷ **Do Not Store Certificates and Requests In the CA Database:** When you configure this option, certificate issuance information and certificates are not stored in the CA database. This is useful in the event that you want to issue a certificate that cannot be revoked.

▷ **Do Not Include Revocation Information In Issued Certificates:** Configuring this item stops the revocation information from being included in the certificate. This means no revocation check can be performed against the certificate. This is useful for issuing certificates to devices that aren't connected to a network.

▶ **Issuance Requirements:** This tab, shown in Figure 7-6, allows you to specify whether the certificate must be approved before being issued by a Certificate Manager. It is possible to configure this setting so that multiple Certificate Managers must approve the certificate prior to it being issued.

▶ As most users wouldn't know how to do this anyway, you're better off enabling key archiving so that an administrator can restore the private key as necessary.

▶ This is only really useful in organizations that have sophisticated security requirements. For most organizations, the default value is fine.

▶ These precautions are only necessary for high-security templates, such as Key Recovery and Data Recovery Agents, as certificates based off these templates provide special access to private data.

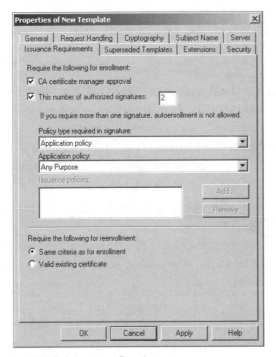

FIGURE 7-6: Issuance Requirements

▶ **Superseded Templates:** On this tab you can specify the certificate templates that the current template supersedes. When used with autoenrollment, you can ensure that all current certificate holders have their certificates updated to use the new template.

▶ **Extensions:** On this tab, you can configure certificate extensions, such as which applications the certificate can be used for, certificate template information, issuance policies, and restrictions on key usage.

▶ This is another setting that you are unlikely to need to change unless your organization has specific security requirements.

▶ **Security:** The Security tab, shown in Figure 7-7, allows you to determine which security principals have specific permissions on this template. If you want to configure a certificate template so that it supports autoenrollment, you must do it by assigning the autoenrollment permission on this tab.

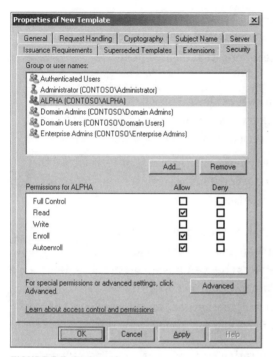

FIGURE 7-7: CA Security

UTILIZING CERTIFICATE AUTOENROLLMENT

The great advantage to enterprise CAs over stand-alone CAs, and perhaps one of the great advantages of a fully integrated solution from Microsoft over deploying third party CAs, is the process of autoenrollment. In a nutshell, *autoenrollment* allows you to configure certain certificate templates so that certificates based on these templates can be automatically issued to security principals that meet specific criteria, usually group membership. The benefit of this is it vastly reduces the amount of effort required to issue and manage certificates. For example, in a Windows 2000 environment, if you had an organization that had 1000 users and you wanted to use a centralized, certificate-based Encrypting File System (EFS) solution, you'd have to come up with some way of issuing an individual EFS certificate to each of the 1000 users in the organization. What would make this even more cumbersome is that you'd have to find a way to have each individual user request this certificate from the CA, even if you configured each certificate to be automatically approved when requested.

To configure a certificate template to support autoenrollment, you need to take the following steps:

▶ Ensure that the certificate is a level 2 or level 3 template. Most certificate templates are level 1, so it is likely that you will need to duplicate an existing template to configure that template for autoenrollment.

▶ Configure the autoenroll security permission for the security principal that you want to allow to automatically enroll in the certificate on the Security tab of the certificate template's properties.

▶ Autoenrollment should be configured in the Default Domain Policy GPO.

Once these two steps have been taken on the certificate template, you need to configure Group Policy to support autoenrollment and renewal. To configure autoenrollment, configure the Certificate Services Client - Autoenrollment Policy. This policy is located in the User Configuration\Windows Settings\Security Settings\Public Key Policies node. The Enrollment Policy Configuration node for autoenrollment of computer certificates is displayed in Figure 7-8 and has the following settings:

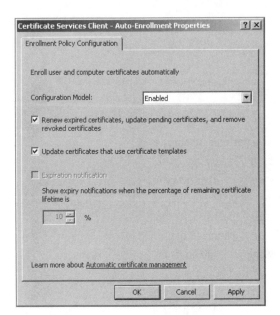

FIGURE 7-8: Configure autoenrollment.

▶ **Configuration Model:** Can be set to Enabled, Disabled, or Not Configured. Set this to Enabled to allow autoenrollment.

▶ **Renew expired certificate, update pending certificates, and remove revoked certificates:** Configuring this setting ensures that certificates are automatically renewed when they expire. Revoked certificates will also automatically be removed from the local certificate store.

▶ **Update certificates that use certificate templates:** Configuring this setting enables autoenrollment in new certificate templates that are configured to supersede existing templates.

▶ **Expiration notification:** Determines whether a user is prompted to trigger reenrollment based on remaining certificate lifetime.

RECOVERING CERTIFICATES

The default settings of a Windows Server 2008 R2 enterprise CA do not have the private keys of issued certificates stored on the server. This means that if a user loses his private key or leaves the organization, any data that might be encrypted to that private key is potentially lost to the organization. *Key archiving and recovery* allows private keys to be recovered from the AD CS database in the event that the user loses his private key.

Key archiving allows centralized backup of private keys, but must be enabled on the CA and enabled within individual certificate templates. To enable a Key Recovery Agent (KRA) on a CA:

▶ First ensure that KRA certificates have been issued to users that will perform the Key Recovery Agent function. To do this you will need to configure a CA to actually issue keys from the Key Recovery Agent Certificate, as this is not enabled by default. Once this is done, you can configure a user account to request a KRA certificate.

▶ Enable key recovery by selecting Archive the key on the Recovery Agents tab of the CA's properties, as shown in Figure 7-9.

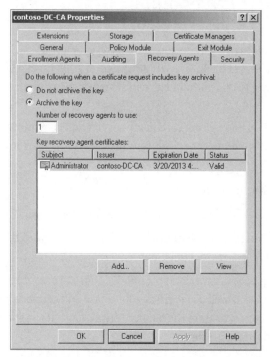

FIGURE 7-9: Key Recovery Agents

Once these steps are taken, configure individual certificate templates to support key archiving. Once you've done this, the private keys from certificates issued from this template can be recovered by a user that holds an appropriate KRA certificate by using the following command on the CA:

```
CertUtil -GetKeySerialNumber EFSKEY.cer
```

Here, `SerialNumber` is the certificate serial number, which can be determined by looking through the list of issued certificates. You can't recover a private key without knowing its serial number.

> **NOTE** A KRA for a CA can only recover certificates issued since the KRA certificate was configured for that CA. So if Rooslan was issued a KRA certificate on the 1st of Jan 2012, and the CA was configured to use Rooslan's public KRA key on the 1st of Jan 2012, Rooslan could only recover keys issued after that date, even if other KRAs were configured for the CA prior to that. When you configure a new KRA, it is a good idea to forcibly reenroll all current certificate holders to ensure that their private certificates can be recovered by the new KRA.

BACKING UP CERTIFICATE SERVICES

Certificate services is backed up entirely when you perform a system state backup. As you can configure Windows Server Backup in Windows Server 2008 R2 to perform scheduled system state backups, this is perhaps the safest way of ensuring that certificate services is backed up.

You can also manually backup and restore certificate services on computers running Windows Server 2008 R2. To manually back up certificate services, perform the following steps:

1. Open the Certification Authority console.

2. Right-click on the CA, click on All Tasks, and then click on Back Up CA.

3. On the Welcome to the Certification Authority Backup Wizard page of the Certification Authority Backup Wizard, click Next.

4. On the Items to Back Up page, shown in Figure 7-10, choose to back up the Private key and CA certificate as well as Certificate database and certificate database log. Specify the location to store the backup, ensuring that the specified directory is empty, and then click Next.

5. Specify a password for the private key backup, and then click Next. When the backup completes, click Finish.

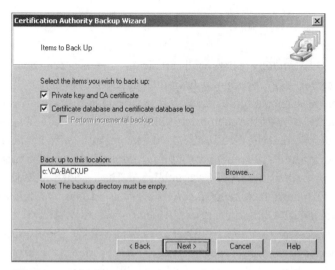

FIGURE 7-10: CA Backup

To restore a certification authority database and private key, either do a system state restore or, if you only want to restore the CA database, use the Certification Authority console. To restore the database using the Certification Authority console, perform the following general steps:

1. Open the Certification Authority console.

2. Right-click on the CA, click on All Tasks, and then click on Restore CA.

3. You will be asked to stop Active Directory Certificate Services before you are able to continue with the restore. To do this, click OK.

4. On the Welcome to the Certification Authority Restore Wizard page of the Certification Authority Restore Wizard, click Next.

5. On the Items to Restore page, shown in Figure 7-11, select the items that you wish to restore and the location of the certificate services backup. Click Next, and then click Finish. When the restore completes, you will be prompted to restart Active Directory Certificate Services.

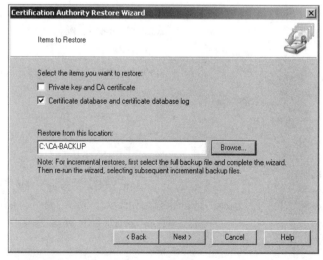

FIGURE 7-11: CA Restore

REVOKING CERTIFICATES

Certificate Revocation Lists (CRL) are lists of all certificates that have been revoked on the certificate server. A *CRL Distribution Point (CDP)* is a location where a CRL is hosted. When a computer encounters a new digital certificate, it checks the information in that certificate to locate the appropriate CDP and then downloads and checks the CRL to determine whether the certificate it has been presented with has been revoked. A *delta CRL* is a mini-CRL that only contains information about certificates that have been revoked since the last CRL was published. The default publication interval for CRLs on Windows Server 2008 R2 CAs is every seven days. The default publication interval for delta CRLs is every day. If your organization rarely revokes certificates, it isn't necessary to publish CRLs or delta CRLs quickly. The drawback is that the validity period of a CRL is defined by its publication period, so if you need to rapidly revoke a bunch of certificates and you have a CRL publication period of a month, it might be a month before clients recognize those certificates as revoked.

Configuring CRL Locations

CRL locations are configured on the Extensions tab of a CA's properties under the CDP Extension item. This information is included in certificates issued by the CA so that clients can check the validity of the certificate. By default, CRLs are published to the following locations:

- ► `C:\Windows\system32\CertSrv\CertEnroll\<CaName><CRLNameSuffix><Delta CRLAllowed>.crl`

- ► `Ldap:///CN=<CATruncadedName><CRLNameSuffix>,CN=<ServerShortName>,CN= CDP,CN=Public Key Services,CN=Services,<ConfigurationContainer><CDPO bjectClass>`

- ► `http://<ServerDNSName>/CertEnroll<CaName><CRLNameSuffix><DeltaCRLAll owed>.crl`

- ► `File:// <ServerDNSName>/CertEnroll<CaName><CRLNameSuffix><DeltaCRLAl lowed>.crl`

► *If you change CDPs, you should attempt to forcibly reenroll all current certificate holders. Although this may cause some disruption, it might be a better option than waiting for all current certificates to expire.*

While you can add and remove locations, be aware that these new locations will only be present in the information of certificates issued after the change is made. Checks against certificates issued earlier will use the CDPs that were specified at the time those certificates were issued.

> **NOTE** You can configure a CDP on a DFS share to ensure that revocation checks can be performed in the event that the original issuing CA becomes unavailable.

If you are publishing certificates that are to be used by external third parties, the CDPs and AIA points will need to be hosted on computers that are accessible to those third parties, such as a server on a perimeter network.

Using Online Certificate Status Protocol Arrays

Online Certificate Status Protocol (OCSP) arrays allow clients to check the revocation status of individual certificates without having to download entire CRLs and delta CRLs. This makes CRL checks significantly faster, as certificate servers that have been in operation for some time can have large CRLs. OCSP arrays have the following benefits:

▶ OCSP arrays minimize bandwidth required to support revocation queries. The client submits a query based on the certificate's serial number and receives a response from the OCSP array.

▶ OCSP arrays are scalable, as it is possible to add extra OCSP servers to an array. These servers can be at multiple sites to provide local OCSP services.

▶ OCSP arrays can host revocation data for multiple CAs. This is done by adding additional revocation configurations to the array. An organization might have one array that supports all of the CAs.

To configure an OCSP array, perform the following tasks:

▶ Add the Online Responder role service to a computer running Windows Server 2008 or Windows Server 2008 R2.

▶ Configure an enterprise CA running Windows Server 2008 or Windows Server 2008 R2 to issue certificates using the OCSP Response Signing template. CAs do not issue this template by default.

▶ Configure the Authority Information Access settings of each CA to point to the address of the OCSP array.

▶ Enroll the computer or computers that will host the OCSP array in certificates created off the OCSP Response Signing template. This can be done automatically but is usually done manually.

▶ Create a revocation configuration using the Online Responder Management console. You can create multiple revocation configurations to provide online responder services to multiple CAs.

NOTE Once all these steps have been taken, you might again consider reen-rolling all current certificate holders so that they switch from using the old CDPs to the new OCSP arrays.

SUMMARY

CAs can be deployed as enterprise root, enterprise subordinate, stand-alone root, and stand-alone subordinate. The most common configuration for organizations that have less than 300 users is a single enterprise root CA. The most secure configuration for organizations that have more than 300 users is an offline root CA with one or more enterprise subordinate CAs used for issuing certificates.

The CA Administrator role allows security principals to manage a CA, configure permissions, and backup the CA database. Configuring key archiving allows users that have been issued a KRA certificate to be able to recover a user's private key from the CA database. You need to enable key archiving on an appropriate certificate template before this is possible.

Certificate templates allow organizations to customize certificates. You must duplicate a level 1 certificate template if you want to alter anything other than the template permissions. Level 2 templates support features such as autoenrollment. Level 3 templates can only be issued from CAs running Windows Server 2008 or Windows Server 2008 R2 but support features such as Cryptography Next Generation, an advanced security option likely only to be used by organizations that have rigorous security standards.

A CRL is a list of all certificates that have been revoked on the CA. A delta CRL is a list of all certificates that have been revoked since the publication of the last CRL. An OCSP array is a more efficient way of handling CRL traffic. Both CRLs and OCSP arrays need to be in locations that are accessible to clients that will use the certificate. This means that if a third party client needs to be able to use the certificate, that third party client needs to be able to access the appropriate CRL distribution point or OCSP site. The easiest way of doing this is publishing the CRL distribution point or OCSP site on the perimeter network.

Additional Sources

Certification Authority Hierarchies

http://technet.microsoft.com/en-us/library/cc781292(WS.10).aspx

Implement Role Based Administration

http://technet.microsoft.com/en-us/library/cc732590(WS.10).aspx

Install an Enterprise Subordinate Certification Authority

http://technet.microsoft.com/en-us/library/cc784465(WS.10).aspx

Managing Certificate Templates

http://technet.microsoft.com/en-us/library/cc772457(WS.10).aspx

Setting Up a Certification Authority

http://technet.microsoft.com/en-us/library/cc770827(WS.10).aspx

Specify CRL Distribution Points

http://technet.microsoft.com/en-us/library/cc753296(WS.10).aspx

PART II

NETWORK INFRASTRUCTURE AND SECURITY SECRETS

Network Addressing

Administrators have been warned for years that the world is running out of public IPv4 addresses. In 2011, the pool is close to depletion, and IPv4 address blocks in some geographic registries are already exhausted. Although you're likely to work for an organization that already has a couple of public IPv4 addresses, the time for procrastinating about IPv6 is past, and you'll need to prepare your organization for its deployment.

Although you can keep IPv4 on your internal network, an increasing number of technologies, such as DirectAccess, assume that you have IPv6 or an appropriate transition technology deployed. Such technologies are going to be more prevalent in the future, which means that although you'll be able to keep your private IPv4 address space, you'll need to perform some sort of IPv6 deployment to keep everything working.

In this chapter, you learn how to provision networks with IPv4 addresses, how to configure the necessary infrastructure for appropriate transition technologies, and how to deploy IPv6. The chapter's focus on IPv6 is on unique local IPv6 unicast addresses, which can be deployed to replicate the functionality of the private IPv4 address space.

UNDERSTANDING IPV4 AND DHCP

IPv4 is a familiar technology to almost every experienced systems administrator. You're probably aware of the difference between the public and the private address space and can quickly recognize whether a host is directly connected to the Internet or located on a private network just by looking at the IP address. In this section, you learn a few secrets about IP address configuration and how to effectively use DHCP for IP address allocation.

Configuring IPv4 Addresses

IPv4 addresses can be configured manually or automatically. Although you are likely to use automatic configuration to configure the IP address of a client computer running Windows 7, you are also likely to manually set the IP address of a server. This is because you generally want to ensure that servers have the same IP address at all times rather than one that is dynamically assigned and subject to change. It is, of course, possible to configure DHCP to always assign the same address to a particular computer, but most administrators prefer static IP address configuration for servers, because it is the most reliable way of accomplishing a consistent result. To configure an IP address manually, perform the following steps:

1. In the Search Programs and Files box on the Start menu, type **ncpa.cpl**. This opens the Network Connections control panel.

2. Right-click on the adapter to which you want to assign an address, and then click Properties.

3. Click Internet Protocol Version 4 (TCP/IPv4), and then click Properties.

4. On this dialog box, you can configure basic TCP/IPv4 address settings including whether the computer receives its IP address configuration from DHCP or through static entry.

5. Clicking the Advanced button displays the Advanced TCP/IP Settings dialog, as shown in Figure 8-1. On this dialog, you can add additional IP addresses to a network interface and add additional default gateway addresses.

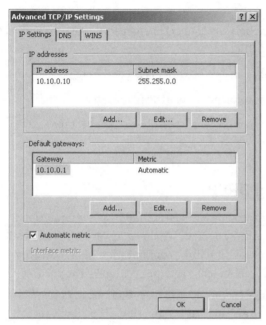

FIGURE 8-1: Advanced TCP/IP settings

6. On the DNS tab, you can add additional DNS servers for the server to query. You can also configure specific DNS suffixes for connections.

7. On the WINS tab, you can configure WINS server addresses, whether or not lookup occurs against the LMHOSTS file and whether NetBIOS over TCP/IP is enabled.

► This is useful if a server has a network interface on the internal network that uses one DNS suffix and another network interface on a perimeter network that uses a separate suffix.

You can also configure TCP/IP address settings from the command line. On servers running the Server Core installation option of Windows Server 2008 R2, this is the primary method of IP address configuration.

NOTE Once you learn how to set an IPv4 address from the command line, you'll find it is much quicker than setting it through the GUI.

The following command line sets the connection named "Local Area Connection" to 10.10.0.10 with a subnet mask of 255.255.0.0 and a default gateway of 10.10.0.1:

```
Netsh interface ipv4 set address "Local Area Connection" static
10.10.0.10 255.255.0.0 10.10.0.1
```

The following command line sets the connection named "Local Area Connection" to retrieve its IP address from a DHCP server.

```
Netsh interface ipv4 set address "Local Area Connection" source=dhcp
```

To configure a DNS server for a computer, use the following command:

```
Netsh interface ipv4 set dnsservers "Local Area Connection" static
10.10.0.20 primary
```

Assigning IPv4 Using DHCP

The DHCP service can be used to provide automatic IP address configuration information to clients configured to use it. By default, Windows Server 2008 R2 computers and clients running Windows 7 seek IP address configuration from DHCP servers. The configuration they get depends on the scope settings configured on the DHCP server.

Windows Server 2008 R2 DHCP servers need to be authorized in Active Directory before they can be used to allocate IP address information. If you don't authorize the DHCP server, it will not provide addresses to the network. The idea behind this is that by requiring authorization, the number of rogue DHCP servers on the network is minimized. DHCP servers can be authorized when you install the role service, as shown in Figure 8-2.

NOTE   Authorization works for only Windows DHCP servers. DHCP servers running on different operating systems or network devices won't be stopped from functioning and can still mess up your network.

To install DHCP on a computer running Windows Server 2008 R2, ensure that the DHCP server is configured with a static IP address and then perform the following steps:

1. Open the Server Manager console, right-click on the Roles node, and then click on Add Roles. This launches the Add Roles Wizard. Click Next.

2. On the Select Server Roles page, select DHCP Server, and then click Next.

3. On the Introduction to DHCP Server page, review the information, and then click Next.

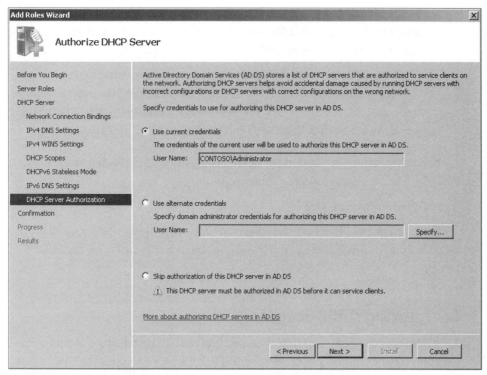

FIGURE 8-2: DHCP authorization

4. On the Network Connection Bindings page, select the network interfaces connected to the network that you want the DHCP server to provide IP addresses on. You can select multiple interfaces. Click Next.

5. On the IPv4 DNS Settings page, you can enter the address of a DNS server. Ensure that the default here is not set to 127.0.0.1. The setting you configure here is used for all scopes, though you can configure different settings on a per-scope basis.

6. On the IPv4 WINS Settings page, specify the address of the network WINS server if one is in use; otherwise, select WINS Is Not Required for Applications on This Network, and then click Next.

7. On the Add or Edit DHCP Scopes page, you can click Add to add a DHCP scope. Creating a DHCP scope is covered later in this chapter.

8. On the DHCPv6 Stateless mode, choose between enabling and disabling stateless mode. Disable stateless mode if you want to use DHCP to provide IPv6 address information.

9. On the IPv6 DNS Settings, confirm that the IPv6 address of the DNS server is present in the Preferred DNS server IPv6 address. Ensure that the IPv6 loopback address ::1 is not present.

10. On the DHCP Server Authorization page, either use the current credentials if the user is a member of the Domain Admins security group or enter alternate credentials of an account that is a member of this group to authorize the DHCP server, and then click Next. Click Install to install the DHCP role service.

As an alternative, ensure that the ServerManager module is loaded into PowerShell and issue the following command:

```
Add-WindowsFeature DHCP
```

When you install DHCP from the command line, you'll need to configure all DHCP settings from the DHCP console. You'll also need to manually authorize the DHCP server.

Configuring DHCP Scopes

A *DHCP scope* is a collection of IP address settings that a client uses to determine its IP address configuration. You configure a DHCP scope for every separate IPv4 subnet to which you want the DHCP server to provide IP address configuration information.

To configure an IPv4 DHCP scope, perform the following steps:

1. Open the DHCP console and click on the IPv4 node.

2. From the Action menu, click on New Scope. This launches the New Scope Wizard. Click Next.

3. On the Scope Name page, provide the scope with a name, and then click Next.

4. On the IP Address Range page, set the start IP address and end IP address and subnet mask. This page is shown in Figure 8-3.

5. On the Add Exclusions and Delay page, you can add DHCP exclusions. Use exclusions to block out parts of the address range that you don't want to assign to clients. This might be because you are configuring a backup scope, or it might be because you statically assign those addresses. You can also set a subnet delay, which determines how long the DHCP server waits before offering an address. This is also used with redundant scopes.

6. On the Lease Duration page, determine how long you want clients to lease addresses. On scopes where the address pool is larger than the number of clients, you can have long lease durations.

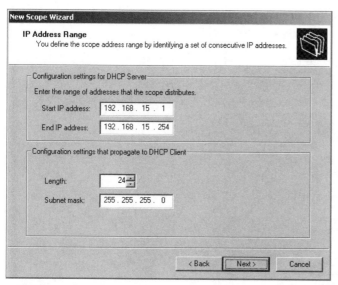

FIGURE 8-3: IP Address Range

NOTE Configure longer leases for scopes where you know the computers are relatively fixed, such as for desktop workstations. Configure short leases for scopes where clients aren't going to be on the network very long, such as for wireless clients.

7. On the Configure DHCP Options page, you can choose to configure scope options or choose to configure options later. Click Finish to finish creating the scope.

8. Once the scope is created, you'll need to click on it, and then click on Activate from the Action menu. This activates the scope.

Configuring Server and Scope Options

DHCP options include additional configuration settings, such as the address of a network's default gateway or the address of DNS and WINS servers. You can configure DHCP options at two levels: the scope level and the server level. Options configured at the scope level override options configured at the server level. There are 61 standard scope options that can be configured on the Scope Options dialog, shown in Figure 8-4.

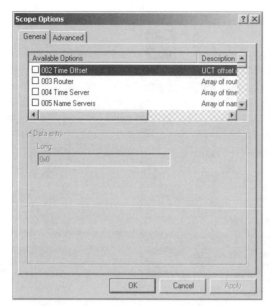

FIGURE 8-4: Scope Options

The most commonly used scope options include:

▶ 003 Router. Default Gateway address.

▶ 006 DNS Servers. DNS server address.

▶ 015 DNS Domain Name. DNS suffix for DNS searches.

▶ 044 WINS/NBNS Servers. WINS server address.

To configure either server or scope level options, right-click on the Scope Options or Server Options node and then click on Configure Options.

> **NOTE** Dynamic updates of DNS are configured to automatically occur from DHCP servers installed on Windows Server 2008 R2. You can configure the dynamic DNS update settings on the DNS tab of the IPv4 properties in the DHCP console.

Creating Superscopes

A *superscope* is a collection of DHCP scopes that can be administered together. Super-scopes allow you to allocate multiple IPv4 subnets to a single physical subnet. This may be necessary in the event that a physical subnet has unpredicted growth, and you aren't able to use supernetting to join together two contiguous subnets. For example, you might have a network 192.168.2.0 /24 assigned to a particular building and the network 192.168.3.0 /24 assigned to another building. If the building with network 192.168.2.0 /24 ends up with more than 254 hosts, you'll need to add another logical subnet. You can't supernet with 192.168.3.0 /24, because it is assigned elsewhere, so you'll need to find another available network and create a superscope.

To create a superscope from an existing scope, perform the following steps:

1. Right-click on the IPv4 node in the DHCP console, and then click New Superscope. This starts the New Superscope Wizard.

2. On the Superscope Name page, enter a name for the superscope, and then click Next.

3. On the Select Scopes page, select the existing DHCP scopes that you want to combine into the superscope, and then click Next. Then click Finish.

Configuring Reservations

Reservations allow you to ensure that a particular computer always receives a specific IP address. You can use reservations to allow servers to always have the same address even when they are configured to retrieve that address through DHCP. If you don't configure a reservation for a computer, it can be assigned any available address from the pool. Although you can configure DHCP to update DNS to ensure that other hosts can connect using the client's hostname, it is generally a good idea to ensure that a server retains the same IP address.

There are two ways to configure a DHCP reservation. The simplest, available only in Windows Server 2008 R2, is to locate an existing IP address lease, right-click on it, and select Add to Reservation. This will then tie that specific network adapter address to that IP address. The only drawback of this method is that the reservation will be for the assigned IP address, and you won't be able to customize it.

If you know the network adapter address of the computer that you wish to configure a reservation for, you can right-click on the Reservations node under the scope that you wish to configure the reservation under, and then click on New Reservation. This brings up the New Reservation dialog box, shown in Figure 8-5. Enter the reservation name, IP address, and network adapter address in this dialog box, and click Add to create the reservation.

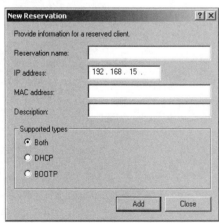

FIGURE 8-5: New Reservation

Utilizing DHCP Relay Agents

DHCP relay agents allow clients on one subnet to use a DHCP server on another to obtain their IP address configuration. DHCP relay agents are necessary when routers do not support forwarding of DHCP traffic. A DHCP relay agent can be a network device, or you can configure a computer running Windows Server 2008 R2 to function as a DHCP relay agent. A computer that functions as a NAT server or as a DHCP server cannot also function as a DHCP relay agent. To configure a computer running Windows Server 2008 R2 to function as a DHCP relay agent, perform the following steps:

1. Install Routing and Remote Access role service of the Network Policy and Access Services role on the server that will function as the DHCP relay agent.

2. Ensure that the LAN Routing role is configured.

3. In the Routing and Remote Access console, right-click on the IPv4\General node, and then click on New Routing Protocol. This will open the New Routing Protocol dialog box, shown in Figure 8-6. Click on DHCP Relay Agent, and then click OK.

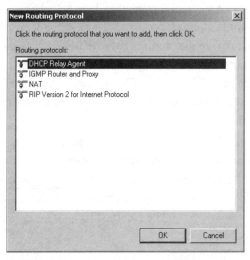

FIGURE 8-6: New Routing Protocol

4. Right-click the IPv4\General\DHCP Relay Agent node, and then click on New Interface. Click the network adapter connected to the local network, and then click OK.

5. On the DHCP Relay Properties page, verify that Relay DHCP Packets is enabled, and then click OK.

6. Right-click on the IPv4\General\DHCP Relay Agent node, and then click Properties. On the DHCP Relay Agent Properties dialog box, enter the IP address of the DHCP server on the remote subnet, as shown in Figure 8-7.

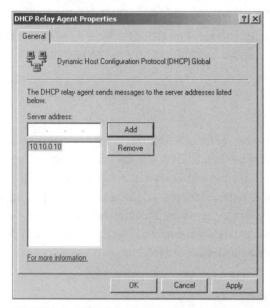

▶ To disable APIPA on a computer, create the following registry key: HKEY_LOCAL_Machine\System\ CurrentControlSet\ Services\Tcpip\Parameters\ _Interfaces\<Adaptername>\ IPAutoconfigurationEnabled: REG_DWORD=0.

FIGURE 8-7: DHCP Relay Agent Properties

Ensuring DHCP Redundancy

If an organization has only one DHCP server and that server fails completely, computers that use DHCP will gradually lose their IP address information. The problem with this sort of failure is that unless you have a monitoring solution in place that will alert you, the nature of DHCP leases will mean that the failure might not be immediately obvious. Just because DHCP fails doesn't mean that clients that have already leased an IP address will stop being able to communicate on the network. Only clients whose leases have expired will experience problems, and few helpdesk staff will assume that there is a problem with DHCP if only one or two calls come in complaining that the network is unavailable.

To ensure that computers in your organization continue to receive IP address information in the event that a DHCP server fails, you should configure scopes so that they are present on more than one DHCP server. You then configure exclusions in the scope so that clients aren't leased the same address from the different DHCP servers. For example:

▶ On DHCP server one, configure a scope for the 192.168.15.0 /24 network and create exclusions for addresses from 192.168.15.200 to 192.168.15.254.

▶ On DHCP server two, configure a scope for the 192.168.15.0 /24 network and create exclusions for addresses from 192.168.15.1 to 192.168.15.199.

DHCP Filtering

▶ The backup DHCP server doesn't have to have enough addresses for the entire subnet, just enough to give you the breathing space required to bring the original or a replacement DHCP service online.

You can configure *DHCP filtering* on the Filters tab of the IPv4 Properties dialog in the DHCP console, as shown in Figure 8-8. DHCP filtering is used in high-security environments to restrict the network adapter addresses that are able to utilize DHCP. For example, you can have a list of all network adapter addresses in your organization and use the Enable Allow List option to lease only IP addresses to this list of authorized adapters. This method of security is not entirely effective, because it is possible for unauthorized people to fake an authorized adapter address as a way of gaining network access.

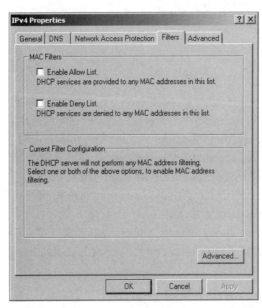

FIGURE 8-8: DHCP filters

NOTE You can enable conflict detection on the Advanced tab of the IPv4 Properties dialog of the DHCP console. Enabling this option ensures that clients aren't leased an address that is already assigned to another computer. This is a rare event but can happen if someone has statically assigned an address that would otherwise be in the DHCP lease pool.

UNDERSTANDING IPV6

As you are probably aware, IPv6 uses 128-bit addresses rather than IPv4's 32-bit address space. These addresses can be represented in hexadecimal notation by eight groups of four numbers separated by colons. The general problem that most administrators have with getting a handle on IPv6 is that, unlike IPv4 addresses, it is almost impossible to remember IPv6 addresses unless you write them down.

IPv6 can use CIDR notation, so when you write fe80::/64, you're saying that the first bit of the address is fe80:0000:0000:0000, similar to if you wrote 192.168.15.0 /24.

NOTE A convention in writing IPv6 addresses is that you can replace one group of contiguous zeros with two colons. For example, 2001:0000:0000:0000:012b: 3cff:12fe:ffaa can be written as 2001::012b:3cff:12fe:ffaa. You can also remove zeros and write it as 2001:0:0:0:012b:3cff:12fe:ffaa.

There are a number of different types of IPv6 addresses that administrators need to know about. These address types are as follows:

▶ **Link-local address:** This address type is automatically assigned to all network adapters. The link-local address is only accessible to hosts that are on the same network segment. Link-local addresses are always prefixed with fe80::/64, with the last 64 bits being the interface ID.

▶ **Unique local IPv6 unicast address:** This address type is similar in function to the private IPv4 address space in that it is routable on an organization's intranet but cannot be accessed by hosts on the Internet. Unique local IPv6 addresses are prefixed with fc00::/8 or fd00::/8. The next 40 bits are known as the global ID and are used to represent sites. The next 16 bits represent the subnet ID. The last 64 bits represent the interface ID.

▶ **Global unicast address:** This address type is similar in function to the public IPv4 address space in that it is routable to IPv6 hosts on the Internet. Global unicast addresses are always prefixed with 2000::/3.

▶ **Anycast address:** Anycast addresses are assigned to multiple network interfaces. This allows you to give a server with multiple network cards a single network address.

▶ **Special address:** Special addresses are similar to the IPv4 address 127.0.0.1. The following special addresses exist:

  ▷ **::1:** The loopback address, similar in function to 127.0.0.1

  ▷ **ff01::1:** Interface-local scope all-nodes multicast address

  ▷ **ff02::1:** Link-local scope all-nodes multicast address. This functions in a way similar to broadcast addresses in IPv4.

  ▷ **ff02::2:** Link-local scope all-routers multicast address

  ▷ **ff02::5:** Site-local scope all-routers multicast address

  ▷ **ff00::/8:** Multicast address prefix

  ▷ **fe80::/64:** The IPv6 version of an APIPA address. When you see this address you know that the network interface has not picked up an IP address from a local DHCP server.

In general, computers on IPv4 networks have a single IPv4 address. This isn't the case with computers on IPv6 networks, which generally have both a link-local address and either a unique local unicast or global unicast address.

Assigning IPv6 Addresses

Given the problems that most IT professionals have with remembering IPv6 addresses, you shouldn't be surprised to find out that IPv6 addresses are almost always assigned automatically rather than statically. You can, of course, assign an IP address statically by editing the properties of a network interface, as shown in Figure 8-9.

You can also use the netsh command to set an IPv6 address from the command line, as follows:

```
Netsh interface ipv6 set address "Local Area Connection"
fc00:1000:1000:1000:0001:0002:0003:0004
```

▶ If you want to use an IPv6 address in a URL, encase it in square brackets, for example, http://[2001:0000:0000:0000:012b:3cff:12fe:ffaa]

▶ You can force ping to use IPv6 by using the -6 option. For example, to ping a host named Melbourne.contoso.com using IPv6, type ping -6 melbourne.contoso.com. The same -6 switch also works for tracert and pathping.

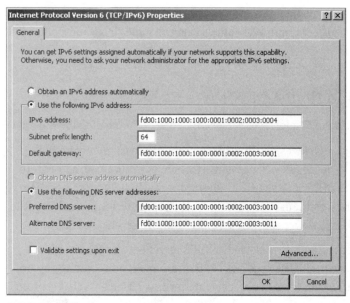

FIGURE 8-9: Manual IPv6 address assignment

> ▶ It is important, if you're going to deploy unique local IPv6 unicast addresses, to have routers that support IPv6. If you deploy unique local IPv6 unicast addresses on a network without routers that support IPv6, you're likely to run into configuration problems.

Creating an Address Scheme

In most cases, an organization is going to keep using an internal IP address scheme, as few internal hosts need to be accessible to the IPv6 Internet. With this in mind, you can use the unique local IPv6 unicast prefix, remembering that the unique local IPv6 addresses are always prefixed with fc00://8, the next 40 bits are known as the global ID and represent sites, and the next 16 bits represent the subnet ID.

For example, if you had two sites and you wanted to have two subnets per site, you can use the following address prefixes when configuring DHCP scopes:

- ▶ Site A, network 1: fc00:3a49:4ef1:6e82/64
- ▶ Site A, network 2: fc00:3a49:4ef1:4d7e/64
- ▶ Site B, network 1: fc00:8ce1:7abc:3a5e/64
- ▶ Site B, network 2: fc00:8ce1:7abc:813e/64

The key is to ensure that the global ID remains consistent at each site. Although you can allocate global and subnet IDs sequentially and in an easier format to remember, the RFC document dealing with unique local IPv6 addresses (RFC 4193) recommends that global IDs that represent sites and the 16 bits that represent the subnet ID be allocated in a random way. Doing so ensures that if at some point a merger occurs between organizations, there is minimal chance that the same global and subnet IDs will be duplicated.

Autoconfiguring IPv6 Addresses

Automatic configuration of IP addresses can occur in one of the three following ways:

▶ **Stateless:** When *stateless mode* is used to automatically configure an IPv6 address, the client uses IPv6 router advertisements to obtain an address. In the event that a DHCP server with an IPv6 scope is available, stateless clients are able to obtain configuration settings that they haven't inherited from the router, such as DNS server addresses, from the DHCP server.

▶ **Stateful:** When *stateful mode* is used, a DHCP server with an IPv6 scope provides the client with its IPv6 address configuration. Clients use stateful address configuration when they receive router advertisements that contain no prefix options when the Managed Address Configuration flag or Other Stateful Configuration flag is set to 1.

▶ **Both Stateless and Stateful:** Both modes can be used together.

When a computer on an IPv6 network boots up, it goes through the following steps to obtain IP address information:

1. The computer assigns itself a link-local address. These addresses have the FE80::/64 prefix.

2. The computer sends three router solicitation messages in an attempt to perform stateless address autoconfiguration. If a router responds to these solicitation messages, the computer uses this data for IPv6 address configuration.

3. If no router responds, or a router responds with a Managed Address Configuration flag and/or the Other Stateful Configuration flag set to 1, a DHCP server with an IPv6 scope is used for IPv6 address configuration.

4. The computer then performs duplicate address detection for every IP address. When an address is proven not to be a duplicate, the computer considers the address valid.

▶ To go against the RFC recommendation, use addresses such as fc00:1:1:1/64 and fc00:1:1:2/64 for networks at the same site and fc00:1:2:1/64 for networks at other sites, and so on. Remember, however, this isn't recommended by those who designed IPv6.

▶ Clients also use stateful address configuration in the event that an IPv6 router is not present on the network.

Assigning IPv6 Scopes Using DHCP

As IPv6 addresses are rather cumbersome to configure on an individual basis, it is likely that you will use DHCP to configure the IP addresses of hosts on your network. Configuring IPv6 scopes is straightforward, though you need to ensure that the DHCP server is configured with a static IPv6 address first. This can either be done through the interface or by using the netsh interface IPv6 set address command.

> **NOTE** You need to configure your routers to support DHCP by setting either or both the Managed Address Configuration flag or the Other Stateful Configuration flag.

Authorized Windows Server 2008 R2 DHCP servers support both IPv4 and IPv6 scopes. Prior to configuring an IPv6 scope, ensure that an appropriate IPv6 address is statically assigned to the appropriate network interface. To configure an IPv6 DHCP scope for the network fc00:3a49:4ef1:6e82/64, perform the following steps:

1. Open the DHCP console.

2. Right-click on the IPv6 node and click on New Scope.

3. On the Welcome to the New Scope Wizard, click Next.

4. On the Scope Name, give the scope a name and click Next.

5. On the Scope Prefix page, enter the prefix fc00:3a49:4ef1:6e82:: (or the prefix you want to use for your network), as shown in Figure 8-10, and click Next.

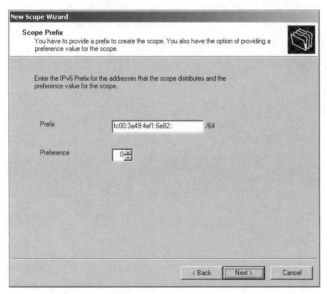

FIGURE 8-10: New IPv6 scope

6. On the Reservations tab, enter any address reservations that your network requires and click Next. For example, you'll want to enter the IPv6 address that you configured for the DHCP server.

7. On the Scope Lease page, enter the preferred lifetime and valid lifetime and click Next.

8. On the Completing the New Scope Wizard page, verify that Activate Scope is set to use and click Finish.

> **NOTE** If you get a ping transmit failure on DHCP assigned IPv6 addresses when statically assigned ones work, you'll need to do one of three things. The first is to set up your routers to configure IPv6 clients with routing information using the otherconfig=true configuration. You can also reinstall DHCP and disable stateless mode on your Windows Server 2008 R2 server as shown in Figure 8-11. Finally you can manually add routes using the **netsh** interface IPv6 add route command.

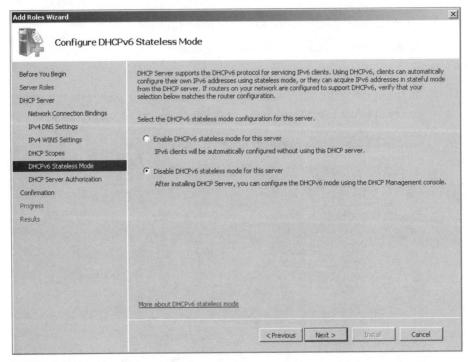

FIGURE 8-11: Disable stateless mode

Configuring IPv6 DHCP Options

As is the case with IPv4 scopes, IPv6 scopes in DHCP allow you to configure a number of options. Using the Scope Options dialog, shown in Figure 8-12, you can configure IPv6 DHCP clients with the following settings:

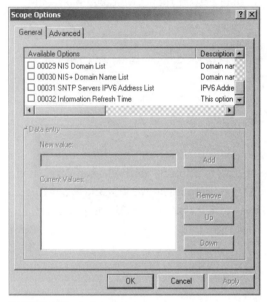

FIGURE 8-12: IPv6 DHCP Scope Options

▶ **SIP Server Domain Name List:** Domain names of Session Initiation Protocol (SIP) servers that the client can access

▶ **SIP Servers IPv6 Address List:** IP address of SIP servers that the client can access

▶ **DNS Recursive Name Server IPv6 Address List:** IP addresses of DNS recursive name servers that the client can access

▶ **Domain Search List:** Domain search list used by DHCP clients to resolve host-names through DNS

▶ **NIS IPv6 Address List:** IP address of Network Information Service (NIS) servers that the client can access

▶ **NIS+ IPv6 Address List:** IP address of the NIS+ servers that the client can access

▶ **NIS Domain List:** Domain names of NIS servers that the client can access

▶ **NIS+ Domain Name List:** Domain names of NIS+ servers that the client can access

▶ **SNTP Servers IPv6 Address List:** IPv6 addresses of Simple Network Time Protocol servers that the client can access

▶ **Information Refresh Time:** How long a client should wait before refreshing information from a DHCP server

> **NOTE** You can configure an IPv6 DHCP relay agent in the same way that you configure an IPv4 DHCP relay agent.

Using Zone IDs

When a Windows Server 2008 R2 computer has multiple network adapters connected to separate network segments, it can distinguish those networks using a *zone ID*. A zone ID appears as a number following a percent sign after an IP address. For example:

▶ fe80::5a49:4ef1:6e82:281a%3

▶ fe80::3df2:7e8e:ab32:75b9%4

▶ fe80::4e82:5d41:87e3:19cf %5

Zone IDs are relative to the host that they are on, so you wouldn't ping a host remotely using a zone ID, just using its IPv6 address.

TRANSITIONING TO IPV6

IPv6 transition technologies allow you to begin transiting to IPv6 without jumping into a full IPv6 implementation all the way at once. Unless you're building a brand new network, there are likely to be hardware and software issues that stop you from going to IPv6 fully all at once. The following technologies and strategies can be used to begin moving your organization towards a full IPv6 deployment.

Setting Up a Dual IP Layer Architecture

A dual IP layer architecture is when a computer uses both an IPv4 and an IPv6 address. Computers running Windows XP, Server 2003, Server 2008, Server 2008 R2,

Vista, and 7 all support a dual IP layer architecture. When you configure computers in this manner, they will attempt to use IPv6 for network communication and fall back to IPv4 in the event that the hosts or services that they wish to access only support IPv4.

Windows Vista, 7, Server 2008, and Server 2008 R2 support dual layer IP architecture by default, and it is necessary to explicitly disable either IPv6 or IPv4 if you want to use a single technology. You need to have both IPv4 and IPv6 enabled to use the ISATAP and Teredo transition technologies.

IPv6 Over IPv4 Tunneling

IPv6 over IPv4 tunneling allows hosts connected to IPv4 networks to use a tunnel to connect to an IPv6 network. This works by having IPv6 packets encapsulated within IPv4 packets. When the IPv4 packet arrives at the IPv6 destination host, the IPv4 header is stripped.

IPv6 over IPv4 tunneling can work according to one of three methods:

> **Router-to-router:** This method allows two separate IPv6 networks to communicate using IPv6 when they are separated by an IPv4-only network, for example, if an organization uses IPv6 internally but has to connect to branch offices through an ISP that only supports IPv4. The 6to4 tunneling transition technology uses router-to-router tunneling.

> **Host-to-router and router-to-host:** This method allows a computer configured with an IPv6 address to connect to a remote IPv6 network when the local network only supports IPv4. Both the ISATAP and Teredo transition technologies can use this type of tunneling.

> **Host-to-host:** This method allows two hosts configured with IPv6 addresses to communicate on networks that only support IPv6. Both the ISATAP and Teredo transition technologies can use this type of tunneling.

Teredo Tunneling

Teredo, which also goes by the name IPv6 network address translator (NAT) traversal (NAT-T) for IPv6, allows IPv6 hosts to communicate across IPv4 NAT gateways. Teredo differs from 6to4 tunneling in that 6to4 requires a 6to4 router with a public IP address. As many organizations use NAT devices on their edge networks, Teredo allows communication until the NAT device is replaced. Teredo clients use the 2001::/32 IPv6 address prefix.

> **NOTE** Teredo is a transition technology of last resort, and you should use it only if native IPv6, ISATAP, or 6to4 tunneling cannot be implemented.

To use Teredo, your organization's NAT device must support UDP port translation. Teredo functions with cone and restricted NAT for clients running Windows Server 2008, Server 2008 R2, Vista and 7.

Teredo host-specific relays are computers that are configured with public IPv4 and IPv6 addresses that are able to forward traffic between the IPv4 Internet and the IPv6 Internet. To configure a Windows Server 2008 R2 computer to function as a Teredo-specific relay, determine the interface that is used with the public IPv6 address and issue the following command:

```
Netsh interface ipv6 set interface interface=InterfaceName forwarding
enabled
```

A Teredo server assists in configuring Teredo clients. Teredo servers also assist in setting up sessions between two Teredo clients or between Teredo clients and IPv6 hosts. You can manually configure a Windows Server 2008 R2 computer to function as a Teredo server by configuring it with two public IPv4 addresses. You then run the following command:

```
Netsh interface Teredo set state server FirstPublicIPAddress
```

You can configure Teredo clients to use this server by issuing the command:

```
Netsh interface Teredo set state server=FirstPublicIPAddress
```

You can also configure clients using the Computer Configuration\Administrative Templates\Network\TCPIP Settings\IPv6 Transition Technologies\Teredo Server Name policy.

ISATAP Tunneling

The *Intra-Site Automatic Tunnel Addressing Protocol (ISATAP)* transition technology allows IPv6 hosts to communicate on IPv4 networks through a combination of the IPv6 and IPv4 addresses. ISATAP addresses use the following format:

▶ On private networks, ISATAP addresses use the 0:5EFE:w.x.y.z format, where w.x.y.z is the private IPv4 address.

▶ On public networks, ISATAP addresses use the 200:5EFE:w.x.y.z format, where w.x.y.z is the public IPv4 address.

Windows 7, Windows Vista, Windows Server 2008, and Windows Server 2008 R2 computers have ISATAP enabled by default. They will have an ISATAP address for every IPv6 address assigned. As these clients all have a link-local address that uses the fe80::/64 prefix, they will also automatically be assigned ISATAP addresses of fe80::5efe:w.x.y.z if they have a private IPv4 address or fe80::200:5efe:w.x.y.z. For example, a computer that has the IPv4 address 10.10.0.10 will have the ISATAP address fe80::5efe:10.10.0.10.

An ISATAP address cannot communicate directly with a native IPv6 address or an IPv4 address, only with another ISATAP address. ISATAP does allow two hosts on the same IPv4 network segment to communicate directly with each other, with the IPv6 packets encapsulated within IPv4 packets. ISATAP routers allow communication between computers with ISATAP addresses and computers with native IPv6 addresses. ISATAP routers broadcast their address details, and IPv6 hosts that support ISATAP use ISATAP routers as their default gateway. ISATAP hosts learn the location of an ISATAP router through a DNS query for the name ISATAP.

You can configure a Windows Server 2008 R2 computer that has both a native IPv6 address and an ISATAP address to function as an ISATAP router by registering the name ISATAP in DNS and issuing the following command:

```
Netsh interface ipv6 set interface ISATAPInterfaceName
advertise=enabled
```

You can determine the ISATAPInterfaceName by using the `ipconfig` command. You need to then get the prefix of the IPv6 native network and use it in the following command:

```
Netsh interface ipv6 add route IPv6Prefix ISATAPInterfaceName
publish=yes
```

For example, if you are using fc00:1:1:1::/64 as the prefix for your IPv6 network, and the hostname of the computer that will function as the router is `isatap.contoso.com`, use the command:

```
Netsh interface ipv6 add route fc00:1:1:1::/64 isatap.contoso.com
publish=yes
```

Once this is done, issue the following command, substituting LANInterface for the name of the network interface that has the native IPv6 address:

```
Netsh interface ipv6 set interface LANinterface forwarding=enabled
```

For example, if the network interface with the native IPv6 address is Local Area Connection, you would issue the command:

```
Netsh interface ipv6 set interface "Local Area Connection"
forwarding=enabled
```

The final step is to configure the ISATAP router to advertise routes. This is done by issuing the command:

```
Netsh interface ipv6 add route ::/0 LANinterface nexthop=IPv6Address
publish=yes
```

For example, if the Local Area Network connection was assigned the IPv6 address fc00:1:1:1::1, you would issue the command:

```
Netsh interface ipv6 add route ::/0 "Local Area Connection"
nexthop=fc00:1:1:1::1
```

6to4 Tunneling

6to4 tunneling tunnels IPv6 packets over an IPv4 network. A computer configured with a 6to4 address can communicate with 6to4 hosts on the same network, with 6to4 hosts in other sites across the IPv4 Internet, and with IPv6 hosts on the IPv6 Internet.

6to4 tunneling stores the IPv4 address of the 6to4 router in the IPv6 address, but the addresses are written entirely in hexadecimal, so the IPv4 address isn't as apparent as it is in an ISATAP address. 6to4 addresses use the 2002::/16 prefix.

6to4 tunneling is intended for hosts on the public Internet rather than hosts on private IPv4 networks. It is possible to connect to the IPv6 Internet through a 6to4 relay even if your organization's ISP supports only IPv4.

If you configure a public IPv4 address to a network interface on a computer running Windows Server 2008 R2 and a global prefix is not received through a router advertisement, the following happens:

- ▶ A 6to4 address is configured on the 6to4 Tunneling Pseudo-Interface.
- ▶ A 2002::/16 route is created that forwards all 6to4 traffic to the 6to4 Tunneling Pseudo-Interface. Traffic forwarded by this host to other 6to4 hosts is encapsulated with an IPv4 header.
- ▶ A DNS query is performed to locate the IPv4 address of a 6to4 relay router on the Internet. If the query returns a result, a route is added to the 6to4 Tunneling Pseudo-Interface with the next-hop address set to the 6to4 address of the relay router.

SUMMARY

Although you can configure an IPv4 DHCP reservation, many systems administrators manually configure addresses for important servers. DHCP servers assign IP address configuration automatically to clients. You can configure additional configuration options through the use of scope and server options. Windows Server 2008 R2 can be configured as a DHCP relay agent to forward DHCP traffic to servers across routers from physical networks with no DHCP server. Windows Server 2008 R2 computers are configured with a link-local address by default. If you want to configure your network with the IPv6 equivalent of the IPv4 private address space, use a unique local IPv6 unicast address. A global unicast address is equivalent to a public IPv4 address. Several transition technologies exist to allow clients on IPv4 networks to communicate with IPv6 hosts.

Further Links

DHCP Server

http://technet.microsoft.com/en-us/library/cc896553(WS.10).aspx

IPv4

http://technet.microsoft.com/en-us/library/dd379485(WS.10).aspx

IPv6

http://technet.microsoft.com/en-us/library/dd379498(WS.10).aspx

IPv6 Transition Technologies

http://technet.microsoft.com/en-us/library/dd379548(WS.10).aspx

CHAPTER 9

Securing the Network: Windows Firewall and Network Access Protection

The idea of the firewall is to put a barrier between a host or a protected network and a potentially hostile network. This idea came from a time when administrators had complete control over all the computers on their organizations' local area networks, and most computers were desktop workstations. Computers that rarely move are easier to manage than those that move often. While laptops were around back then, they were not commonly used as a person's primary workstation. In those days, administrators weren't too concerned about people plugging unknown computers into the network, because there weren't a lot of them.

Today, those core assumptions no longer hold. The sales of portable computers exceed the sales of desktop computers, and many people use a laptop computer as their main work computer. These people are taking their computers in and out of the office each day. When the computers are out of the office, they are generally beyond the administrator's ability to manage. Unfortunately, when a computer is off the protected cul-de-sac of the corporate network, it is most likely to become unhealthy. The networks in people's homes and coffee shops are far more hostile and likely to lead to infection than the protected fortress you have built for the organization. It is when computers return to the protected network after being in more hostile environments that things become problematic.

Much of today's malware attempts to replicate itself by probing the local network environment and attempting to infect unprotected hosts. This means an infected laptop computer plugged into your network is going to attack all hosts the moment it gets an IP address. Unless you've got some way to ensure that every computer plugged into your network is healthy, you should treat your local area network as if it is as hostile an environment as the Internet. In this chapter, you learn some tricks about how to protect computers from hostile environments and how to ensure that only healthy computers get access to your protected networks.

UNDERSTANDING WINDOWS FIREWALL WITH ADVANCED SECURITY

Windows Firewall with Advanced Security (WFAS) is a bi-directional, host-level firewall. This means, not only can you set it to protect a host from incoming traffic, you can also have it block all or specific outgoing traffic. Later in this chapter, you learn how to configure WFAS so that only authorized applications and services are able to communicate with external hosts on the network.

Generally, you can control outbound traffic only on very sensitive hosts. Controlling outbound traffic minimizes the chance of malware infecting the server phoning home. On sensitive hosts, you should allow outbound traffic on a per-application rule. For example, you should create a rule to allow a specific browser to communicate with the Internet rather than just allowing outbound traffic on port 80.

WFAS allows for the creation of rules based on program, port, or predefined rule. There are 37 predefined rules, which include categories such as Remote Desktop, Windows Firewall Remote Management, File and Printer Sharing, and Core Networking. One of the useful things about WFAS is that it generally enables the appropriate firewall rules when you enable a specific role, role service, or feature. These default rules are appropriate most of the time, but you may wish to edit the properties of these rules to make them more secure. You learn about editing advanced rule properties later in this chapter.

Exporting the Firewall and Group Policy

You can apply WFAS rules to a collection of computers using *Group Policy*. While this simplifies the application of similar new rules to a large number of computers, it does present a challenge when testing and developing those rules. A better way of testing rules is to create firewall policies on an individual computer running Windows Server 2008 R2, export those rules into a file in .wfw format, and then import them into a GPO that you apply to a number of computers. Exporting firewall settings includes not only incoming and outgoing settings but also per profile settings, IPsec settings, and connection security rules.

To export firewall policy, perform the following steps:

1. Open Windows Firewall with Advanced Security and right-click on the Parent node. Click Export Policy.

2. In the Save As dialog box, enter the name and location of the firewall settings to be exported.

To import a firewall policy into a Group Policy, perform the following steps:

1. Open the Group Policy Management Console.

2. Select the Group Policy Objects node, and then right-click on the GPO that you want to edit. This opens the Group Policy Management Editor.

3. Navigate to the Computer Configuration\Windows Settings\Security Settings\ Windows Firewall with Advanced Security node in the GPO.

4. Click the Windows Firewall with Advanced Security item under this node. In the Actions menu, click Import Policy as shown in Figure 9-1.

▶ Unless you've done it before, it is a good idea to check out which firewall rules are enabled on a server before and after you install a role feature. When you perform a default install of a nondomain-joined member server with no roles or features installed, 23 out of the 88 built-in rules are enabled.

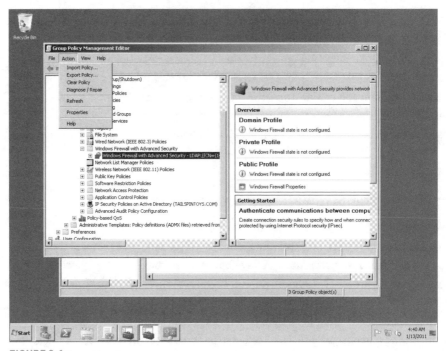

FIGURE 9-1: Import policy

Creating Firewall Profiles

Firewall profiles allow you to treat traffic differently depending on the network to which the computer is connected. For example, the same server might be connected to the following:

- ▶ A remote site through a VPN connection that has the private profile applied

- ▶ A perimeter network by a network adapter, where the connection has the public profile applied

- ▶ To the organization's internal network through a second adapter that has the domain profile applied

> **NOTE**   Some call a perimeter network the "Demilitarized Zone," perhaps because they like using military terminology. Some call the perimeter network the "screened subnet." Whatever name you give it, the perimeter network exists logically, often physically, between your organization's direct Internet connection and the internal network. Place computers here that need to provide services to hosts on the Internet without opening the internal network directly.

The advantage of separate profiles is that each one allows you to have separate sets of firewall rules applied. You might allow Distributed File System (DFS) traffic on one profile, Web traffic on another, and SMTP traffic on a third.

Profiles work differently between Windows Server 2008 and Windows Server 2008 R2. In Windows Server 2008, the most restrictive network profile applies to all networks when multiple profiles are active. In Windows Server 2008, it is possible to configure rules that differentiate on the source IP address, but it is often easier to apply different profiles when dealing with different networks. In Windows Server 2008 R2, firewall profiles apply on a per-interface basis and you can have a restrictive profile on one interface and a permissive one on another interface at the same time.

To change which profile applies to a specific interface, perform the following general steps:

1. Open the Network and Sharing Center from the Control Panel.

2. On the list of active networks, choose the network that is associated with the profile you wish to alter and then click on the currently assigned profile. For example, click Public Network.

3. On the Set Network Location dialog shown in Figure 9-2, click the network profile that you wish to assign to this network.

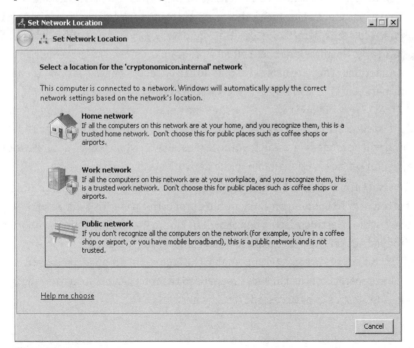

FIGURE 9-2: Network location

Profiles are independent of each other—the settings that you configure for one profile do not apply to other profiles. You can configure the following properties for each profile:

- ▶ **Firewall State:** You can set this to On (default) or Off.

- ▶ **Inbound Connections:** You can set this to Block (default), Block All, or Allow. The Block All setting means firewall rules that allow connections will be ignored.

- ▶ **Outbound Connections:** You can set this to Block or Allow (default).

- ▶ **Protected Network Connections:** This allows you to specify the network connections to which the profile can apply.

- ▶ **Settings:** This allows you to configure whether notifications are displayed, whether unicast responses are transmitted to multicast or broadcast traffic, and whether to merge rules when rules apply both locally and through Group Policy.

- ▶ **Logging:** This allows you to specify logging settings. You learn more about these later in the chapter.

Firewall notifications alert you when the firewall encounters traffic that is blocked by an existing rule. As Figure 9-3 shows, notifications are disabled by default. Some administrators turn off WFAS in frustration, because they can't get firewall rules to work properly. Notifications occur when a program is blocked from receiving incoming connections. They are useful for diagnostic purposes but distracting if enabled for any period of time. *Firewall logs* are written to the %systemroot%\system32\ LogFilres\Firewall\pfirewall.log file. The default settings do not log dropped packets or successful connections, which means that, unless you change the defaults, nothing will be logged. Firewall logging is most useful when you've determined that a particular service is unavailable to the network because of the firewall.

You can turn on firewall logging on a per profile basis by clicking on the Customize button next to Logging on each profile's properties page. This displays the Customize Logging Settings dialog box shown in Figure 9-4. You can then enable logging for dropped packets and successful connections. If you are having trouble with a newly installed service on a server, enable the logging of dropped packets to determine the properties of the packets dropped, so that you can create a firewall rule that allows your service to be accessed from the network.

▶ When something works when the firewall is off but doesn't work when it is on, you need to configure a rule to get it working. To find out what rule you need to create or to have it created automatically, turn on firewall notifications or examine the firewall log.

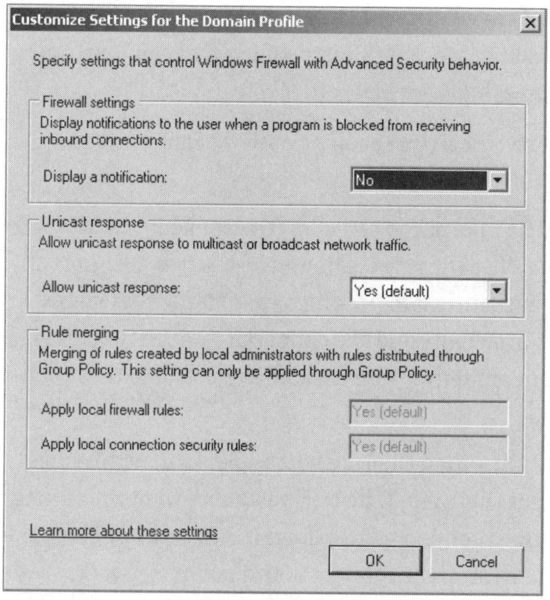

FIGURE 9-3: Firewall notifications

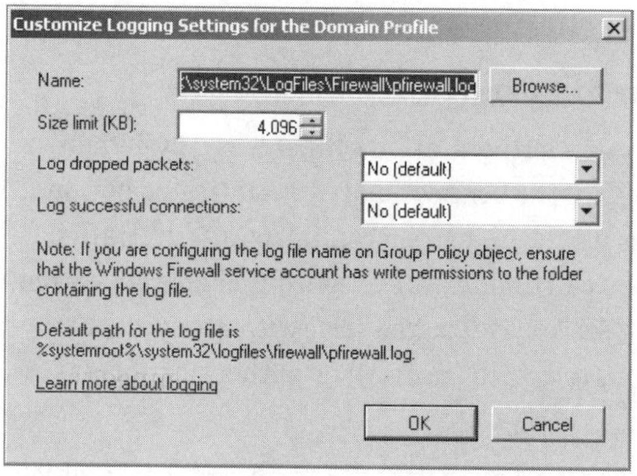

FIGURE 9-4: Logging settings

Creating Inbound Rules

Inbound rules are based on program, port, or one of 27 predefined categories, such as BranchCache Content Retrieval or Network Policy Server. You can also create custom rules that include a mixture of these, where you specify a program and a port as well as rule scope. For example, you can use a custom rule to block all incoming traffic on port 80 to a particular application but not block port 80 traffic to other applications on the server. The basic aspects of creating a firewall rule involve:

- **Specifying a program or port:** When you specify a port, you must choose whether the rule applies to TCP or UDP traffic.

- **Specify what action should be taken:** You can allow the connection, in which case all traffic that matches the rule is allowed by the firewall. You can allow the connection if it is authenticated, in which case traffic that meets the IPsec authentication requirements and the connection security rules is allowed, but traffic that is not properly authenticated according to these conditions is dropped.

- **Specify the network profiles in which the rule will apply:** In general, rules should apply in all profiles, but there might be circumstances where you want to allow traffic from an interface connected to a domain network but block the same traffic if it comes from an interface connected to a public network.

After you have created the rule, you can then edit the rule's properties. Editing the rule's properties allows you to configure more advanced options than are present in the Rule Creation Wizard. By editing a rule's properties, you can:

- Configure a rule to apply to a service rather than just a program.

- Limit the computers that can make authenticated connections. By default, if you configure the Allow Traffic if the Connection is Authenticated option, any computer that can authenticate is able to successfully transmit traffic. By editing a firewall's rules, you can limit traffic to specific computers, rather than all authenticated computers. You can do the same with user accounts, limiting successful connections to specific users when authentication has successfully occurred.

- Edit the rule's scope, which is the local and remote IP address ranges to which the rule applies. You can also do this when you create a custom rule.

- Configure whether the rule applies to specific network interfaces, instead of just network profiles. For example, if your computer has two network adapters, you can configure a rule to apply so that it allows traffic on one adapter but not the other when both adapters have the same profile set.

- Configure whether or not to allow packets that have passed across a Network Address Translation (NAT) device.

Creating Outbound Rules

As you learned earlier, the default settings for Windows Firewall with Advanced Security do not block outbound traffic. In high-security environments, you should consider using outbound rules to block all but authorized outbound traffic.

The process for creating an outbound rule is almost identical to the process for creating an inbound rule. You specify the rule type on the New Outbound Rule Wizard, as shown in Figure 9-5, whether the connection is blocked, allowed, or allowed only if authenticated, and specify the network profiles in which the rule is active. By editing the properties of the rule after the rule is created, you can configure all of the advanced options configurable for inbound rules, such as rule scope, specific network interfaces, and which computers or users the rule allows outbound connections to.

▶ One outbound rule you should consider creating on Internet-facing servers blocks ftp.exe. When attackers attempt to compromise a server, they often use the built-in ftp.exe command-line utility to remotely download a rootkit they use to exploit the server.

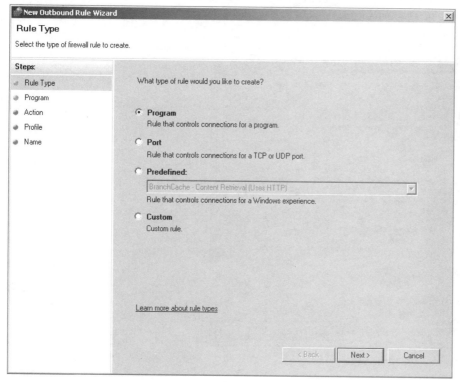

FIGURE 9-5: Outbound rule

Configuring IPsec Settings

The *IPsec Settings* tab of Firewall Properties allows you to configure how IPsec is used when applied in connection security rules. On the tab itself, shown in Figure 9-6, you can configure whether or not you want to customize the IPsec defaults, exempt Internet Control Message Protocol (ICMP) traffic from IPsec, and whether you want to configure IPsec tunnel authorization.

> **NOTE** Exempting ICMP traffic can be useful for diagnostic purposes, as many administrators use the ping utility to diagnose whether a host has network connectivity. If connection security rules are enabled, the default IPsec settings mean that a successful IPsec negotiation must occur prior to an ICMP response being sent. If the IPsec negotiation is the problem, enabling ICMP response allows you to verify that there is network connectivity and that the problem just lies a bit further up the network stack.

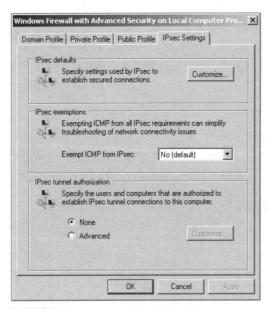

FIGURE 9-6: IPsec Settings tab

If you click Customize next to IPsec defaults, you can change the Key exchange, Data protection, and Authentication method. This dialog is shown in Figure 9-7. The default key exchange uses Diffie-Hellman Group 2 key exchange algorithm with a key lifetime of 480 minutes. You can modify these settings so that they use more secure methods, but, in doing so, you can communicate only with computers running Windows Vista, Windows 7, Windows Server 2008, or Windows Server 2008 R2.

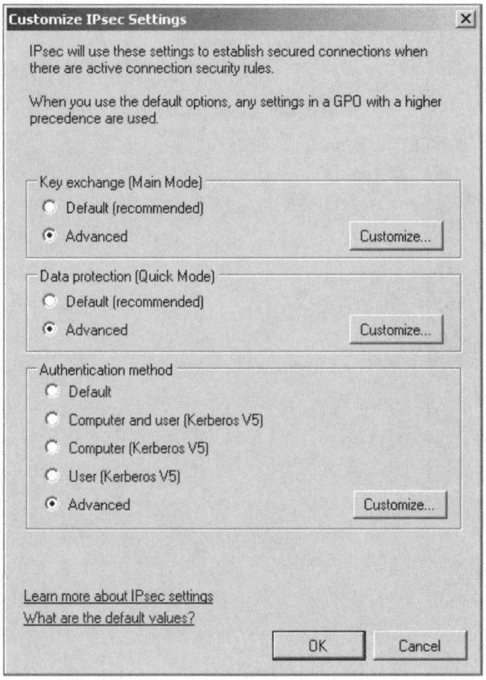

FIGURE 9-7: Customize IPsec settings

The data protection settings allow you to configure the algorithms used for data integrity and encryption. Normally there isn't much reason to change this; however, if you feel you need the strongest encryption possible to protect your organization's network traffic, you can use a different algorithm, such as AES-CBC with a 256-bit key length. In general, the stronger the encryption, the greater the resources needed to support that encryption. Although you can make the protection a lot stronger, it will probably slow computers down and you'll be able to use it only with Windows Vista, Windows 7, Windows Server 2008, and Windows Server 2008 R2 clients.

The default authentication method used for IPsec connections is Computer (Kerberos V5). This means that a domain controller must be present to verify the identity of each computer before an IPsec session can be established. As Figure 9-8 shows, you can also use Computer (NTLMv2), Computer certificate from this certification authority (CA), or a pre-shared key to authenticate IPsec connections. A pre-shared key is not a recommended method of authentication but might be necessary where there is not a certificate services infrastructure and computers aren't members of a domain. It might also be necessary to use pre-shared keys if you are attempting to set up IPsec connections to computers running Linux or Mac OSX.

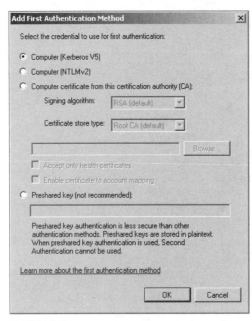

FIGURE 9-8: IPsec authentication

► Connection security rules are about trusting incoming connections based on the identity of the remote host, rather than the remote host's network address or the communication port it uses.

► An authentication exemption can function as a special backdoor access method, in case you make a mistake when creating your connection security rules and lock yourself out of being able to remotely administer the computer.

UNDERSTANDING CONNECTION SECURITY RULES

Connection security rules are a more intelligent type of firewall rule than a simple port-based rule. An interesting adaption to firewalls has been an increase of traffic through ports traditionally used for common applications. BitTorrent, a popular file-sharing protocol, is difficult to block because, unless a sophisticated analysis is done, the traffic appears to be similar to Web traffic.

Creating Authentication Exemptions

Authentication exemptions allow you to create very specific holes in connection security rules. These are useful in the event that you want to remotely manage a server, but all of the servers that would normally authenticate your connection, such as certificate servers or domain controllers, are for some reason unavailable. Authentication exemptions override existing connection security rules.

When you create an authentication exemption, you define the exemption on the basis of the source computer's IP address. As Figure 9-9 shows, you do this using a single IPv4 or IPv6 address, an IP address range, or a pre-defined set of computers. For security reasons, you should limit the number of IP addresses for which you create authentication exemptions to one or two specific management workstations.

▶ You should create authentication exemption rules first because this enables you to remotely connect to a server in the event that you make an error in rule configuration that blocks your access to the server.

FIGURE 9-9: Authentication exemption

To create an authentication exemption, perform the following steps:

1. In Windows Firewall with Advanced Security, right-click the Connection Security Rules node, and then click New Rule. This opens the New Connection Security Rule Wizard. Select Authentication Exemption.

2. On the Exempt Computers dialog, click Add. In the IP Address dialog, enter the IP address, subnet, or IP address range of the computers that you wish to exempt from connection security rules.

3. Select the profile to which you want the rule to apply.

▶ With authentication exemption rules, you should almost always apply them to all profiles, as you create these rules as a failsafe way of accessing a server.

Creating Isolation Rules

Isolation rules allow you to limit communication so that a server or computer communicates only with computers that have authenticated with it. Isolation rules are similar to traditional IPsec rules.

▶ When you configure an isolation rule, it applies to all traffic from all hosts, unlike tunnel or server-to-server rules, which apply to traffic to and from specific hosts.

To create an isolation rule, perform the following steps:

1. In Windows Firewall with Advanced Security, right-click the Connection Security Rules node, and then click on New Rule. This opens the New Connection Security Rule Wizard. Select Isolation, and then click Next.

2. On the Requirements page, as shown in Figure 9-10, choose between requesting authentication on inbound and outbound connections, requiring authentication on inbound and requesting it on outbound, or requiring authentication for both inbound and outbound connections. Requiring authentication on both inbound and outbound connections is the strongest form of protection, as it means that communication can be performed only with authenticated hosts.

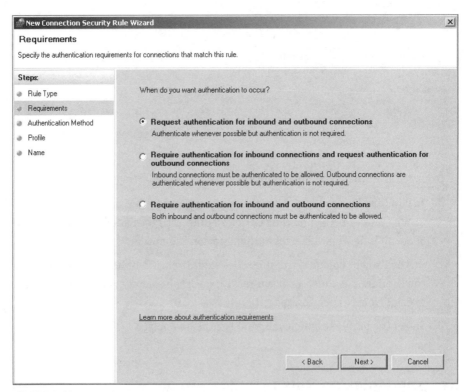

FIGURE 9-10: Authentication requirements for isolation rule

3. Choose the authentication method. The default is to use the authentication method specified on the IPsec Settings tab of Firewall Properties. You learned how to configure these settings earlier in the chapter. You can also

choose between computer and user leveraging Kerberos version 5 or configure advanced authentication options, which include certificate-based authentication, such as a computer certificate or a health certificate, if using Network Access Protection. It is also possible, though not recommended, to use a pre-shared key for authentication, which is useful when you need to communicate with computers running 3rd party operating systems.

4. The final step in setting up a connection security rule is to configure the profiles in which the rule applies. Unless there is a good reason otherwise, you should apply connection security rules in all profiles.

Creating Server-to-Server Rules

Server-to-server rules are used to authenticate communication between two groups of computers. This can be a rule authenticating and encrypting a single, computer-to-computer connection, such as between a web server and a database server, or between computers on two separate subnets. Server-to-server rules differ from isolation rules, as isolation rules apply to communication from all hosts, whereas server-to-server rules apply to specific hosts.

To create a server-to-server rule, perform the following steps:

1. In Windows Firewall with Advanced Security, right-click the Connection Security Rules node, and then click on New Rule. This opens the New Connection Security Rule Wizard. Select the Server-to-Server rule.

2. In the Endpoints dialog, enter the IP addresses of the computers that will be at one end of the connection and the IP addresses of the computers that will be at the other end of the connection. Figure 9-11 shows a connection between a computer at IP address 10.10.0.100 and a computer at IP address 10.10.0.200.

3. On the Requirements page, specify how you want authentication to occur. If you want only this computer to communicate on the profile using encrypted and authenticated connections, select Require authentication for inbound and outbound connections.

4. Specify the authentication method. The default is to use a computer certificate issued by a designated CA. You can also specify Computer-based Kerberos, NTLMv2 or Pre-shared key.

5. Specify the firewall profiles in which this connection security rule applies.

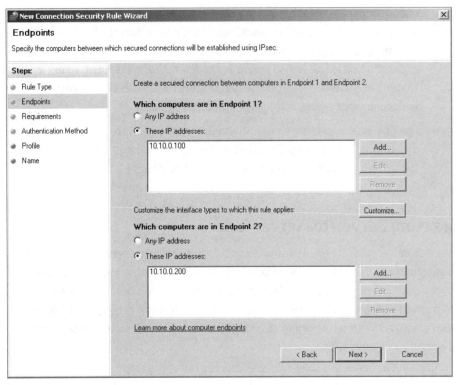

FIGURE 9-11: Server-to-server endpoint

Creating Tunnel Rules

Tunnel rules allow client computers to communicate with computers on a secure network behind a remote gateway. For example, if you have a single server located at a branch office that you want to connect to an internal network at another office, using a tunnel rule, you specify the location of a host that functions as a gateway to that secure network. This allows you to create an IPsec tunnel through which secure communication can occur.

To create a tunnel rule, perform the following steps:

1. In Windows Firewall with Advanced Security, right-click the Connection Security Rules node, and then click on New Rule. This opens the New Connection Security Rule Wizard. Select Tunnel Rule.

2. On the Tunnel Type page, as shown in Figure 9-12, determine the type of tunnel that you want to create. To create the type of rule outlined above, select Client-to-gateway.

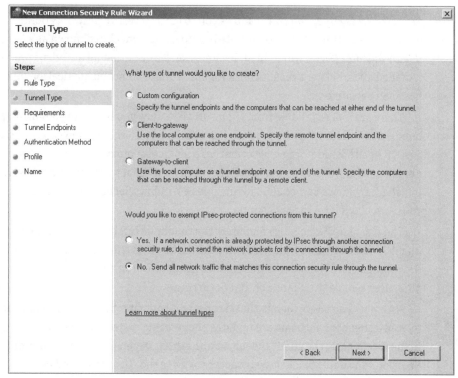

FIGURE 9-12: Tunnel rule

3. Choose whether you wish to require authentication for inbound and outbound connections.

4. Specify the address of the computer that functions as the gateway to the secure network.

5. Specify the authentication method. The default is to use a computer certificate issued by a designated CA. You can also specify Computer-based Kerberos, NTLMv2 or Pre-shared key.

6. Specify the firewall profiles in which this connection security rule applies.

UNDERSTANDING AND CONFIGURING NETWORK ACCESS PROTECTION

Network Access Protection (NAP) allows you to block access to network clients based on their health state. This health state is defined by a checklist known as a *System Health Validator (SHV),* which includes items such as whether an antivirus product is installed and whether a recent check for operating system and application updates has been performed.

There are tools available from Microsoft that allow you to create your own System Health Validators with your own health settings. In theory, you can configure a System Health Validator to check whether a particular proxy has been set for Internet Explorer and to ban computers from the network that have specific software installed. Windows Server 2008 R2 includes a Windows Security Health Validator that you learn about later in this chapter.

The aim of NAP is to stop computers that might be infected with malware or other unauthorized software from accessing the network. As with all security measures, NAP won't ensure that clients infected with malware aren't able to join the network, but it does reduce the chance of that occurring.

▶ Security is never a matter of absolute protection and should be thought of as being about reducing probabilities that something will go wrong.

NAP works on the principle that if the client computer hasn't successfully performed a check for antimalware updates or operating system or application updates in the recent past, the client is deemed unhealthy. Depending on how you configure NAP, you can simply block network access or force the client to go and perform the check. Once it has performed the check and installed any required updates, the client can access the production network.

NAP isn't used to mediate whether a computer running a server operating system is allowed on the network. NAP is a technology for mediating client health. You configure static exemptions for servers with NAP rather than have them subject to the process.

NAP uses the Network Policy Server (NPS) role of Windows Server 2008 R2. Depending on which version of NAP enforcement you use, you may need to install additional components, such as the Health Registration Authority. To install the NPS service to support NAP and then authorize that server in Active Directory, run the following commands from an elevated PowerShell prompt:

```
Import-Module ServerManager
Add-WindowsFeature NPAS-Policy-Server
Netsh ras add registeredserver
```

If you use NAP in your organization, you should have multiple NPS servers. Like domain controllers, if one NPS becomes unavailable, clients can use other NPS servers in the organization.

Once you've installed NAP, you should configure a remediation server group. *Remediation server groups* are collections of servers that hold the necessary updates and virus definitions required for a noncompliant client to become compliant. To create a remediation server group, perform the following steps:

1. Open the Network Policy Server console and click the Remediation Server Group item under the Network Access Protection item.

2. From the Action menu, click New. This opens the New Remediation Server Group dialog. Enter a name for the Remediation Server Group, and then click Add to add the host names of the servers that make up the remediation server group. Figure 9-13 shows a remediation server group with two hosts.

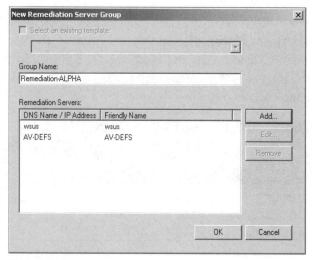

FIGURE 9-13: Remediation group

Configuring SHVs

System Health Validators include a set of tests that a computer must pass to be allowed on the network when you enforce NAP. You configure System Health Validators in the Network Access Protection\System Health Validators\Windows Security Health Validators\Settings node of the Network Policy Server. Windows Server 2008 R2 includes a Windows Security Health Validator that enables you to mediate access based on the following security settings:

- Is a firewall enabled for all connections?
- Is an antivirus application enabled?
- Is the antivirus application up-to-date?
- Is an antispyware application enabled?
- Is the antispyware application up-to-date?
- Is automatic updating enabled?
- Should the minimum severity level for installed updates be Low, Moderate, Important, or Critical?
- How long has it been since a check has been made against the automatic updates server?

Figure 9-14 shows the Windows Security Health Validator for Windows 7 and Windows Vista. The included Windows Security Health Validator for Windows XP is not as comprehensive as the one for Windows Vista and Windows 7. The main difference is that the Windows XP SHV can't be configured to restrict on the basis of whether antivirus and antispyware applications are up-to-date.

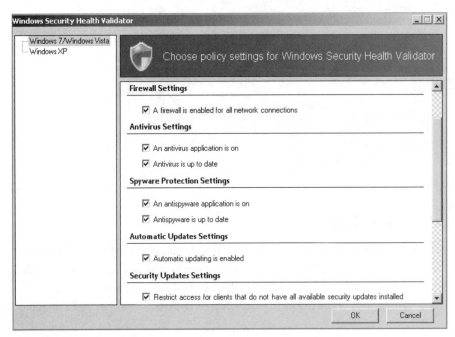

FIGURE 9-14: Windows SHV

NOTE NAP doesn't actually check the version of the antimalware program you are using. Instead, it uses Action Center as a proxy. Almost all modern antivirus and antispyware programs register themselves with Action Center. They feed it information about whether they have been disabled and if they are overdue for definition updates. It isn't that NAP knows your antivirus product doesn't have a specific set of definitions installed; it just knows that the antivirus application has informed Action Center that it hasn't successfully checked for antivirus definitions.

SHVs can make checks only against items that it knows about. If your organization uses an antivirus and antimalware solution that doesn't register itself with the Action Center, then NAP won't be able to tell whether the application is switched on and up-to-date. If you are lucky, your vendor will have created an SHV for NAP.

Configuring Client Policies

For NAP to work, the client computer must have the appropriate NAP client enabled and must have the NAP Agent service running. You configure the NAP client by turning on a specific enforcement client using Group Policy. The relevant policy is located at `Computer Configuration\Windows Settings\Security Settings\ Network Access Protection\Nape Client Configuration\Enforcement Clients`.

Figure 9-15 shows the DHCP enforcement client enabled. You can configure the NAP Agent service to start automatically using the Computer Configuration\Windows Settings\Security Settings\System Services node of the same GPO. It is a good idea to keep these settings in the same GPO and the NAP Enforcement policy settings in their own GPO, rather than integrating them into an existing GPO, such as the Default Domain Policy. Having NAP settings in a separate GPO allows you to unlink and link the GPO to OUs containing computer groups as necessary. Using NAP is a great reason to organize Active Directory computer accounts into their own OUs.

This policy node contains the following enforcement clients that can be used with Windows 7 and Windows Server 2008 R2:

▶ **DHCP Quarantine Enforcement Client:** This client is used with the DHCP enforcement method.

▶ **IPsec Relying Party:** This client is used with the IPsec enforcement method.

▶ **EAP Quarantine Enforcement Client:** This client is used with the 802.1x enforcement method.

▶ **RD Gateway Quarantine Enforcement Agent:** This client is used to support NAP with RD Gateway.

▶ *NAP policies apply to computers rather than users. Collecting computer accounts into OUs and then applying NAP policies to those OUs simplifies the process of deploying NAP in your organization.*

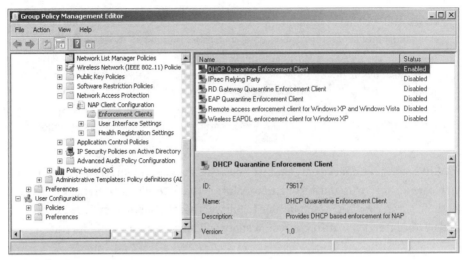

FIGURE 9-15: Enforcement clients

CROSSREF You learn more about RD Gateway in Chapter 17.

In the event that you attempt to configure a stand-alone client in a NAP environment, run the napclcfg.msc command, which opens a NAP-specific console.

Configuring DHCP Enforcement

▶ NAP with DHCP enforcement does not support IPv6. If you are in the process of transitioning to IPv6, you may wish to use a different enforcement method.

DHCP enforcement is the easiest method of NAP to configure. It does not have a certificate services requirement and does not require special hardware. You can deploy it by having the NPS server role and the DHCP role installed on a computer running Windows Server 2008 or Windows Server 2008 R2. If your organization uses DHCP servers running a different operating system, it is not possible to use this method of NAP enforcement.

One drawback of NAP with DHCP enforcement is that a clever user can get around NAP with DHCP enforcement by manually configuring his own IP address. Of course, this might be overstating the threat, as you will find that the majority of users are unable to set their own IP address manually, and even if they could, they probably would not be able to specify the correct IP address settings for the particular subnet of the network that their computer is hosted on.

Another drawback of NAP with DHCP enforcement is that you need to configure a shorter DHCP lease span than the default. The NAP assessment is performed only when the DHCP lease is renewed, so if a client falls out of compliance, the lease duration determines how long it takes before that state of noncompliance is recognized. If you have a lease duration set to 30 days, and a client stops updating its antivirus software for some reason, it may be several weeks before the computer is pushed into remediation. The other methods of NAP discussed in this chapter automatically address clients falling out of compliance.

To configure NAP with DHCP enforcement, perform the following steps:

1. Ensure that the policy that applies to the NAP clients has the NAP Agent service running and that the DHCP Quarantine Enforcement Client policy is enabled.

2. Ensure that client computers are configured to use DHCP for IP address configuration.

3. Ensure that the DHCP and NPS services are installed on the same server. Open the DHCP Management console and view the properties of the scope that you want to use with NAP. You should configure the IPv4 scope that you want to use with NAP with a name that indicates that it is to be used with NAP. You should also configure a shorter lease.

4. Right-click on the scope that you wish to configure, and then select Properties. Click on the Network Access Protection tab. Click the Enable for this scope option, as shown in Figure 9-16. It is only necessary to use the custom profile option if you have configured special conditions within NPS. The default Network Access Protection profile is suitable in almost all cases. Click OK.

5. In the DHCP console, under the scope that you are configuring for NAP, right-click the Scope Options node, and then click Configure Options. Click the Advanced tab. Ensure that the User Class is set to Default User class, and then verify the settings for options such as DNS server and default gateway that you wish to configure for NAP-compliant computers.

6. Change the User Class to Default Network Access Protection Class, and then configure the options, such as DNS server, that are used for the computers that are not NAP-compliant. Click OK.

7. In the NPS console, click the NPS node at the console root. In the Details pane, click Configure NAP. This launches the Configure NAP Wizard. On the Select Network Connection Method for Use with NAP page, click Dynamic Host Configuration Protocol (DHCP), and then click Next.

▶ It's unlikely the average user will set his own IP address, but plan your network security around the idea that the person trying to subvert the network is smart. He may use his own computer, so the rights you configure to block him might be irrelevant.

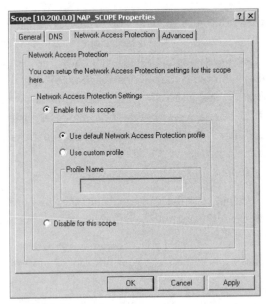

FIGURE 9-16: DHCP NAP

8. If your NPS server is separate from your DHCP server, you need to add the NPS role to those servers, and then add them as RADIUS clients. If you are using the computer that hosts the NPS and DHCP roles, ignore this step, and then click Next.

9. On the Specify DHCP Scopes page, add the scope that you started configuring in step 3. If you want to deploy NAP to additional scope, you can add it to the NAP policy.

10. On the Machine Groups page, specify whether you want this policy to apply to all computers or just specific computers.

11. On the Remediation Server Groups page, specify the remediation server group. You should also specify a troubleshooting URL. This allows you to inform users what they need to do to become compliant if they are using a product that does not automatically update. For most products, being pushed into remediation triggers the Action Center to automatically attempt to update noncompliant components.

12. On the Define NAP Health Policy page, specify all of the SHVs that the client must comply with to be deemed healthy. On this page, shown in Figure 9-17, you can also specify whether clients are provided with full network access if they are noncompliant. When you are first implementing NAP, it is better to

use this test mode until you are sure that the vast majority of computers will be compliant. Click Next, and then click Finish.

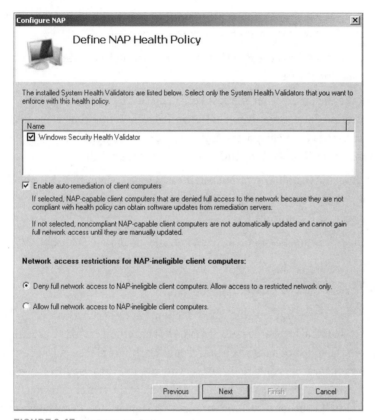

FIGURE 9-17: NAP Health Policy

Deploying IPsec Enforcement

NAP with *IPsec enforcement* works on the basis of a special type of computer certificate known as a *health certificate*. Health certificates are issued only to computers that have passed their NAP health check. NAP with IPsec enforcement is more complicated than NAP with DHCP enforcement, because it is necessary to deploy Active Directory Certificate Services to support NAP. Prior to deploying NAP, ensure that all computers that are not subject to NAP have an exemption certificate. An *exemption certificate* is a permanently assigned health certificate that you deploy to servers so that they can authenticate with the clients running IPsec without having to go through the health check process to obtain the certificate. To deploy NAP with IPsec enforcement, you need to:

- ▶ Configure and deploy the Active Directory Certificate Services on a computer running Windows Server 2008 or Windows Server 2008 R2.

- ▶ Configure and deploy the Health Registration Authority (HRA) on the computer hosting the NPS role.

- ▶ Configure the Connection Request Policy. Do this by navigating to the Health Registration Settings node under Network Access Protection in the GPO that applies to the client computers, right-click on the Trusted Server Groups node, and then click New. Add the URL of the HRA to this group.

- ▶ Configure and install exemption certificates for all computers that should not be subjected to the NAP policy. This allows clients to communicate with these hosts once NAP is enforced.

- ▶ Run the policy process on the NAP server, specifying the IPsec option.

Using 802.1X Enforcement

802.1x enforcement works by checking whether clients are healthy. Healthy clients are placed onto a virtual local area network (VLAN) that connects to the production network. Clients that do not meet the health benchmarks are placed onto a restricted VLAN that gives them access only to infrastructure necessary to support remediation. To use 802.1x enforcement, you need to ensure that all of the switches in your organization support 802.1x authentication. Switches that support 802.1x authentication tend to be more expensive, and many organizations transition to this method of NAP after they have proven that the technology works through DHCP or IPsec enforcement. To use NAP 802.1x enforcement, you need to ensure the following conditions are met:

- ▶ You have enabled the NAP EAP enforcement client and enabled the NAP service on all computers that use NAP.

- ▶ You have created a NAP policy on the NAP server where all of the 802.1x switches are configured as RADIUS clients.

SUMMARY

Firewalls are necessary on internal networks, as there is no guarantee that hosts on internal networks are not infected by malware. WFAS has multiple profiles that allow you to apply different sets of firewall rules depending on the network to which the network interface connects. There are three profiles available to WFAS Windows Server 2008 R2: the Domain Profile, the Private Profile and the Public Profile. All profiles block all traffic except that which is explicitly authorized by default. All profiles allow outgoing traffic by default.

Firewall rules can be based on programs or ports. You can also use predefined rules for a list of 27 different, common Windows network traffic scenarios. You can configure a rule to allow a connection, allow a connection if it is authenticated using IPsec, or block a connection that matches the rules. Using a rule's advanced properties, you can also configure rule scope, limiting the rule to specific incoming or outgoing IP address ranges, authenticated users and authenticated computers. Firewall rules can be applied using Group Policy.

Connection security rules allow you to deny or block traffic specifically based on a set of authentication criteria. You should configure an authentication exemption for one IP address so that it is possible to connect to the computer in question in the event that authentication servers, such as domain controllers or certificate servers, become unavailable.

Network Access Protection (NAP) allows you to require clients to pass a health check before they are allowed on the corporate network. For LAN connections you can do this through DHCP, IPSec, or 802.1x enforcement.

Additional Sources

Common Troubleshooting Situations using Windows Firewall with Advanced Security

http://technet.microsoft.com/en-us/library/cc749242(WS.10).aspx

NAP with IPsec Enforcement

http://technet.microsoft.com/en-us/library/cc771899.aspx

NAP with DHCP Enforcement

http://technet.microsoft.com/en-us/library/cc733020.aspx

NAP with 802.1x Enforcement

http://technet.microsoft.com/en-us/library/cc770861.aspx

Understanding Connection Security Rules

http://technet.microsoft.com/en-us/library/cc772017.aspx

Windows Firewall with Advanced Security

http://technet.microsoft.com/en-us/library/cc754274.aspx

PART III

SHARED FOLDER AND DATA PROTECTION SECRETS

Secrets behind Shared Folders

The humble file server, while being one of the most prevalent servers on organizational networks, gets scant consideration from most administrators. This is because file servers are relatively easy to set up and often require little in the way of ongoing maintenance. Although file servers don't require a substantial amount of attention from systems administrators, there are ways to tune file servers to perform better so they require even less attention than is currently necessary. There are also ways to extend file server functionality through client-side caching and replication to ensure files are almost always accessible under a variety of network conditions.

In this chapter, you learn about the tools in Windows Server 2008 R2 that can reduce the burden on your time caused by file servers. You learn about File Server

Resource Manager, a tool that provides advanced quotas, file screening, and file expiration functionality. You also learn about the Share and Storage Management console, which assists in the rapid provisioning of storage and shares. You also learn about configuring Distributed File System, BranchCache, and Offline File policies to best meet your organization's needs.

USING THE SHARE AND STORAGE MANAGEMENT CONSOLE

The Share and Storage Management console enables you to provision and monitor shared folders on file servers running the Windows Server 2008 R2 operating system. Although it is possible to create shares directly at the folder level, the Share and Storage Management console enables you to quickly determine which shares are hosted on a particular server; what the local path of those shares is; whether quotas, file screens, and shadow copies have been configured for the shares; and the amount of free space that remains available on the volumes that host the shares.

▶ The advantage of the wizard is it incorporates all aspects of the creation of the share, such as the name of the share and permissions, to connection limits, quotas, file screens, and publishing to an existing Distributed File System (DFS) namespace.

You can use the Share and Storage Management Console to access the Provision a Shared Folder Wizard. This wizard allows you to easily create shared folders and apply settings to those folders. Although it is possible to do all of this by editing the properties of a folder through Explorer and other tools, having all of this functionality in the same place can save a substantial amount of time. In the following section you'll learn more about creating shares and provisioning volumes.

Creating Shares

▶ The benefit of the console is that common volume and shared folder tasks are located in the same area, so you don't have to switch consoles when creating a new shared folder and volume at the same time or to perform management tasks against all shares hosted on the server.

The Share and Storage Management console centralizes access to common tools related to volumes and shares. Where you manage shares using the Provision a Shared Folder Wizard, volumes are managed through the Provision Storage Wizard. The Provision Storage Wizard enables you to create a new volume on a directly attached disk or to create a new Logical Unit Number (LUN) on a Storage Area Network (SAN) device to which the computer has connectivity. This wizard works in a way that is similar to the process you go through when creating volumes using the Disk Management node of the Server Manager console.

To use the Provision Storage Wizard to create a volume on a local, directly attached disk, perform the following general steps:

1. Ensure the disk on which you want to provision storage has been initialized. The easiest way to do this is to ensure that the disk is connected and then open the Storage\Disk Management node of Server Manager. When you do this with a newly attached disk, you'll encounter a pop-up asking if you want to initialize the disk, as shown in Figure 10-1. You should choose the GPT style if your disk is greater than 2 TB in size.

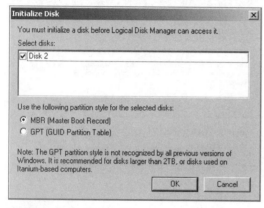

FIGURE 10-1: Initialize disks.

2. In the Administrative Tools menu, open Share and Storage Management. In the Actions menu, click Provision Storage.

3. On the Storage Source page, select one or more disks available on this server option, and then click Next.

4. On the Disk Drive page, select the disk on which you wish to create the volume, and then click Next.

5. On the Volume Size page, specify the size of the volume, and then click Next.

6. On the Volume Size page, choose a volume letter, and then click Next.

7. On the Volume Creation page, provide a volume label and select whether you want to perform a quick format. Click Next, and then click Create to finish provisioning storage. Click Close when the wizard completes.

After you prepare the volume where you will host the shared folder, you can create the shared folder. To do this, you need to start the Provision Shared Folder Wizard,

▶ Generally speaking, a quick format will meet most of your needs. The difference between a quick and a full format is that the quick format doesn't check for errors on the disk.

which you can do by clicking on Provision Share on the Actions Pane of the Share and Storage Management Console.

To provision a share using Share and Storage Manager, perform the following general steps:

1. Open Share and Storage Management.

2. In the Actions pane, click the Provision Share item. This opens the Provision a Shared Folder Wizard, shown in Figure 10-2.

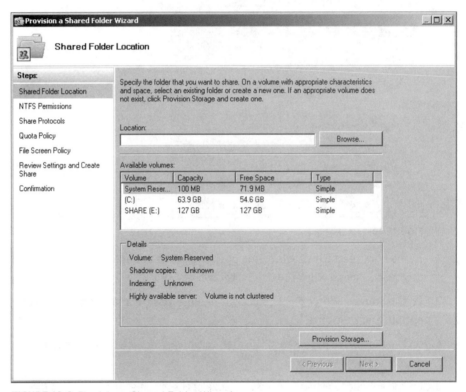

FIGURE 10-2: Provision a Shared Folder Wizard

3. Specify the location that will host the share, and then click Next.

4. Determine whether you want to alter the default NTFS permissions assigned to the folder that will host the share.

5. On the Share Protocols page, select SMB and/or NFS. Enter the share name, and then click Next.

▶ Remember that the more restrictive combined NTFS and Share permissions will apply to clients accessing files from the network.

> **NOTE** You can create a Network File System (NFS) share, which is accessible to UNIX clients, but only if Services for NFS is installed on the computer that runs Windows Server 2008 R2. Because most modern UNIX or Linux clients come with a service named SAMBA, allowing access to the default SMB protocol used by Windows file servers, NFS shares are increasingly unnecessary.

6. On the SMB Settings page, click the Advance button to display the Advanced window shown in Figure 10-3. On the first tab of this window, you can limit the number of users that can concurrently connect to the share. You can also enable access-based enumeration. You can use the Caching tab to configure offline file settings. Click OK, and then click Next.

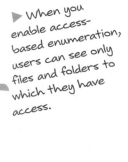

▶ When you enable access-based enumeration, users can see only files and folders to which they have access.

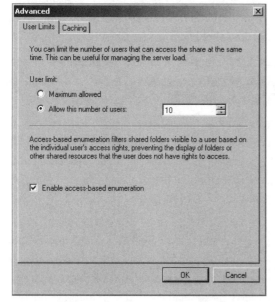

FIGURE 10-3: Enable access-based enumeration.

7. On the SMB permissions page, configure the share-level permissions.

8. If you have installed the File Server Resource Manager, you'll get the option to select a Quota policy and a File Screen Policy, otherwise you'll be presented with the DFS Namespace Publishing page of Step 10. On the Quota Policy page of the Provision a Shared Folder Wizard, you can choose to apply a quota derived from a File Server Resource Manager template.

▶ It is usually better to use the Custom Share Permissions option here and assign permissions directly to the group that has primary use of the share. Some administrators forget to set share permissions later on, so better to do it from the start.

▶ Unless there is an excellent reason to do otherwise, you should always apply a quota to a shared folder to minimize the chance that the volume hosting the share will run out of space.

9. On the File Screen Policy page, choose to apply a file screen derived from an existing file screen template.

10. On the DFS Namespace Publishing page, you can configure the shared folder to be published to an existing Distributed File System (DFS) namespace.

11. The final pages of the wizard give you a chance to review your settings and, if you are happy with them, you can click Create to provision the share.

Another reason why the provision storage and create share functionalities are tied into the same console is that doing so encourages systems administrators to create a separate volume for each share. If you put all of your shares on the same volume and run out of disk space, it will impact the users of all shares.

In general, it is a good idea to configure a separate share for each significant group, rather than configuring a small number of shares and then using the directory structure to differentiate groups. You should do this for the following reasons:

▶ **Simplified permissions:** Even experienced administrators mess up share and NTFS permissions, especially when a user is a member of multiple groups, each of which is assigned permissions at the share and file and folder level.

▶ **Simplified maintenance:** Performing maintenance on a share that is used by 500 people is far more disruptive than performing maintenance on a share used by 50 people. It is easier to move smaller shares to new volumes. Smaller shares, by their nature, involve the storage of smaller amounts of data. This means that you can move them to new volumes more easily than larger shares.

▶ **Easier Management:** Larger numbers of small shares enable easier application of different share-level quotas and file screen policies. For example, if you have separate shares for Accounting and Finance, it is easier to apply different quotas and file screens to the separate shares than it is to apply different quotas and file screens if all data is hosted off the same share.

Managing Shares

One of the most difficult things about managing a file server is ensuring that people don't have open files when you need to perform a reboot to complete routine maintenance. No matter how much warning of an impending reboot you give, you'll still have a number of users who ignore or otherwise don't receive the message to close

> ▶ If you provision a separate volume for each share, running out of disk space on the volume that hosts one share will have no impact on the functionality of other shares on the server.

> ▶ Reducing the number of users that access a specific share reduces the complexity of the permissions that need to be assigned to support the share.

all open files on the server. There are two tools available from the Share and Storage Management console that enable you to view who is connected to shared folders and which shared folder items are open. You can use these tools to do the following:

- ▶ **Manage sessions:** The Manage Sessions tool enables you to view which users are connected to shared folders. You can view how long these users have remained connected and each user's idle time. You can use the Manage Sessions item to close individual sessions or close all sessions connected to the server.

- ▶ **Manage open files:** The Manage Open Files item enables you to view each file that is opened by network clients, including information about which network user has opened the file. You can use the Manage Open Files item to disconnect users from specific files or to disconnect them from all files that are remotely opened on a particular server.

USING FILE SERVER RESOURCE MANAGER

After you have created shares, you use the *File Server Resource Manager (FSRM)* to manage those shares. FSRM is a tool that enables you to manage the minutiae of shares, such as controlling how much data can be written to a share and what types of data can be written to shares. It also enables you to develop strategies to deal with the various sorts of data stored on shares.

You can use FSRM to manage the following:

- ▶ Quotas
- ▶ File screens
- ▶ Storage reports
- ▶ File classification
- ▶ File management tasks

To install File Server Resource Manager, ensure that the File Services role is installed on your Windows Server 2008 R2 computer and then add the File Server Resource Manager role service. As an alternative, install RSAT if you want to remotely manage file servers from an administrative workstation running Windows Vista or Windows 7.

You can install FSRM quickly from PowerShell by loading the ServerManager module and issuing the command:

```
Add-WindowsFeature FS-Resource-Manager
```

Configuring Quotas

In the best of worlds, we wouldn't need quotas, because users would store only reasonable amounts of data on file shares and wouldn't keep copying files across file shares until the volumes hosting them were full. Unfortunately, experience has shown that some users keep copying data across to file shares until they reach a hard limit. Instead of using a hard limit for the capacity of the volume that hosts the share, quotas allow you to limit the amount of storage data packrats can consume.

You might know that quotas have been on Windows Server operating systems for some time. The main issue has been that although quotas have been supported, the quota functionality available is less than likely to inspire enthusiasm in the hearts of systems administrators. These quotas, often labeled NTFS quotas, have the following properties:

▶ **Apply to the entire volume:** NTFS quotas apply across the volume. They are also cumulative across the volume. This means if users have access to two different shared folders hosted on the same volume, their quota usage is calculated based on the total amount stored across both shares.

▶ **No user notification:** When a user exceeds his warning or quota limit, an event is written to the log. Without some serious mucking about with event log triggers, the user is unaware that he has exceeded the warning level and will realize he has exceeded the quota only when he is unable to save files to the shared folder.

The quotas you can create using FSRM address these concerns in that they allow e-mail messages to be sent to users when they exceed a certain percentage threshold of their quota, can apply on a per share basis, and are not cumulative across a volume. You create quotas by assigning a quota template to a folder. That quota template then applies cumulatively across all subfolders of the parent folder. To create a quota template, perform the following steps:

1. Open FSRM, navigate to the Quota Management\Quota Templates node, and then click Create Quota Template in the Actions menu. This opens the Create Quota Template window shown in Figure 10-4.

▶ The 80/20 rule has many applications to IT planning. It has been suggested that 20 percent of users consume 80 percent of the space allocated to shared folders, and 20 percent of users are responsible for 80 percent of support calls.

▶ Without some type of notification mechanism, users are more likely to call the support desk to inquire about quota issues than they are to realize they have exceeded a quota.

2. Enter a template name. This name should mention the quota limit, as you will use this template when applying a quota.

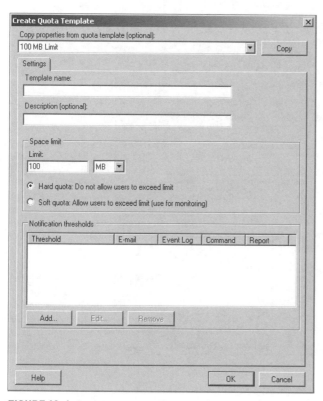

FIGURE 10-4: Create quota templates.

3. Enter the space limit. You can choose between a hard quota and a soft quota. A soft quota is primarily used for monitoring. A hard quota blocks users from saving files to the shared folder if they exceed the quota value. You can over-allocate, because most users won't bump up against their quota.

4. Click Add to open the Add Threshold window. Here, you can configure an e-mail to be sent to a user whose disk usage exceeds a set value. Figure 10-5 shows a threshold at which the user will receive an e-mail if he exceeds 85 percent of the quota value. You can also configure an item to be written to the event log, configure a storage report to be generated, or run a specific command or script.

▶ A good rule of thumb when setting limits is to work out how many users will access the share, divide the total amount of storage you want to allocate to these users by this number, and then multiply it by about 1.2.

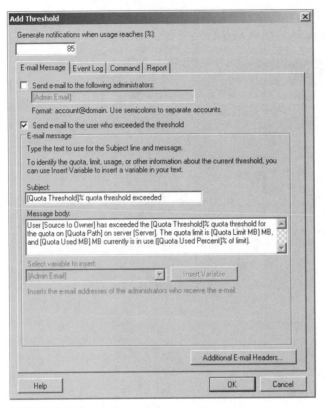

FIGURE 10-5: Create threshold.

After you create the quota template, you can apply it on a per-folder basis. You apply quota templates to the root folder of the share to which you want the quota to apply. To apply a quota template, perform the following general steps:

1. Open FSRM and navigate to the Quota Management\Quotas node. In the Actions pane, click Create Quota.

2. In the Create Quota window, specify the local path of the root folder of the share. Use the drop-down list to select a quota template to apply. Figure 10-6 shows that the quota template 1 GB limit is applied to the share hosted at path E:\Accounting. Click Create to apply the quota.

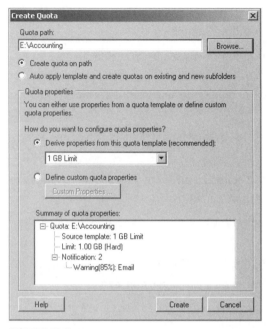

FIGURE 10-6: Apply quota.

Configuring File Screens

If all users did was store documents in the common Office formats on file shares, there would rarely be a need for quotas, and it would be unusual for file shares to run out of space. An administrator who investigates the storage habits of the users he manages is likely to find all sorts of odd files being stored on departmental file shares. *File screens* enable you to block certain file types from being written to shared folders on the basis of a file name. File screens are usually implemented on the basis of a file's extension, though it is possible to create blocks based on any part of a file's name.

▶ Rather than wonder why users have decided to store MP3, AVI, and MOV files on shared folders, it is simply easier to block these files from being written to these locations.

BLOCKING WITH FILE GROUPS

File groups are collections of file extensions that are commonly related to a specific type of file. For example, the Office Files file group contains file name extensions related to Office files and the Image Files file group contains file name extensions related to image files. File groups are comprehensive collections of extensions related to specific file types, but they are not always complete. You can add extra extensions as necessary or create your own custom file group for a specific class of files. The file groups that are included in FSRM by default are as follows:

- ▶ **Audio and Video Files:** This file group blocks 36 file extensions related to audio and video files, such as .avi, .mov, and .mp3. Note that, by default, files in .mkv format are not blocked, though it is simple to add this file type by editing the file group.

- ▶ **Backup Files:** This file group blocks .bak, .bck, .bkf, and .old files from being stored.

- ▶ **Compressed Files:** This file group blocks 26 different file extensions related to compressed files, including .zip, .tgz, and .rar.

- ▶ **E-mail Files:** This file group blocks nine file extensions related to e-mail files, such as .mbx and .pst.

- ▶ **Executable Files:** This file group blocks 20 different file extensions related to scripts and executable files, such as .ps1, .bat, .msi, and .exe.

- ▶ **Image Files:** This file group blocks 18 different file extensions related to image files, such as .jpg, .gif, and .bmp.

- ▶ **Office Files:** This filegroup blocks 86 different file extensions related to Office documents, including .doc, .docx, and .xls.

- ▶ **System Files:** This file group blocks five different file types related to system files, including .dll and .sys files.

- ▶ **Temporary Files:** This file group blocks file names often used by temp files, including files that have a name beginning with the tilde (~) and .tmp files.

- ▶ **Text Files:** This file group blocks files with the .asc, .text, and .txt extensions.

- ▶ **Web Page Files:** This file group blocks 13 different file types related to web content, including files that have the .htm, .php, and .aspx extensions.

> **NOTE** File screens do not stop users from renaming file extensions to get past a file screen. For example, if a user renames an MP3 file with the .doc extension, he can store the file on a file share to which a file screen that blocks the Audio and Video file group applies. Although these sorts of issues are technically feasible, in general, the only people who are able to think around this type of simple block are already working in the IT department. You can also use storage reports to look for suspiciously large files. A user who is constantly storing suspiciously large documents will be noticeable in a properly configured storage report.

To add a file type to an existing file group, for example, to add the .mkv file extension to the Audio and Video file group, perform the following steps:

1. Open File Server Resource Manager.

2. Navigate to the File Screening Management\File Groups node.

3. Click the Audio and Video file group. In the Actions menu, click on the Edit File Group Properties. This opens the File Group Properties for Audio and Video Files window.

4. Enter *.mkv, as shown in Figure 10-7, and then click Add. Click OK to close the File Group Properties for the Audio and Video Files window.

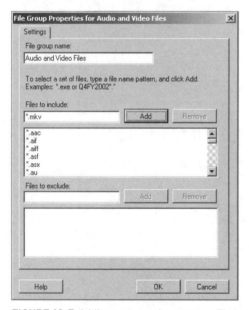

> File screens almost entirely use file name extensions to identify files, but you can use wildcards to add an entry to a file group. Although *.txt blocks text files, you can add an entry to a file group of the form budget.*, which blocks files named budget, irrespective of extension.

FIGURE 10-7: Adding an extension type to a file group

APPLYING FILE SCREEN TEMPLATES

You apply file screen templates to a path to create a file screen. A *file screen template* includes a screening type, a set of file groups, and a set of configurable actions that occur when a match is found with any of the file groups. You can set screening types to active or passive, with the difference as follows:

▶ **Active screening:** When enabled, active screening blocks users from saving files with name types that are specified in the file group.

▶ **Passive screening:** When enabled, passive screening allows users to save file types that are specified in the file groups but also allows events to be triggered, such as event logs.

When you configure a screen in either Active or Passive mode, you can also configure the screen to initiate actions. These actions include:

► **Sending an e-mail message:** As Figure 10-8 shows, you can configure an e-mail message to be sent to the user who attempted to save the file and/or to one or more administrator accounts. Configuring e-mail alerts will limit the number of users that ring the help desk trying to figure out why they can't save files of a specific type to the file share.

► This will only work if you have e-mail addresses associated with Active Directory accounts.

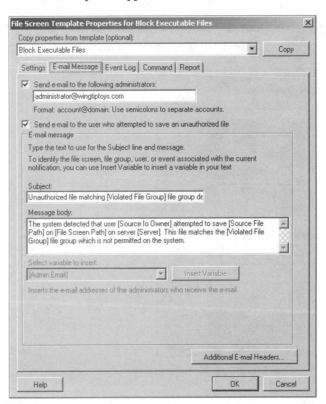

FIGURE 10-8: E-mail alert

► **Generating an event log message:** You can also configure file screen templates to generate an event log message each time an attempt is made to write an item in a configured file group to a shared folder. This is useful only if you want to check the event logs for this sort of event. Most administrators lack the enthusiasm necessary for this to be worthwhile.

► **Run a command:** This option enables you to run a command every time someone attempts to write an item specified within a file group to a shared folder. You can configure these commands to be run under the Local Service, Network Service, or Local System account.

▶ **Generate a report:** You can configure any of the available storage reports to be created and, if you want, you can forward them to administrators and/or the user who attempted to save the blocked file.

You can edit an existing template to configure these options or set them when you create a new file screen template. To create a file screen template, perform the following general steps:

1. Open File Server Resource Manager and select the File Screen Templates node under File Screening Management. Click Create File Screen Template.

2. In the Create File Screen Template window, enter a name for the template, and then select the file groups that the template will be configured to block. You can configure the actions that the template will take beyond the block, such as e-mailing notifications to users who attempt to save verboten files. Figure 10-9 shows a template named General Block that blocks audio, video, executable, and system files. When you have configured the appropriate actions, click OK to create the template.

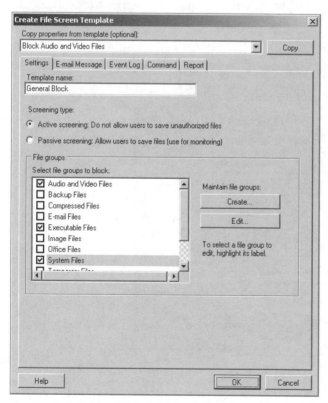

FIGURE 10-9: Custom file screen template

CREATING FILE SCREENS

After you have configured an appropriate template, you can apply that template to a volume or directory tree by creating a file screen. Like quotas, file screens are applied to folders, which can include the root folder of a volume, and they are inherited by all child folders under that parent folder. Unlike quotas, with file screens, you can also apply a *file screen exception*. For example, you might create a template that blocks audio, video, image, and executable files and then apply that template to a volume that hosts several shares. One of the shares is used by members of the marketing department who need to save images to a specific shared folder. You could allow this to occur by applying a file screen exception to that particular share. File screen exceptions override file screens.

To create a file screen, perform the following steps:

1. From the FSRM, select the File Screening Management\File Screens node. In the Actions pane, click on Create File Screen.

2. On the Create File Screen window, enter the path that the file screen applies to, and then select the file screen template that you wish to apply. Figure 10-10 shows the General Block template applied to volume E. Click Create to apply the file screen.

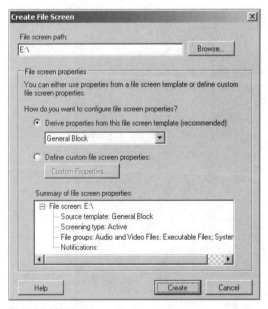

FIGURE 10-10: Create file screen.

To create a file screen exception, perform the following steps:

1. From the FSRM, select the File Screening Management\File Screens node. In the Actions pane, click on Create File Screen Exception.

2. On the Create File Screen Exception window, specify the path that the exception applies to and the file groups that you wish to exclude from screening. Figure 10-11 shows the exception applying to the E:\Accounting folder for the Audio and Video Files file group.

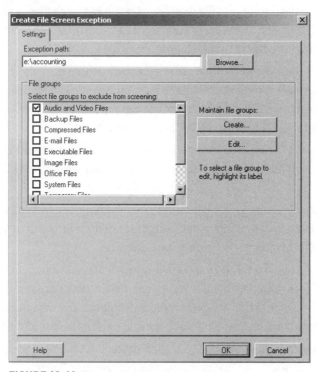

FIGURE 10-11: File screen exception

Configuring Storage Reports

Storage reports enable you to gain information about files that are stored on specific volumes on your organization's file servers. You can configure storage reports to run locally on each server, and storage reports are saved, by default, in the %systemdrive%\ StorageReports\Sheduled folder. You can also configure storage reports to be e-mailed to one or more e-mail addresses on a regular basis. Storage reports can be created in DHTML, HTML, XML, CSV, and text formats.

You can create storage reports for the following:

▶ **Duplicate Files:** A list of files that appear to be the same based on their size and last access time

▶ **File Screening Audit:** Enables you to identify users or applications that are regularly triggering file screens. You can configure the report to specify the number of days since the last file screen event occurred.

▶ **Files by File Group:** Enables you to determine the prevalence of files based on file group. You can configure file groups under the File Groups node of File Screening Management. The report defaults to reporting on all file groups, but you can configure the report to search for specific file groups.

▶ **Files by Owner:** Enables you to group files by owner. This report helps you determine which users are consuming the most disk space. The report defaults to a search for files by all owners, but you can customize the report so that it only searches for files owned by specific users.

▶ **Files by Property:** Enables you to generate information based on a file classification. You will learn how to configure file classifications later in this chapter.

▶ **Large Files:** Enables you to locate files that are consuming the most disk space. By default, the report only searches for files that are larger than 5 MB, but you can edit this to set a larger minimum file size.

▶ **Least Recently Accessed Files:** Enables you to locate files on shared folders that have not been accessed for more than a specified number of days. Use this report to locate files that can be moved to an archive. The default option generates a report on files that have not been accessed in the last 90 days.

▶ **Most Recently Accessed Files:** Enables you to locate files that have been accessed recently, ensuring that it is frequently backed up. The default setting shows you all files accessed in the last seven days.

▶ **Quota Usage:** Enables you to determine which users are using more than a specified percentage of their quota. For example, you can use this report to determine which users have exceeded 80 percent of their assigned quota.

▶ Systems administrators deluge themselves in data; the reaction is to ignore it. If you set alerts for everything, you train yourself not to respond to them. If you configure reports and alerts for important things, you'll keep track of important things.

You can configure reports to run on demand or according to a schedule. Only configure reports to run on a schedule if you intend to review the reports at a later stage, as it is a trivial exercise to configure a report to run immediately. To configure a report to run immediately, perform the following general steps:

1. Open File Server Resource Manager, and navigate to the Storage Reports Management node.

2. In the Actions pane, click the Generate Reports Now item.

3. On the Storage Reports Task Properties window shown in Figure 10-12, click Add to specify the volumes that you want to check, and use the checkboxes to select which reports you want to run. Click OK to run the report(s). During this process, you have the option of waiting for the reports to be generated and then displayed, or having the reports generated in the background for later review.

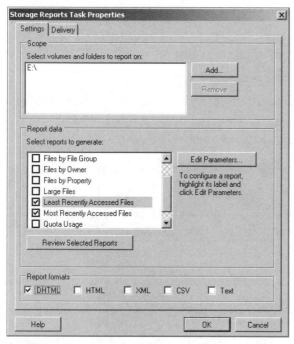

FIGURE 10-12: Storage reports

Configuring File Classification

File classification enables you to assign metadata to a file based on its properties. You can perform a simple classification based on the file's location or a more complex classification based on the contents of the file. The first step in configuring file classification is to set classification properties. Classification properties support the following types:

▶ **Yes/No:** A Boolean value

▶ **Date-Time:** The date and time

▶ **Number:** An integer value

▶ **Multiple Choice List:** Where multiple values can be assigned

▶ **Ordered List:** Values that have an order

▶ **String:** A text-based value

▶ **Multi-string:** Allows the assignment of several text-based values in a classification

For example, to create a classification property named Importance, which has the possible values High, Medium, and Low, perform the following general steps:

1. Open File Server Resource Manager and navigate to the Classification Management\Classification Properties node.

2. In the Actions menu, click Create Property.

3. In the Create Classification Property Definition window, enter the property name as **Importance**. Change the property type to Ordered List and enter the items **High**, **Medium**, and **Low** as shown in Figure 10-13. Click OK.

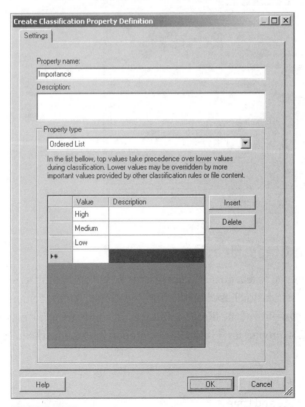

FIGURE 10-13: Classification property

After you have a classification property defined, you can create a rule to assign that property. For example, you can automatically classify all files in the folder E:\ Managers with the Importance classification property of High. To do this, perform the following steps:

1. Open File Server Resource Manager and navigate to the Classification Management\Classification Rules node.

2. In the Actions pane, click Create a New Rule. This will open the Classification Rule Definitions window. Enter a rule name, click Add, and then select the E:\ Managers folder.

3. Click the Classification tab. Ensure that Folder Classifier is selected, and then ensure that the Importance property value is selected and the property value is set to High, as shown in Figure 10-14.

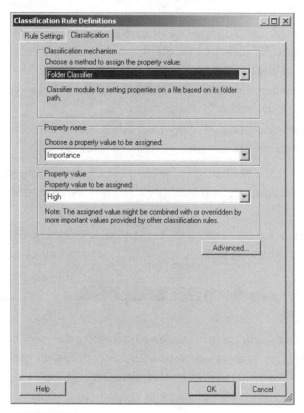

FIGURE 10-14: Classification rule definition

Instead of using the Folder Classifier option on the Classification tab, you can use the Content Classifier. This option works by searching for text or patterns within the file. Use the Advanced button to select how the search will occur. You have the option of searching for regular expressions, strings, or case-sensitive strings.

After you have configured the classification properties that you want to assign and the classification rules by which those properties are assigned to files, you can configure a schedule against which the classification rules can be run. The default schedule is to run the classification rules on the file server every day at 9am.

Configuring File Management Tasks

Using the file management tasks capabilities of the File Server Resource Manager, you can configure certain actions to be taken on files based on their properties. The default action is the file expiration task. The *file expiration task* allows you to automatically move files from the share to a separate location after they have not been accessed for a certain amount of time. For example, you might use the file expiration task to automatically move files to an archive server. These moved files will be stored in a directory structure that mirrors that of the original location, so it won't be a matter of all expired files being lumped into the same folder.

To configure a file management task that moves all files that have not been accessed for 365 days on volume E to volume F, perform the following steps:

1. Open FSRM and click the File Management Tasks node. In the Actions pane, click Create File Management Task. This opens the Create File Management Task window.

2. On the General pane, enter a name for the task and select the volume(s) and/ or folder(s) against which the task will run. In this example, I will choose the E: drive.

3. On the Action tab, ensure that File Expiration is selected and set the Expiration Directory to **F:**.

▶ *You should never set the Expiration Directory to a subdirectory of the directory against which you are running the expiration task.*

4. On the Notification tab, click Add to have an e-mail sent to the user whose file is about to expire. Specify how much warning you want to give the user that the file is going to be moved to a different location.

5. On the Condition page, specify the conditions for expiration. Figure 10-15 shows a condition of 365 days since last access, but it is also possible to configure conditions based on file creation date, last modification of the file, and file name.

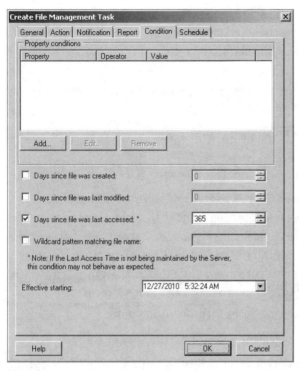

FIGURE 10-15: File expiration

6. On the Schedule tab, configure a schedule for the file expiration task to run against. The default schedule is for the task to run every day at 9am.

By default, Windows Server 2008 R2 does not track the last file access time. To ensure that last access time is tracked, you need to run the following command from an elevated command line and then reboot the server.

```
Fsutil behavior set disablelastaccess 0
```

WORKING WITH THE DISTRIBUTED FILE SYSTEM

The *Distributed File System (DFS)* enables you to replicate shared files and folders across the network in a highly efficient manner. DFS also provides highly available access to shared files. Traditionally, when the server hosting a shared folder fails, the files stored in the shared folder are not available until the server is restored. When a server hosting a DFS replica fails, clients are redirected to the closest available replica and are still able to access those files. This works automatically across WAN links, with the client perhaps only being aware of the failure because there is a delay in accessing the files from a remote location, rather than from the server down the hall.

To install DFS on a server that is part of an Active Directory domain, perform the following steps:

1. Open an elevated PowerShell session and run the following commands:

```
Import-module ServerManager
Add-WindowsFeature FS-DFS,FS-DFS-Namespace,FS-DFS-Replication
```

Once you have installed the DFS-related role services, you need to create a namespace. A *namespace* is a collection of the shared folders in the organization and looks similar to the UNC pathname where you use \\servername\share, except with DFS it is \\domainname with all shared folders that are part of the hierarchy under this DFS root. An advantage of DFS over a basic shared folder infrastructure is that, when configured properly, all shared folders can be found under the DFS root.

► This saves a lot of time when looking for a shared folder, as they are all stored in the same place. You don't need to know which server hosts the file; you just have to look under the DFS namespace for everything.

To create a DFS namespace, perform the following steps:

1. Open the DFS Management console from the Administrative Tools menu.

2. Click the Namespaces node. Click New Namespace in the Actions pane.

3. Click Browse to select a namespace server. The namespace server needs to have the DFS Namespace role service installed.

4. Enter a name for the namespace. This name appears after the domain name in a domain-based DFS namespace. If you name it shares, and you are in the wingtiptoys domain, it's as \\wingtiptoys\shares.

5. Select the Namespace Type. You should select Domain-based namespace, as this allows you to have multiple servers as roots. Figure 10-16 shows the Namespace Type selection page of the New Namespace Wizard.

6. Review your settings and create the namespace.

7. After the namespace is created, expand the Namespaces node, right-click on the namespace, and then click on Add Namespace Server. This enables you to add additional namespace servers, ensuring that the namespace remains available in the event that one namespace server fails.

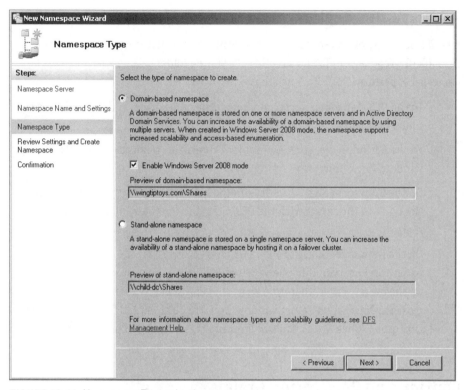

FIGURE 10-16: Namespace Type selection page

Adding Shares to the DFS Namespace

After you have configured the DFS namespace, you can add shares to that namespace.
To add an existing share to an existing namespace, perform the following steps:

1. In the DFS Management console, select the namespace, and then click New
   Folder in the Actions pane.

2. In the New Folder window, enter a name for the folder. In general, this should
   mirror the name of the shared folder. Click Add under Folder Targets. This
   opens the Add Folder Target dialog box.

3. On the Add Folder Target window, click Browse. On the Browse for Shared
   Folders dialog, select a shared folder, and then click OK. You can also use this
   window to create a new, shared folder to add to the DFS namespace. Click OK
   twice to close the Add Folder Target and New Folder dialog boxes.

Adding a DFS Replica

A *replica* is a copy of a shared folder on another server that is kept up-to-date through DFS replication. To add a replica of a shared folder that you've added to the namespace, perform the following steps:

1. In the DFS Management console, select the namespace, and then click on the folder that you wish to create a replica of.

2. In the Actions pane, click Add Folder Target. This opens the New Folder Target window. Click Browse.

3. On the Browse for Shared Folders dialog box, click Browse, and then enter the name of the server with the DFS role installed that you want to host the replica.

4. On the Browse for Shared Folders window, ensure that the server name is set to the target server. Click New Shared Folder, and then specify the location on the target server where you want the replica hosted. Click OK. Click OK to close the New Folder Target window. You will be prompted to create a replication group. Click No, as you will be doing this in the next procedure.

Configuring Replication Groups

Replication groups enable you to ensure that replication occurs between replica folders in your DFS hierarchy. To configure replication, perform the following general steps:

1. In the DFS Management console, click on the Replication item. In the Actions pane, click New Replication Group. This opens the New Replication Group Wizard.

2. Choose Multipurpose replication group, as this will allow updates to occur at all servers that are members of the group.

3. Enter a name for the replication group and specify the domain to which the replication group belongs.

4. Add servers to the replication group. You must add a minimum of two servers to a replication group.

5. Select the type of replication topology that you want to use. Full-mesh topology allows any DFS server to update any other DFS server, though this might

not be practical for certain WAN configurations. If you have a central server and many branch office servers, you might choose a Hub and Spoke topology.

6. Configure a replication schedule. You have the option of configuring replication to occur continuously or according to a schedule.

7. Specify the primary member of the replication group. This will be the server that has the initial content that you wish to replicate to other members.

8. Specify which folders you wish to have replicated. You should specify the local path on the server that hosts the share. On the target server, specify the path that hosts the DFS replica share.

UTILIZING BRANCHCACHE

BranchCache enables clients in branch office networks to utilize local copies of files cached on computers on the branch office network, rather than dragging fresh copies of the same files over the WAN from the central office. The locally cached copies are only used if a check finds them to be the same as the version stored on the remote server. From the perspective of the branch office user, they appear to be accessing the file on the central server, but it occurs more quickly. The big advantage of BranchCache is that it speeds up access to files over the WAN without having to go to the trouble of deploying a DFS replica on each branch office network. BranchCache can be used with clients and servers that aren't members of a domain, but doing so requires significantly greater effort to configure the clients and the server than accomplishing the same goal in a domain environment.

▶ The drawback to BranchCache is that you can only use it if the host servers are running Windows Server 2008 R2, and the clients are running Windows 7 Professional, Enterprise, or Ultimate editions.

BranchCache works with both Internet Information Services (IIS), Windows Server Update Services (WSUS), and with the file server role. To enable BranchCache on a server that functions as either an IIS, WSUS, or file server, perform the following general steps:

1. Open an elevated PowerShell session.

2. Import the Server Manager module by running the command:

```
Import-module ServerManager
```

3. Install the BranchCache features by running the following command:

```
Add-WindowsFeature BranchCache,FS-BranchCache
```

4. Start the BranchCache service by running the following command:

```
Start-Service BranchCache
```

To ensure that BranchCache works with WSUS, you need to configure the WSUS server to store content locally. To ensure that clients accessing file shares on the file server can use BranchCache, you need to take the following steps:

CROSSREF   You will learn more about configuring WSUS in Chapter 15.

1. From the Run dialog box on the Start menu, type **gpedit.msc** to open the Local Group Policy Editor.

2. Navigate to the Computer Configuration\Administrative Templates\Network\ Lanman Server node and edit the properties of the Hash Publication for BranchCache policy.

3. Ensure that you configure the policy as Enabled and that the value is set to Allow Hash Publication for All Shared Folders, as shown in Figure 10-17.

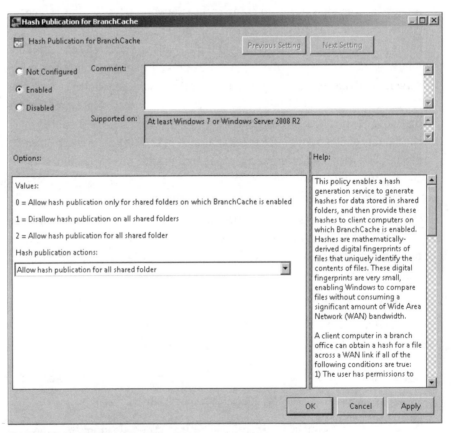

FIGURE 10-17: Enable hash publication.

4. Open the Share and Storage Management console and edit the properties of each share. Click the Advanced button, and then navigate to the Caching tab. Ensure that the Enable BranchCache item is selected, as shown in Figure 10-18.

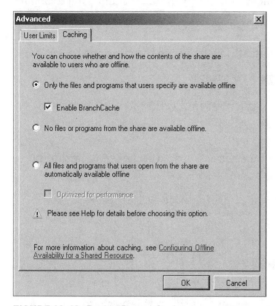

FIGURE 10-18: Enable BranchCache.

BranchCache clients are configured through the Computer Configuration\Administrative Templates\Network\BranchCache node of Group Policy. BranchCache clients can function in one of two modes, and you select the appropriate mode when configuring the group policy items. These two modes function as follows:

▶ **Distributed Cache mode:** This mode uses the computers running Windows 7 at a branch office site to host the file cache. Each computer at the branch office site hosts parts of the cache. The drawback to distributed cache mode is that if a computer that hosts a cached file is shut down, then the file must be retrieved again over the WAN link. You need to configure clients to use BranchCache to function in this mode.

▶ **Hosted Cache mode:** This mode enables a server at the branch office, running the Windows Server 2008 R2 operating system, to function as a caching server. This means that all files that are transferred to the BranchCache will be stored on this server rather than stored on branch office clients running Windows 7. To use hosted cache mode, you need to configure a server running the Windows Server 2008 R2 operating system at the branch site to function as a local BranchCache server.

To configure a branch office computer running the Windows Server 2008 R2 operating system to function as a local BranchCache server, perform the following steps:

1. Open an elevated PowerShell session.

2. Import the Server Manager module by running the following command:

   ```
   Import-module ServerManager
   ```

3. Install the BranchCache feature by running the following command:

   ```
   Add-WindowsFeature BranchCache
   ```

4. Start the BranchCache service by running the following command:

   ```
   Start-Service BranchCache
   ```

5. Configure the server to function as a hosted cache server by running the following command:

   ```
   Netsh branchcache set service mode=HOSTEDSERVER
   ```

WORKING WITH OFFLINE FILES

Offline file policies allow users to access files that reside on shared folders while they are not connected to the network. Offline file policies work by storing the files on specially configured shared folders in an encrypted local cache on users' PCs. From the perspective of the user working with the files, everything appears the same. When the user who has been working with an offline file reconnects to the network, the offline file is synchronized with the copy stored on the shared folder as required. In the event that there is a conflict, which will only occur if the file on the shared folder has been edited in the period in which the user has modified the file in the offline cache, the user is notified and given the option of creating an additional copy, discarding his changes, or overwriting the copy of the file that is stored on the file share and was edited.

The default setting for offline files allows users to mark certain files as available offline. You configure the offline file settings for each shared folder by performing the following steps:

1. Open the Share and Storage Management console.

2. In the Shares list, locate the file share for which you wish to enable offline files.

3. Right-click the share and choose Properties. On the Sharing tab of the Properties window that appears, click the Advanced button. Then select the Caching tab in the Advanced window, shown in Figure 10-19. This interface allows you to configure offline file settings for the share.

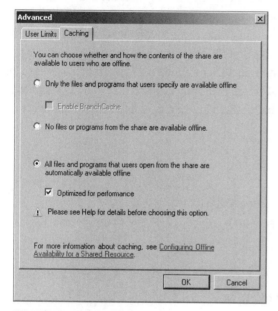

FIGURE 10-19: Offline files

Offline file settings can be configured for each individual share. This means that you can block offline files for sensitive shares while allowing offline files for less sensitive files. The offline file settings that you can configure through advanced shared folder properties are as follows:

▶ **Only the Files and Programs that Users Specify Are Available Offline:** This default setting requires users to configure specific files as available offline.

▶ **No Files or Programs from the Share Are Available Offline:** This option disables offline files for the share.

▶ **All Files and Programs that Users Open from the Share Are Automatically Available Offline:** This option ensures that any file that users open will be available offline. These files will be stored in the Offline Files cache on the client and will synchronize when the client is connected to the network until such time as the cache reaches capacity or the user deletes the file.

SUMMARY

The Share and Storage Management console enables you to provision storage as well as create file shares. It has the benefit of centralizing all shared folder tasks. File Server Resource Manager allows you to configure quotas and file screens, and run storage reports and file classification tasks against volumes that host shares. Distributed File System allows important file shares to be replicated to multiple servers throughout your organization. BranchCache allows users in branch offices to locally cache and share files retrieved across WAN links. Offline files allow users to continue to utilize files that were originally stored on shared folders without manually making a separate, local copy of the file.

Further Links

BranchCache for Windows Server 2008 R2

http://technet.microsoft.com/en-us/library/dd996634(WS.10).aspx

Distributed File System

http://technet.microsoft.com/en-us/library/cc753479(WS.10).aspx

Using File Server Resource Manager

http://technet.microsoft.com/en-us/library/dd758759(WS.10).aspx

What Is New in Offline Files

http://technet.microsoft.com/en-us/library/ff183315(WS.10).aspx

CHAPTER 11

Keeping Data Private

IN THIS CHAPTER

▸ **Using Encrypting File System**
▸ **Using BitLocker Drive Encryption**
▸ **Understanding Active Directory Rights Management Services**

For many organizations, the most important asset is data.
Organizations don't want to lose it, and they don't want it getting into the hands of their competitors. As workers become increasingly mobile through portable computers, the chances that data can end up in the hands of unauthorized third parties through loss of equipment or theft increases. Tens of thousands of laptop computers each year are stolen or lost, and IT news sites regularly carry stories of companies reporting the exposure of sensitive data because a laptop computer was left in the back of a taxi or at an airport security checkpoint.

In this chapter, you learn about three technologies that can ameliorate the chances of an unauthorized third party retrieving sensitive data in the event that the computer that hosts that data is lost or stolen. Each of these technologies works in a slightly different way, and they can all be used together to minimize the chance that important files are seen by those who are not authorized to do so.

ENCRYPTING FILE SYSTEM

Encrypting File System (EFS) is a file-level encryption technology. Users can encrypt their files with EFS by right-clicking on the file, clicking Advanced and then checking the Encrypt Contents to Secure Data option. EFS can also be enabled at the folder level. When this is done, every new file created in that folder, or every existing file copied to that folder, will become encrypted. To configure a folder to use EFS, right-click on the folder and on the General Properties tab, click Advanced, and then check the Encrypt Contents to Secure Data checkbox, as shown in Figure 11-1.

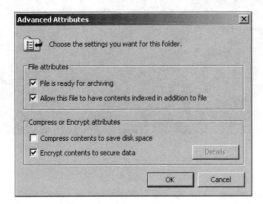

FIGURE 11-1: Folder-level EFS

> **NOTE** The main drawback to EFS is that it is cumbersome to use on the level of the individual user. Ways around this include using the cipher.exe command-line utility as a part of a logon script to automatically apply EFS encryption to specific files and directories, such as a special directory on the user's network drive. Users can then encrypt files just by copying them to a special folder.

As long as you retain access to your EFS certificate, you can transparently access the file. Transparent means that you can access the file without having to type in a password or jump through any other hoops. The encrypted file behaves normally, and you can open it using an appropriate application. The only way you can tell that a file is encrypted is by viewing its properties or if you notice that Windows Explorer has rendered its text green.

EFS-encrypted files cannot be read by users who do not have access to the private key of the EFS certificate used to encrypt the file. For example, if you have an EFS-encrypted file stored in a shared folder and the file was encrypted by Rooslan, only Rooslan will be able to open that file, even if other users have read and write permissions to that file. The only way that other people can gain access to that file is if Rooslan gives them access to his private EFS key, or if Rooslan adds their public EFS key to the encrypted file.

EFS is most useful when restricting access to files stored on file shares. A great problem in storing data on file shares is that, unless you are really careful with permissions, it is likely that someone who shouldn't be able to access the file will be able to do so. While most files stored on file shares aren't all that interesting, there is bound to be some data stored on file shares that should only be accessed by authorized people. Using EFS adds another layer of protection.

▶ A good use of EFS is to restrict administrators from accessing sensitive files.

> NOTE If you want to store EFS-encrypted files on a USB key, the USB key must be formatted with the New Technology File System (NTFS). This is important, because USB keys are almost always formatted as FAT32. A user copying an EFS-encrypted file from the hard disk to a USB key formatted with FAT32 might not realize that the file is automatically decrypted as part of the copying process. If the user wants to access an EFS encrypted file stored on a USB key on his home computer, he'll need to export his EFS certificate and transfer it to that computer.

A user can encrypt a file so that another user can access it only if he has access to that user's encryption certificate. How this works depends on whether a Certificate Authority (CA) has been configured to issue EFS certificates. A user can encrypt only files that can be accessed by another user if he has access to that user's public key. This can happen if both users have logged on to the same computer and encrypted files, the user has direct access to the public key, or the public key is published with the certificate in Active Directory. To give another user access, you use the cipher. exe command with the ADDUSER option, or you can edit the file's properties by clicking Advanced, clicking Details, and then clicking Add. This displays the dialog box shown in Figure 11-2, where you can encrypt a file to more than one user.

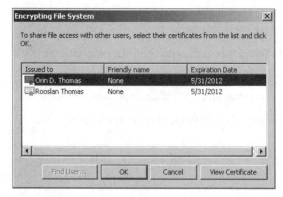

FIGURE 11-2: EFS multiple users

Using Local and Centralized EFS Certificates

When a person encrypts a file using EFS on a computer running Windows XP, Vista, 7, Server 2003, 2008, or 2008 R2 in an environment that does not have a Certificate Authority and centralized EFS certificates deployed, the local computer generates an EFS certificate for that user. Although this is fine if the user is logged on to a specific machine and only encrypting files locally, it becomes a problem if the user is constantly shifting machines, as he may not always take his EFS private key with him.

Although you can export a local EFS certificate from one computer and import it onto other computers, doing so is a manual process and most users aren't savvy enough to do it. A much better solution is to use a Certificate Authority to centrally manage and publish EFS certificates.

The best way to deploy EFS is to use certificates issued from an enterprise CA. When you do this, EFS certificates are stored in Active Directory. This means that the user will have one EFS certificate throughout the organization to encrypt and decrypt data no matter how many machines he or she logs on to. When certificates are published in Active Directory, other users will also be able to encrypt files against a user's public certificate without having to import that public certificate manually.

▶ Only enterprise root or subordinate CAs can issue EFS certificates.

Creating Advanced EFS Certificate Templates

The EFS template that ships with an enterprise CA in Windows Server 2008 R2 has not been altered since the release of Windows 2000. This means that if you use EFS certificates with the out-of-the-box settings, you won't get a chance to utilize all of the new features available, such as autoenrollment, key archiving, and ensuring that the user's public certificate is published in Active Directory.

To create a version 3 EFS certificate template, perform the following steps:

1. On a computer that has the enterprise root or enterprise subordinate Active Directory Certificate Services role installed, open the Certification Authority console from the Administrative Tools menu.

2. Right-click on the Certificate Templates node, and then click Manage. This opens the Certificate Templates console.

3. Right-click on the Basic EFS Template, and then click Duplicate Template.

4. On the Duplicate Template dialog, select Windows Server 2008 Enterprise, and then click OK.

5. On the General tab, set the Template display name to Advanced EFS and ensure that Publish Certificate in Active Directory is selected, as shown in Figure 11-3.

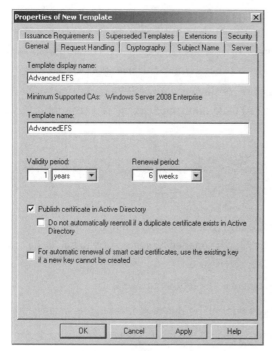

FIGURE 11-3: Publish Certificate in AD.

6. On the Request Handling tab, ensure that Archive Subject's Encryption Private Key is selected. This allows the key to be recovered in the event that it is lost if you have configured key archiving in your organization.

7. On the Superseded Templates tab, click Add, and select Basic EFS.

8. On the Security tab, configure the autoenroll permission for the user groups that will use this certificate. You'll also need to configure autoenrollment in Group Policy by setting the Computer Configuration\Policies\Windows Settings\ Public Key Policies\Certificate Services Client - Auto-Enrollment policy in the default domain GPO.

9. Click OK to create the certificate template. Go back to the Certification Authority console, right-click on Certificate Templates, click on New, Certificate Template to Issue, and then click on Advanced EFS.

▶ If you use autoenrollment, you can ensure that everyone in the organization is issued an EFS certificate without requiring them to encrypt a file.

Recovering EFS-Encrypted Data

The drawback of allowing users to encrypt data on an individual basis is that unless you take specific precautions, the data will be irretrievable in the event that the user leaves the organization without decrypting the data or providing access to his EFS certificates. For example, Bob uses EFS to encrypt sensitive files stored on the local file server. One morning, Bob gets hit by a bus. Access to Bob's encrypted files will be a challenge unless precautions were taken prior to this event occurring.

There are two ways of preparing for the recovery of EFS-encrypted data: configuring a Data Recovery Agent (DRA) or configuring EFS templates to support a Key Recovery Agent (KRA).

> **CROSSREF** Configuring a KRA was covered in Chapter 7, "Managing Active Directory Certificate Services."

When you configure a DRA, all files that are encrypted in the domain are encrypted in such a way that they can be opened by someone who holds the target user's EFS certificate and the DRA certificate.

To configure a DRA for EFS, perform the following steps:

1. Determine which user or users will be able to recover EFS-encrypted files.

2. Issue the user certificates based off the EFS Recovery Agent certificate template.

3. Edit the default domain GPO. Navigate to the Computer Configuration\Policies\Windows Settings\Public Key Policies\Encrypting File System node.

4. Remove any existing DRA certificates. By default, the first Administrator account in the domain is configured as a DRA.

You can also choose not to have a DRA and rely entirely on recovering users' EFS keys in the event that you need to recover encrypted data. The advantage of this is that encrypted data can be only recovered on a per-user basis by recovering that user's EFS key.

▶ Create a new certificate template based on the EFS Recovery Agent template and ensure that issued certificates are published to Active Directory. This ensures the DRA public certificate will be available to all computers in the domain.

▶ Once you've issued the DRA certificate, you can export it from the local user's certificate store, delete it from the certificate store, and put the exported certificate in a secure location.

▶ The drawback in having a DRA is that the person or people enrolled with the DRA certificate are able to view all EFS-encrypted data in the organization. Depending on the security practices at your organization, this may be a security risk.

To remove the first Administrator account in the domain as a DRA, or any other configured EFS DRAs, perform the following steps:

1. Open the default domain GPO and navigate to the Computer Configuration\ Policies\Windows Settings\Public Key Policies\Encrypting File System node.

2. Click on the Administrator item, and then press Delete. Click Yes when asked if you want to permanently delete the certificate.

3. If necessary, delete any other certificates that are set up to be used for EFS recovery.

▶ It isn't necessary to have a DRA if you've configured key archiving, as data is still recoverable; the process is simply more cumbersome.

ENCRYPTING WITH BITLOCKER

BitLocker drive encryption is a full-disk encryption technology. This technology can be used to protect the data on a disk drive in the event that the disk is removed from a computer and mounted elsewhere by an unauthorized third party intending to recover data. When a disk encrypted with BitLocker is used normally, the encryption is transparent and doesn't impact the normal functioning of the computer. When a BitLocker-protected disk is moved to another computer, the disk is unreadable unless the person attempting to access it has the BitLocker recovery tool and the appropriate decryption key or DRA certificate.

BitLocker is primarily used on portable computers to prevent the recovery of data in the event that the computer is lost or stolen. BitLocker also provides *boot integrity protection*. Boot integrity protection is used to stop attacks, such as those where the attacker boots off a customized boot device and uses an intrusion tool to reset the local Administrator password. Boot integrity protection can also prevent malware attacks that modify the boot environment. BitLocker usually requires that a computer have a Trusted Platform Module (TPM) chip installed, though it is also possible to use a startup USB key as an alternative if the appropriate Group Policy item is configured.

BitLocker can be used in conjunction with EFS. EFS protects data from being read by unauthorized users, whether they are inside or outside of the organization. BitLocker only protects against unauthorized users attempting to recover data from a volume on a computer that they are unable to boot into and log onto manually. To recover EFS-encrypted files from a volume protected by BitLocker, it is first necessary to perform BitLocker recovery and then recover the EFS-encrypted files.

▶ You should consider using BitLocker on servers that are located in insecure places, such as branch office locations without server rooms.

To install BitLocker on a computer running Windows Server 2008 R2, either add the BitLocker Drive Encryption feature using the Server Manager console or, with the Server Manager module loaded, use the following PowerShell command:

```
Add-WindowsFeature BitLocker
```

Once installed, BitLocker can be enabled either through the BitLocker Drive Encryption Control Panel item, shown in Figure 11-4, or by using the following Manage-Bde command, where volume represents the drive that you wish to protect:

```
Manage-bde -on volume: -rp -rk
```

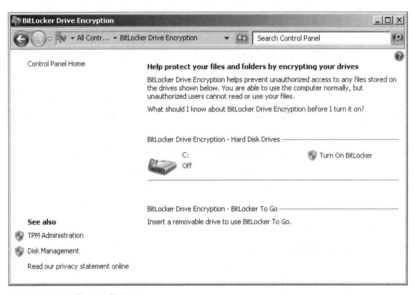

FIGURE 11-4: Enable BitLocker.

Protecting Removable Drives with BitLocker To Go

BitLocker To Go is a full-volume encryption technology that you can use with removable drives. As removable drives continue to get larger, people are storing more and more data on them. Unfortunately, as the drives are remaining about the same size, people are also still losing them. Just as organizations don't want some unknown third party recovering data from a lost laptop, they don't want an unknown third party recovering data from a USB stick. Unlike BitLocker, BitLocker To Go does not utilize a TPM chip.

Although BitLocker To Go is generally less relevant for server administrators, it is possible, through the use of Group Policy, to restrict users in an organization from writing data to removable disks that are not protected by BitLocker To Go. Doing so allows an organization to ensure that, if sensitive data is transferred to a removable disk and that removable disk is subsequently lost, the data cannot be recovered by anyone other than an authorized user.

Configuring BitLocker Group Policy

BitLocker works fine without having to configure Group Policy, but when you are thinking of using BitLocker with more than a couple of computers, you should configure BitLocker settings, such as automatically backing up BitLocker passwords centrally to Active Directory through Group Policy. You can configure advanced BitLocker settings through the following Group Policies:

▶ **Computer Configuration\Windows Settings\Public Key Policies\BitLocker Drive Encryption:** This policy enables you to configure a DRA for BitLocker.

Remaining policies are located under the Computer Configuration\ Administrative Templates\Windows Components\BitLocker Drive Encryption node. These policies are as follows:

▶ **Store BitLocker Recovery Information in Active Directory Domain Services:** Enabling this policy allows you to ensure that BitLocker recovery passwords and keys are backed up to Active Directory. You can stop drives from being encrypted unless these items have been backed up. This allows recovery of drives in the event that you have not configured a DRA for BitLocker.

▶ **Choose Default Folder for Recovery Password:** This policy enables you to specify a location for the BitLocker recovery password to be written. This isn't important if you're backing up recovery data to Active Directory.

▶ **Choose How Users Can Recover BitLocker-Protected Drives:** This policy only applies to computers running Windows Server 2008 (not 2008 R2) and Windows Vista and determines whether a 48-digit recovery password or 256-bit recovery key is used for recovery. Windows 7 and Windows Server 2008 R2 support backup to Active Directory and a DRA.

▶ **Choose Drive Encryption Method and Cipher Strength:** This policy enables you to specify which encryption algorithm and key length is used for BitLocker. The default is AES 128-bit with Diffuser, which should be suitable for all but the highest security organizations.

▶ **Provide the Unique Identifiers for Your Organization:** This policy provides an identifier field for BitLocker-protected volumes. This policy is necessary if you want to configure a DRA. It is also necessary if you want to limit users from writing to removable drives, unless they are protected by BitLocker and use a specific BitLocker identifier.

▶ **Prevent Memory Overwrite on Restart:** This security setting stops computer memory from being overwritten when a reboot occurs. It can speed up restarts, but at the cost of possibly allowing BitLocker data to be exposed to sophisticated attacks.

▶ **Validate Smart Card Certificate Usage Rule Compliance:** This policy associates a smart card certificate's object identifier with a BitLocker drive. This setting is only necessary if you want to use smart cards with BitLocker, and when this policy is not configured, a default object identifier is used.

▶ **Operating System Drives:** This node contains policies related to the operating system or boot drive. The policies under this node do not apply to additional disks in the computer.

  ▷ **Require Additional Authentication at Startup:** This setting relates to whether you allow BitLocker on computers that do not have a TPM chip to use BitLocker with a startup USB flash drive. You can also configure whether a startup PIN and/or a startup key is required to boot a computer protected by BitLocker if it does have a TPM chip. There is a separate policy with an identical name for computers running the Windows Vista or Windows Server 2008 operating systems.

  ▷ **Allow Enhanced PINs for Startup:** This policy enables you to configure more complex PINs for startup. Not all computers support complex BitLocker startup PINs.

  ▷ **Configure Minimum PIN Length for Startup:** This policy enables you to specify how many digits a startup PIN requires. It can be set to between 4 and 20.

  ▷ **Choose How BitLocker-Protected Operating System Drives Can Be Recovered:** This policy enables you to configure BitLocker to use a DRA. You can also configure BitLocker keys to be backed up to Active Directory using this policy.

  ▷ **Configure TPM Platform Validation Profile:** This policy enables you to configure settings related to the TPM security hardware. Unless you are in a very high-security environment, you are likely to be fine in not configuring this policy.

▶ **Fixed Data Drives:** This node contains policies related to additional fixed disks, as opposed to removable disks, in the computer. These policies are as follows:

 ▷ **Configure Use of Smart Cards on Fixed Data Drives:** Use this policy to require a user to insert a smart card to access a BitLocker-protected fixed drive.

 ▷ **Deny Write Access to Fixed Drives Not Protected by BitLocker:** Enabling this policy blocks users from writing data to any fixed drive that has not been configured with BitLocker.

 ▷ **Allow Access to BitLocker-Protected Fixed Data Drives from Earlier Versions of Windows:** When enabled, this policy allows BitLocker-protected FAT32 volumes to be accessed through the BitLocker To Go Reader, in a read-only manner, from computers running Windows XP SP2, Windows Vista, and Windows Server 2008.

 ▷ **Configure Use of Passwords for Fixed Data Drives:** This policy enables you to require a password to unlock a fixed data drive.

 ▷ **Choose How BitLocker-Protected Fixed Data Drives Can Be Recovered:** This policy enables you to configure BitLocker to use a DRA for fixed drives. You can also configure BitLocker keys for fixed drives to be backed up to Active Directory using this policy.

▶ **Removable Data Drives:** This node contains policies related to the protection of removable data drives by BitLocker To Go.

 ▷ **Control Use of BitLocker on Removable Drives:** Through this policy, you can allow users to configure BitLocker To Go on removable data drives. You can also separately allow users to decrypt BitLocker To Go data drives. When the policy is not configured, users can use BitLocker To Go on removable disks if their computer is running a compatible operating system.

 ▷ **Configure Use of Smart Cards on Removable Data Drives:** This policy enables you to require a smart card to access a BitLocker To Go-protected removable disk.

 ▷ **Deny Write Access to Removable Drives Not Protected by BitLocker:** This policy enables you to block users from writing data to removable drives that have not been configured with BitLocker To Go and the local organization's identifier.

▷ **Allow Access to BitLocker-Protected Removable Data Drives from Earlier Versions of Windows:** Similar to the policy detailed earlier for fixed drives, when enabled, this policy enables BitLocker-protected volumes to be accessed through the BitLocker To Go Reader, in a read-only manner, from computers running Windows XP SP2, Windows Vista, and Windows Server 2008.

▷ **Configure Use of Passwords for Removable Data Drives:** This policy enables you to configure BitLocker To Go so that a password must be entered when the removable disk is connected to another computer. You can also configure a password complexity policy for the BitLocker To Go-protected removable drive.

▷ **Choose How BitLocker-Protected Removable Drives Can Be Recovered:** This policy enables you to configure BitLocker to use a DRA for removable drives. You can also configure BitLocker keys for removable drives to be backed up to Active Directory using this policy.

Configuring BitLocker to Use a DRA

Like Encrypting File System, BitLocker can be configured to use a Data Recovery Agent. This means that you don't have to worry about recovering BitLocker keys from Active Directory to recover data from BitLocker-encrypted drives. Unlike EFS, where there may be some security concerns about configuring a DRA, using a DRA with BitLocker does not increase the risk of a security breach. This is because BitLocker provides transparent encryption and is only designed to protect data from people outside the organization. It doesn't matter that the person that holds the DRA certificate can recover BitLocker-encrypted data, because the only time that data needs to be recovered is in the event that the host computer fails or the BitLocker To Go password is forgotten.

To configure BitLocker to use a DRA, perform the following steps:

1. Ensure that you have a DRA certificate template on your enterprise CA. You can create a DRA certificate template by creating a duplicate template of the EFS Recovery Agent template and calling it DRA Certificate. You should configure the template to publish the certificate to Active Directory.

2. Edit a GPO that applies to the computer accounts for which you want to configure the DRA and navigate to the Computer Configuration\Windows Settings\Public Key Policies\BitLocker Drive Encryption node.

3. Right-click the BitLocker Drive Encryption node and then click on Add Data Recovery Agent. This will launch the Add Recovery Agent Wizard.

4. On the Select Recovery Agents page, click Browse Directory, if you've configured your DRA certificates to be published to Active Directory; or Browse Folders, if you're using an EFS Recovery Agent certificate; and select the certificate.

▶ It is a good idea to have one DRA for the organization rather than having separate DRAs for different organizational units.

5. Navigate to the Computer Configuration\Administrative Templates\ Windows Components\BitLocker Drive Encryption node.

6. Edit the Provide the Unique Identifiers for Your Organization node policy and specify the BitLocker Identification Field and the Allowed BitLocker Identification Field settings, as shown in Figure 11-5.

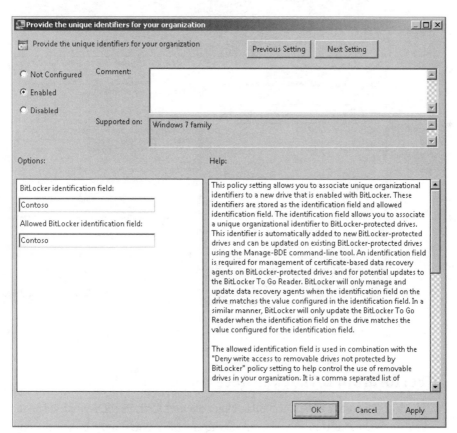

FIGURE 11-5: BitLocker Identification Field

7. Configure the following policies to allow the use of a Data Recovery Agent:

▷ Choose How BitLocker-Protected Operating System Drives Can Be Recovered. This policy is shown in Figure 11-6.

▷ Choose How BitLocker-Protected Fixed Drives Can Be Recovered.

▷ Choose How BitLocker-Protected Removable Drives Can Be Recovered.

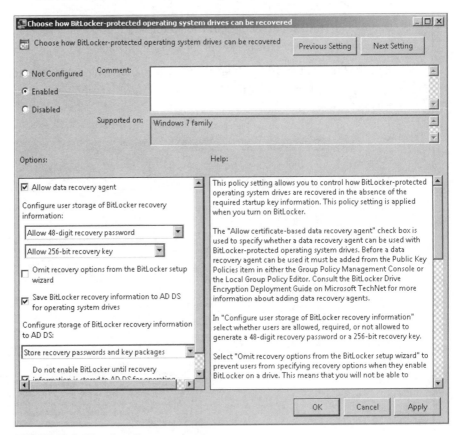

▶ Be aware that you need to set all this up prior to encrypting drives with BitLocker. That way the DRA recovery hooks are inserted into the BitLocker encrypted drives. If you do it after you've deployed BitLocker, it won't work.

FIGURE 11-6: Allow Data Recovery Agent.

▶ Performing recovery using a DRA in a large environment is much simpler than recovering recovery keys from Active Directory and using them in the manage-bde tool.

Performing BitLocker Recovery

There are two ways to perform BitLocker recovery. Using a DRA or using the recovery key. To perform BitLocker recovery using the DRA, you'll need to use a computer running Windows Server 2008 R2 or Windows 7 and ensure that you've got the appropriate Data Recovery Agent certificate in the local certificate store. Once you've done that, perform the following steps:

1. Connect the drive that you want to recover to the computer that you are using for recovery.

2. Open an elevated command prompt.

3. Determine the thumbprint of the DRA by running the following command, substituting volume for the drive letter of the drive that you are attempting to unlock:

   ```
   Manage-bde -protectors -get volume:
   ```

4. Locate the key protector listed as Data Recovery Agent (Certificate Based) and copy the certificate thumbprint.

5. Use the thumbprint in the following command to unlock the drive:

   ```
   Manage-bde -unlock volume: -cert -ct thumbprint
   ```

To unlock a drive using the recovery key, you need access to that key. If you have it backed up to Active Directory, you can extract it using the Active Directory Users and Computers console. To do this, you need to run Windows Server 2008 R2 or Windows 7 with the Remote Server Administration Tools installed. If you are using Windows 7, use the Turn Windows Features On or Off feature to enable the BitLocker Password Recovery Viewer and run the regsvr32.exe BdeAducExt.dll command from the Run dialog box.

To recover the key using Active Directory Users and Computers, perform the following steps:

1. Locate the computer account in Active Directory Users and Computers.

2. View the computer account properties and click on the BitLocker Recovery tab. This will list the BitLocker recovery information related to that computer.

3. Right-click on the appropriate recovery password and then click Copy Details.

4. Open an elevated command prompt and run the following command where Volume is the volume you want to unlock and RecoveryPassword is the recovery password extracted from Active Directory:

   ```
   Manage-bde -unlock Volume: -RecoveryPassword RecoveryPassword
   ```

▶ BitLocker recovery functionality only becomes apparent in Active Directory Users and Computers once a domain-joined computer running BitLocker has its BitLocker keys backed up to Active Directory.

USING ACTIVE DIRECTORY RIGHTS MANAGEMENT SERVICES

Active Directory Rights Management Services (AD RMS) allows an organization to apply rights management technology to AD RMS-enabled applications, such as Microsoft Office and Exchange. An organization can use AD RMS to stop sensitive e-mails from being printed, copied, or forwarded outside the organization. AD RMS can stop sensitive documents from being opened, copied, or printed by anyone that is not on a specific list of authorized individuals. EFS and BitLocker ensure, when properly implemented, that sensitive information cannot be recovered in the event that the media that hosts it is lost or stolen, whereas AD RMS provides this service and can also be used to ensure that sensitive data is not leaked to unauthorized third parties.

When you use AD RMS, the usage rights information is encoded in the document. For example, when a user attempts to open at home a Microsoft Word document that is protected by AD RMS, Microsoft Word performs a check to see if the user is able to open the document and the conditions under which that is allowed. Usage rights include the following:

- ▶ **Full control:** User can exercise all rights, even if those rights have not been explicitly granted. In general, if a right is not granted to a user, a user cannot exercise that right.

- ▶ **View:** Allows the user to view the protected content

- ▶ **Edit:** Allows the user to modify the protected content

- ▶ **Save:** Affords the same as the Edit right

- ▶ **Export:** Allows the user to use the Save As functionality, potentially removing AD RMS protection from the content

- ▶ **Print:** Allows the user to print AD RMS-protected content

- ▶ **Forward:** Allows the user to forward a protected message

- ▶ **Reply:** Allows the user to reply to a protected message, including the content of the original message

- ▶ **Reply all:** Allows the user to use the Reply All function to respond to all recipients of an AD RMS-protected message

- ▶ **Extract:** Allows the user to copy and paste content from an AD RMS-protected document. This includes taking screen shots.

▶ **Allow macros:** Allows the user to run macros in the AD RMS-protected
document

▶ **View rights:** Allows the user to view rights that are assigned in the AD RMS-
protected document

▶ **Edit rights:** Allows the user to modify rights assigned to the AD RMS-
protected document

Documents and e-mail can also be configured to expire. This means that once a
certain date and time has passed, the document is no longer accessible. Figure 11-7
shows how an expiration policy can be configured for a specific AD RMS template. AD
RMS protects data using encryption, so if a user attempts to access a protected document or e-mail using client software that is not AD RMS-enabled, he will be unable to
view the document's contents.

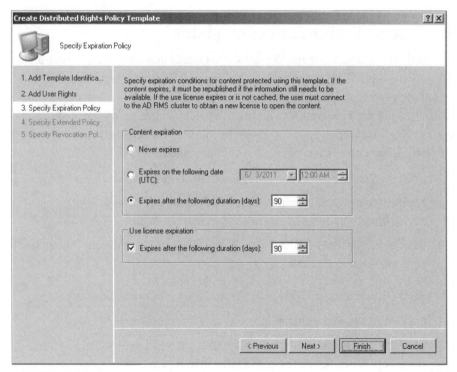

FIGURE 11-7: Content expiration

To install AD RMS, either add the role using Server Manager or, if the Server
Manager module is loaded, the following PowerShell command:

```
Add-WindowsFeature ADRMS
```

▶ The AD-RMS
client is included with
the Windows Vista
and Windows 7 client
operating systems.

When installing AD RMS, you must configure a special domain user account for the AD RMS service to run under. This account should be a standard domain user account with no additional permissions. If you are installing AD RMS on a domain controller, this account must be a member of the Domain Admins or Enterprise Admins group, so for security reasons it is better to install AD RMS on a member server. As AD RMS also installs a Web server component, you should think carefully about co-locating the AD RMS server on any server that is used to serve up web content.

Microsoft recommends configuring an SQL Server 2008 or 2008 R2 instance to host the AD RMS database; though, if you only want to install one AD RMS server in your organization, you can use the default Windows Internal Database. The only drawback of this is that you can't have more than one AD RMS server if you use the Windows Internal Database.

Distributing Rights Policy Templates

Rights policy templates allow you to control what rights users or groups have to an AD RMS-protected file. When an author decides to use AD RMS to protect a specific file, she chooses a specific rights policy template to apply. The AD RMS client on Windows Vista and a Windows 7 computer retrieves the available rights policy templates from the AD RMS server through an automated scheduled task. To create this task, perform the following steps on client computers in your organization:

1. Open the Task Scheduler from the Administrative Tools menu.
2. Navigate to the Task Scheduler Library\Microsoft\Windows\ Active Directory Rights Management Services Client node.
3. Double-click on the AD RMS Rights Policy Template Management (Automated) task and then click Enable.

To specify the location of rights policy templates, perform the following steps:

1. Create a shared folder that allows read access for the Everyone group.
2. Open the AD RMS console from the Administrative Tools menu and navigate to the Rights Policy Templates node as shown in Figure 11-8.
3. From the Action menu, click Properties, check the Enable Export checkbox, then enter the shared folder path where templates will be stored, and then click OK.

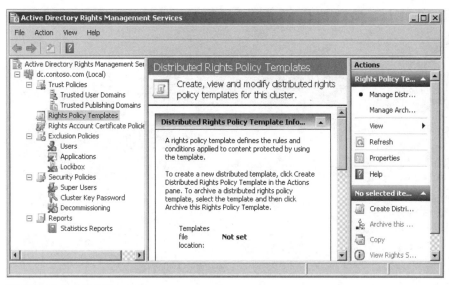

FIGURE 11-8: AD RMS console.

Creating Rights Policy Templates

Some applications, such as Microsoft Exchange Server 2010, come with a basic set of AD RMS policy templates. AD RMS also allows you to create your own set of rights templates from the AD RMS console. Once these templates have been distributed to clients, they will be able to utilize them to protect content from AD RMS-enabled applications.

To create a new rights policy template, perform the following steps:

1. Open the AD RMS console from the Administrative Tools menu and click the Rights Policy Templates node.

2. In the Actions pane, click Create Distributed Rights Policy Template. This opens the Create Distributed Rights Policy Template Wizard.

3. On the Add Template Identification Information page, click Add. Enter a template name and provide a description.

4. On the Add User Rights page, click Add. Specify a user or group. The user or group must have an e-mail address associated with them.

5. Use the checkboxes to specify which rights you want to assign to a particular group in this template, as shown in Figure 11-9.

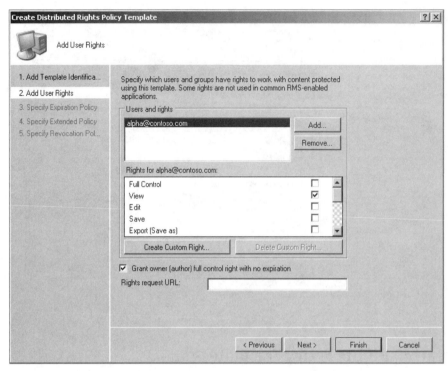

FIGURE 11-9: Add RMS rights.

> When creating rights policy templates, it is best to specify security groups rather than individual users. You can specify an e-mail address on a group's properties page, but it is better to use mail-enabled groups in Microsoft Exchange for this purpose.

6. On the Specify Expiration Policy page, specify whether the content expires, whether it expires after a specific date, or whether it expires after a specific number of days. After content expires, users will be unable to access it anymore.

SUMMARY

EFS is a file-level encryption technology. It allows users to encrypt files for themselves and other users so that they can be accessed only by the people that the files are encrypted to. You can configure both a DRA and a KRA for EFS-encrypted files. A DRA allows anyone that holds the appropriate certificate to read all encrypted files under the scope of the DRA policy. A KRA allows a person that holds the KRA certificate to recover an EFS user's private key and then access files encrypted with that key.

BitLocker is a hard-disk drive encryption technology and a boot integrity protection technology. BitLocker is almost always used on computers that have a TPM chip, though it is possible, using Group Policy, to configure a computer to use BitLocker with a USB startup key. Through Group Policy, you can configure BitLocker keys to be backed up to Active Directory. You can also configure BitLocker to use a DRA, which allows all BitLocker-encrypted drives in the organization to be recovered using a single certificate, rather than having to extract the individual password associated with the volume that you are intending to recover.

AD RMS allows you to configure usage rights for AD RMS-enabled applications, such as Microsoft Exchange and Office. These rights include allowing or blocking users from editing, saving or printing documents or forwarding or replying to e-mail. You can also configure AD RMS-protected content with an expiration policy, which means that the content will not be able to be accessed once it has expired. Expiration can be configured to occur after a specific date or after a specific number of days have passed.

Additional Sources

Active Directory Rights Management Services

http://technet.microsoft.com/en-us/library/cc772403.aspx

BitLocker Drive Encryption

http://technet.microsoft.com/en-us/library/cc731549(WS.10).aspx

Encrypting File System

http://technet.microsoft.com/en-us/library/cc721923(WS.10).aspx

Using Data Recovery Agents with BitLocker

http://technet.microsoft.com/en-us/library/dd875560(WS.10).aspx

CHAPTER 12

Backup and Recovery

Organizations use computers to generate and store data.
Data is a form of organizational memory, from the spreadsheets that track expenditures to the e-mail servers that store communications. Protecting that data and making sure that it is recoverable is important because when an organization loses data, it is as though it has lost part of its memory. Backup and recovery aren't just about ensuring that a server remains available to the people who use it; it is also about ensuring that the organization has a reliable memory.

Windows Server Backup is the backup and restoration utility that ships with Windows Server 2008 and Windows Server 2008 R2. This utility has significant differences from the NTBACKUP utility that shipped with Windows NT4, Windows 2000, and Windows Server 2003. In this chapter, you learn how Windows Server Backup differs from previous backup tools, what the limitations of Windows Server Backup are, and what you can accomplish with Windows Server Backup when it comes to protecting your organization's servers running Windows Server 2008 R2.

USING AND CONFIGURING WINDOWS SERVER BACKUP

Windows Server Backup replaces NTBACKUP, the backup utility that shipped with previous versions of the Windows Server operating system. Windows Server Backup is not an enterprise-level backup utility. You can certainly use it to perform regular, local backups of individual servers, but it should not be used to manage the backups of a large number of critical servers.

Windows Server Backup provides single-server backup and system recovery protection, and it does it well. It differs significantly from NTBACKUP, and, if you are new to Windows Server Backup, you should be aware of the following things:

- ▶ It doesn't allow you to write backup data to or restore backup data from tape drives.

- ▶ It can be configured to write scheduled backup data to local volumes, disks, or remote shared folders.

- ▶ You can't use it to restore data that was backed up using NTBACKUP. Keep in mind that you'll still need to find drivers to get your tape drive running with Windows Server 2008 before you can use this special version of NTBACKUP to recover data from your old backups.

- ▶ You don't directly perform full, differential, and incremental backups anymore. When you perform a full-server backup, the next backup taken stores only the blocks that have changed since the last full-server backup. This enables you to store more backups on a disk than would otherwise be possible if you were performing a traditional file-based, incremental, or differential backup.

- ▶ Backups of volumes are written in VHD format. This means that it is possible to mount backups in Windows Explorer if you want to recover data without running Windows Server Backup.

▶ An enterprise-level backup solution has a monitoring console that enables you to quickly determine whether any of the regular backups done on the servers in your organization have encountered errors.

▶ There is a version of NTBACKUP for Windows Server 2008 R2 (downloadable from Microsoft's website) that allows you to restore data from backups taken using NTBACKUP.

▶ VHD stands for Virtual Hard Disk. VHD can be mounted in Hyper-V or even configured as an operating system boot device.

▶ It is designed to require a minimal amount of administrator intervention after it is configured. After Windows Server Backup is scheduled, full server backups are configured and the service monitors available remaining space. When the backup disk becomes full, the oldest backup is replaced by the newest backup. This means that Windows Server Backup isn't useful as a data archiving tool, but you can set it up to run and know that you'll be able to perform a full-server recovery to the last backup without having to worry about tracking down tapes or other storage devices.

If you are familiar with Windows Server Backup from Windows Server 2008 and figure that not much has changed between Windows Server 2008 and Windows Server 2008 R2, think again. Windows Server Backup in Windows Server 2008 R2 has several features that were not available in Windows Server Backup in the original release of Windows Server 2008. These features include:

▶ The ability to back up individual files and paths from a volume. In the RTM release of Windows Server 2008, the minimum item that you could back up was a full volume.

▶ The ability to exclude individual files and file types from a backup. For example, you can configure Windows Server Backup in Windows Server 2008 R2 to back up an entire volume except for MP3 and AVI files. You could not screen files from a backup in the RTM version of Windows Server Backup.

▶ You can perform scheduled backups to network shares or a specific volume on a disk. The RTM version of Windows Server Backup required that you dedicate an entire local disk as the target for scheduled backups. The drawback of this additional functionality is that if you configure a scheduled backup to be written to a network share, you will have only one backup from which to restore. Each scheduled backup to a network folder always overwrites the previous backup.

▶ The ability to perform a System State only backup as a scheduled job and as a one-off job from the GUI. You could not perform a GUI-based backup of only the System State data using the RTM version of Windows Server Backup, though you could accomplish this from the wbadmin.exe command-line utility.

> **WARNING** You should be aware that Windows Server Backup cannot be used to back up more than 2 TB of data per volume. While it is possible to partition large drives so that they remain under 2 TB in size, if you are looking at backing up this volume of data, you should consider an enterprise backup solution. Given that disks on servers routinely exceed 2 TB in size, the 2 TB limit may be raised in a later Windows Server 2008 R2 service pack.

Installing Windows Server Backup

Many administrators are surprised to find that Windows Server Backup is not installed by default on computers running the Windows Server 2008 R2 operating system. Previous versions of the Windows Server operating system have always come with the NTBACKUP utility, and, to some administrators, having to go to the effort of installing a backup utility, is like having to install Notepad.

Although you can add Windows Server Backup through the Add Features functionality of the Server Manager console, it is often quicker and easier to add features like Windows Server Backup using PowerShell commands. PowerShell commands allow you to accomplish in one or two lines what may take a couple of pages of an installation wizard to accomplish as an alternative.

To install Windows Server Backup using PowerShell, perform the following steps:

1. Open an elevated PowerShell session.

2. Import the Server Manager module with the command:

```
Import-Module ServerManager
```

Remember that to import PowerShell modules, you have to run the Set-ExecutionPolicy Unrestricted command on the server at some point in the past.

3. Install Windows Server Backup with the following command:

```
Add-WindowsFeature Backup-Features,Backup,Backup-Tools
```

Performing a One-Time Backup

Generally with Windows Server Backup, you'll want to set up a scheduled backup and then forget about it until it becomes time to perform a restore. This is one of the best things about Windows Server Backup: no longer worrying about whether or not tapes have been rotated, if you're running out of disk space, or if you should switch from differential to incremental backup. With Windows Server Backup, you just turn it on, and it worries about itself.

One-time backups allow you to back up files, folders, volumes, or the entire server in a one-off action. One-time backups might suit you for compliance and archiving purposes, where you perform a one-time backup of a server once a month and then ship the removable hard-disk drive on which you performed the backup to an off-site location. As Windows Server Backup relies on local storage, you'll need the occasional one-time backup to ensure that you're able to recover in the event that an ice cream truck, or a meteorite, hits your server room.

To perform a single backup of specific items using Windows Server Backup, perform the following steps:

1. Open Windows Server Backup from the Administrative Tools menu.

2. In the Actions pane, click Backup Once. On the Backup Options page of the Backup Once Wizard, verify that Different Options is selected, and then click Next.

3. Choose Custom and click Next.

4. On the Select Items for Backup page, click Add Items.

5. On the Select Items page, place a check next to all the items that you want to back up. Figure 12-1 shows a selection where the e:\Accounting folder is backed up. Click OK.

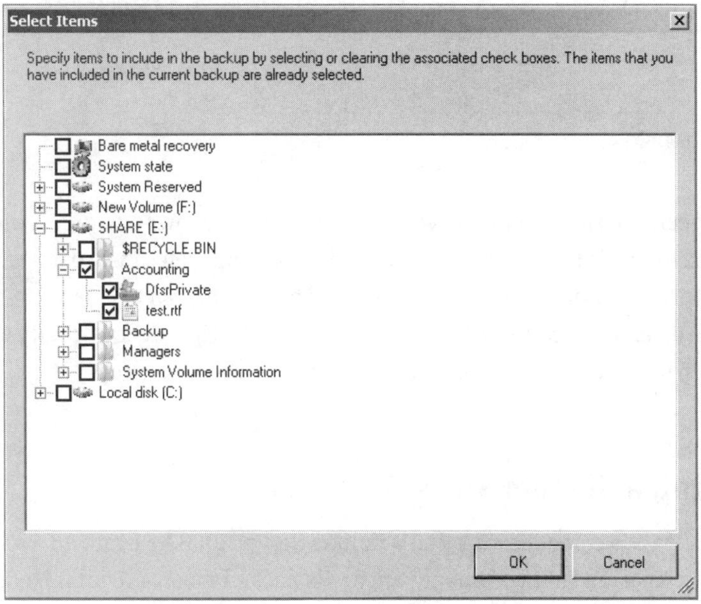

FIGURE 12-1: Select items for a single backup

6. If you want to exclude specific items from the backup, click the Advance Settings button on the Select Items for Backup page of the Backup Once Wizard.

7. On the Exclusions tab, click Add Exclusion to add file type exclusions. Figure 12-2 shows the exclusion of all MP3 files. Click OK, and then click Next.

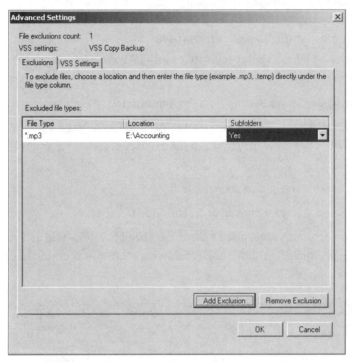

FIGURE 12-2: Add exclusions

8. For Specify Destination Type, you can select either a local drive or a remote shared folder. When performing a one-time backup, you can also use writable optical media as a destination drive, though this isn't generally recommended, as the backup most likely has to span multiple disks. Specify the backup destination volume, click Next, and then click Backup.

Performing a System State Backup

The System State of a computer running Windows Server 2008 R2 contains a lot of important information that you should ensure is backed up on a regular basis. Usually this isn't a problem, as when you perform a full-server backup, the System

State data is automatically included. If you are only backing up files and folders from a server, whether you bother backing up the System State depends on the role the server has in your organization. Depending on the roles installed on the computer running Windows Server 2008 R2, the System State can contain the following items:

- Registry
- COM+ Class Registration database
- Boot files
- Active Directory Certificate Services (AD CS) database
- Active Directory database (ntds.dit)
- SYSVOL directory
- Cluster service information
- Microsoft Internet Information Services (IIS) metadirectory
- System files under Windows Resource Protection

To perform a System State only backup from Windows Server Backup, ensure that you select the System State item in the Select Items dialog box, as shown in Figure 12-3.

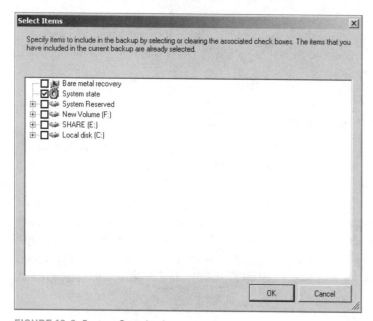

FIGURE 12-3: System State backup

You can quickly perform a System State backup from the command line using the WBADMIN command. For example, to perform a backup of a server's System State to the network share \\storage\backup, run the following command from an elevated command prompt or PowerShell session:

```
Wbadmin START SYSTEMSTATEBACKUP -backuptarget:\\storage\backup
```

Backing Up an Application

When you perform a full-server backup, Windows Server Backup takes specific note of certain applications that have registered themselves with the service. An example of an application that registers itself with Windows Server Backup is Exchange Server 2010. When you perform a full-server backup of a server that hosts an application that has registered itself with Windows Server Backup, Windows Server Backup retains separate catalog information about those files. This means that during recovery, it is possible to restore just the data related to that application.

When you perform a custom backup, you are not given the option of just backing up the application. Applications that have registered themselves with Windows Server Backup are backed up automatically. You only have the option to separately restore applications if the application has registered itself with Windows Server Backup. It is important to note that not all applications have this functionality, though it is becoming increasingly prevalent in Microsoft server-based applications, such as the System Center and ForeFront Suites. You learn about recovering applications later in this chapter.

Creating a Scheduled Backup Job

▶ When people who worked in IT at small- and medium-sized businesses were quizzed about whether their backups were up-to-date, one of the most common excuses given for not having recent backups was the hassle involved in managing backup tapes.

Windows Server Backup excels at providing you with a quick, full-server recovery option in the event that you lose the hard-disk drive hosting the operating system. You turn on a scheduled, full-server backup as a daily task and the architecture of Windows Server Backup ensures that this backup will continue to be taken, with the oldest backup data being replaced by the newest, but always in such a way that a full-server recovery is possible (assuming you don't do something silly like store backup data on the same physical disk as the operating system!). Windows Server Backup provides you with a "set it up and forget it" recovery solution. The only time you need to really think about backup with Windows Server Backup is when it comes time to perform a recovery.

To create a scheduled job that ensures you have an up-to-date set of backups from which to recover, perform the following steps:

1. Ensure you have a disk that you can dedicate to storing backup data. This disk should be able to hold approximately 2.5 times the size of the current total amount of data stored on the server. This disk can be mounted internally or attached by USB, eSATA or FireWire cable.

2. Open Windows Server Backup from the Administrative Tools menu.

3. In the Actions pane, click Backup Schedule. This opens the Backup Schedule Wizard. On the Getting Started page, click Next.

4. On the Select Backup Configuration page, choose Full Server, and then click Next.

5. On the Specify Backup Time page, select when you want the backup to occur. You can specify a backup to be taken at multiple times during the day, though the more backups that are taken, the smaller your restoration window will be. If you want to take more than one backup each day but keep a large restoration window, attach a really big hard disk to the server to store backups.

6. Choose your backup destination on the dialog shown in Figure 12-4. You can back up to a dedicated hard disk, which is recommended because it protects you against the failure of one of the hard disks that hosts your operating system or data files. You can also back up to a volume on an existing disk; though, because of performance issues, this isn't recommended, as the same disk could host other volumes that store important data, and, if that disk fails, you'll be in trouble. Although it is possible to perform a scheduled backup to a network share, each backup overwrites the previous backup, and you can restore data only from the previous backup.

7. If you have chosen the dedicated hard-disk option, you are asked to select which hard disk stores the backups. This disk is wiped of all current data and is used only to store backup data from Windows Server Backup.

8. Review your settings and click Finish.

In the future, when you click Backup Schedule, you will have the chance to modify the settings of this job. You can change any of the settings, from what gets backed up to where it gets backed up when modifying the backup schedule. This is because you can use Windows Server Backup to schedule only one backup job. You

▶ Consider doing bi-weekly, one-off backups of critical servers and storing those backups on separate, removable storage devices. Take those separate devices off-site and keep the dedicated disk connected to the server for scheduled backups.

▶ You won't be able to see this disk from within Windows Explorer anymore, as it is directly visible only to Windows Server Backup.

cannot use Windows Server Backup to schedule one job that backs up one set of items to one location and another job that backs up a different set of items to an alternate location.

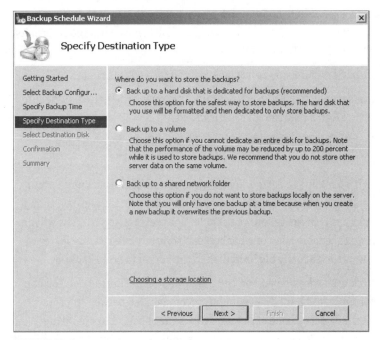

FIGURE 12-4: Backup destination

Optimizing Backup Performance

You can optimize backup performance for Windows Server Backup by opening the Windows Server Backup console and clicking on the Configure Performance Settings item in the Actions pane. Doing so launches the Optimize Backup Performance dialog shown in Figure 12-5.

Through this dialog box, you can configure the following settings:

▶ **Normal Backup Performance:** When you select this option, all backups created are full backups, but additional space used is only for data blocks that have changed since the last full backup on the source volumes. Windows Server Backup creates a separate full backup every 14 days that includes all blocks from the source volumes, not just changed blocks.

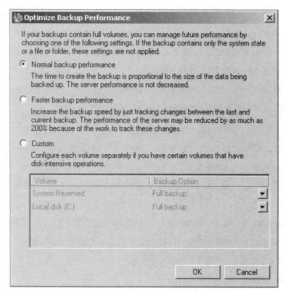

FIGURE 12-5: Optimize backup performance

▶ **Faster Backup Performance:** This option uses a shadow copy on the source volumes to track changes since the last full backup. Rather than transferring and calculating which blocks are different since the last full backup, this data already exists separately within the shadow copy, so the backup occurs more quickly. The drawback of this option is that enabling shadow copies does degrade disk write performance on the source volume, which might have a detrimental effect on volumes that have a lot of data written to them.

▶ **Custom:** Using this setting allows you to configure different volumes to use either normal or faster backup performance settings.

Modifying the Optimizing Backup Performance settings applies only when you are performing backups of full volumes. If you are just backing up a couple of folders or the System State, this does not have an impact.

ENABLING SHADOW COPIES OF SHARED FOLDERS

The idea behind Shadow Copies of Shared Folders is to get users to perform a lot of the file recovery tasks that, up until now, have had to be performed by support staff.

When Microsoft researched the sort of tasks that support staff spent time on, they found that file recovery consumed a significant fraction of support hours. When they investigated further, they found that the vast majority of file restorations performed by support staff involved files that had become deleted or corrupted in the last week. By giving users the ability to recover their own files, users get their files recovered more quickly, and the IT support desk can concentrate on other tasks.

Shadow Copies of Shared Folders is enabled on a per volume basis. When you enable Shadow Copies of Shared Folders on a volume, it enables Shadow Copies of Shared Folders for all shared folders on that volume. There is a maximum of 64 shadow copies per volume. When the limit is reached, the oldest copy is deleted. Keep this 64 limit in mind when deciding on the schedule to create shadow copies. You can have one copy generated every day for 64 days or two every day for 32 days. The more frequently you create shadow copies, the less data people lose when they have to recover a file, but the cost of this is a smaller recovery window.

> ▶ Enabling Shadow Copies of Shared Folders on a volume leads to a decrease in write performance on that volume.

To enable Shadow Copies of Shared Folders for a share, perform the following steps:

1. Open the Share and Storage Management console.

2. On the Shares tab, determine the volume that hosts the Share for which you want to enable Shadow Copies of Shared Folders.

3. On the Volumes tab, select the volume that hosts the share. On the Actions pane, click Properties. This displays the Volume Properties dialog box.

4. Click the Shadow Copies tab and click Enable. Review the performance warning, and then click Yes.

5. Click Settings. This opens the Shadow Copies of Shared Folders Settings dialog, which is shown in Figure 12-6. It enables you to configure the maximum amount of space consumed by shadow copies as well as how often shadow copies are made.

6. Click Schedule to create a new schedule for how often shadow copies are created. The default schedule has shadow copies being created at 7am and 12pm every weekday. You can add additional shadow copies creation events or modify the existing schedule.

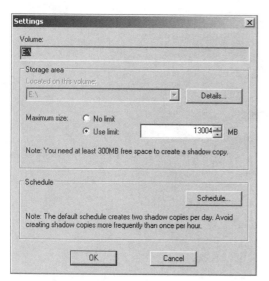

FIGURE 12-6: Shadow Copies of Shared Folder Settings

The trick to Shadow Copies of Shared Folders is not implementing the infrastructure. This is relatively simple. The trick is training your users to be able to recover their own files from shared folders on volumes that support Shadow Copies of Shared Folders. You can do this by creating a document outlining the procedure and then having the support desk walk users through the procedure whenever they need to recover a file or folder. The procedure should include the following general steps:

1. On your computer, navigate to the parent folder that hosted the file or folder that you want to recover. Right-click on this folder, and then click Restore Previous Versions.

2. This opens the folder's Properties dialog box on the Previous Versions tab, which appears similar to what is shown in Figure 12-7. Select the snapshot version of the folder taken prior to the event that required you to perform a restore, and then click Open.

3. Locate the file that you want to restore, right-click on that file, and then click Copy. Paste the file to your Desktop and verify that its contents meet your needs. Once you have verified that the file does meet your needs, close the folder's Properties dialog box and return the file to the shared folder where it was originally located.

▶ The most effective method of quickly educating users how to restore their own files is a short video using screen capture software like Camtasia Studio. Video works better than a checklist of how to accomplish the same task.

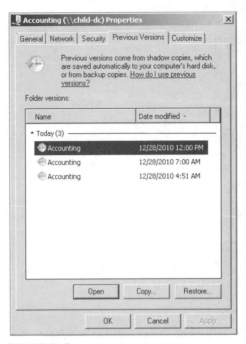

FIGURE 12-7: Previous Versions dialog

PERFORMING RECOVERY

Recovery is a bit like house insurance—something that's nice to have but something you hope you will not have to use. Just as backup has been simplified in the Windows Server Backup application, so has the process of recovery. One of the greatest advantages of performing recovery with Windows Server Backup is that, because it doesn't rely on tapes, you don't have to hunt around the server room to find the right combination of full and incremental backups when you want to restore data. All of your backup data is in one place, and recovery is just a matter of clicking on the right items in a wizard.

Recovering Files and Folders

The most common type of recovery that a systems administrator has to perform is the recovery of the accidentally deleted file or folders. While hard-disk drive and server technology has become more reliable over the decade and a half since the release of Windows NT 4, people's propensity to accidentally delete important data has remained the same. True, from time to time, files become hopelessly infected by malware or become corrupt and need to be restored from backup, but you are far more likely to have to perform a recovery because a user has deleted an important file than you are because a user has caused a file to become infected with a nasty malware.

The first thing that you should do prior to attempting to recover files and folders is to check whether or not you can recover the items by using the Previous Versions functionality. If you've enabled Previous Versions functionality and the items that you want to recover were only recently deleted, it is likely that you'll be able to recover them through an existing shadow copy. Remember, items exist as shadow copies even when they've been deleted from the volume that hosts them. If you are having trouble finding the items, start at the volume level and work your way down the tree.

To recover specific files and folders, perform the following general steps:

1. Open Windows Server Backup, and then click Recover in the Actions pane.

2. On the Getting Started pane, select the location of the backup, and then click Next.

3. On the Select Backup Date page, select the date from which you want to recover, and then click Next.

4. On the Select Recovery Type page, select Files and Folders, and then click Next.

5. On the Select Items to Recover dialog box, as shown in Figure 12-8, expand the items to locate the files and folders that you want to recover, and then click Next.

▶ Minimize the chance that you'll overwrite something important and always restore to an alternate location. Don't overwrite files and folders at the original location.

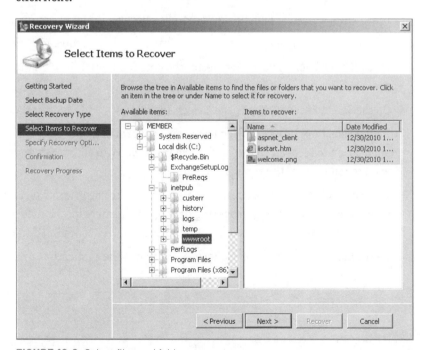

FIGURE 12-8: Select files and folders to recover

▶ In general, it is a
good idea to recover
permissions.

6. On the Specify Recovery Options page, choose whether to recover to the original location or to an alternate location. In both instances, you can choose
whether or not you restore the NTFS permissions assigned to the files and
folders that you are recovering. If you choose to recover to the original location, you can select between one of the following options:

  ▷ Create copies so you have both versions.

  ▷ Overwrite the existing versions with the recovered versions.

  ▷ Do not recover items that exist on the recovery destination.

7. On the Confirmation page, click Recover.

Recovering Applications

You can use Windows Server Backup to recover applications separate from the recovery
of files and folders. As you learned earlier, certain newer applications, like Exchange
Server 2010, register themselves with Windows Server Backup. When they do this,
they provide information to the backup service about which data needs to be backed
up to allow the application to be recovered in its entirety.

To recover an application, perform the following general steps:

1. Open Windows Server Backup, and then click Recover in the Actions pane.

2. On the Getting Started pane, select the location of the backup and click Next.

3. On the Select Backup Date page, select the date from which you want to
   recover, and then click Next.

4. On the Select Recovery Type page, select Applications, and then click Next.

5. On the Select Application to Recover page, as shown in Figure 12-9, select the
   application to recover. In the case of Exchange, you can choose whether you
   want to roll forward the application database.

6. You have the option of recovering the application to the original location or
   to an alternate location. Recovering data to an alternate location does not
   recover the application to this location, just the relevant application data.

7. On the Confirmation page, click Recover to recover the application.

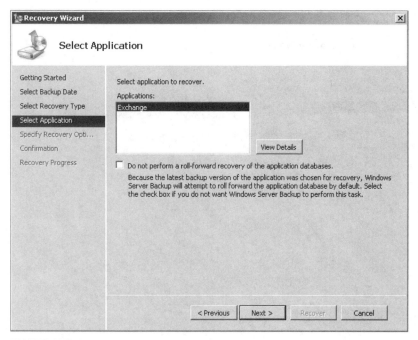

FIGURE 12-9: Restore application

Recovering the System State

In some cases, such as when you want to perform an authoritative restore of Active Directory or when you want to restore the Certificate Services database, you want to restore the System State of a computer running Windows Server 2008 R2 without recovering the entire server. You do this by performing a System State recovery.

To recover the System State data using Windows Server Backup, perform the following steps:

1. Open Windows Server Backup, and then click Recover in the Actions pane.

2. On the Getting Started pane, select the location of the backup and click Next.

3. On the Select Backup Date page, select the date from which you want to recover, and then click Next.

4. On the Select Recovery Type page, select System State, as shown in Figure 12-10, and then click Next.

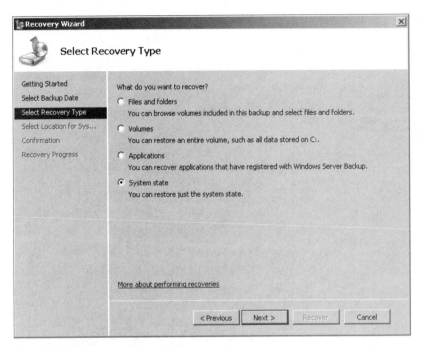

FIGURE 12-10: Recover System State

5. Choose to recover the System State data to the original location, which necessitates a reboot of the computer, or to an alternate location. You might want to recover the System State data to an alternate location when you want to mount a previous instance of Active Directory to verify that it contains the correct version of objects that you want to recover prior to attempting a restore.

6. On the Confirmation page, click Recover to perform the recovery.

You can also use the WBADMIN command-line utility to recover System State data. Prior to doing this, you need to know which versions of the System State data have been backed up. You can determine this by running the command:

```
WBADMIN get versions
```

Figure 12-11 shows a version identified as 12/28/2010-01:20, which includes System State data, can be restored.

To recover this System State backup to the local server and then perform a reboot after the recovery has completed, run the command:

```
WBADMIN START SystemStateRecovery -version:12/28/2010-01:20 -autoreboot
```

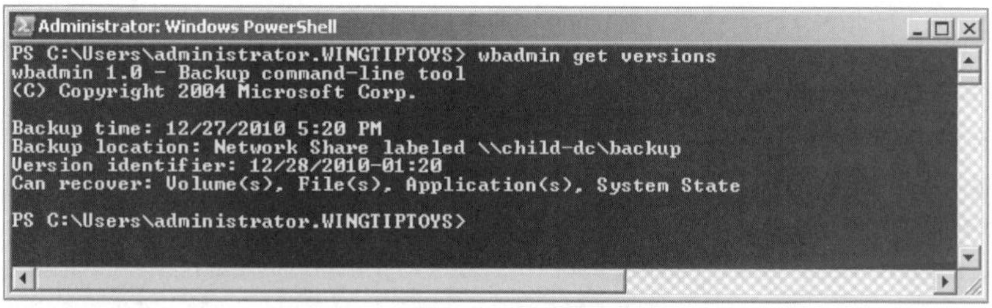

FIGURE 12-11: Backup versions

If you want to restore a System State backup from another location, use the backupTarget parameter to specify the location. For example, if the version desired is located on the server at \\storage\backup, you would issue the command:

```
WBADMIN Start SystemStateRecovery -version:12/28/2010-01:20
-backupTarget:\\storage\backup -autoreboot
```

Recovering Backup Catalog

The backup catalog contains information about backups that have been taken. When you begin to perform a recovery, the backup catalog is queried to allow you to determine what you can recover. In some cases this information is lost and you need to recover the backup catalog. When this happens, Windows Server Backup provides you with a warning that the catalog is missing or corrupted. You can recover backup catalogs from previous full-server backups.

To recover a backup catalog, perform the following steps:

1. Open Windows Server Backup and click Recover Catalog.

▶ The Recover Catalog item is present only if the current catalog is corrupt.

2. On the Specify Storage Type page, choose between Local Drives and Remote Shared Folder, depending on the location of the available backup. Specify the location of the backup from which you will recover the catalog. As an alternative, if you just want to delete the corrupt catalog, click the I Do Not Have Any Usable Backups item.

3. On the Confirmation page, click Finish to recover or delete the catalog.

You can also use the WBADMIN command-line utility to restore a catalog. For example, if you want to restore a backup catalog from the share \\storage\backup, use the command:

```
WBADMIN RESTORE CATALOG -backupTarget:\\storage\backup
```

Recovering a Server or Operating System

You perform a full-server recovery in the event that the server operating system somehow becomes so corrupted that it is simpler to roll back to a working version of the operating system than it is to undo whatever has gone wrong with the server. Bare metal recovery, covered later in this chapter, differs from full-server recovery in that, during bare metal recovery, you boot from the operating system media, whereas during server recovery, you still boot off the hard-disk drive.

Although it is possible to perform a full-system restore over the network, this process is time intensive. It is far quicker to copy the backed up system image to a removable storage device and connect that removable storage device to the computer that you want to recover, than it is to perform a full-server recovery over even a gigabit network. In some circumstances, however, this may not be practical.

To perform a full-server recovery, perform the following steps:

1. Reboot the computer and press F8. This displays the Advanced Boot Options menu shown in Figure 12-12. Select Repair Your Computer, and then press Enter.

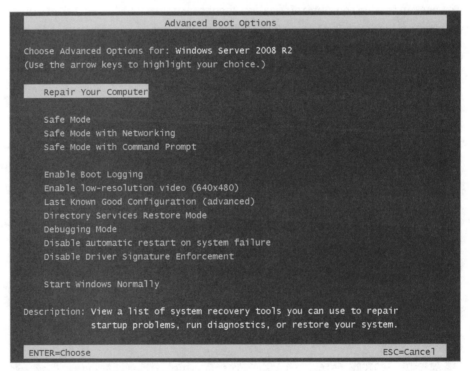

FIGURE 12-12: Repair Your Computer

2. On the System Recovery Options dialog, select your keyboard language, and then click Next.

3. On the System Recovery Options dialog, enter the password of a local administrator account. This is only necessary when performing a full-server recovery from the Repair Your Computer option. This is not necessary when performing a bare metal recovery.

4. On the Choose a Recovery Tool dialog, shown in Figure 12-13, click System Image Recovery.

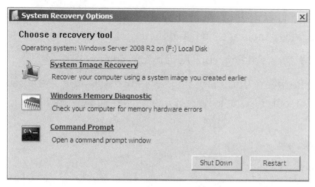

FIGURE 12-13: Choose a Recovery Tool

5. On the Select a System Image Backup, you can choose to restore the most recent image or select from a list of backed up system images. If you want to restore an image from a network location, you need to use the Select a System Image option and then click Advanced. You then need to provide credentials and the location of a network share that holds a copy of the system image you want to restore.

6. Depending on the recovery, you have the option of formatting and repartitioning disks and/or restoring only the system drives. Selecting the latter option leaves data volumes intact but restores the volumes' hosting operating system data. You can also load any drivers for the disks that may be required in the event that the disks haven't been automatically detected.

7. How long the restore process takes depends entirely on how much data needs to be restored. As the data is being restored from disk, the restoration process is much quicker than it would have been if it had occurred from tape. If all goes well, the server can reboot at the end of the restoration process.

▶ When performing full-server recovery, restore from the most recent image. An exception is when you know a server has become irrecoverably corrupt by malware and you want to wipe the server clean, returning it to a state that is free of infection.

Performing Bare Metal Recovery

Bare metal recovery is similar to full-server recovery except the hardware chassis on which you are recovering the operating system does not have an existing operating system installed, either because you are restoring to a brand new disk or a completely new and fresh server. To perform bare metal recovery, you need to do the following:

1. Boot from the installation media of the operating system that you want to restore.

2. At the Install Windows dialog, select your language, time and currency format, and keyboard or input method, and then click Next.

3. On the Install Windows dialog, click Repair Your Computer.

4. On the System Recovery Options dialog, as shown in Figure 12-14, select Restore Your Computer Using a System Image That You Create Earlier, and then click Next.

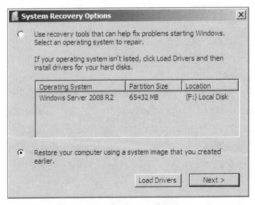

FIGURE 12-14: System Recovery Options

5. From this point, the recovery process is the same as that outlined from step 5 of a full-server recovery. You can perform a bare metal recovery from a network folder, choose whether to overwrite specific volumes, and choose whether you want to format or repartition disks, as shown in Figure 12-15.

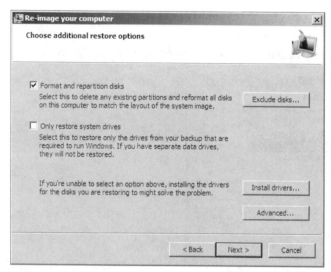

FIGURE 12-15: Additional restore options

USING SYSTEM CENTER DATA PROTECTION MANAGER

If you need to back up a large number of servers and have data archiving requirements, you need to move beyond using Windows Server Backup and start using an
enterprise-level data protection product. Enterprise-level data protection products
offer features not available in Windows Server Backup, including multiple server protection and recovery, data archiving and deduplication functionality. System Center
Data Protection Manager is Microsoft's enterprise backup solution. Like most enterprise-level backup solutions, Data Protection Manager (DPM) is designed with a cli-
ent-server architecture. This means you install the DPM client on each computer that
you want to protect and then use one or more DPM servers to back up those clients.
Each DPM server is connected to its own storage array on which it can store backups.
You can also connect a tape drive to the DPM server—though tape drives are almost
exclusively used for data archiving purposes—allowing you to regularly move tapes
to a secure, off-site location to ensure compliance with data archiving regulations.

To configure System Center Data Protection Manager 2010 to protect a server, perform the following general steps:

1. Open the System Center Data Protection Manager (DPM) console.

2. The first thing you need to do is provision storage. This is where server backups
   are stored. Click the Management item in the Ribbon, and then click the Disks
   tab. In the Actions menu, click Add. On the Add Disks to Storage Pool dialog,

shown in Figure 12-16, select and then add disks to the storage pool. You receive a warning that any disks added to the storage pool will be converted to dynamic disks and any existing volumes will be converted to simple volumes.

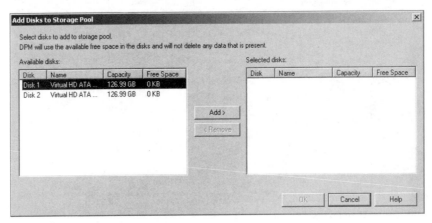

FIGURE 12-16: Add disks to storage pool

3. After you have provisioned storage, you need to install the DPM agent on the servers you wish to protect. To do this, click the Agents tab and then click on Install. This launches the Protection Agent Installation Wizard. Select Install Agents for Computers in the Same Domain, and then click Next.

4. Select, by name, the computers on which you wish to add the DPM agent. Figure 12-17 shows that the DPM agent will be deployed to the computer named DC. Next, provide credentials for a user account that is authorized to install software on the target computers and then determine whether or not you want to manually or automatically restart the target computers should it be necessary. Click Install to deploy the DPM agent and review the results of that deployment.

5. When the DPM agent is successfully installed, you need to create a protection group and add the server with the agent on it to the protection group. To accomplish this goal, click the Protection item in the Ribbon, and in the Actions pane, click Create Protection Group. This launches the Create New Protection Group Wizard.

6. On the Select Protection Group Type page, choose between creating a server and a client protection group. On the Select Group Members page, select the computers that you want to protect. Figure 12-18 shows that all shares, volumes, and the system for server DC are protected. Provide the protection group with a name. You can configure long-term protection using tape if you have installed a tape drive on the server running DPM; otherwise, you can configure short-term protection using disk.

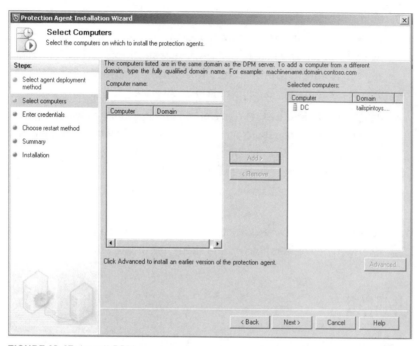

FIGURE 12-17: Install DPM agent

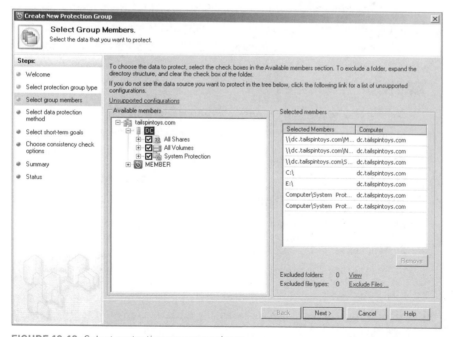

FIGURE 12-18: Select protection group members

7. On the Specify Short-term Goals page, specify how long you want data to be retained and how often you want data to be synchronized. The default is a five-day retention range with a 15-minute synchronization. This means that you can restore data on a protected server to a recovery point within 15 minutes of the failure that triggered the recovery.

8. On the Choose Replica Creation Method dialog, choose how you want the initial synchronization of data to occur. You can schedule it to occur immediately or at a later date. Replica creation generates a complete copy of the computer to be protected. In most organizations, you'd configure this to occur at some time in the morning after 2am because this minimizes its impact on protection network traffic.

9. Configure DPM to run a consistency check whenever a replica becomes inconsistent, review the summary, and then click Create Group.

SUMMARY

Windows Server Backup is a lightweight backup utility that allows you to set up a regular, scheduled backup to a locally attached storage device. It allows you to perform a full-server, volume, application, System State, and file- and folder-level recovery. You should enable shadow copies of shared folders on file servers, as accidentally deleted items from shared folders are the items that IT departments must most often restore.

Additional Sources

Backup and Recovery Overview for Windows Server 2008 R2
http://technet.microsoft.com/en-us/library/dd979562(WS.10).aspx

Recovering the Operating System or Full Server
http://technet.microsoft.com/en-us/library/cc755163.aspx

Shadow Copies of Shared Folders
http://technet.microsoft.com/en-us/library/cc771305.aspx

System Center Data Protection Manager TechCenter
http://technet.microsoft.com/en-us/systemcenter/dm/default

Wbadmin
http://technet.microsoft.com/en-us/library/cc754015(WS.10).aspx

Windows Server Backup Cmdlets in Windows PowerShell
http://technet.microsoft.com/en-us/library/ee706683.aspx

PART IV

INFRASTRUCTURE SERVICES

Internet Information Services

Internet Information Services (IIS) 7.5 is Windows Server 2008 R2's built-in Web and FTP server platform. Many organizations use IIS to host both their public facing website as well as internal intranet services. IIS also supports many different roles, from Outlook Web Access in Exchange Server deployments through to SharePoint, Windows Server Update Services, and Certificate Services Web enrollment.

In this chapter, you learn about how to perform Web server administration tasks, from basic tasks such as configuring new websites and virtual directories, to more advanced topics such as configuring application pool recycling settings, setting FTP sessions to require SSL, and delegating administrative privileges.

MANAGING SITES

You perform website management in IIS 7.5 through the IIS Manager console. This console, which first appeared in Windows Server 2008, is substantially different than previous IIS management tools, which stayed relatively unchanged from Windows NT 4 through Windows Server 2003. The key to understanding the IIS Manager console, shown in Figure 13-1, is that when you select a particular node in the Connections pane, such as the Web server itself, the Applications Pool node, or individual websites, you are presented with a Details pane that allows you to configure items depending on the configuration node selected. For example, if you open the Authentication node at the Server level, it configures authentication options for the server. If you have a specific website selected, opening the same Authentication item configures authentication for only that website. If you want to configure an item and the item isn't present, you need to verify that the relevant role service is installed.

▶ Unlike previous versions of the Web server, in IIS 7.5 specific configuration items are present only when the appropriate role service is installed, and many items commonly used in previous IIS versions are not installed by default.

FIGURE 13-1: IIS Manager console

Adding a Website

The only practical limit for the number of websites that a server that runs IIS 7.5 can host is hardware-related. Although you can probably run 10,000 different sites off the same computer, the hardware needed to support that number of sites so that they run in a fast and responsive manner is prohibitively expensive.

To run more than one site on IIS 7.5, the sites need to be different in one of the following ways:

▶ **Unique IP address:** You can configure a different site for each IP address associated with the server. Although this isn't useful when you use one of the limited supply of IPv4 addresses, it is useful when it comes to the more plentiful IPv6 addresses. You can use IP address differentiation to ensure that website traffic utilizes a specific network adapter.

▶ **Hostname:** If your server runs IIS 7.5 and has only one IP address, you can still run multiple sites. You just need to ensure that each site uses a unique hostname. IIS 7.5 parses the hostname in the HTTP request and directs the client to the appropriate site.

▶ **Port number:** You can also configure different sites that use the same IP address and hostname by assigning them different port addresses. The port address is a less popular way of differentiating websites, because, although it is an effective technique, most people have difficulty remembering to add a separate port address to a URL.

To add a website to an existing server, perform the following steps:

1. Open the IIS Manager console from the Administrative Tools menu.

2. Right-click on the Server node, and then click Add Web Site.

3. On the Add Web Site dialog box, shown in Figure 13-2, enter the following information:

   ▷ **Site name:** The name that represents the site on the server.

   ▷ **Application pool:** The application pool with which the site is associated. The default settings create a new application pool for each new site. You can click the Select button to select a different application pool.

   ▷ **Physical path:** Where the website files are stored. You can configure site files to be stored on a remote network share. When you do this, you need to specify the authentication credentials used to connect to the network share. The default credentials use the Web user's identity, so you'll need to configure authentication settings if you aren't using a specific account

   ▷ **Type:** Allows you to specify whether the site uses HTTP or HTTPS.

▷ **IP address:** Determines whether the site uses all unassigned IP addresses or a specific IP address assigned to the server.

▷ **Port:** Determines whether the site uses the default port 80 or 443 for HTTPS sites.

▷ **Host name:** The hostname associated with the site.

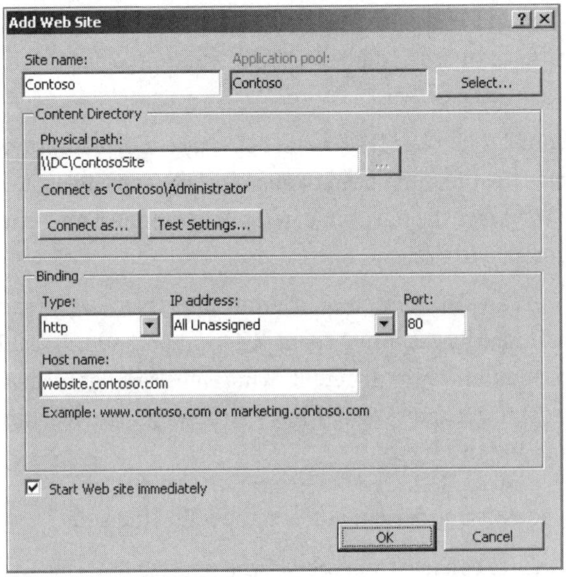

FIGURE 13-2: Add Web Site.

To create a site using AppCmd.exe, the IIS 7.5 command-line administration utility, use the following syntax:

```
Appcmd.exe add site /name:sitename /physicalPath:path /bindings:string
```

▶ AppCmd .exe is located in the \Windows\ System32\inetsrv directory. This directory is not part of the standard path environment variable. You need to modify the path environment variable if you end up using AppCmd .exe on a regular basis.

For example, to create a site named Fabrikam, the path C:\Fabrikam and the HTTP protocol on port 80 associated with the hostname www.fabrikam.com, issue the following command:

```
Appcmd.exe add site /name:fabrikam /
physicalPath:c:\fabrikam /
bindings:http/*:80:www.fabrikam.com
```

To view a list of sites on a server, run the following command:

```
APPCMD.exe list sites
```

Adding Virtual Directories

You use *virtual directories* when you want to create a directory on the website that does not map to a corresponding folder in the existing website folder structure. For example, the site www.fabrikam.com might map to the c:\fabrikam folder on a computer running IIS 7.5. If you create the folder c:\fabrikam\products, people can access that folder by navigating to the URL www.fabrikam.com/products. Instead, if you put the Products folder on another volume, you can use a virtual directory to map the URL www.fabrikam.com/products to that alternate location.

To add a virtual directory using the IIS Manager console, perform the following steps:

1. Open the IIS Manager console and navigate to the site for which you wish to add the virtual directory.

2. Right-click on the site, and then click Add Virtual Directory.

3. In the Add Virtual Directory dialog box, shown in Figure 13-3, enter the alias for the virtual directory and the path to the virtual directory. If specifying a remote network share, you can configure which account is used to connect to that share.

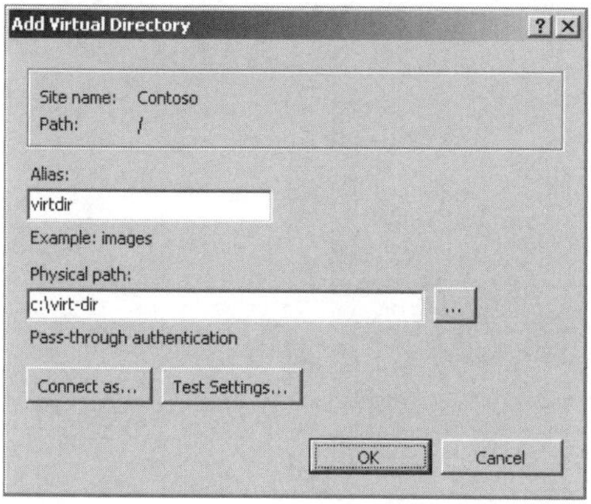

FIGURE 13-3: Add Virtual Directory.

To add a virtual directory using AppCmd.exe, you need to know what application is associated with a particular site. You can find this by running the following command:

```
Appcmd.exe list apps
```

In general, the application name is the same as the site name, but with a slash (/) after it. To add a virtual directory named alpha to the website Contoso with the path c:\alpha, use the following command:

```
Appcmd.exe add vdir /app.name:Contoso/ /path:/alpha /
physicalPath:c:\alpha
```

After you create a website, you can change the settings of the site by viewing its advanced settings, as shown in Figure 13-4. This can be done by clicking on the site in the IIS Manager console and then clicking the Advanced Settings item in the Actions pane.

FIGURE 13-4: Advanced website settings

Adding Web Applications

A *Web application* is a collection of content, either at a website's top level or in a separate folder under the website's top level. Applications can be collected together in application pools. Application pools allow you to isolate one or more applications in a collection. When you create a website, it automatically creates a Web application associated with that website. This Web application has the same name as the website.

To create a Web application, perform the following steps:

1. Open the IIS Manager console and navigate to the site for which you want to create a Web application.

2. Right-click on the site, and then click on Add Application.

3. In the Add Application dialog, shown in Figure 13-5, enter the alias of the application, choose which application pool the application is a member of, and specify the path to the application on the server.

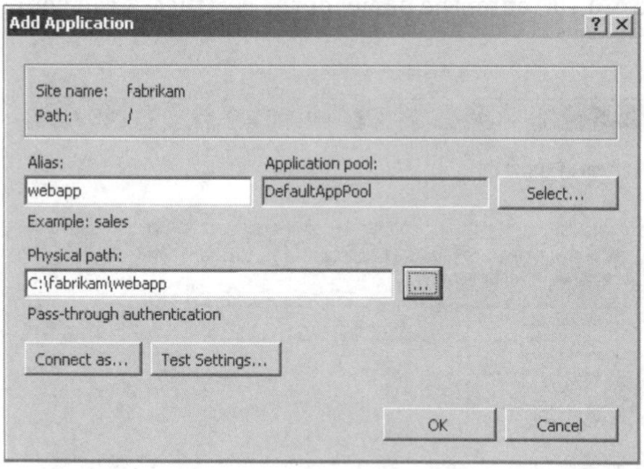

FIGURE 13-5: Add Web Application.

To add a Web application using AppCmd.exe, use the following syntax:

```
Appcmd.exe add app /site.name:websitename /path:websitepath /
physicalPath:Folderpath
```

For example, to add a Web application in the location www.fabrikam.com/webapp associated with the c:\fabrikam\webapp folder, issue the following command:

```
Appcmd.exe add app /site.name:fabrikam /path:/webapp /physicalPath:c:\
fabrikam\webapp
```

Configuring SSL Certificates

SSL certificates allow clients to both encrypt their session with the Web server, minimizing the chance that communication between the client and the server can be intercepted, and serve as an identity verification mechanism. You can configure SSL to be required at the server, site, Web application, virtual directory, folder, and file level.

The first step you need to take prior to requiring SSL on a particular site is to request and then install a certificate. To do this, perform the following steps:

1. Open the IIS Manager console, select the Server node, and then double-click on the Server Certificates item in the Details pane.

2. Click the Create Certificate Request item. In the Request Certificate dialog box, shown in Figure 13-6, enter the name for the certificate and your organization's details.

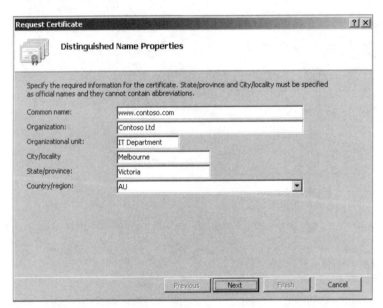

FIGURE 13-6: Create certificate request.

3. On the Cryptographic Service Provider Properties page, enter the cryptographic service provider and the key length that you wish to use for the SSL certificate and then click Next.

4. Enter a name for the certificate request file. After the certificate request file is created, forward it to a CA.

▶ As an alternative, you can use the Create Domain Certificate to request a certificate from an enterprise CA.

5. After the certificate has been issued, open the Server Certificates item, and then click Complete Certificate Request.

6. On the Specify Certificate Authority Response page of the Complete Certificate Request Wizard, specify the location of the certificate issued by the CA and a friendly name with which to identify the certificate, and then click OK. This installs the certificate.

After the certificate is installed, you can configure the site, virtual directory, folder, or file to request or require SSL. To accomplish this goal, perform the following steps:

1. In IIS Manager, select the site on which you wish to configure SSL.

2. Click Edit Bindings, and then click Add. In the Add Site Binding dialog box, ensure that HTTPs is selected on the Type drop-down menu and the SSL certificate that you installed is selected on the SSL certificate drop-down menu, as shown in Figure 13-7.

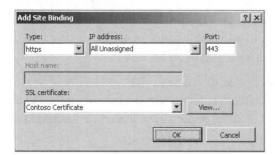

FIGURE 13-7: Add site binding.

3. Select the site, virtual directory, folder, or file on which you wish to enforce SSL settings.

4. Double-click on the SSL Settings item in the Details pane.

5. On the SSL Settings page, ensure that Require SSL is selected, and then click Apply.

Configuring Site Authentication

Authentication methods determine how a user authenticates with a server or a website. You can configure authentication at the server level or at the site level. If there is a conflict between the authentication methods configured at the server and the site level, then the site-level authentication settings have precedence.

▶ **Active Directory Client Certificate:** This form of authentication works by checking client certificates. These are almost always issued by an internal certificate authority.

▶ **Anonymous Authentication:** This is the most typical form of authentication for a Web server. Clients can access the web page without entering credentials.

▶ **ASP.NET Impersonation:** Use ASP.NET impersonation when it is necessary to execute an ASP.NET application under a different security context.

▶ **Basic Authentication:** Basic authentication works with all web browsers, but has the drawback of transmitting unencrypted base64-encoded passwords across the network. If you use Basic Authentication, you should also configure the site to require an encrypted SSL connection.

▶ **Digest Authentication:** Digest authentication occurs against a Domain Controller and is used when you want to authenticate clients that may be accessing content through a proxy, something that can be problematic for clients if you configure a server to use Windows authentication.

▶ **Forms Authentication:** This method is used when you redirect users to a custom web page on which they enter their credentials. Once they've been authenticated, they are returned to the page that they were attempting to browse.

▶ **Windows Authentication:** Use this method for Intranet sites when you want clients to authenticate using Kerberos or NTLM. It works best when client computers are members of the same forest as the computer hosting the Web server role.

Remember that you need to disable Anonymous authentication if you want to force clients to use a different authentication method. Web browsers always request content from a server anonymously the first time you attempt to access content. If Anonymous authentication is enabled, other forms of authentication are ignored. To enable a specific form of authentication for a website, perform the following steps:

1. Open the IIS Manager console from the Administrative Tools menu.
2. Click the Web server node. In the Content pane, scroll down, and then double-click on the Authentication item.

▶ Unlike previous versions of Windows, where you enabled authentication methods through a checkbox, in IIS 7.5, you can enable only authentication methods that you've installed. If you can't see the method you're looking for, you probably haven't installed it!

3. On the list of available authentication technologies, shown in Figure 13-8, click the authentication technology that you want to enable, and then click Enable in the Actions pane.

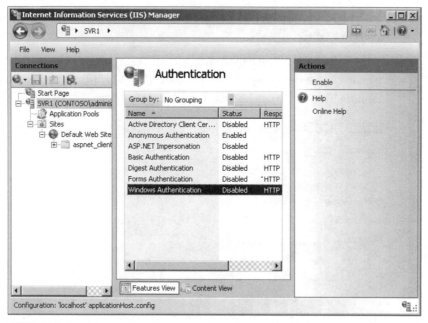

FIGURE 13-8: Configure authentication.

You can configure authentication options using AppCmd.exe. For example, to enable Windows authentication on the default website using AppCmd.exe, issue the following commands:

```
appcmd unlock config /section:windowsAuthentication
appcmd set config "default website" /
section:windowsAuthentication /enabled:true
```

Modifying Custom Error Response

Many sites customize their error responses so that users are provided with something more meaningful than a simple error message. Although the default error messages are perfectly serviceable, many organizations feel that they lack character and like to customize the most popular error messages, such as the 404 error message displayed by the Web server when a page is not found.

To modify custom error message settings, perform the following steps:

1. Open the IIS Manager console and select the Server node.

2. Scroll down in the Details pane and double-click on the Error Pages item.

3. On the Error Pages pane, select the error code that you want to modify, and then click Edit.

4. In the Edit Custom Error Page dialog, shown in Figure 13-9, choose forwarding clients to a static page based on file location, to a URL on the server, or an absolute URL, which can be a page on another website.

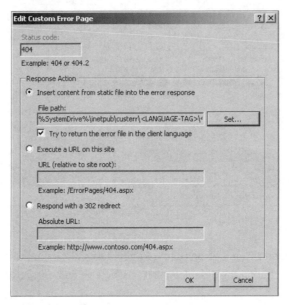

FIGURE 13-9: The Edit Custom Error Page

Adding or Disabling the Default Document

The *default document* is the document that loads when a client navigates to a web page but doesn't specify which page to load. The Default Documents role service is installed in a default installation of IIS 7.5, though this can be removed if you so choose. On servers running IIS 7.5, the following default documents are used:

► Default.htm

► Default.asp

► index.htm

- index.html

- iisstart.htm

- default.aspx

If more than one of these documents is present in the same folder, the document that is higher on the list overrides the documents that are lower on the list. You can add or disable default documents using the IIS Manager console by double-clicking on the Default Document item either at the server or the website level.

To add a default document using AppCmd.exe, use the following syntax:

```
AppCmd.exe set config /section:defaultDocument /+files.
[value=' filename']
```

To remove a default document using AppCmd.exe, use the following syntax:

```
AppCmd.exe set config /section:defaultDocument /-files.
[value=' filename']
```

Directory Browsing

Directory browsing allows clients to view the files that are stored in a folder. Directory browsing works only if the default document is not present or has been disabled. To enable directory browsing, the Directory Browsing role service must be installed.

▶ Microsoft suggests that enabling directory browsing is a security risk. This is because it might allow clients to see the underlying structure of the site.

To configure directory browsing, perform the following steps:

1. Open the IIS Manager console and select the site on which you want to enable directory browsing.

2. Scroll down in the Details pane and double-click on the Directory Browsing item.

3. When Directory Browsing is shown in the Details pane, click Enable and select the items that you want to allow to be displayed when the client is browsing. By default the filename, time, size, extension, and date information are displayed.

To enable directory browsing from AppCmd.exe, issue the following command:

```
Appcmd.exe set config /section:directoryBrowse /enabled:true
```

IP Address and Domain Name Filtering

IP address and domain name restrictions allow you to block or allow access to a site based on a client's address. You can configure two types of rules: *allow rules* and *block rules*. When you configure an allow rule, only hosts that are on the Allow List are able to access your website. When you configure a block rule, hosts with an address on your Block List are blocked from accessing your site. You can configure allow and block rules at the server, site, application, virtual directory, folder, and file level in IIS 7.5. You need to have the IP and Domain Restrictions role service installed to use IP address and domain name filtering.

▶ Using Block Lists does not stop determined attackers, as they are likely to be able to spoof an address that is not on your Block List.

To configure an IP address and domain name restriction, perform the following steps:

1. Open the IIS Manager console and select the site on which you want to implement an Allow List.

2. Double-click on the IP Address and Domain Restrictions item.

3. If you want to configure an Allow List entry, click Add Allow Entry and on the Add Allow Restriction Rule dialog box, shown in Figure 13-10, enter the IP address range or IP address that you want to allow.

FIGURE 13-10: IP address restriction

4. If you want to configure a Deny entry, click Add Deny Entry and on the Add Deny Restriction Rule dialog box, enter the IP address range or IP address that you want to block.

URL Authorization Rules

URL authorization rules allow you to grant or deny access to specific computers, groups of computers, or domain access to sites, Web applications, folders, or specific files. For example, you can use URL authorization rules to block everyone except the Managers group from accessing specific pages on the organization's Intranet server. You can also configure URL authorization rules to apply only when the client attempts to use specific HTTP verbs, such as GET or POST. To use URL authorization rules, you need to ensure that the URL Authorization role service is installed on the server. There are two types of authorization rules: Allow rules and Deny rules.

To create an authorization rule, perform the following steps:

1. Open IIS Manager and navigate to the site, virtual directory, folder, or file on which you want to create the authorization rule.

2. Double-click on the Authorization Rules item in the Details pane.

3. Click Add Allow Rule or Add Deny Rule depending on the type of authorization rule that you wish to create.

4. On the Add Allow Authorization Rule or Add Deny Authorization Rule dialog box, specify the users or groups you wish to configure the rule for and any specific HTTP verbs that you wish to trigger the rule. Figure 13-11 shows the Add Allow Authorization Rule dialog box.

▶ If you want to block access to everyone except a specific group of users, remove the default All Users Allow rule and replace it with a rule that allows only the user group in question.

FIGURE 13-11: Add Allow Authorization Rule.

To create an authorization rule using the AppCmd.exe command-line utility, use the following syntax:

```
AppCmd.exe set config /section:system.webServer /security /
authorization /+ "[accessType='Allow/Deny',
roles=' string', users=' string', verbs=' string']"
```

Configuring Request Filters

Request filters allow you to block clients from making certain types of requests of your Web server. Request filters allow you to block a common form of attack against Web applications, one where the attacker enters a specially formatted HTTP request in order to elicit an unplanned response from the Web application. SQL injection attacks are one such kind of specially formatted HTTP request. There are several different types of request filters you can configure using the Request Filtering item. Request filters can be configured at the server, site, and file level. To use request filtering, you need to ensure that you install the Request Filtering role service on the server.

> **NOTE** Request filtering provides the features of the UrlScan tool, which was an add-on for previous versions of IIS.

You can configure the following types of request filters:

▶ **File Name Extensions:** This type of filter allows you to specify which type of files clients are not allowed to request from the Web server on the basis of file extension. The default request filtering settings block 43 different file extensions, and it is relatively easy to add additional extensions by clicking Deny File Name Extension on the File Name Extensions tab of the Request Filtering item.

▶ **Rules:** Allows you to configure specific rules that check either the URL, query string, or both. If a match occurs, the request is blocked.

▶ **Hidden Segments:** Allows you to set a list of URL segments that will be blocked to requesting clients. A *URL segment* is the section of a URL path that lies between slash (/) characters.

▶ **URL:** Allows you to specify a set of URL sequences (such as setup/config.xml) that the Request Filtering role service blocks to clients. All instances of the URL sequence are blocked within the scope of the filter.

▶ **HTTP Verbs:** Allows you to restrict which HTTP verbs can be used in requests by clients. For example, you might block clients from using the PUT verb in requests.

▶ **Headers:** Allows you to specify a maximum URL size for a specific HTTP request header.

You can modify the general request filtering settings, as shown in Figure 13-12, by clicking on Edit Feature Settings in the Actions pane. Using this dialog, you can configure the following options:

▶ **Allow unlisted file name extensions:** If this box is not checked, file extensions that are not explicitly allowed cannot be requested by clients.

▶ **Allow unlisted verbs:** If this box is not checked, HTTP verbs that are not explicitly allowed are blocked.

▶ **Allow high-bit characters:** If this box is not checked, unusual non-ASCII characters are blocked.

▶ **Allow double escaping:** If this box is not checked, URLs can contain double escape characters.

▶ **Maximum allowed content length:** This textbox specifies the maximum size of content that a request can process. Keep this figure small if you do not allow HTTP uploads to your site.

▶ **Maximum URL length:** Allows you to restrict the maximum size of a URL request sent to your site.

▶ **Maximum query string:** Allows you to restrict the maximum query string size in a URL request sent to your site.

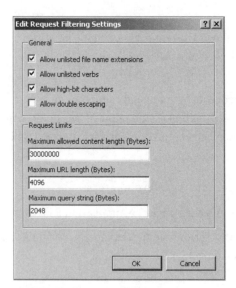

FIGURE 13-12: Request filtering settings.

MANAGING APPLICATION POOLS

Application pools are collections of Web applications that are served by a worker process or a group of worker processes. When you create a new website in IIS 7.5, IIS automatically creates an associated application pool. One of the ideas behind application pools is that by separating Web applications into their own pools, the failure of one Web application does not impact the functioning of other Web applications. Application pools allow you to do the following:

▶ Collect sites and applications that use the same configuration settings.

▶ Improve security by allowing the use of a custom security account to run an application.

▶ Silo resources in such a way that one Web application cannot address or influence resources in another Web application.

Creating an Application Pool

Although new application pools are created each time you create a new site, there are reasons why you want to configure a new application pool. Prior to creating a new application pool, you need to know what pipeline mode you want to use to process requests for managed code. *Managed pipeline mode* determines how IIS 7.5 processes requests for managed code. The difference between the two managed pipeline modes is as follows:

▶ **Integrated:** This newer mode allows the request-processing pipelines of IIS and ASP.NET to process the request. Most Web applications are likely to use this mode.

▶ **Classic:** This mode forwards requests for managed code through aspnet_isapi .dll. This is the same method used for processing requests on servers running IIS 6.0. Use this mode if an older Web application does not function well in integrated mode.

To create a new application pool, perform the following steps:

1. Open the IIS Manager console, and then click the Application Pools node.

2. Click Add Application Pool in the Actions menu. This opens the Add Application Pool dialog box shown in Figure 13-13.

FIGURE 13-13: Add Application Pool.

3. Enter a name for the application pool, choose the .NET Framework version for the application pool, or choose to have no managed code, and choose which managed pipeline mode you are going to use.

Configuring Application Pool Recycling Settings

Not all developers write code that functions correctly over an extended period of time. If you find that a Web application that you need to host on a computer running Windows Server 2008 R2 starts to develop problems after it has run for a lengthy amount of time, you can deal with this by configuring *application pool recycling settings* to recycle the processes related to the application on a regular basis. You configure application pool recycling settings on the Edit Application Pool Recycling Settings dialog box shown in Figure 13-14. You can configure an application pool to be recycled when the following thresholds are met:

▶ After a certain amount of time has elapsed. By default all application pools automatically recycle every 1,740 minutes.

▶ After an application pool has processed a certain number of requests

▶ At specific times of the day

▶ After an application pool exceeds a certain virtual memory threshold

▶ After an application pool exceeds a specific private memory threshold

Through the Advanced Settings dialog box, shown in Figure 13-15, you can configure basic settings such as the pipeline mode and recycling settings. You can also configure settings including processor affinity, CPU limits, process orphaning, request limits, and rapid fail protection settings.

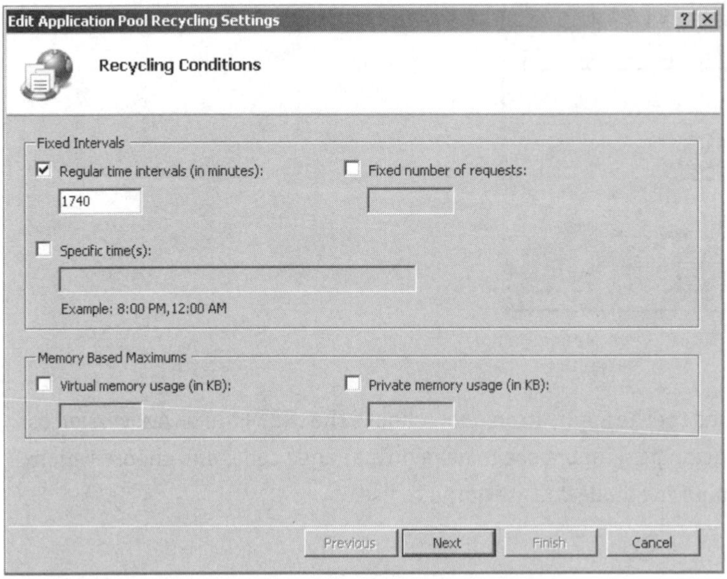

FIGURE 13-14: Application pool recycling settings

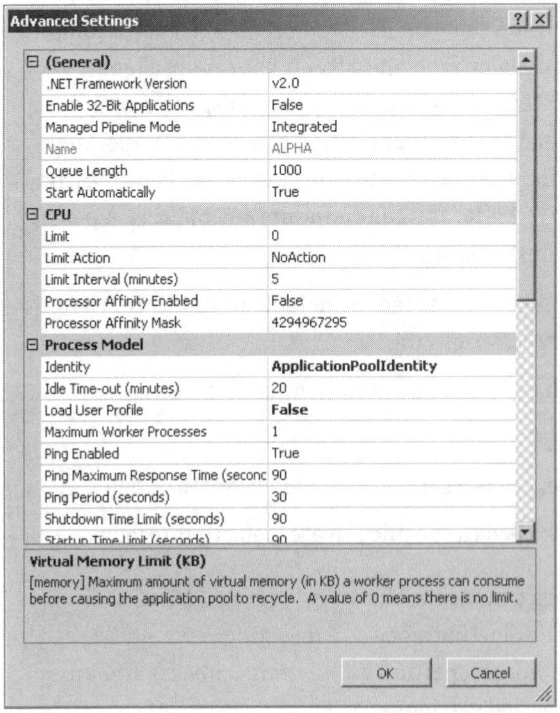

FIGURE 13-15: Application pool advanced settings

IIS USERS AND DELEGATION

IIS 7.5 allows you to delegate the management of specific websites and Web applications. This means that you can allow a specific user to manage a website without giving him logon privileges to the server or control over any other site or Web application hosted by IIS.

When you install IIS, it is configured so that it does not allow remote management using the IIS Manager console. You configure IIS to allow remote management using the Management Service item at the server level in the IIS Manager console. Using the Management Service item, you can configure the following remote management properties:

▶ **Enable Remote Connections:** This item must be enabled for remote administration connections using IIS Manager Console to work.

▶ **Identity Credentials:** Allows you to specify whether administrators can connect using Windows credentials or IIS Manager credentials. The default setting only allows Windows user accounts.

▶ **Connections:** Allows you to specify whether remote management connections can occur on any IP address interface, or whether they are limited to a specific IP address interface. You can also specify which SSL certificate will be used to protect remote administration sessions.

▶ **IPv4 Address Restrictions:** Allows you to specify which IP addresses or networks are allowed to successfully connect using IIS Administrator

> ▶ To allow IIS 7.5 to be remotely managed using the IIS Manager console, you need to install the Management Service role service and configure the service to start automatically.

IIS 7.5 User Accounts

IIS 7.5 allows you to create user accounts that exist only in IIS. These user accounts do not have any privileges outside IIS and cannot be used to log on locally to the server. This allows you to assign administrative permissions to users without having to create a corresponding machine local or domain user account.

To create an IIS Manager user, perform the following steps:

1. Open the IIS Manager console and double-click on the IIS Manager Users item when the Server level is selected in the IIS Manager console.

2. Click Add User in the Actions pane. This opens the Add User dialog box shown in Figure 13-16. Enter the user name and password for the IIS user.

FIGURE 13-16: Add an IIS user.

Delegating Administrative Permissions

After you have enabled remote management and, if you choose to create IIS users, configured the appropriate IIS user accounts, you can delegate management permissions on a site or Web application through the IIS Manager Permissions item. You can check precisely which permissions users have been delegated by viewing the Feature Delegation item at the server level. You can also modify which configuration items are delegated using the Feature Delegation item.

To delegate administrative permissions over a site, perform the following steps:

1. Open the IIS Manager console and select the website for which you want to delegate administrative permissions.

2. Double-click the IIS Manager Permissions item in the Details pane.

3. In the Actions pane, click Allow User. On the Allow User dialog box, shown in Figure 13-17, select the Windows or IIS Manager User, and then click OK.

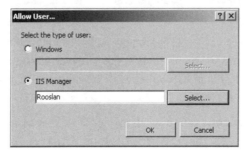

FIGURE 13-17: User delegation

MANAGING FTP

FTP in Windows Server 2008 R2 is substantially different than the FTP server software that was included with Windows Server 2008 and Windows Server 2003. Two big differences are that the FTP server now supports SSL connections, and that FTP can be managed from the IIS Manager console rather than having to install management tools for the previous version of IIS. From the IIS Management console you can configure the following:

▶ **FTP Authentication:** Allows you to enable or disable Anonymous or Basic authentication. The default settings have both forms of authentication disabled.

▶ **FTP Authorization:** Allows you to specify which users or groups are allowed to connect to the FTP server, and whether they have read and write permissions when using FTP

▶ **FTP Directory Browsing:** Allows you to specify whether MS-DOS or UNIX-style directory listings are provided. Also allows you to specify if virtual directory, available bytes, and four-digit years information is displayed.

▶ **FTP Firewall Support:** Allows you to configure the FTP server to accept passive connections from a perimeter network firewall

▶ **FTP IPv4 Address and Domain Name Restrictions:** Allows you to block or allow FTP clients based on IPv4 address or client domain name

▶ **FTP Logging:** Allows you to configure the FTP logging settings, including how often log files are rotated

▶ **FTP Messages:** Allows you to configure FTP banner settings. This is the informational text that is presented to new FTP sessions.

▶ **FTP Request Filtering:** Using this item, you can configure the following:

  ▷ Configure FTP to allow or block specific file name extensions from transfers.

  ▷ Block segments, such as sensitive folders, from being accessible in FTP.

  ▷ Block particular FTP URLs.

  ▷ Block specific FTP commands from being used during a session.

▶ **FTP SSL Settings:** Allows you to specify which server certificate is used for SSL sessions. Also allows you to force the use of SSL as well as enforce 128-bit encryption on FTP SSL sessions.

▶ **FTP User Isolation:** Allows you to limit which folders an FTP user can navigate. You can configure a user to start in the FTP root directory or a specific user name-related directory.

To add a new FTP site, perform the following steps:

1. Open the IIS Manager console, right-click on the Sites node, and then click on Add FTP Site.

2. On the Site Information page, enter a name for the site and the directory path that is used to host the site's files.

3. On the Binding and SSL Settings page, shown in Figure 13-18, specify which IP addresses the FTP site listens on, whether the FTP site uses a virtual host name, whether the site starts automatically, whether SSL is allowed or required, and which server certificate is used in conjunction with the FTP site.

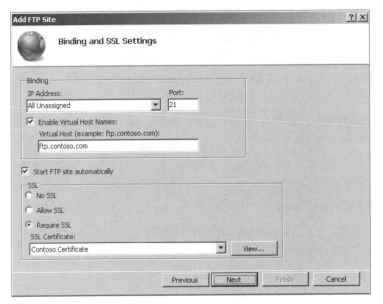

FIGURE 13-18: Add FTP Site.

4. On the Authentication and Authorization Information page, specify whether you'll allow Anonymous and/or Basic authentication. On the Authorization drop-down menu, specify whether you want to allow access for the following:

   ▷ All users

   ▷ Anonymous users

   ▷ Specified roles or user groups

   ▷ Specified users

If you choose to allow access only to specified roles or user groups, you need to specify which roles, users, or user groups you want to grant access.

SUMMARY

IIS 7.5 is modular and has only a minimum number of modules installed by default when you install the Web server software. If a feature that you want to configure doesn't appear in the IIS Manager console, it is likely because you haven't installed the associated role feature yet. IIS allows you to delegate the management of individual websites, either to Windows users and groups or to IIS users. The IIS Manager console can be used to remotely administer IIS only if remote management has been enabled. The FTP Service in Windows Server 2008 R2 supports forcing clients to use SSL encrypted sessions.

Additional Sources

Getting Started with AppCmd.exe

http://learn.iis.net/page.aspx/114/getting-started-with-appcmdexe/

IIS 7 Operations Guide

http://technet.microsoft.com/en-us/library/cc732976(WS.10).aspx

Web Server

http://technet.microsoft.com/en-us/library/cc753433(WS.10).aspx

CHAPTER 14

Configuring Hyper-V Virtual Machines

IN THIS CHAPTER

▶ **Configuring Hyper-V settings**

▶ **Allocating Hyper-V dynamic memory**

▶ **Taking virtual machine snapshots**

▶ **Creating virtual hard disks**

▶ **Understanding physical to virtual migration**

Hyper-V is Windows Server 2008 R2's built-in virtualization solution. The Hyper-V role allows computers running Windows Server 2008 R2 with processors that support virtualization to host up to 384 virtual machines (VMs). On the Datacenter edition of Windows Server 2008 R2, Hyper-V supports up to 1 TB of physical memory that can be allocated to VM guests. Hyper-V is available on the Standard, Enterprise, and Datacenter editions of Windows Server 2008 R2 in both the typical and server core configurations.

> **NOTE** Windows Server 2008 R2 Datacenter edition includes unlimited virtual instance image rights. This means that if you have 1 TB of memory on a computer running the Datacenter edition and can run those 384 virtual machines, you don't need to purchase additional operating system (OS) licenses. Once you host a certain number of VMs, the licensing benefits can save your organization a substantial amount of money.

CONFIGURING HYPER-V

▶ Just because a computer has an x64 processor, doesn't mean that virtualization support is enabled in BIOS.

Unlike Windows Server 2008, which comes in versions that can be installed on x86 processors, you can install Windows Server 2008 R2 only on computers that have x64 processors. This means that you can install the Hyper-V role on the Standard, Enterprise, and Datacenter editions of Windows Server 2008 R2 without having to worry that you're running the 32-bit version of the OS rather than the 64-bit. Hyper-V is not supported on the 32-bit version of Windows Server 2008.

You can install the Hyper-V role using the Server Manager console or by using the following PowerShell command when the Server Manager module is loaded:

```
Add-WindowsFeature Hyper-V
```

▶ The benefit of installing Hyper-V on a computer running the Server Core installation option is that it reduces the number of times you need to reboot the host machine to install security updates.

Allocating Virtual Processors

Hyper-V supports up to 64 logical processors on the host server, with each processor core representing a virtual processor. You configure a VM's processor settings when the Processor item is selected in the virtual machine properties dialog, as shown in Figure 14-1. Through this dialog, you can allocate the number of logical processors assigned to the VM, the percentage of processor resources reserved for the machine, the maximum percentage of allocated processor resources that the VM can consume, and the relative weight of the VM when there is contention for processor resources. If you leave VMs with the default settings, Hyper-V allocates processor resources equally across all running virtual machines, assuming that resource contention exists. You can allocate a maximum of four virtual processors to a single virtual machine. The default setting for a VM allocates only one logical processor.

▶ Use the Virtual Machine Reserve setting to ensure that a critical VM is not starved of processor resources.

Allocating Dynamic Memory

Until the release of Service Pack 1 for Windows Server 2008 R2, Hyper-V would allow you to allocate only a static amount of RAM to a VM. This meant that if you wanted to allocate more or less RAM to a virtual machine, you needed to shut down the VM and modify that VM's properties. When you allocate a static amount of RAM to a VM, powering on the VM allocates all that RAM to the VM. If the amount of allocated RAM is not available to the system, you won't be able to power on the VM, even if the VM doesn't actually need all the RAM to start up.

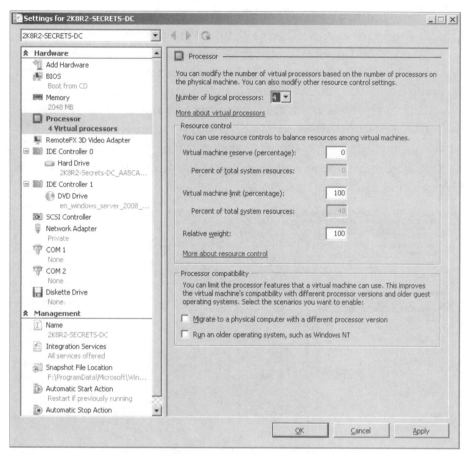

FIGURE 14-1: Processor resources

Rather than allocating a fixed amount of RAM to each VM, *dynamic memory*, a feature available only in Windows Server 2008 R2 with Service Pack 1 or later, allows you to allocate memory dynamically to virtual machines. When you do this, you set a minimum and maximum amount of memory for the VM, and the VM utilizes as much as it needs. Rather than guessing how much memory a specific VM needs when configuring it, dynamic memory allows the VM to request only the memory it needs, leaving the rest of it to the OS. As most VMs use less memory than systems administrators usually allocate to them, this often means that you can run more VMs simultaneously. The minimum amount of RAM that you specify is allocated when the VM is started up; however, the VM releases RAM back to the OS if it isn't required.

To utilize dynamic memory, it is necessary to ensure that you have installed the latest integration tools on the VM. If you don't install the integration tools that come with Service Pack 1 or later on Windows Server 2008 R2, the VM does not utilize dynamic memory. When you configure a VM to use dynamic memory, you can configure a *memory buffer*. This is the amount of RAM, expressed as a percentage of the current demand that Hyper-V allocates to the VM over its current utilization. This allows applications to quickly consume more memory before the VM has to request an extra allocation from the Hyper-V host. You can also configure a *memory weight* for the virtual machine, which determines how much memory is allocated to the VM beyond its minimum when there is contention for memory resources.

You configure dynamic memory settings when the Memory item is selected on the VM's properties, as shown in Figure 14-2.

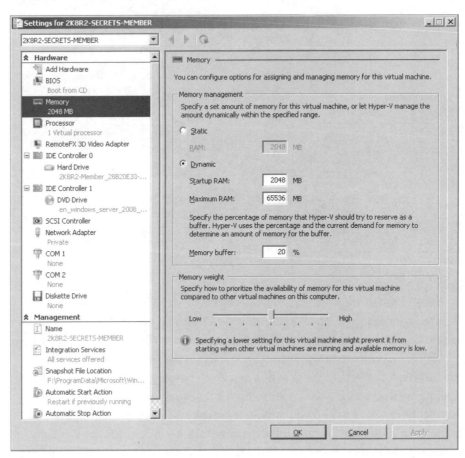

FIGURE 14-2: Dynamic memory settings

Dynamic memory can be used by VMs running the following OSes:

- ▶ Windows Server 2008 R2 (Recommended with SP1 or later)
- ▶ Windows Server 2008 with SP2 or later
- ▶ Windows 7 RTM (Recommended with SP 1 or later)
- ▶ Windows Vista with SP1 or later
- ▶ Windows Server 2003 R2 with SP2 or later
- ▶ Windows Server 2003 with SP2 or later

Using Integration Services

Integration services are components that include OS drivers for all Hyper-V components, such as synthetic network adapters and with Windows Server 2008 R2 SP1,
dynamic memory support. Integration services also support certain communication
functionality between the VM and the Hyper-V host.

You install integration services after you complete the installation of the virtual
machine by selecting the Insert Integration Services Setup Disk option from the
Actions menu. Doing this mounts a virtual DVD-ROM that contains all of the necessary integration services files for all supported VM OSes. When these components are
installed, you can enable or disable specific integration services functionality by
selecting the Integration Services item on the virtual machine properties, as shown
in Figure 14-3. The functionality of each integration service is covered over the next
few pages.

TIME SYNCHRONIZATION

The *time synchronization service* allows the virtual machine to synchronize time settings with the Hyper-V host. This ensures that VMs that use private or internal networks and are unable to synchronize with an external time source do not have their
clocks drift. Clock drift can be a significant problem for VMs that spend a substantial
amount of time shut down or paused. It also ensures that VMs that are reverted from
a previous snapshot are brought up to the current time, rather than being stuck at
the time the snapshot was taken.

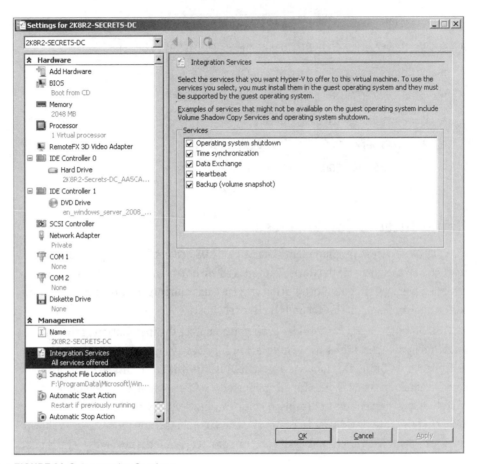

FIGURE 14-3: Integration Services

HEARTBEAT

The *heartbeat service* allows the Hyper-V host to automatically detect whether a guest VM has become unresponsive. Heartbeat works by sending a heartbeat request to the VM on a periodic basis. In the event that a response is not received from the VM, an item is written to the event log. You can configure monitoring solutions, such as System Center Operations Manager 2012, to raise an alert when heartbeat events are issued to the event log.

SHUTDOWN

The *shutdown service* allows you to initiate a clean shutdown of a VM through the Hyper-V console without having to log directly on to that VM and initiate shutdown manually. This functionality allows you to use products such as System Center Orchestrator 2012 to cleanly shut down VMs as a part of a scheduled maintenance process. If you have to manage several hundred VMs, being able to shut them down through the console, rather than having to log on directly, can save a substantial amount of time.

DATA EXCHANGE

The *key/value pair exchange service* allows a VM to share data with the Hyper-V host or to allow the host to forward that data to third-party management tools without having to install an agent directly on the VM.

BACKUP (VOLUME SNAPSHOT)

The *volume shadow copy services (VSS)* integration services component allows the parent partition to request synchronization and quiescence of a VM, assuming that the VM supports VSS. If this functionality is supported, it is possible to back up VMs through products that support VSS snapshots, such as System Center Data Protection Manager 2012.

UNDERSTANDING VIRTUAL HARD DISKS

Virtual hard disks are binary files that use the VHD extension. Hyper-V VMs use these files to store all the data associated with a volume. If you want to create a VM that has two simulated hard-disk drives, you create two separate VHD files. VHD files aren't just used by Hyper-V but can also function as:

- ► The default format in which Windows Server Backup writes backup files
- ► A bootable device on which you can install the Windows Server 2008 R2 or Windows 7 OS
- ► A device that can be mounted as a disk drive on computers running Windows Server 2008 R2 or Windows 7

When you create a virtual hard disk, you can choose between creating a fixed disk, a dynamically expanding disk, or a differencing disk, as shown in Figure 14-4.

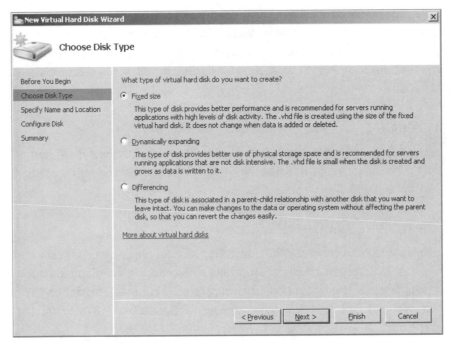

FIGURE 14-4: New virtual hard disk

Creating Fixed Disks

When you create a *fixed virtual hard disk*, a file that is the same size as the hard disk is created and stored on the target volume. The benefit of a fixed virtual hard disk is that, at creation, all virtual hard-disk space is allocated. While this takes longer than creating other forms of virtual hard disks, it also minimizes the chance that the VHD will become fragmented. Another benefit of fixed disks is that they always remain the same size and do not expand to the point where they consume all space on the host volume.

Creating Dynamically Expanding Disks

The drawback of *dynamically expanding disks* is that, as they grow only when new space is required on the VM, they tend to be substantially more fragmented than virtual hard disks of a fixed nature. Substantial fragmentation can reduce overall performance. Another drawback of dynamically expanding disks is that, if insufficient care is taken, the dynamically expanding disk may continue to grow until all space on the host volume is consumed. This can be problematic if you don't regularly moni-tor the volumes on which you host VHD files.

Creating Differencing Disks

A *differencing disk* records all the changes made to a parent disk without applying those changes to that parent disk and instead applying them only to the differencing disk. Differencing disks are a special type of dynamic disk. Hyper-V snapshots use chains of differencing disks to allow you to use the computer as it was configured at different points in time. A differencing disk hierarchy that has multiple levels is also called a *chain*. A single parent disk can have multiple children. Figure 14-5 shows the properties of a differencing virtual disk, including the disk's parent disk.

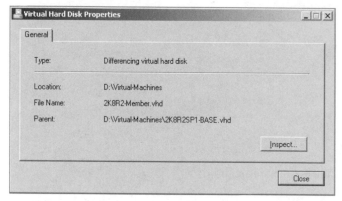

FIGURE 14-5: Differencing virtual disk

If a differencing disk's chain is broken, you can reconnect the differencing disk to its parent, assuming the parent disk still exists. To accomplish this goal, perform the following steps:

1. Open the Hyper-V Manager console, select a VM, and then click Inspect Disk in the Actions pane.

2. Locate the virtual disk that you wish to reconnect to the parent and then click Open.

3. On the Virtual Hard Disk Properties dialog box, click Reconnect. This launches the Edit Virtual Hard Disk Wizard.

4. In the Edit Virtual Hard Disk Wizard, click Browse to navigate to the location of the parent virtual hard disk.

▶ When using differencing disks, you should configure the parent disk as read- only to minimize the chance that changes can be made that will cause corruption.

▶ One way of rapidly deploying VMs is to create a VM, install the OS, run the sysprep.exe utility, and then shut the OS down. Take the VHD file from that VM, make it read-only, and then deploy new VMs by creating VMs that use a differencing disk that uses the sysprepped VHD as a parent.

You can use the Edit Virtual Hard Disk Wizard to merge a child disk with its parent hard disk, as shown in Figure 14-6. You accomplish this goal in one of two ways. The first involves merging the child disk into its parent, which effectively applies all the changes recorded in the child VHD to the parent VHD. The other option is to use the merge operation to create a brand new VHD while retaining the original child and parent VHDs.

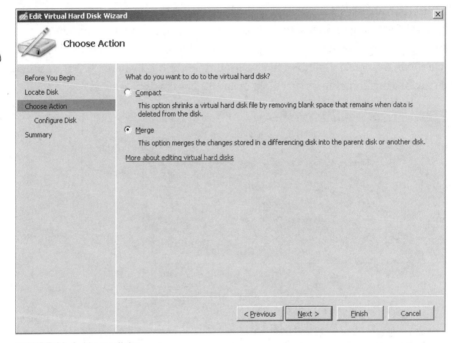

FIGURE 14-6: Merge disks.

Connecting Pass-Through Disks

▶ Microsoft does not recommend using differencing disks on VMs hosted on clusters.

Pass-through disks allow you to connect a physical disk directly to a VM, rather than connecting the VM to a virtual hard-disk file hosted on a physical disk. Pass-through disks can also be connected to the server running Hyper-V as an LUN on a storage area network (SAN). The main benefit of pass-through disks, as opposed to virtual hard disks, is that pass-through disks are not subject to the 2040-gigabyte size limitation. The drawback of pass-through disks is that they do not support Hyper-V's snapshot functionality.

To configure a VM to use a pass-through disk, first take the disk offline using Disk Management. After this is done, you'll be able to select either an IDE or SCSI controller, click Add Hard Drive, select the Physical Hard Disk drop-down, and then choose the offline disk that you want to allocate to the VM.

Copying Physical Disks to VHD

Hyper-V allows you to create VHD files that are duplicates of existing physical hard-disk drives. You can use the New Hard Disk Wizard to perform this task under the following conditions:

▶ You can use the New Hard Disk Wizard only to convert physical disks. It is not possible to convert partitions.

▶ The New Hard Disk Wizard cannot be used to migrate the disk that hosts the OS. It is possible to migrate only data disks.

▶ You need to ensure that the host OS does not access the disk being converted during the conversion process. You can do this by removing the drive letter associated with the disk in the Disk Management console.

To copy an existing physical disk to VHD, run the New Virtual Hard Disk Wizard, create a dynamically expanding disk, and then, on the Configure Disk page, choose the Copy the Contents of the Specified Physical Disk option, as shown in Figure 14-7.

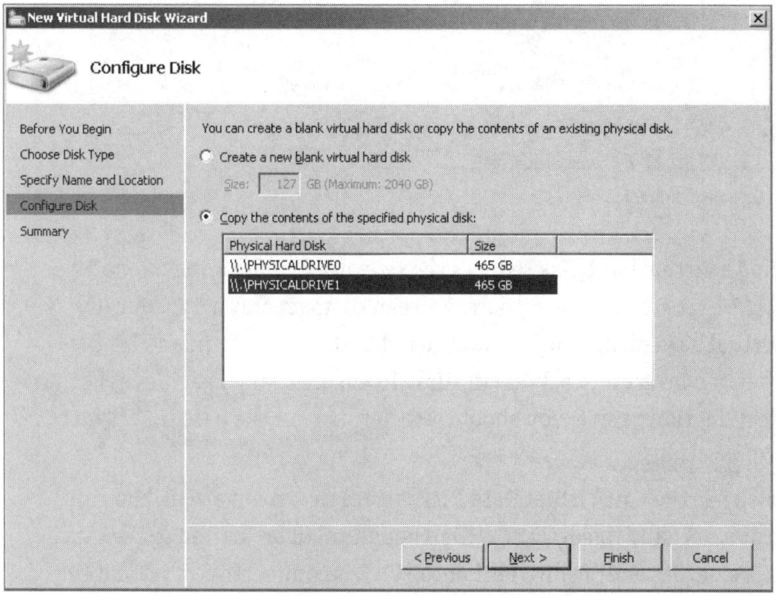

FIGURE 14-7: Copy physical disks.

Converting, Expanding, and Compacting VHDs

Hyper-V allows you to convert virtual hard disks that were originally set up as dynamic so that they become fixed and disks that were originally set up to be fixed so that they become dynamic. What happens when you perform a conversion is that a new VHD of the target type is created, and the contents of the source VHD are copied across to it. After this has happened, the source disk is deleted. To perform this procedure, you need to ensure that you have double the VHD's size available prior to attempting the conversion. You use the Edit Virtual Hard Disk Wizard to perform the conversion process, as shown in Figure 14-8.

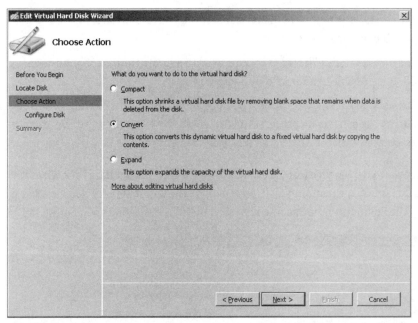

FIGURE 14-8: Convert disk.

Compacting a virtual hard disk reduces the size of a VHD file on a volume by removing blocks that are not storing data. You can compact only a dynamically expanding virtual hard disk, so if you want to reduce the size of a fixed VHD file, you'll need to first convert it to a dynamic disk. To ensure that you achieve the maximum possible reduction in size, you should also defragment the hard disk prior to performing compaction.

▶ To defragment a virtual hard-disk drive, you need to shut down the VM, mount the VHD in the host Hyper-V OS, perform defragmentation, and then dismount the VHD.

You can also use the Edit Virtual Hard Disk Wizard to expand a VHD. You can expand both dynamic and fixed-sized VHDs, though you'll be limited to the maximum allowable size, depending on whether the VHD is connected to a virtual IDE or virtual SCSI adapter.

Connecting Virtual SCSI and IDE Adapters

Virtual hard disks, pass-through disks, and virtual DVD-ROM drives connect to virtual disk drive controllers. Hyper-V supports both virtual IDE controllers and virtual SCSI controllers. A computer can have a maximum of two virtual IDE controllers and a maximum of four virtual SCSI adapters. Each virtual IDE device supports up to two attached devices. Each virtual SCSI device supports up to 64 attached devices.

Virtual hard disks connected to a virtual IDE controller cannot be larger than 127 GB. Virtual hard disks connected to a virtual SCSI controller cannot be larger than 2040 GB.

UNDERSTANDING HYPER-V NETWORKS

Hyper-V networks determine how the VM communicates with the host machine and computers on external networks. By creating a virtual network and then connecting a virtual network adapter to that network, you configure how the VM is able to communicate. Hyper-V VMs can use three different types of network:

- **External:** External networks allow a virtual network adapter to be bound to a physical network adapter on the Hyper-V host machine. You use an external network when you want to allow the VM to communicate through that network adapter with computers on external networks. VMs can be automatically or manually assigned IP addresses on the same subnet as the host machine's network adapter.

- **Internal:** Internal networks allow the virtual machine to establish network communication with the Hyper-V host machine. For example, you could use the ping utility to verify connectivity between the host and the VM if the VM's network adapter is connected to an internal network. VMs connected to the same internal network on the same Hyper-V host can communicate with each other.

- **Private:** Private networks are isolated from the Hyper-V host machine's network. The Hyper-V host cannot use the ping utility to establish network connectivity with a VM connected to a private network. VMs connected to the same private network on the same Hyper-V host can communicate with each other.

▶ It is important to remember that Hyper-V VMs can boot off only virtual hard disks attached to virtual IDE controllers.

▶ Hyper-V on Windows Server 2008 R2 supports adding or removing virtual hard disks from a powered on virtual machine without requiring a reboot, as long as integration services is installed and the disks are attached to virtual SCSI adapters.

You manage Hyper-V networks through the Virtual Network Manager dialog box shown in Figure 14-9.

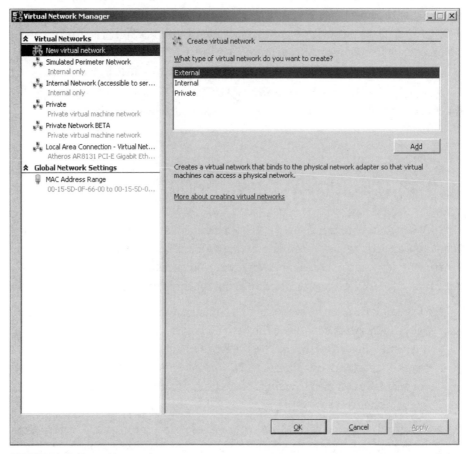

FIGURE 14-9: Hyper-V networks

To create a Hyper-V network, perform the following general steps:

1. Open the Hyper-V Manager console from the Administrative Tools menu.

2. Click Virtual Network Manager from the Actions pane.

3. On the Virtual Network Manager dialog, select the type of virtual network that you wish to create, and click Add.

4. Enter a name for the network. If you are choosing to create an External network, select the network adapter that the new virtual network will be mapped to. You can also choose whether you want to enable virtual LAN identification and specify a VLAN ID.

Connecting Network Adapters

A Hyper-V network adapter can be connected only to a single Hyper-V network. If you want to configure a VM to be connected to multiple Hyper-V networks, you need to set the VM up to have multiple network adapters, each connected to a separate network. To connect a specific adapter to a specific network, use the Network drop-down when the Network Adapter item is selected on the virtual machine's properties dialog box, as shown in Figure 14-10.

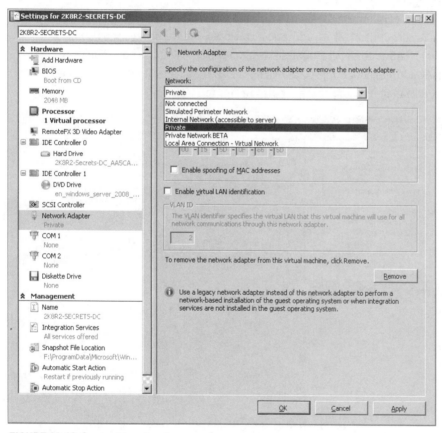

FIGURE 14-10: Connect to network.

There are two different types of network adapters that you can add to a Hyper-V VM: the *network adapter* and the *legacy network adapter*. The first type, sometimes called a *synthetic network adapter*, uses drivers that are included in recent OSes, such as Windows 7 and Windows Server 2008, or which can be installed with the integration services components. Synthetic network adapters aren't functional until the OS has properly booted. A VM can have a maximum of eight synthetic network adapters.

The legacy network adapter, also called the *emulated network adapter*, emulates
a virtual Multiport DEC 21140 adapter. This is useful when you have guest OSes that
don't work with the synthetic network adapters, because there are no appropriate
integration services drivers available for that OS. Most OSes do support the Multiport
DEC 21140, so if you can't get a synthetic network adapter working, configure the VM
to use a legacy network adapter. Legacy network adapters are also necessary if you
want to PXE boot a virtual machine, as they are available prior to the OS booting up.
A virtual machine can have a maximum of four legacy network adapters.

You can configure a virtual network adapter with either a static or a dynamic
Media Access Control (MAC) address. A static MAC address stays consistent. A
dynamic MAC address is configured through the MAC address pool. You configure
the MAC address pool range by selecting the MAC Address Range item on the Virtual
Network Manager dialog box, as shown in Figure 14-11.

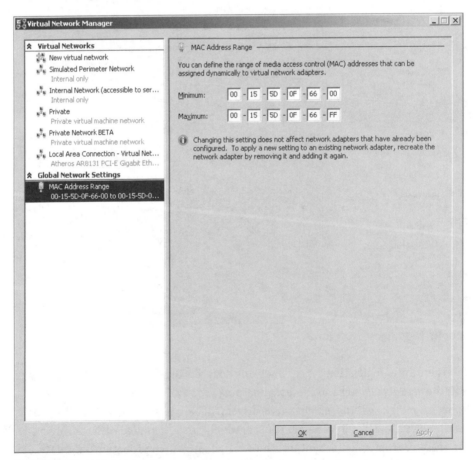

FIGURE 14-11: MAC Address Range

You can also enable MAC address spoofing on a per-virtual network adapter basis. Most of the time you won't want to do this as it presents a security risk, though some applications, such as Network Load Balancing, require a virtual machine network adapter to support MAC address spoofing. To enable MAC address spoofing, check the Enable Spoofing of MAC Addresses check box on the virtual network adapter's properties.

Configuring VLANs

Hyper-V supports using VLANs to partition network traffic. When you configure VLANs, network traffic is isolated so that hosts, or virtual hosts, on one VLAN are unable to communicate with hosts on another VLAN unless routing between those VLANs is explicitly configured. You can configure VLANs on external and internal virtual machine networks, but not private virtual machine networks. VLAN IDs can also be configured on a per-virtual network adapter basis.

To configure a VLAN ID for a specific virtual network, open the Virtual Network Manager, select the network that you want to configure the VLAN ID for, check the Enable Virtual LAN Identification for Management Operating System item and then enter a VLAN ID, as shown in Figure 14-12.

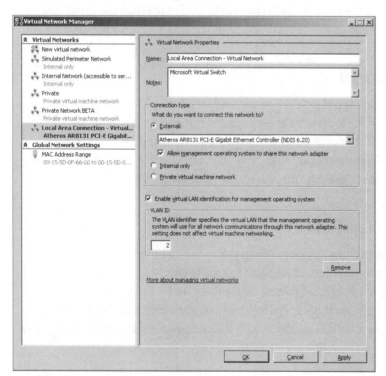

FIGURE 14-12: VLAN ID

To configure a VLAN ID for a specific virtual network adapter, perform the following steps:

1. Open Hyper-V Manager and edit the virtual machine's properties.

2. Select the adapter to which you want to assign a VLAN ID.

3. Select the Enable Virtual LAN Identification checkbox.

4. Enter the appropriate VLAN ID.

USING VIRTUAL MACHINE SNAPSHOTS

Virtual machine snapshots allow you to capture the state of the VM at a particular point in time. VM snapshots can be taken when the VM is powered on or when the VM is shut down. VM snapshots include not only the current state of the VM, but the current VM's configuration. For example, if you take a snapshot, add an additional hard disk, and then revert back to that snap shot, the VM will be configured as though you'd never added the hard-disk drive in the first place. By viewing the settings of a snapshot, you can check how the VM was configured at the time the snapshot was taken, but you will be unable to make any modifications to this configuration.

Creating Snapshots

▶ Snapshots taken when a computer is powered down require less disk space, because they don't have to store the contents of the system's RAM. They are also easier to work with because the VM is in a consistent state.

To create a VM snapshot, right-click on the VM in the Hyper-V Manager console, and then click Snapshot. This creates a new snapshot, visible in the console, which has the VMs name and the current date and time. In the Actions pane, you can click Rename to give the snapshot another, more descriptive, name. You can create a maximum of 50 snapshots for each virtual machine hosted by Hyper-V.

Applying Snapshots

▶ If you have a lot of snapshots and none of them have meaningful names, it can be difficult to figure out precisely which existing snapshot you wish to restore at a future point in time.

You can apply an existing snapshot. When you do this, all changes since the previously taken snapshot are lost. If you want to keep those changes, take an additional snapshot. Applying a snapshot doesn't delete other snapshots, it just reverts the VM to a known pre-existing state. If you apply an earlier snapshot, make changes to the VM, and then take another snapshot, you'll create a new branch on the snapshot tree.

For example, Figure 14-13 shows two different branches of snapshots of a virtual machine. If you applied the snapshot taken at 5:46 pm and then took another snapshot, yet another branch would be created under this snapshot node.

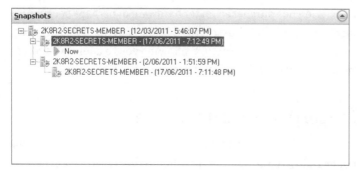

FIGURE 14-13: Snapshot tree

Reverting to Snapshots

Clicking Revert from the Hyper-V Manager console when a VM is selected applies the most recently taken snapshot, discarding any changes that have been made to the VM since then. Reverting always returns the VM to the most recent snapshot. You can revert to a VM only if a snapshot currently exists. You use reversion when you want to return a VM to a previously known configuration.

Deleting Snapshots

When you delete a snapshot, you have the option of deleting just that snapshot or the entire snapshot tree. When you delete a link in a snapshot chain, the changes represented in that link are merged back in such a way that the integrity of the remaining snapshots is preserved. For example, if you create a snapshot of a server at 9 am on Monday, Tuesday, and Wednesday, you can delete the snapshot taken on Tuesday without losing the other two snapshots. The changes that were recorded in the deleted Tuesday snapshot are merged in a way that allows you to maintain the integrity of the Monday and Wednesday snapshots, freeing up disk space. You can use the Delete Snapshot Subtree option to delete all snapshots in a branch.

MIGRATING VIRTUAL MACHINES

From time to time, you'll want to move data from one Hyper-V server to another, perhaps because your organization has purchased faster hardware or perhaps because you simply want to consolidate your VM infrastructure. Tools also exist to virtualize your existing traditionally deployed infrastructure, allowing you to migrate a server that runs on a traditional physical chassis so that it now runs as a VM.

Importing and Exporting Virtual Machines

▶ You might encounter problems when exporting and migrating between a Hyper-V host with a processor made by one vendor and a Hyper-V host with a processor made by a different vendor.

You can import or export only VMs that are in a powered off state. You can export a VM from a specific snapshot by right-clicking on the snapshot in the Hyper-V Manager console and then clicking on Export. This displays the Export Virtual Machine dialog shown in Figure 14-14.

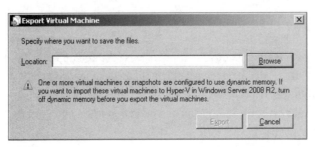

FIGURE 14-14: Export Virtual Machine.

When you import a VM, you can choose to make a copy of the VM, allowing you to place it in a different location, or add the VM to the current Hyper-V server, allowing it to remain at its current location. If you want to import the VM again at a later stage or on another server, you need to select the Duplicate All Files so the Same Virtual Machine Can Be Imported Again option. If you don't do this, you won't be able to import the VM using the Hyper-V Manager console.

When you import a VM, you need to choose whether or not to use the existing virtual machine ID or have Hyper-V generate a new virtual machine ID, as shown in Figure 14-15. You need to create a new virtual machine ID if you are importing the VM back onto the same server that hosts the original. If you attempt to import a VM back onto the same server that hosts the original without changing the virtual machine ID, the import operation fails.

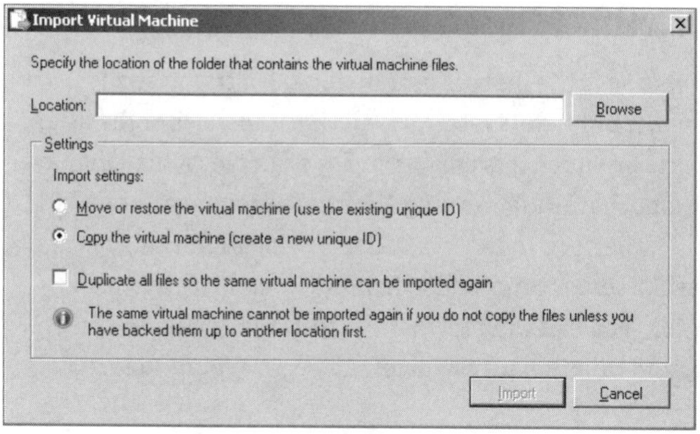

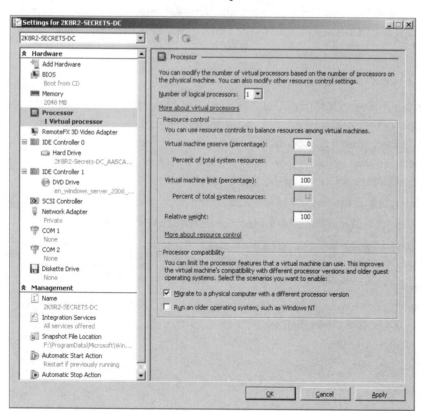

FIGURE 14-15: Import Virtual Machine.

If you are migrating from a host running a newer processor to an older processor, you need to enable the processor compatibility option. You can do this under the Processor settings, shown in Figure 14-16, by enabling the Migrate to a Physical Computer with a Different Processor Version option.

▶ You can use Virtual Machine Manager 2012 to directly transfer VMs from one Hyper-V server to another one.

FIGURE 14-16: Migrate to a different processor version.

Using Physical to Virtual Migration

Physical to virtual (P2V) migration is the process of transferring a traditionally deployed server to a virtual machine while retaining all the properties of the original server except the platform on which it is deployed. For example, you might have a server deployed on traditional hardware running Microsoft Exchange Server 2010 that you want to virtualize. By performing a physical to virtual migration, you can create a virtualized copy of the server running Exchange Server 2010. When you have completed the migration, you can shut down the traditionally deployed server as its name, configuration, and functionality will now all be present in the virtualized copy.

▶ You can perform an offline P2V migration by booting the source server off a specially configured boot device. It is possible to prepare a PXE boot image and perform an offline migration this way. Offline migrations are faster than online migrations.

To perform a physical to virtual migration, you need to use a tool such as System Center Virtual Machine Manager 2012. Virtual Machine Manager 2012 allows you to perform a conversion while the original server is online without disruption to the functionality of that original server. You can perform an online physical to virtual migration using Virtual Machine Manager 2012 of physical servers running the following OSes: Windows Server 2003 SP1 or later, Windows Server 2003 R2, Windows Server 2008, and Windows Server 2008 R2. An online P2V migration is wizard-driven, and you can perform this migration from the Virtual Machine Manager 2012 console.

Using Live Migration

Live migration moves a VM from one node in a failover cluster to another node without data loss or service interruption. You can use live migration only to move VMs between cluster nodes; it isn't possible to accomplish this service continuity when moving between stand-alone Hyper-V hosts. Windows Server 2008 R2 supports Hyper-V live migration on up to 16-node failover clusters.

▶ Remember that the different processor version option allows migration to earlier versions of the same vendor's processor, not to Hyper-V hosts running processors from other vendors.

Live migration is supported under the following conditions:

All nodes in the Hyper-V cluster are located on the same TCP/IP subnet.

All nodes in the Hyper-V cluster have access to shared storage.

All nodes in the Hyper-V cluster use the same processor model from the same vendor.

You can initiate live migration either through the Failover Cluster Manager console, through a WMI or PowerShell script, or through System Center Virtual Machine Manager 2012.

SUMMARY

Installing Hyper-V on a computer running the Server Core installation option minimizes the number of times that you need to reboot the Hyper-V host to apply updates. Hyper-V dynamic memory allows you to allocate RAM on the basis of VM need rather than guesswork. Virtual SCSI adapters support up to 64 devices, while virtual IDE adapters only support two devices. VMs can be booted off only a virtual IDE device or a legacy network adapter. Dynamic virtual hard disks grow over time but can become fragmented on the host volume. Fixed hard-disk drives consume space on the volume equivalent to their size once they are created.

External virtual networks allow a virtual machine to communicate with external hosts as well as locally hosted VMs. Internal virtual networks allow a virtual machine to communicate with the host server and locally hosted VMs. Private virtual networks allow only virtual machines to communicate with other locally hosted VMs on the same private network. Internal and external virtual networks and virtual adapters can be configured with VLAN IDs.

Snapshots allow you to create a point-in-time configuration freeze of a VM that you can roll back to when necessary. You can use the Hyper-V console to import and export virtual machines and, when hosted on a Windows Server 2008 R2 failover cluster, you can leverage Hyper-V live migration to transfer VMs between nodes without an interruption of service.

Additional Sources

Converting Physical Computers to Virtual Machines in VMM (P2V Conversions)

`http://technet.microsoft.com/en-us/library/bb963740.aspx`

Hyper-V R2 FAQ

`www.microsoft.com/hyper-v-server/en/us/faq.aspx`

Hyper-V Dynamic Memory Configuration Guide

`http://technet.microsoft.com/en-us/library/ff817651(WS.10).aspx`

System Center Virtual Machine Manager 2012

`www.microsoft.com/systemcenter/en/us/virtual-machine-manager.aspx`

CHAPTER 15

Patch Management with WSUS

IN THIS CHAPTER

▶ Installing Windows Server Update Services on Windows Server 2008 R2
▶ Configuring WSUS groups
▶ Configuring WSUS approvals
▶ Rolling back WSUS updates
▶ Choosing the right WSUS topology
▶ Verifying Update Deployment
▶ Using System Center to manage updates

You have finally reached the stage where the servers that you are responsible for managing work perfectly. There are no errors in the event logs. You get no complaints about performance from those that use the server on a daily basis. The systems that you are responsible for managing are running like clockwork. Then, Microsoft publishes a security bulletin indicating that one of the products installed on your servers needs an update. This leaves you in an uncomfortable position: You do not want your servers to be exposed to the vulnerability the update addresses, but you are wary of altering a configuration that appears to be functioning flawlessly.

You feel this way because you do not want to change something that is working without a problem. You may even have had the unfortunate experience of installing an update only to have the update cause endless problems. Some administrators have successfully tested updates in a development environment, only to find that update wreaking havoc when deployed on a production system.

This chapter focuses on Windows Server Update Services (WSUS) as a method of deploying and managing updates on computers running Windows Server 2008 R2. WSUS is a built-in role, like the DNS and DHCP roles, that you can add to any computer running Windows Server 2008 R2. Of course, it is possible to manually deploy updates to each computer in your organization, but the advantage of using WSUS is that it gives you a basic framework for managing updates, including approval, deployment, and rollback. Having a basic process for the deployment of updates makes managing those updates across a large number of servers easier.

DEFINING AN UPDATE PROCESS

Systems administrators have the enthusiasm for process that eight-year olds have for visiting the dentist. Most administrators want to get things done as soon as possible. Many lack interest in writing out lengthy plans, submitting those plans, waiting for those plans to be approved, and then finally doing the work that they could have done much earlier if they didn't need to go around submitting plans all the time. Update management is a tricky area when it comes to approvals. Tricky, because no one really wants to approve something that may make a bigger mess than it solves. Tricky, because, to be honest, most people do not really understand what the majority of updates do or the nature of the threats they address. Although Microsoft does release security bulletins with each update, updates generally boil down to "If you don't apply this software, your server may be vulnerable to attack." In the back of each system administrator's head is the addendum, "If I do deploy the update, it may cause more problems than it is worth." We systems administrators are professional pessimists and, if things didn't go wrong on a regular basis, most of us would be out of a job!

Depending on your organization, you may have a complicated process when it comes to managing updates, or you might be a little more ad-hoc in your approach. I know many administrators who simply take a full backup and then deploy each update Microsoft publishes without testing. They figure that, over the long term, they will spend less time resolving the rare problem that an update causes than they would spend if they rigorously tested each update before putting it into production.

While there is a certain logic to this approach, you would want to ensure that management is fully informed of this strategy. It may be rather challenging to explain why you didn't go through any form of update testing after you deployed an update that takes a mission-critical server offline for a couple of hours.

You should have some form of an update management plan. The most basic update management plan should include the following components:

- **Understand what the update addresses:** Know if the update resolves a security issue or if it addresses a functionality issue.

- **Determine how urgent the update is:** Does this update deal with a minor functionality issue or does it patch a remotely exploitable vulnerability? Microsoft attaches ratings to its updates. Has Microsoft rated the update Critical or just Important?

- **Prioritize the update:** Rarely will you have only one update to deploy during any specific cycle. Determine the order in which you will apply updates based on their priority.

- **Test the update:** Spend some time running the update on development servers and then in limited production environments.

- **Have a rollback plan:** Know how you are going to get back to a stable configuration if something goes wrong.

- **Deploy the update.**

- **Verify that the update has been successfully deployed.**

INSTALLING AND DEPLOYING WSUS

Installing WSUS on previous versions of the Windows Server operating system could be a bit of a trial. There was likely a lot of mucking about ensuring that you had all the necessary prerequisite software installed before you actually got to the point where you installed the WSUS role. The inclusion of WSUS as a role on Windows Server 2008 R2 greatly simplifies deployment. The only additional software that is necessary is the Microsoft Report Viewer 2008 Redistributable, and you can install the Report Viewer after you have installed WSUS 3.0 SP2. As WSUS is a role, you can add WSUS to a server running Windows Server 2008 R2 just as you would add roles such as DHCP, DNS, or Active Directory Certificate Services.

To install WSUS, perform the following general steps:

1. Ensure the computer that hosts WSUS has all current updates installed. Unless you are configuring a WSUS server on a disconnected network, ensure that the server can connect to the Internet.

2. Open the Server Manager console, click the Roles node, and then click Add Roles.

3. If you are presented with the Before You Begin page, click Next.

4. On the Select Server Roles page, select Windows Server Update Services, and then click Next. When presented with the Add Role Services Required for Windows Server Update Services? dialog box, click Add Required Role Services. Click Next.

5. On the Introduction to Web Server (IIS) page, click Next.

6. On the Select the Role Services to Install for Web Server (IIS) page, click Next.

7. On the Introduction to Windows Server Update Services page, click Next. On the Confirm Installation Selections page, click Install.

8. When the WSUS role has installed, you are presented with the Windows Server Update Services 3.0 SP2 Setup Wizard, as shown in Figure 15-1. Click Next.

FIGURE 15-1: After you install WSUS, you have the option of starting the configuration process.

9. On the License Agreement page, click I Accept the Terms of the License Agreement, and then click Next.

10. If you receive a message about the Report Viewer Distributable, make a note that you need to obtain this software and install it after you have deployed WSUS, and then click Next.

11. On the Select Update Source page, choose whether you are going to store updates locally. The default option is to store updates in the C:\ WSUS directory. Microsoft recommends that you have at least 6 GB of free disk space on the volume on which you choose to store updates. Click Next.

▶ You might configure a WSUS server to issue only update approval information if you have clients on the Internet, where it makes more sense to retrieve updates directly from Microsoft's servers rather than over a VPN or DirectAccess connection.

12. On the Database Options page, you can choose to install the Windows Internal Database on the server that will host WSUS or point at an existing SQL instance hosted locally or on another computer. Unless you are going to develop advanced WSUS reports, you should just use the Windows Internal Database on the local computer.

13. On the Web Site Selection page, you can choose between using the existing default IIS website or creating a separate WSUS-specific website. You should only choose to create a separate WSUS-specific website if you intend to host other websites on the WSUS server.

14. On the Ready to Install Windows Server Update Services 3.0 SP2 page, click Next.

15. On the Completing the Windows Server Update Services 3.0 SP2 Setup Wizard, click Finish. Click Cancel if you do not want to perform configuration, and then click Close.

▶ From this point, you can either start to configure the WSUS server, or you can click Cancel if you want to perform configuration later.

Performing Initial WSUS Configuration

When you finish installing WSUS, the wizard prompts you to begin configuration and offers to start the configuration wizard. You can choose to perform this configuration by running the wizard immediately or choose to run the wizard at a later point in time. If you don't want to use the wizard, you can configure each WSUS setting directly through the relevant item Options node. You learn about WSUS options later in this chapter.

To complete initial WSUS configuration using the wizard, perform the following steps:

1. From the Administrative Tools console, open the Windows Server Update Services console.

2. Expand the console nodes and locate the Options node. Open the WSUS Server Configuration Wizard item.

3. Click next on the Before You Begin and on the Join the Microsoft Update Improvement Program pages.

4. On the Choose Upstream Server page, choose between synchronizing the server against Microsoft Update or against an upstream WSUS server within your organization. Having multiple WSUS servers in your organization enables you to implement different update deployment strategies for diverse groups of clients. You learn more about using multiple WSUS servers in the section "Understanding WSUS Topologies" later in this chapter.

5. On the Specify Proxy Server page, specify any necessary proxy server settings, including whether specific authentication credentials are required to utilize the proxy.

6. Click Start Connecting to connect either to the upstream WSUS server or the Microsoft Update servers to determine the types of updates that can be obtained, the list of products for which updates are available, and the languages for which those updates are available. Synchronization takes a few minutes. After it completes, click Next.

▶ You can significantly reduce the number of updates that you need to download by limiting updates to languages used in your organization.

7. On the Choose Languages page, select the languages that you need to support. For example, if you need to support only computers running English versions of Microsoft products, select English. If you need to support computers running English and Russian versions of Microsoft products, choose both English and Russian. When you use multiple servers in an upstream/downstream WSUS topology, downstream servers are limited to the update languages that they can obtain from the upstream servers.

8. On the Choose Products page, select the Microsoft products that you need to keep up-to-date. The simplest solution when using this dialog is to select all products. This means you have to perform a massive number of approvals, but at least you'll know that you'll be covered for the updates for all Microsoft products in your organization. You can go through and select individual products, but administrators often miss products, because they forget or are unaware that products are deployed on some client or server somewhere on the organizational network. When making selections on this dialog box, you need to balance the annoyance of an increased number of approvals versus the risk that you might have missed a product on your network that you aren't aware of.

9. Classifications determine what type of updates WSUS should provide to WSUS clients. You can select all classifications or one or more of the following: Critical Updates, Definition Updates, Drivers, Feature Packs, Security Updates, Service Packs, Tools, Update Rollups, and Updates. Most administrators choose everything, giving them the option of rejecting specific updates, rather than not being offered the update option in the first place.

▶ It is important to remember that WSUS downloads only updates that you approve for the WSUS server.

10. On the Set Sync Schedule page, choose whether to perform synchronization manually or perform synchronization according to a schedule. Choosing to perform synchronization according to a schedule ensures that updates are ready to be approved when you open the WSUS console. Performing synchronization manually means that you need to wait until after synchronization has occurred before you have an up-to-date list of updates awaiting approval.

11. The final page of the wizard allows you to choose whether you want to begin initial synchronization. Initial synchronization takes a substantial amount of time. Subsequent synchronizations will be shorter.

▶ You can change any of the selections you have made when running the configuration wizard using the appropriate items in the Options node.

Configuring WSUS Options

The Options node of the WSUS console enables you to configure all aspects of WSUS, including aspects that you cannot configure using the WSUS wizard. You can use the items in the Options node to configure the following settings:

▶ **Update Source and Proxy Server:** Configures whether WSUS synchronizes against Microsoft Update or another WSUS server in your organization. You can also use this dialog box to configure WSUS as a replica. You learn more about WSUS replica servers later in this chapter.

▶ **Products and Classifications:** Configures the Microsoft products and update classifications that you want to synchronize. There is little need to download updates for products that aren't deployed in your organization, but make sure you have an accurate list.

▶ **Update Files and Languages:** As shown in Figure 15-2, this option configures whether you want WSUS to download updates directly from Microsoft Update or an upstream WSUS server. You can choose whether to download only approved updates, download all updates, or download express installation files. You can also use the Properties dialog box to determine which update languages you will retrieve.

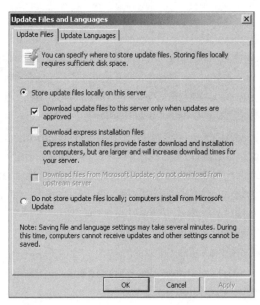

FIGURE 15-2: Update Files and Languages.

▶ **Synchronization Schedule:** Specifies whether WSUS synchronizes with Microsoft Update or the upstream server on a scheduled basis, or whether you want to perform synchronization manually.

▶ **Automatic Approvals:** Configures automatic approvals. You learn more about automatic approvals later in this chapter.

▶ **Computers:** Configures how WSUS assigns computers to groups. You can choose between having WSUS groups populated through Group Policy or through manual assignment. You learn more about assigning computers to groups later in this chapter.

▶ **Server Cleanup Wizard:** Runs a maintenance task that allows you to delete unused, expired, superseded, or unneeded updates. You can also use it to remove computer accounts that have not reported to the WSUS server in more than 30 days. Be careful with this second option as you may remove the computer account of someone who has gone on a long holiday!

▶ **Reporting Rollup:** Specifies whether you want WSUS replica servers to provide computer and update status data to this server

▶ **E-Mail Notifications:** Configures WSUS to send e-mail notifications when new updates are synchronized. You can also use this item to configure WSUS to send status reports according to a configurable schedule.

▶ Computers that are offline for a substantial period of time may also have their computer password out-of-sync.

- **Microsoft Update Improvement Program:** Specifies whether you want data from WSUS reported back to Microsoft. Reported data includes the number of computers in the organization and how many of those computers successfully install and fail to install each update.

- **Personalization:** Configures whether a WSUS server will display computers and status information from replica downstream servers. You can also configure which items show up as To Do List items for the server. This includes whether the server will remind you if the server database is nearly full, SSL is not enabled, and new products and classifications have been added.

- **WSUS Server Configuration Wizard:** Runs the configuration wizard. This is the same wizard that you are prompted to run after you install WSUS for the first time.

Creating the Update Database

The update database is a directory on a WSUS server that stores all the update files that WSUS provides to clients on your network. By default, the update database is stored in the c:\WSUS\WsusContent folder. As the update database will probably store a fair amount of data, you probably shouldn't accept the default option that puts the database on the volume hosting your operating system. If you choose the default setting, at some point there is a good chance that the volume hosting the operating system will fill up leading to all kinds of excitement. Keep an eye on the amount of disk space left on the volume hosting the update database, because this is an important part of WSUS administration.

You should configure event viewer to send an e-mail alert when space on that volume starts to get scarce.

You have the option of storing updates locally on the WSUS server or on Microsoft's Update servers. When you have updates stored locally, clients retrieve those updates from the WSUS server. This puts more pressure on the WSUS server but reduces your overall use of external bandwidth. When you don't store updates locally, clients look to the WSUS server to figure out which updates they should install but still retrieve the updates themselves from the Microsoft Update servers on the Internet. This option works well when it isn't practical to have clients retrieve updates from the WSUS server, such as when the clients are located in very small branch offices or are indirectly accessing the WSUS server over the Internet. You configure whether update files are stored locally or stored on Microsoft's servers using the Update Files and Languages item within the Options node of the WSUS console.

When you choose to store updates locally, you can select whether WSUS only downloads approved updates or automatically downloads all update files. The default setting has WSUS download only approved updates. Some administrators configure WSUS to automatically retrieve all updates prior to approval, because they have these files downloaded during off-peak network times, such as at 3am. If WSUS only downloads updates after they are approved, you will need to then choose when you want those approved updates downloaded to the WSUS server. This delay is important when considering your testing strategy. Having a test group of computers will allow you to leverage the strategy of only downloading approved updates without having to deploy those updates widely. You learn more about test groups later in this chapter.

All clients of a specific WSUS server either get their update files from that WSUS server or from the Microsoft Update servers on the Internet. You cannot configure some clients of a WSUS server to obtain update files from the server and other clients of the same WSUS server to obtain update files from the Microsoft Update servers on the Internet. If you want to configure your update infrastructure so that some clients download updates from WSUS and others from the Microsoft Update servers, you will need to configure multiple WSUS servers. You learn about configuring multiple WSUS servers later in this chapter in the section Understanding WSUS Topologies.

MIGRATING WSUS METADATA AND THE PATCH DATABASE

WSUS metadata is the information that you create when configuring WSUS. WSUS metadata includes approval data and computer group membership. If you have spent 12 months tuning your WSUS server with the perfect collection of groups, and you've finally gotten your approval list under control, the last thing you want to do is go through that process again from the beginning.

You might want to set WSUS up on a disconnected network or migrate the WSUS role to a new server without having to download all of the updates that you have already obtained.

To migrate the WSUS database, perform the following steps:

1. Install WSUS on the target server.

2. You need to manually ensure that the Download Express Installation Files option and the Update Languages option in the Update Files item in WSUS Options are the same on both source and destination servers.

3. Copy the contents of the \WSUS\WSUSContent folder from the source computer to the \WSUS\WSUSContent folder on the destination server.

4. Use the WSUSutil.exe utility, usually found in the `c:\program files\ Update Services\Tools` directory to issue the following command on the source server:

```
Wsusutil.exe export export.cab export.log
```

5. Copy the export.cab and export.log files from the source server to the destination server.

6. Issue the following command on the destination server:

```
Wsusutil.exe import export.cab import.log
```

7. Depending on the size of the patch update, this process may take several hours.

Configuring Windows Server 2008 R2 as a WSUS Client

When you deploy WSUS, you need to configure computers running Windows Server 2008 R2 as WSUS clients. This is accomplished on stand-alone computers by editing the local Group Policy or by editing a GPO that applies to a computer when that computer is a member of a domain. The WSUS-related policy settings are located in the `Computer Configuration\Administrative Templates\Windows Components\ Windows Update` area of a Windows Server 2008 R2 Group Policy object. The policies that you can configure are as follows:

▶ **Do Not Display 'Install Updates and Shut Down' Option In Shut Down Windows Dialog Box:** This setting enables you to configure the properties of the Shut Down Windows dialog box. It is more relevant to provisioning client computers with updates than it is for configuring updates on servers.

▶ **Do Not Adjust Default Option to 'Install Updates and Shut Down' In Shut Down Windows Dialog Box:** This policy allows you to configure whether Install Updates and Shut Down is the default option in the Shut Down Windows dialog. This setting is also more relevant to client computers than it is to servers.

▶ **Enable Windows Update Power Management to Automatically Wake Up the System to Install Scheduled Updates:** This setting allows computers that are put into hibernation to wake from hibernation to install updates at a scheduled time. As servers rarely go into hibernation, this feature is more relevant when deploying updates to clients.

▶ **Configure Automatic Updates:** This policy enables you to configure automatic update settings. There are three settings that can be configured as well as letting the local Administrator choose:

  ▷ **Notify for Download and Notify for Install:** You will need to log on locally to download and install the updates published on the WSUS server.

  ▷ **Auto Download and Notify for Install:** You will need to log on locally to install the updates published on the WSUS server.

  ▷ **Auto Download and Schedule the Install:** The updates will be downloaded and then installed automatically at the scheduled time. This may lead to an automatic reboot of the server in the event that the update requires a restart to complete installation. Many updates require such a restart.

▶ **Specify Intranet Microsoft Update Service Location:** This setting allows you to configure which WSUS server will be used. When you enable this policy, you need to specify the WSUS server as both the intranet update service for detecting updates and the intranet statistics server.

▶ **Automatic Updates Detection Frequency:** This policy determines how often the client checks in with the WSUS server to see whether there are any new approved updates.

▶ **Allow Non-Administrators to Receive Update Notifications:** This setting allows non-administrators to install updates. This setting is more client than server related, and there are likely to be very few scenarios where you want to allow a user that isn't a member of the local Administrators group on a server to install updates on that server.

▶ **Turn On Software Notifications:** This policy is also primarily client related and determines whether or not users see detailed update information. As you are using WSUS to review and deploy updates, configuring this policy isn't really necessary on servers.

▶ **Allow Automatic Updates Immediate Installation:** This policy allows you to configure the automatic installation of updates that do not require a service interruption or a restart of Windows. You should enable this policy on servers as it minimizes the number of updates where installation is pending until the server restarts.

▶ **Turn On Recommended Updates Via Automatic Updates:** This setting configures the client to download updates marked as recommended. As WSUS clients will download updates that you approve, it is not necessary to configure this policy.

- **No Auto-Restart with Logged On Users for Scheduled Automatic Updates Installations:** This policy relates to client update installation behavior and whether the computer will wait for a user to log off before performing a scheduled update installation.

- **Re-Prompt for Restart with Scheduled Installations:** This setting relates to prompts that the operating system displays to the logged on user before a scheduled restart. This policy is less relevant to servers than it is to client computers.

- **Delay Restart for Scheduled Installations:** This policy allows you to configure how long the server will wait to restart after it has completed the installation of approved updates. If this policy is not configured, a server will wait until 15 minutes after updates have installed before it begins the restart process.

- **Reschedule Automatic Updates Scheduled Installations:** This setting determines the amount of time for the automatic update process to wait before it initiates a scheduled installation if the server was powered off at the time the installation should have occurred.

- **Enable Client-Side Targeting:** This setting enables you to assign the computer to a WSUS computer group.

- **Allow Signed Updates from an Intranet Microsoft Update Service Location:** This setting enables you to configure clients to accept updates from a Microsoft Update server where the updates are not digitally signed by Microsoft but are signed by a third party.

Computers running a Server Core variant of Windows Server 2008 R2 that are members of a domain can have their Windows Update settings applied through Group Policy. Stand-alone computers running a Server Core variant of Windows Server 2008 R2 can be configured to use WSUS by editing the registry. To do this you need to modify registry keys in two areas of the registry. The first set of keys is located in the HKEY_LOCAL_MACHINE\Software\Policies\Microsoft\Windows\WindowsUpdate area. They keys you should configure are:

- **TargetGroup:** Use this key to specify the WSUS group to which the computer belongs.

- **TargetGroupEnabled:** Set this key to 1 to enable client-side targeting.

- **WUServer:** This key specifies the URL of the WSUS server.

- **WUStatusServer:** This key must be set to the same URL as that specified in the WUServer key.

The second set of keys is located in the `HKEY_LOCAL_MACHINE\Software\Policeis\ Microsoft\Windows\WindowsUpdate\AU` area. The keys you should configure are:

- ▶ **UseWUServer:** This value must be set for the WUServer key to be used.
- ▶ **NoAutoUpdate:** When set to zero, this key enables automatic updating. When set to 1, it disables automatic updating.

You can of course use the registry to configure non-Server Core instances of Windows Server 2008 R2 rather than using local Group Policy or Group Policy inherited from the domain environment. It is just a lot simpler to configure these settings through Group Policy than it is to edit the registry!

One of the big issues around the automatic deployment of updates is whether you want to allow your server operating systems to automatically reboot. Factors that should influence your decision include:

- ▶ You want to ensure that a server does not reboot itself to install updates during peak usage times.
- ▶ Do you want to have updates automatically deployed to the server to be installed at a later stage?
- ▶ If you want to configure automatic restarts, you need to configure updates to be downloaded to the server but installed at a separate time. This can be done by configuring the Configure Automatic Updates policy, selecting the Auto Download and Schedule the Install option and then configuring the scheduled installation time to a specified period, such as Saturday at 3am, as shown in Figure 15-3. Keep in mind, if you configure all your servers with the same setting, it is possible that they will all install the update and reboot at the same time, which may cause dependency problems.

To optimize network bandwidth, you should also enable BITS peer caching. Peer caching allows clients on the local network to share update files, reducing the load on the WSUS server and optimizing bandwidth usage for WSUS clients located on branch office networks that do not have a local WSUS server. You can accomplish this by enabling the Allow BITS Peer Caching policy that is located in the Computer Configuration\Administrative Templates\Network\Background Intelligent Transfer Service node of a standard Group Policy object.

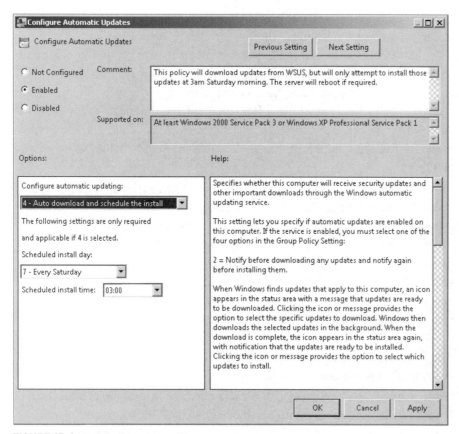

FIGURE 15-3: Automatic update settings

DEPLOYING UPDATES

Prior to rolling out an update to production servers, you should perform testing in a development environment. Testing in a development environment allows you to determine if the update causes any obvious critical faults, such as deploying an update that causes an instant STOP error (the technical term for the Blue Screen of Death). Within WSUS, you can configure a special group and populate it with your test servers. If you have configured WSUS to download updates only once you approve them, deploying to your test servers will have the added benefit of populating your WSUS server with update files, which speeds eventual deployment to your production systems.

Your testing phase should last long enough so that you are reasonably confident that deploying the updates will not cause a critical fault on your production servers. The best test environments involve a select group of users performing tasks that replicate what actually happens on production systems. Many systems administrators assume that simply deploying the update and being able to successfully run all the server's applications constitutes sufficient proof that the update does not cause problems. In many cases, problems caused by updates can be subtle, and only someone who is extremely familiar with the applications running on the server may notice issues.

▶ A virtual copy of a server makes an excellent update test bed.

Your test environment should mirror your production environment as closely as possible. Virtualization provides you with a great way to replicate your production environment. You can ensure that your virtual environment matches your physical environment relatively closely by performing physical to virtual conversions, which you learned about in Chapter 14, "Configuring Hyper-V Virtual Machines." Virtualization will not provide you with a foolproof test environment, as you cannot use it to replicate your server's hardware configuration, such as specific hardware drivers. Virtualization does give you an effective platform on which to test your software configuration. Of course, if most of your production servers are virtualized, using a virtual test environment that mirrors the production environment is an obvious strategy for the update-testing phase.

Staggering the deployment of updates gets you an additional round of testing without a full deployment to the production environment. For example, you may be in the process of rolling out an update for Exchange Server 2010. You test the update in a virtual environment first. After you are reasonably certain that no problems will arise, you can deploy the update to a site that has a smaller number of users. If no problems arise when you deploy updates in a limited production environment, you can then deploy the updates to all necessary systems. Inconveniencing 30 users of Exchange Server 2010 at a branch office site is a better result than inconveniencing 300 users of Exchange Server 2010 at your organization's head office location.

Using WSUS Groups

WSUS groups allow you to deploy updates to specific collections of computers. Using WSUS groups, you can deploy an update to one collection of servers on Tuesday and deploy the same update to a separate collection of servers on Wednesday. WSUS groups are not related to Active Directory security groups and exist only in your

WSUS hierarchy. Unlike Active Directory security groups, a computer can only be a member of a single WSUS group.

It is possible to nest groups. Figure 15-4 shows that the DHCP Servers, DNS Servers, and File Servers groups are nested under the Production Servers group. You should design your WSUS groups from general to specific.

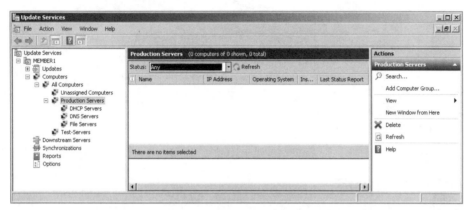

FIGURE 15-4: Nested WSUS groups

As you learned earlier in the chapter, you can either populate WSUS groups automatically through client-side targeting policy or manually by adding computers to specific groups using the WSUS console. If you use client-side targeting and configure a client to use a WSUS group that is not configured on the WSUS server, the computer account ends up in the Unassigned Computers group. All computers that contact the WSUS server that do not use client-side targeting also end up in the Unassigned Computers group.

▶ If you can't find a computer account in WSUS, check the Unassigned Computers group.

Understanding Update Approvals

You approve updates on a per computer group basis. When you approve an update for a specific computer group, groups under that group in the hierarchy will inherit the update approval. If you want to approve an update for a group but do not want to approve the update for some groups further down the hierarchy, you can set the status of the update to Not Approved for those groups. Figure 15-5 shows an update that is approved for the Production Servers group and, by inheritance, the DHCP Servers group, is configured to install on a specific deadline for the File Servers group, and is set to Not Approved for the DNS Servers group.

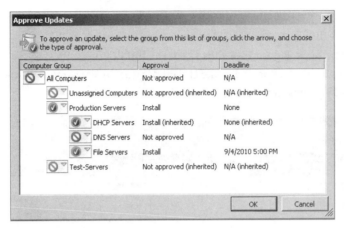

FIGURE 15-5: Approvals and removals

APPROVING UPDATES

To approve updates, perform the following general steps:

1. Locate the update that you want to approve in the list of updates. You can use the search function to find a specific update. You can also configure updates to be displayed by:

   ▷ **Approval Status:** Unapproved, Approved, Declined, or Any Except Declined

   ▷ **Update Status:** Failed or Needed, Installed/Not Applicable or No Status, Failed, Needed, Installed/Not Applicable, No Status, or Any

2. Select the update. In the Actions pane, click Approve. This opens the Approve Updates dialog box. This dialog box lists all the WSUS computer groups. Select a computer group and use the drop-down menu to select Approved for Install. The approval will be inherited by all groups under this group in the WSUS hierarchy.

3. After you have configured the update as Approved for Install, you can also configure a deadline for the update. An update deadline ensures that WSUS clients install the update by a certain date. If you want to force an update to install immediately, set a deadline for a date one day prior to the current date.

REMOVING UPDATES

Even when you test updates prior to deployment, there will be times when an update that you have rolled out causes a problem that your testing did not uncover. This is because even reasonably rigorous testing cannot cover every possible usage scenario. You can remove updates deployed by WSUS by following a similar process to that used to approve the update. Instead of selecting the Approved for Install option, you instead select the Approved for Removal option. Once the Approved for Removal option is set, you should configure a deadline for the removal. If you want the update removed as soon as possible, you should configure a removal deadline for a date one day prior to the current date. You should note that doing this might cause the servers in that group to reboot automatically after the update is removed.

If you want to remove an update from a specific server but not from all servers within a WSUS group, you can manually remove the update using the Programs and Features item in the Control Panel. To remove an update using this method, perform the following general steps:

1. Open the Programs and Features item from the Control Panel.

2. Click View Installed Updates.

3. Select the update that you want to install, and then click Uninstall.

To remove an update from a single computer running the Server Core version of Windows Server 2008 R2, perform the following steps:

1. Obtain the update file. This file is in .msu format. Make this file available to the computer running the Server Core version of Windows Server 2008 R2.

2. At the administrative command prompt, run the command:

```
Wusa /uninstall update-name.msu /quiet
```

SETTING UP AUTOMATIC APPROVALS

In general, most administrators are reluctant to configure automatic update approvals for computers running server operating systems. When you configure an automatic approval, you are essentially bypassing any update testing process to get the update deployed as quickly as possible. Administrators are more likely to configure automatic distribution of anti-virus and anti-malware definitions to clients, though most anti-virus and anti-malware technologies use their own internal update mechanism that bypasses the WSUS process. You should also note that, by default, the WSUS server itself is configured to automatically approve any updates to WSUS and will automatically approve new revisions of updates you have already approved, and automatically decline updates when a new revision causes those updates to expire. You can configure these options through the Automatic Approvals item in the Options node of the WSUS console.

To configure automatic updates, perform the following general steps:

1. Open the Automatic Approvals item from the Options node of the WSUS console. This will open the Automatic Approvals dialog box, shown in Figure 15-6.

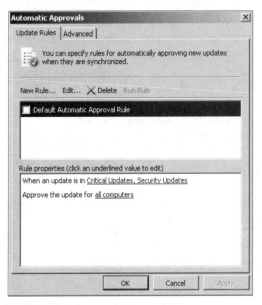

FIGURE 15-6: Automatic Approvals

2. Click New Rule to create a new rule. This will open the Add Rule dialog box.

3. Select the update Classification.

4. Select the product the update will apply to.

5. Set the deadline for the approval.

6. Select the group to which automatic approval applies. Note that the automatic approval will be inherited by any child groups and cannot be overridden at the child group level like a normal approval can.

Figure 15-7 shows an automatic approval rule for Definition Updates for Forefront Endpoint Protection 2010 for the Production Servers group with a deadline set to seven days after the automatic approval.

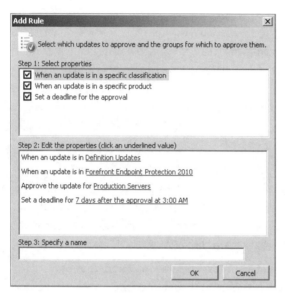

FIGURE 15-7: Automatic approval rule

UNDERSTANDING WSUS TOPOLOGIES

All clients of a WSUS server either retrieve their updates off that WSUS server or pull down the updates approved on the WSUS server off the Windows Update servers on the Internet. If you want to have some clients pull their updates off the WSUS server and other clients pull their update files off Microsoft's servers on the Internet, you need to configure more than one WSUS server. In this section, you learn about the different WSUS topologies, upstream and downstream servers, and WSUS replicas.

Most organizations have more than one site. This provides several challenges to those responsible for the automatic deployment of updates. These challenges include answering the following questions:

▶ Do you deploy one WSUS server and let clients in other sites pull their updates over the WAN link?

▶ Do you configure WSUS so that clients in all sites pull their approvals from the WSUS server but individually download their updates from the Microsoft Update servers on the Internet?

▶ If you deploy multiple WSUS servers, do you want to approve updates on each WSUS server or approve updates only once?

WSUS servers can function as upstream servers, downstream servers, or both. Both approvals and update files flow from upstream servers to downstream servers depending on configuration settings. Reporting data can flow back to upstream servers. Using the Update Source and Proxy Server item and the Update Files and Languages option in the WSUS console's Options node, you can configure a variety of combinations for update file and approval flow to downstream servers. These combinations include the following:

▶ **Configure downstream servers as replicas:** All configuration options, approvals, and updates replicate to the downstream server. This option involves the smallest administrative burden but can place stress on WAN links, as all update files must be replicated to branch office sites. All reporting data automatically replicates back up to the server at the top of the hierarchy.

▶ **Download approvals from upstream server. Download update files from upstream server:** This option is similar to the replica configuration but allows a local WSUS administrator to override approval configuration, if necessary.

▶ **Download approvals from upstream server. Download update files from Microsoft Update:** This solution works well for organizations that do not want to flood WAN links with update files. These files are instead retrieved from the Microsoft Update servers based on approvals configured on the upstream server.

▶ **Perform approvals locally. Download updates from upstream server:** In this option, an administrator performs his own approvals, but the updates are retrieved from the upstream server rather than from the Microsoft Update servers on the Internet. The local WSUS administrator is limited to being able to approve or decline updates that are available on the upstream server, rather than all updates available on the Microsoft Update servers.

VERIFYING UPDATE DEPLOYMENT

Deploying updates is one thing. Verifying that the updates have been successfully deployed is quite another. WSUS provides you only with information about computers that report back to it as a part of the WSUS process. If you install an update manually on a computer rather than through WSUS, WSUS is unable to tell you about it, as the installation of that update is not a part of the WSUS process. It is important to note that even when clients retrieve updates from WSUS, they don't always success-fully report back. Sometimes updates that don't install successfully are reported as installed, and sometimes updates that do install successfully aren't registered by WSUS. Multiple WSUS servers in the same organization complicate reporting consis-tency. Reporting consistency is especially problematic with laptop computers that move from site to site.

The most obvious way to check whether a specific update has been installed is to check the Installed Updates section of Programs and Features, shown in Figure 15-8. This console has a search input box that enables you to look for a specific update within the collection of installed updates. Although this works if you want to check only one server, auditing the status of a specific update using this method on all servers in your organization is unnecessarily laborious. In this section, you learn about several tools that you can use to determine which updates are installed on the servers in your organization.

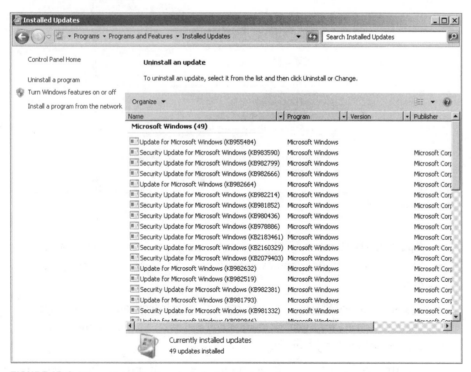

FIGURE 15-8: The updates that are installed on a particular server

Running WSUS Reports

WSUS offers a number of reports that you can run based on information stored within the WSUS database. It is important to stress that this is information that WSUS has collected when clients report back to the service: The WSUS server itself does not interrogate clients to determine whether specific updates have actually been installed. Reports are available from the Reports node in the WSUS console, as shown in Figure 15-9. The reports that you can view are as follows:

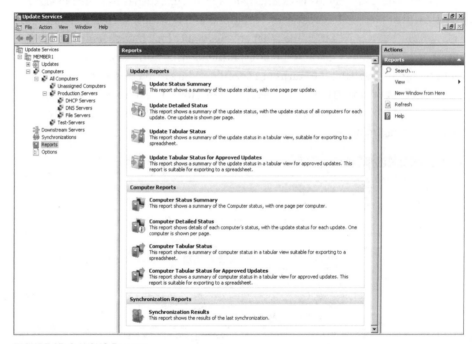

FIGURE 15-9: WSUS Reports

▶ **Update Status Summary:** This report provides information on a per update basis, summarizing the approval status of each update on a per computer group basis.

▶ **Update Detailed Status:** This report provides information on a per update basis, providing information on approval status on a per computer, rather than per computer group, basis.

▶ **Update Tabular Status:** This report provides similar information to the Update Status Summary report, except this report is presented in tabular format and can be exported to Excel.

▶ **Update Tabular Status for Approved Updates:** This report provides update status information in tabular format for updates that have been approved.

▶ **Computer Status Summary:** This report provides summary information about each computer that reports to the WSUS server.

▶ **Computer Detailed Status:** This report provides information on each computer's status along with the status of each update on that computer.

▶ **Computer Tabular Status:** This report provides information on computers where updates are needed, where they have failed to install, or where no status exists.

▶ **Computer Tabular Status for Approved Updates:** This report provides a spreadsheet view of approved updates on a per computer basis. It provides information on computers where updates have failed to install, are needed, or where no status information exists.

▶ **Synchronization Results:** This report provides information on previous synchronizations, including the number of new and revised updates.

Using MBSA

The *Microsoft Baseline Security Analyzer (MBSA)* is a free tool that allows you to scan a collection of computers to determine whether they have all approved updates installed. You can download the MBSA tool from Microsoft's website and run it on a computer that has Windows Server 2008 R2, Windows Server 2008, Windows Vista, or Windows 7 installed. The MBSA tool has the advantage of a GUI, which makes configuring it to scan different groups of computers a simple process.

Using the MBSA, you can determine one of the following:

▶ Whether all relevant updates that have been published by Microsoft have been installed on the target computers.

▶ Whether all updates approved on a specific WSUS server have been installed on the target computers.

The ability to check against a list of WSUS approved updates, rather than all updates published by Microsoft, enables you to better tailor the update check for your organization. If you attempt to scan a computer that does not use WSUS, you receive an error. As you can see in Figure 15-10, you can check on the basis of domain name and IPv4 address range. You can also scan for common administrative vulnerabilities and update the Windows Update agent on any computer that is subject to the scan.

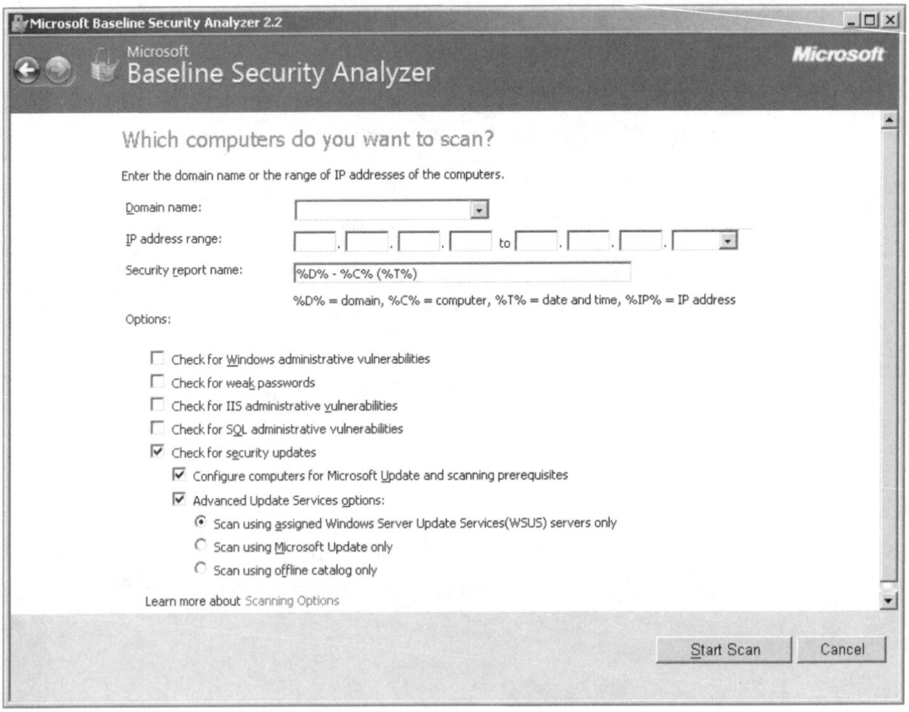

FIGURE 15-10: MBSA scan options

To run the MBSA tool, you need to have local Administrator permissions on the computer against which you are running the scan. This is relatively straightforward when all the servers that you are scanning are members of the same domain. It is somewhat more complicated when servers are configured as stand-alone computers and require separate unique credentials for logon.

Using Get-Hotfix

The MBSA tool isn't the only way that you can assess whether specific updates have been deployed to a server. You can use PowerShell v2's Get-Hotfix command to determine whether specific updates are present on a computer. To use Get-Hotfix to query remote computers, you need to have enabled remote management on the target computer. You learned about enabling remote management for PowerShell in Chapter 2, "The Windows Server 2008 R2 Administrator's Toolkit."

The default output of the Get-Hotfix cmdlet is a list of hotfixes present on the target computer. You can specify the target computer using its NetBIOS name, Fully Qualified Domain Name, or IP address.

You can use Get-Hotfix to query based on source, description, HotfixID, installation date, and the account used to install the update. The two most common update descriptions are Update and Security Update. HotfixID is the knowledge base article number associated with the update. For example, to check if a hotfix with the id KB123456 is installed on the local computer, run the following command:

```
Get-Hotfix -id KB123456
```

If the hotfix is present, the command will return information including when the update was installed, the type of update and the account used to install the update.

You can use the Get-Hotfix cmdlet as part of a larger PowerShell script to determine whether computers in your organization are missing a specific hotfix. For example, the following PowerShell commands will scan through the list of computers listed in the file computers.txt to determine whether Hotfix KB123456 has been installed. The name of any computer that is found to be missing the hotfix will be written to the file KB123456.txt.

```
$x = Get-Content computers.txt
$x | foreach { if (!(Get-Hotfix -id KB123456 -computername $_))
{ Add-Content $_ -path KB123456.txt }}
```

GOING FURTHER

The great advantage of WSUS is that it is a free add-on to Windows Server 2008 R2. A disadvantage is that while it does some things well, it is a free product and hence lacks more comprehensive patch management functionality found in products that require a paid license. Microsoft makes two products that allow you to take patch management further. These products are SCE and SCCM. These products provide the following additional functionality:

- ▶ SCE and SCCM both enable you to deploy updates to non-Microsoft products. As Microsoft has become more rigorous in applying its security development lifecycle, attackers are moving on to other applications. Keeping your servers up-to-date means more than keeping Windows Server 2008 R2 up-to-date; you need to keep your third party applications up-to-date as well.

- ▶ SCE 2010 allows you to publish updates from vendors other than Microsoft. SCE 2010 works in a slightly different manner than System Center Configuration Manager, publishing updates using a special method through WSUS, rather than using a special agent on the client computer.

▶ SCE allows computers to be members of multiple groups, and SCCM allows computers to be members of multiple collections. This enables you to target updates more effectively than is possible with WSUS, where a computer can belong only to a single group.

▶ SCCM provides a greater scope to schedule the deployment of updates. With WSUS, once you approve an update, all clients within the scope of that approval begin detecting and installing the update. With SCCM, you can choose a specific time of day for updates to be installed. Clients pre-stage the updates and then install them during the assigned maintenance window.

▶ SCCM allows updates to be deployed using Wake On LAN technologies. This enables a shut down computer to wake up in the middle of the night so that it can install an update. This is less important for servers than it is for client computers.

▶ SCCM has more detailed reporting functionality than WSUS. SCCM fully integrates with SQL Server Reporting Services. You can use SCCM's query functionality to build new collections, such as "All servers without a specific update."

▶ You can use SCCM to monitor the configuration of servers as a part of your change management process to determine if server configuration has varied from the established norm. This can be very useful if you have more than one administrator in your organization, and it isn't clear whether updates have been deployed.

SCE offers a subset of the functionality available in System Center Operations Manager, System Center Virtual Machine Manager and System Center Configuration Manager. Microsoft targets SCE at networks that have 50 or fewer servers and 500 or fewer clients that might not need the greater functionality present in the enterprise-level products. While you can use SCE to schedule the deployment of updates from vendors other than Microsoft, you will be unable to deploy features such as Wake On LAN or desired configuration management. Additional products that you can use for update management include but are not limited to: GFI LANguard, ManageEngine Security Manager Plus, WinINSTALL, and Ecora Patch Manager.

SUMMARY

The WSUS role provides a free patch management solution that you can host on computers running Windows Server 2008 R2. Through the use of WSUS groups, you can stagger the deployment of updates, deploying first to a test environment, then to limited production, and then finally to all production servers in such a way that you minimize the chance that problems with the update might impact directly the services your servers host. You can configure Group Policy in such a way that updates are only installed at a specific time each week, though you need to ensure that you stagger this time across servers, as having all servers in your organization reboot to install an update at the same time might result in unintended consequences. If you want to go further than WSUS, Microsoft offers several products in its System Center range that provide greater patch management functionality. There are also comprehensive products available from third-party vendors in the event that the Microsoft solutions do not meet your organization's precise needs.

Further Links

Microsoft Baseline Security Analyzer

`http://technet.microsoft.com/en-au/security/cc184924.aspx`

Get-Hotfix

`http://technet.microsoft.com/en-us/library/dd315358.aspx`

WSUS Support Team Blog

`http://blogs.technet.com/b/sus/`

WSUS TechNet Home

`http://technet.microsoft.com/en-us/library/dd939796(WS.10).aspx`

System Center Essentials

`www.microsoft.com/systemcenter/en/us/essentials.aspx`

System Center Configuration Manager

`www.microsoft.com/systemcenter/en/us/configuration-manager.aspx`

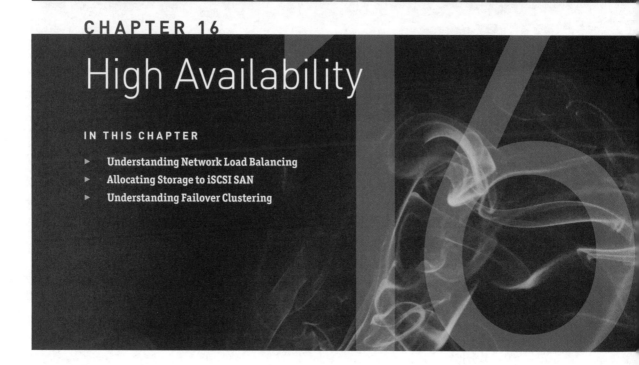

High Availability

High availability allows administrators to ensure that network resources remain available in the event that one or more of the servers that host those resources goes offline. You can use Windows Server 2008 R2 in several ways to achieve high-availability objectives. The most common ways are Network Load Balancing and failover clustering. Each of these techniques has its place in a high-availability strategy, and in this chapter, you learn which technology is appropriate for making a particular service, such as a Web server or a DNS server, highly available.

UNDERSTANDING NETWORK LOAD BALANCING

Network Load Balancing (NLB) is a high-availability technology that allows servers that host the same content to work together to provide that content to network clients. NLB works by creating a virtual network adapter with incoming traffic to this adapter spread across multiple hosts. The virtual network adapter has its own IP address and physical or MAC address. The advantage of NLB is that it automatically reconfigures itself as nodes join and leave the cluster. You can configure Windows Server 2008 R2 NLB clusters with up to 32 nodes.

▶ In reality, performance deteriorates if you have more than eight nodes in an NLB cluster. If clusters larger than this are required, you use multiple clusters with eight nodes and load balance them using DNS round robin.

For example, if you have four Web servers that host the same web pages, you can use Network Load Balancing to configure things so that clients are able to address the servers using a single address. When a client makes a request of the NLB cluster, the node under the least load is the one to respond to that request. In the event that one of these servers fail, clients of the NLB cluster can still access the other servers in the cluster using that one address, as NLB automatically detects node failures. Should the failed node return to service, new clients are automatically redirected to it.

NLB works well if you want to:

▶ Make a Web server highly available.

▶ Make a set of Remote Desktop servers highly available.

NLB works because, in these cases, it is possible to ensure that each node has precisely the same content. The Web servers host the same files and the Remote Desktop servers the same applications. This is a stateless service, because no matter which node a client accesses, it gets the same content.

You can't use Network Load Balancing to make a file share highly available, because there is no way to set up a file share so that it would be consistent across all nodes in a network load balanced environment. A change made to a file on node A wouldn't necessarily be replicated to node B. File shares are *stateful applications*— they keep data in a single place—and can't be network load balanced.

You can use Network Load Balancing to make websites that use SQL Server database back-ends on separate servers highly available, but only if the websites are load balanced and the SQL Server database is not. Because it is a stateful application, you must use failover clustering with SQL Server, to make it highly available.

It is possible to use NLB with different versions of the Windows Server operating system on each node, though generally not a good idea to do so. The Standard, Enterprise, and Datacenter editions of Windows Server 2008 R2 all support Network Load Balancing.

Understanding Unicast and Multicast

When you create a new NLB cluster, you have to determine which cluster operation mode to use. Cluster operation mode is primarily dependent on the number of network adapters installed on each cluster node. NLB has two modes of operation: *unicast* and *multicast*. All servers within a cluster must operate in one mode or the other. You cannot mix the two operation modes. Configuring the operations mode is shown in Figure 16-1.

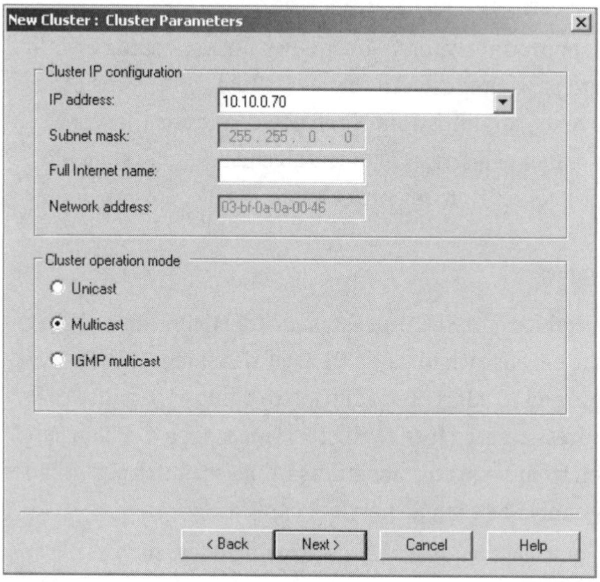

FIGURE 16-1: Cluster operation mode

OPERATING NLB UNICAST

The MAC address created for the virtual network adapter is shared among the participants in the cluster. If the cluster nodes have only one network card, the cluster's virtual MAC address logically replaces the physical MAC address for that network card, and the server will respond to network traffic targeted at the virtual MAC address.

Although the server still retains its original IP address, that original IP address resolves to the virtual MAC address rather than the physical MAC address.

When you use NLB unicast mode on servers that have a single network adapter, only computers in the same subnet as that server are able to communicate with that server using the original IP address. This means that if you need to perform management tasks on that server, you need to connect from the same subnet as the NLB cluster. For example, suppose that one of the servers in a unicast-mode NLB cluster has an original IP address of 192.168.1.10 and the cluster IP address is 192.168.1.100. You have configured NLB to support a Web server, and a port rule is set up for port 80. If you wanted to connect to this server using Remote Desktop, you would be able to make a connection to IP address 192.168.1.10 only from a host on the same subnet. You would not be able to make a successful Remote Desktop connection to IP address 192.168.1.10 from a remote subnet, because the unicast configuration replaces the physical MAC address with the cluster's virtual MAC address.

NLB unicast mode is most appropriate when there are two network cards installed on a host. The first network card participates in the cluster, while you use the other for management and inter-server communication. When you configure a server to have two network cards as a member of a unicast-mode NLB cluster, you can make management connections to the server from remote subnets.

OPERATING NLB MULTICAST

NLB multicast mode is more suitable than NLB unicast mode for computers that have single network adapters. This is because when using NLB multicast mode, the server retains its original MAC address and IP address in addition to being able to use the virtual MAC address and IP address created for the cluster. This means that you can perform remote administration from separate subnets, as in the scenario described earlier, even though the server only has a single network card.

The only drawback of NLB multicast mode is that network devices, such as switches and routers, must support multicast MAC addressing. As modern devices almost always do so, NLB multicast mode works as a good default mode for Windows Server 2008 R2 NLB clusters.

OPERATING IGMP MULTICAST

IGMP multicast mode is a special version of NLB multicast mode that enhances network performance by limiting switch flooding. Enabling IGMP support means that multicast traffic passes through only switch ports that service the NLB cluster rather than all switch ports, which is the case with standard NLB multicast mode. It is possible to use IGMP multicast mode only if your switch hardware supports this technology.

Creating NLB Clusters

To create an NLB cluster, ensure that the Network Load Balancing feature is installed on all hosts that will participate as nodes in the cluster. You can do this from PowerShell by using the following command:

```
Add-WindowsFeature NLB
```

After this has been done, open the Network Load Balancing Manager console from the Administrative Tools menu and perform the following steps:

1. From the Cluster menu, click New. This opens the New Cluster: Connect dialog. Enter the address of the first node that you want to be a member of the NLB cluster. Click Next.

2. On the New Cluster: Host Parameters page, click Next.

3. On the New Cluster: Cluster IP Addresses page, enter the IP address of the cluster, and then click Next.

4. On the New Cluster: Cluster Parameters page, select the Cluster Operations Mode, and then click Next.

5. On the New Cluster: Port Rules page, review the port rules, and then click Finish.

6. In Network Load Balancing Manager, on the Cluster menu, click Add Host. This allows you to add a second node to the cluster.

7. On the Add Host to Cluster: Connect dialog, enter the address of the second node, and then click Connect. Click Next twice, and then click Finish.

Managing NLB Clusters

You manage NLB clusters using the Network Load Balancing Manager console, accessible from the Administrative Tools menu. Using this tool, you can perform tasks such as altering the port rules and parameters under which the cluster operates. To manage NLB clusters, you must be a member of the local Administrators group on each node of the cluster.

To remove hosts from NLB clusters through the Network Load Balancing Manager, simply right-click the host that you want to remove and select Delete Host. You can remove the entire cluster by right-clicking the cluster and selecting Delete Cluster. If you want to perform maintenance on a cluster node, you have the option of blocking incoming connections while retaining existing connections. You can then wait for the existing connections to terminate before performing your maintenance task. You have the following options for controlling NLB cluster nodes:

▶ **Start:** Starts a cluster that has been stopped

▶ **Stop:** Stops a cluster. This terminates any active connections.

▶ **Drainstop:** This stops a cluster node from receiving any new connections but does not terminate existing connections.

▶ You use Drainstop prior to shutting down a cluster node gracefully.

▶ **Suspend:** This pauses the cluster node until the Resume command is issued. This differs from the Stop option in that Stop shuts down the cluster service on the targeted node.

▶ **Resume:** Resumes the cluster node after it has been suspended

Understanding NLB Port Rules

NLB port rules allow you to control how NLB clusters deal with traffic to a specific port, such as port 80 for Web traffic. Port rules are set on the Port Rules tab of the Cluster Properties dialog box. Port rules must match for each host in the NLB cluster. When you configure port rules on the cluster level, the port rules for all nodes in the cluster are configured automatically. A node is unable to join the cluster if it has a different set of port rules. The default port rule for an NLB cluster redirects all traffic in a balanced way to all nodes in the cluster. You should delete this default rule if you want to create specific rules.

When creating an NLB cluster port rule, you choose a *filtering mode*. Filtering modes allow you to specify whether only a single node, some nodes, or all nodes in the cluster respond to requests from a single client during the session. This is important for some applications, such as e-commerce websites, because they require all session traffic to occur only between a single host and the client.

The available filtering modes are as follows:

▶ **Single Host:** A single node handles all traffic sent to the cluster matching the port rule.

▶ **Disable Port Range:** Use this mode to configure the cluster not to respond to traffic on specific ports. NLB discards traffic sent to the cluster IP on these ports.

- **Multiple Host Filtering**: This mode allows traffic to be directed to all nodes in the cluster. When you configure multiple host settings, you also configure an affinity setting. Affinity settings work as follows:

  - **None**: All requests are distributed equally across the cluster, even if a client has an established session.

  - **Network**: This is similar to netmask ordering and directs clients to the closest node on the basis of the subnet.

  - **Single**: After a client establishes a session, all subsequent requests in the session will be directed to the same node in the cluster. This allows sessions that require stateful data, such as e-commerce transactions, to be completed. This is the default filtering mode on port rules.

ALLOCATING STORAGE TO ISCSI SAN

For the uninitiated, getting Windows Server 2008 R2 to work with a storage area network, such as an iSCSI LUN, can seem counter intuitive. Depending on your licensing, Windows Server 2008 R2 can be configured to run as an iSCSI target, meaning that you can allocate storage on one Windows Server 2008 R2 computer as a SAN disk to another Windows Server 2008 R2 computer. Windows Storage Server 2008 R2 is essentially Windows Server 2008 with this functionality added in. The Microsoft iSCSI target software, which is available to some customers, allows you to add this functionality to an existing server.

▶ Running a Windows Server 2008 R2 box as a dedicated SAN device is a bit like running it as a packet router. It accomplishes a particular task, but you're probably better off buying dedicated hardware.

Configuring iSCSI Targets

Configuring an iSCSI target involves ensuring that iSCSI clients are able to connect. This can be done by configuring some firewall rules to allow the necessary traffic and to configure how authentication works.

> **NOTE** There are many different options for an iSCSI host, and it is likely that the method that you use to configure iSCSI on your system will depend on the iSCSI solution you purchase. It is possible to configure certain Linux distributions to function as iSCSI targets in the event that you don't want to use Windows to host this role.

To configure an iSCSI target, perform the following general steps:

1. Configure firewall rules to allow communication to the server that hosts the iSCSI target software. This can be done by issuing the following sets of commands:

```
Netsh advfirewall firewall add rule name="Microsoft iSCSI Software
Target Service-TCP-3260" dir=in action=allow protocol=TCP
localport=3260

netsh advfirewall firewall add rule name="Microsoft iSCSI Software
Target Service-TCP-135" dir=in action=allow protocol=TCP localport=135

netsh advfirewall firewall add rule name="Microsoft iSCSI Software
Target Service-UDP-138" dir=in action=allow protocol=UDP localport=138

netsh advfirewall firewall add rule name="Microsoft iSCSI Software
Target Service" dir=in action=allow program="%SystemRoot%\System32\
WinTarget.exe" enable=yes

netsh advfirewall firewall add rule name="Microsoft iSCSI Software
Target Service Status Proxy" dir=in action=allow program="%SystemRoot%\
System32\WTStatusProxy.exe" enable=yes
```

2. Open the Microsoft iSCSI Software Target application from the Administrative Tools menu. This utility is shown in Figure 16-2. Right-click on the iSCSI Targets node, and then click on Create iSCSI Target.

3. On the first page of the Create iSCSI Target Wizard, click Next.

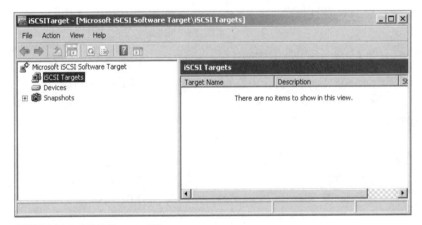

FIGURE 16-2: iSCSI Target utility

4. On the iSCSI Target Name box, enter a name for the target, such as
   LUN-ALPHA, and click Next.

5. On the iSCSI Initiators Identifiers page, click Advanced. On the Advanced
   Identifiers page, click Add.

6. On the Add/Edit Identifiers page, enter the IP address or FQDN of the server
   that will access the LUN from the network, and then click OK. Figure 16-3
   shows access configured for a host at IP address 10.10.0.24. When you have
   populated the addresses of all devices that will access the LUN, click OK, and
   then click Next.

7. Click Next, and then click Finish.

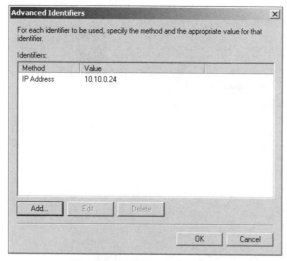

FIGURE 16-3: Advanced Identifiers

Creating iSCSI LUNs on Windows Server 2008 R2

Creating an iSCSI LUN is a matter of taking existing storage space on Windows Server
2008 R2 and making it available, through the iSCSI target, to computers with properly configured iSCSI connections. To do this, you create a VHD file that will then be
made available to clients that want to configure storage. To create an iSCSI LUN using
the Microsoft iSCSI Target software, perform the following steps:

1. In the iSCSI Target console, right-click on Devices, and then click Create
   Virtual Disk.

2. On the Create Virtual Disk Wizard, click Next.

3. Enter the address of the file that you wish to create that will be made available as a storage device to SAN clients, and then click Next. For example, enter `d:\disks\lun-alpha.vhd`.

4. Specify the size of the storage that will be made available to SAN clients, and then click Next.

5. Provide a description of the VHD, and then click Next.

6. On the Access page, shown in Figure 16-4, click Add and specify which iSCSI targets will be able to access the virtual disk. Click Next, and then click Finish.

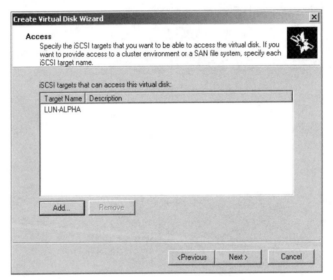

FIGURE 16-4: iSCSI Access

Using iSCSI Initiator

The *iSCSI Initiator* is a component built into Windows Server 2008 R2 that allows you to connect to an iSCSI LUN through an iSCSI target. Assuming that you have configured iSCSI correctly on the SAN, making a connection requires performing the following steps:

1. Open iSCSI Initiator from the Administrative Tools menu. When prompted to start the service automatically, click Yes.

2. On the Targets tab of iSCSI Initiator properties, shown in Figure 16-5, enter the IP address of the iSCSI target, and then click Quick Connect.

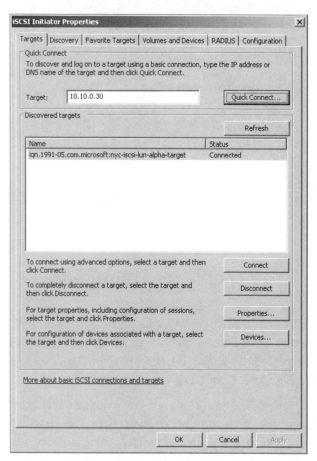

FIGURE 16-5: iSCSI Quick Connect

3. On the Volumes and Devices tab, click Auto Configure. Verify that volumes are mounted. Click OK.

To provision storage, once you have connected to an LUN, use the Disk Management console. Here you can bring disks online and then manipulate them, such as creating volumes, as necessary. Figure 16-6 shows the Disk Management console when connected to an iSCSI LUN where Disk 3 is an unconfigured disk. The disk needs to be brought online before it can be managed and formatted. Once formatted, it can be brought online on other nodes as necessary.

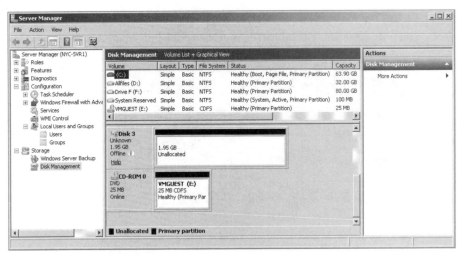

FIGURE 16-6: LUN connected

UNDERSTANDING FAILOVER CLUSTERING

Failover clustering allows two or more servers to host an application, with another server taking over in the event that the current host of the application fails. Failover clusters on Windows Server 2008 R2 support two types of application: *single-instance* and *multiple-instance applications*. These two types differ in the following ways:

▶ Single-instance applications run on one server at a time. An example of a single-instance application is an authentication server. If you have multiple authentication servers, clients might receive conflicting responses when they request authentication. When an application runs as a single-instance application, it runs only on one cluster node at a time and other nodes in the cluster operate in a standby configuration.

▶ Multiple-instance applications can share data or partition it in such a way that one node can provide an answer for a particular segment of the data. Some e-mail servers and advanced database servers operate in this fashion, but, in general, multiple-instance applications are less common than their single-instance counterparts.

To run on a Windows Server 2008 R2 failover cluster, an application must meet the following criteria:

▶ The application must use an IP-based protocol.

▶ Applications that require access to local data must allow you to configure where data is stored, such as configuring a database to be hosted on a SAN volume rather than a local hard-disk drive.

▶ If an application needs access to data independent of what node it is running on, the data must be shared on a shared-disk resource such as an iSCSI LUN, Serial Attached SCSI, or Fibre Channel.

▶ Applications that run and store data locally should use the Node Majority or Node and File Share Majority quorum model. It will also be necessary to have a separate file replication and application data technology.

▶ When an application fails over to an alternate node, client sessions need to be able to reestablish connectivity automatically. Applications that time out when a network connection is broken are generally not suited for failover clusters.

To install failover clustering, you must be running the Enterprise or Datacenter versions of Windows Server 2008 R2. You can install failover clustering as a feature, rather than a role, using the Server Manager console. To install failover clustering from PowerShell, ensure that the Server Manager module is loaded and run the following command:

```
Add-WindowsFeature Failover-Clustering
```

Selecting Cluster Quorum Models

Clusters provide protection against failure; however, even the most robust failover cluster will itself stop running after a certain number of failures to protect data integrity or failed communication attempts between nodes. A cluster's *quorum model* determines the number of failures that can occur before the cluster stops functioning. Quorum exists as a database in the registry and is maintained on the witness disk or witness share. The witness keeps a copy of cluster configuration data so that servers are able to enroll in the cluster. One server in a cluster manages quorum data at any time, but all nodes in the cluster host copies. A quorum model is recommended when you create a Windows Server 2008 R2 cluster, but you can select an alternate model if you want to. There are four quorum models available to Windows Server 2008 R2 models:

▶ Always go with the recommended quorum model unless you really know what you are doing.

▶ **Node Majority:** This model suits cluster deployments with an odd number of nodes. A cluster that uses Node Majority retains quorum if the number of available nodes exceeds the number of failed nodes. For example, in a five-node cluster, the cluster remains online if two nodes fail, but loses quorum when three nodes go offline. Node Majority is suited to geographically dispersed clusters.

▶ **Node and Disk Majority:** This model is suited to cluster deployments with an even number of nodes. As long as the witness disk is available, a Node and Disk Majority cluster will remain online as long as half or more of its nodes are available. For example: A cluster with four nodes will remain online if two nodes and the witness disk remain available. Three nodes need to be available in the event that the witness disk fails.

▶ **Node and File Share Majority:** Similar to Node and Disk Majority, in this model the quorum is stored on a network share rather than a witness disk. It is suited to clusters with an even number of nodes but is less preferable to Node and Disk Majority.

▶ **No Majority: Disk Only:** This model is used for clusters with odd numbers of nodes. As long as the disk hosting the quorum remains available, the cluster remains online. This mode is not recommended for production environments, as the disk containing quorum is the single point of failure.

To view the current quorum configuration, open Failover Cluster Manager and under More Actions select Configure Cluster Quorum Settings. The current model is shown in the second page of the wizard as shown in Figure 16-7.

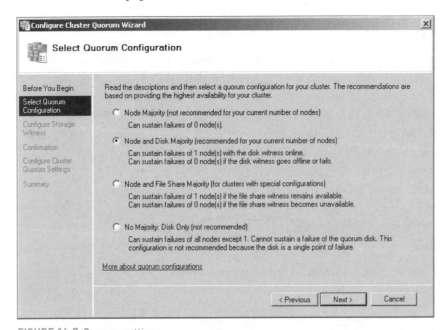

FIGURE 16-7: Quorum settings

Validating a Cluster Before You Create It

To check a cluster's configuration to ensure that it is compatible and can be created, you validate it. You can validate a cluster using the Failover Cluster Manager. Prior to validating a cluster, you should ensure that all potential nodes are online and have access to necessary shared resources. For example, you would make sure that you have configured your potential witness disk and shared-storage drive before attempting to validate the cluster configuration.

Validating a cluster configuration checks the following tests, which are shown in Figure 16-8.

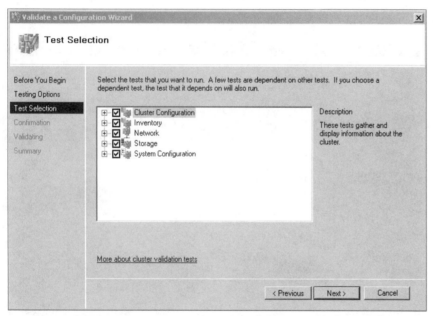

FIGURE 16-8: Validation test

- ▶ **Cluster Configuration:** Checks that the cluster-level components are compatible with the cluster configuration

- ▶ **Inventory Test:** Creates a list of components and settings on each node

- ▶ **Network Test:** Ensures that network settings are compatible with cluster configuration

- ▶ **Storage Test:** Verifies that storage is compatible with the cluster configuration

- ▶ **System Configuration Test:** Checks system settings across all nodes

To validate a cluster, perform the following steps:

1. Open Failover Cluster Manager from the Administrative Tools menu.

2. In the Actions pane, click Validate a Configuration. On the first page of the validation wizard, click Next.

3. Enter the names of the servers that you want to be members of the cluster in the Select Servers or a Cluster dialog. Click Next.

4. Choose to run all tests, and then click Next.

5. On the Confirmation page, click Next.

6. The validation will proceed as shown in Figure 16-9.

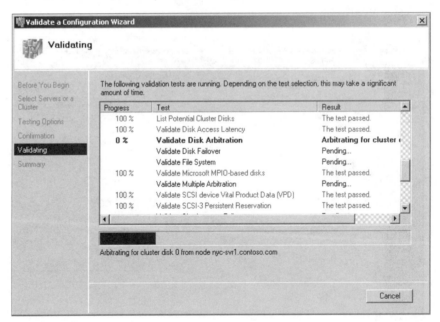

FIGURE 16-9: Cluster test

7. The most common warning received is that redundant networks haven't been detected. This warning will not stop a cluster from being successfully created, though it is a good idea to have redundant networking when building a failover cluster.

In general, your cluster nodes should be as identical as possible. That way, when a service fails across to another node, users will not have a dramatically different experience. Cluster nodes should run the same version of Windows Server 2008 R2, and you should avoid situations where you plan to have different versions and editions of the operating system being part of one cluster.

To create a cluster, perform the following steps:

1. Open the Failover Cluster Manager on one of the cluster nodes.

2. On the Actions menu, click Create a Cluster.

3. In the Create a Cluster Wizard, click Next.

4. On the Select Servers page, add the servers that you want to be members of the cluster, and then click Next.

5. On the Access Point for Administering the Cluster page, enter a name for the cluster and provide a cluster address. This page is shown in Figure 16-10. Click Next.

▶ Remember to create small witness disks on the SAN. They don't need to be very large to do what they do, and there is no need to waste storage on the SAN that will not be used for anything other than storing quorum configuration data.

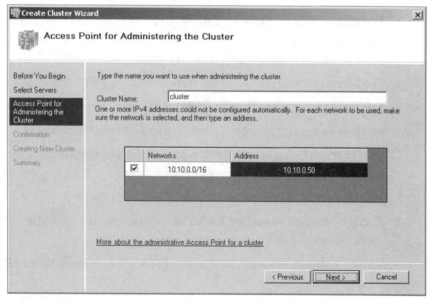

FIGURE 16-10: Cluster Access Point

6. On the Confirmation page, review the configuration information, and then click Next. The cluster will now be created. On the Summary page, click Finish.

Configuring Services for High Availability

Once the cluster has been created, you can configure a service or application to become highly available. This is always done after you create the cluster. For example, if you want to create a clustered server running SQL Server 2008 R2, you would install SQL Server 2008 R2 after you create the cluster.

To make a service highly available, use the High Availability Wizard. Several applications and services have specific settings and are available for selection from within the High Availability Wizard. Services and applications not listed within the wizard should use the Generic Service, Generic Application, or Generic Script option. Services and applications specifically listed in the wizard include the following:

- ▶ **DFS Namespace Server**: Provides a virtual view of an organization's shared folders

- ▶ **DHCP Server**: Provides IP address information to clients

- ▶ **Distributed Transaction Coordinator (DTC)**: Provides support for distributed applications that are used to perform transactions. A transaction is a set of tasks that must either succeed or fail together.

- ▶ **File Server**: Provides the ability to store files on the network

- ▶ **Internet Storage Name Service (iSNS)**: Provides a directory of iSCSI targets

- ▶ **Message Queuing**: Is used by distributed applications for communication

- ▶ **Other Server**: Provides both a client access point and storage for an application that you configure after creating the cluster

- ▶ **Print Server**: Manages the printer queue for a shared printer

- ▶ **Remote Desktop Connection Broker**: Allows sessions to be load-balanced across a Remote Desktop Server farm

- ▶ **Virtual Machine**: Allows a virtual machine to be highly available on a Hyper-V cluster

- ▶ **WINS Server**: Allows the Windows Internet Naming Service (WINS) server to remain available

▶ How this wizard functions depends on what service you choose to make highly available. In this case, the File Server role is being made highly available.

To make a service highly available, perform the following steps:

1. In the Failover Cluster Manager console, click on Configure a Service or Application in the Actions pane.

2. On the Select Service or Application page, shown in Figure 16-11, select the service that you want to make highly available, and then click Next.

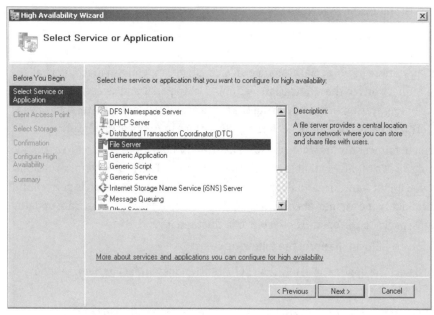

FIGURE 16-11: Select Service or Application

3. Enter a name and IP address for the clustered resource, and then click Next.

4. Specify the storage volume that will be assigned to the application, and then click Next.

5. On the Confirmation page, click Next. After high availability has been configured, click Finish.

Managing Clusters

Cluster management is performed in the Failover Cluster Manager console. Expanding a cluster reveals available options for that cluster, including nodes, networks, cluster events, and storage.

To pause a node, select the node and then, from the Actions menu, click Pause. To resume the node, click the node and then select Resume. You can also use the Cluster .exe command-line tool to pause and resume nodes. To pause the SRV1 node of the cluster CLUSTER using the command line, type the following at the command prompt:

```
cluster CLUSTER node SRV1 /pause
```

Type the following to resume the node:

```
cluster CLUSTER node SRV1 /resume
```

If you want to perform maintenance on an application, you can disconnect all active connections to the application by right-clicking on it and selecting Take the Service or Application Offline. To bring the application back online after it has been taken offline, right-click and select Bring the Service or Application Online.

Manual failover occurs when you force a different node in the cluster to gracefully take control of a highly-available application or service. There are several situations where you might want to manually perform failover. The most common is performing maintenance. For example, at certain times it is necessary to apply software updates or service packs to the operating system of a cluster node.

To force a failover, perform the following steps:

1. Select the application in Failover Cluster Manager under the Services and Applications node.

2. From the Action menu, click Move This Service or Application to Another Node.

If your cluster nodes are identical, you probably don't care which specific node has control of a highly-available application or service. If nodes are not identical,

▶ When you perform software updates on cluster nodes, always update the passive node first. Once you have updated the passive, you can perform a manual failover so that the passive node becomes active. This allows you to update the other cluster nodes without disrupting service to clients.

you may want to ensure that a service returns to a specific node automatically after a failover occurs. This is known as configuring failback. To configure a service to automatically failback to a node after a specific amount of time, edit the service's properties and configure the Allow Failback option as shown in Figure 16-12.

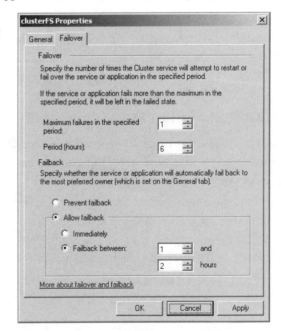

FIGURE 16-12: Allow failback

SUMMARY

Network Load Balancing is supported on all versions of Windows Server 2008 R2 and allows you to balance traffic across multiple nodes that host identical content. NLB clusters can operate in unicast or multicast modes, with multicast being a better option as long as your network hardware supports it. The Enterprise and Datacenter editions of Windows Server 2008 R2 support failover clustering. Failover clustering works best when you have a shared-disk resource, such as an iSCSI volume, that can host cluster quorum data.

Additional Sources

Network Load Balancing Deployment Guide

`http://technet.microsoft.com/en-us/library/cc754833(WS.10).aspx`

Failover Cluster Requirements

`http://technet.microsoft.com/en-us/library/ff182359(WS.10).aspx`

PART V

REMOTE ACCESS SECRETS

CHAPTER 17

Presentation and Application Virtualization

Presentation virtualization allows an application to run on one computer with the graphical output of that computer displayed on another. The benefit of presentation virtualization is that it allows relatively resource-poor clients to run resource-intensive applications remotely. Rather than deploy powerful computers to each user in the organization, you can deploy thin clients, allowing users to run powerful applications remotely across the network.

In Windows Server 2008 R2, the Remote Desktop Services role allows you to leverage presentation virtualization to provide applications to users across the network. Another benefit of presentation virtualization is that it allows you to manage, update, and deploy applications rapidly as they are all hosted in a central location.

Application virtualization is a technology that allows you to partition an application from the host operating system. This means applications that might be incompatible with that operating system are able to run in a special virtual environment on it. Application virtualization works by streaming those parts of the application that the user needs across the network, rather than streaming the whole application. In this chapter, you learn how to configure Windows Server 2008 R2 to support both presentation and application virtualization.

UNDERSTANDING REMOTE DESKTOP SESSION HOST

▶ The key to a successful RD Session Host server deployment is ensuring that you provision the server well with bandwidth, processor power, and RAM. Use tools such as Windows System Resource Manager to ensure that resources are distributed equitably across user sessions.

Remote Desktop (RD) Session Host provides a full desktop environment to a user. Users connect to the RD Session Host server from a thin client, such as Windows Thin PC or the Remote Desktop Connection client that ships with Windows operating systems. An RD Session Host provides a full screen or window that reproduces a Windows desktop, including taskbar, Start menu, and desktop icons.

The benefits of using RD Session Host include:

▶ It allows users to connect from clients, such as Windows Thin PC, that run a minimal operating system. Windows Thin PC can be installed on older hardware that might not run an operating system like Windows 7, because it does not meet the system requirements.

▶ You can deploy an application to many users by installing it on a small number of RD Session Host servers. Users can run applications on RD Session Host servers that might be incompatible with their operating systems.

▶ Application updates are simplified. You update an application on the RD Session Host server rather than having to push the patch down to individual operating systems.

▶ It allows you to grant access to a standardized corporate desktop experience for users who have chosen to use their own computer at work.

▶ It allows you to grant access, through a VPN, to a standardized corporate desktop for users at remote locations or who telecommute.

▶ It allows you to grant access to applications for operating systems that do not support RD Web Access or RD RemoteApp.

▶ RD Session Host clients exist for most operating systems, allowing applications such as Office 2010 to run on iPads, Macs, or Linux without a local installation. The drawback is that they don't often support Network Level Authentication, the strongest authentication available on an RD Session Host server.

Configuring RD Session Host Servers

Although you'll probably find the default settings appropriate for most of your organization's needs, you can configure RD Session Host server protocol-level settings and server-level settings to tune your organization's RD Session Host experience. You can also configure these settings through Group Policy if you have a large number of RD Session Host servers to manage.

PROTOCOL-LEVEL SETTINGS

Most of the important RD Session Host server configuration settings are set at the protocol level. At the Remote Desktop Protocol (RDP) level, you can set configuration items such as session security level, logon settings, and the number of sessions an individual user can establish. You can edit settings at the protocol level by performing the following steps:

1. Open the Remote Desktop Session Host Configuration console, located in the Remote Desktop Services folder of Administrative Tools in the Start menu.

2. Right-click the RDP-TCP item in the Connections area, and click on Properties. This will bring up the RDP-TCP Properties dialog box.

3. Navigate to the tab that hosts the setting that you wish to configure. You use the following tabs to configure specific settings:

   ▷ **General:** On this tab, you can set the security layer level with your options being RDP Security Layer or SSL/TLS 1.0. SSL is more secure but requires that an appropriate computer certificate be installed. The Encryption Level option allows you to set Client Compatible, High, or FIPS (Federal Information Processing Standard) Compliant. The setting you use depends on the key strength supported by the client. On this tab, you can configure RD Session Host to force clients to use Network Level Authentication.

   ▷ **Log On Settings:** On this tab, you can configure a logon session to use the credentials provided by the client or to use a generic account for all sessions.

   ▷ **Sessions:** On this tab, shown in Figure 17-1, you can specify how long an RD Session Host server allows active connections to last and how to treat idle and disconnected sessions. You can use these settings to ensure that disconnected and idle sessions don't consume unnecessary resources.

▶ Network Level Authentication is supported only in clients running Windows XP SP3, Windows Vista, or Windows 7, and it might be difficult to find clients for Linux or IOS that include support for this feature.

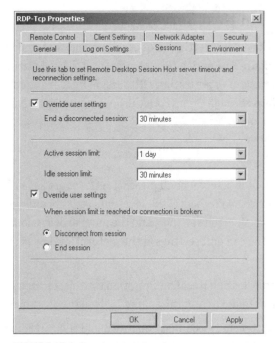

FIGURE 17-1: Sessions tab

▷ **Environment:** You can use this tab to configure whether a specific program runs when the user logs on.

▷ **Remote Control:** This tab allows you to configure whether remote control can be used to view currently connected sessions. The default setting requires a user's permission for a remote control session to be established, and you can use this tab to configure the level of interactivity a user has when viewing an existing Remote Desktop session.

▷ **Client Settings:** On this tab, you can configure the maximum color depth and maximum number of monitors an RDP client can use. You can also disable access to drives, printers, ports, the Clipboard, video and audio playback, and audio recording.

▷ **Network Adapter:** You can use this tab to set whether a specific network adapter is used to service incoming RDP connections. You can also specify the maximum number of allowed connections. The default allows unlimited connections to the RD Session Host server.

▶ Setting a maximum number of sessions allows you to ensure that the RD Session Host doesn't get swamped with more sessions than it can support.

▷ **Security:** This tab allows you to control which users are able to log on to the RD Session Host server. The default setting has the local Remote Desktop Users group able to connect. Most organizations create a domain-based group and add it to this local group on each RD Session Host server.

SERVER-LEVEL SETTINGS

Protocol-level settings cover most of what you might want to configure for connections to an RD Session Host server. You can access the server Properties settings by right-clicking on an item under Edit Settings, and then clicking Properties. You can use the following tabs to configure settings:

▶ **General:** As Figure 17-2 shows, use this tab to configure whether a user is restricted to a single session, whether temporary folders are used for each session, and whether those temporary folders are deleted on exit. You can also use these settings when you need to perform maintenance on the server, allowing you to block new connections but allowing existing connections to reconnect. You do this to gradually reduce the number of sessions on the server, allowing you to minimize disruption when the server needs to be rebooted.

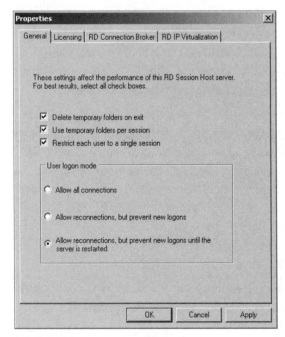

FIGURE 17-2: Server Properties tab

▶ **Licensing:** This tab allows you to control which licensing mode is used for the RD Session Host server and also allows you to specify the address of RD license servers.

▶ **RD Connection Broker:** This tab allows you to control RD Connection Broker *farm* settings, including which farm the RD Session Host server belongs to and the relative weight of the server in the farm. A farm is a group of RD Session Host servers.

▶ **RD IP Virtualization:** Using this tab, you can enable IP virtualization for RD sessions. This is necessary for applications that use unique IP addresses to differentiate user sessions. Normally, all RD Session Host sessions use the same IP address. Enabling RD IP Virtualization allows each RD Session Host session to appear to have its own IP address.

CONFIGURING RD SESSION HOST SERVERS WITH GROUP POLICY

Although configuring RD Session Host server settings using Properties dialog boxes is feasible if you only have a couple of RD Session Host servers to manage, Group Policy allows you to do this more efficiently when you need to configure a large number of servers.

The Computer Configuration\Policies\Administrative Templates\ Windows Components\Remote Desktop Services\RD Session Host server node of Group Policy contains several policies whose functionality mirrors the settings that can be applied on the server. The coverage here is brief, as there are a vast number of policies, and you've already learned about the functionality that most of them implement.

▶ **Connections:** Through the Connections node, you can access the following policies: Automatic Reconnection, Allow Users to Connect Remotely Using Remote Desktop Services, Deny Logoff of an Administrator Logged In to the Console Session, Configure Keep-Alive Connection Interval, Limit Number of Connections, Set Rules for Remote Control of Remote Desktop Services User Sessions, Allow Reconnection from Original Client Only, Restrict Remote Desktop Services Users to a Single Remote Session, Allow Remote Start of Unlisted Programs, and Turn Off Fair Share CPU Scheduling.

▶ **Device and Resource Redirection:** Through the Device and Resource Redirection node, you can configure the following policies: Allow

Audio Redirection, Do Not Allow Clipboard Redirection, Do Not Allow COM Port Redirection, Do Not Allow Drive Redirection, Do Not Allow LPT Port Redirection, Do Not Allow Supported Plug and Play Device Redirection, Do Not Allow Smart Card Device Redirection, and Allow Time Zone Redirection.

▶ **Licensing:** You can access the Licensing node to configure the following policies: Use the Specified Remote Desktop License Servers, Hide Notifications About RD Licensing Problems that Affect the RD Session Host Server, and Set the Remote Desktop Services Licensing Mode.

▶ **Printer Redirection:** Through the Printer Redirection node, you can configure the following policies: Do Not Set Default Client Printer to Be Default Printer in a Session, Do Not Allow Client Printer Redirection, Specify RD Session Host Server Fallback Printer Driver Behavior, Use Remote Desktop Services Easy Print Printer Driver First, and Redirect Only the Default Client Printer.

▶ **Profiles:** You can find the following policies in the Profiles node: Set Remote Desktop Services User Home Directory, Use Mandatory Profiles on the RD Session Host Server, and Set Path for Remote Desktop Services Roaming User Profile.

▶ **RD Connection Broker:** You can find the following policies in the RD Connection Broker node: Join RD Connection Broker, Configure RD Connection Broker Farm Name, Use IP Address Redirection, Configure RD Connection Broker Server Name, and Use RD Connection Broker Load Balancing.

▶ **Remote Session Environment:** You can use the Remote Session Environment node to locate the following policies: Limit Maximum Color Depth, Enforce Removal of Remote Desktop Wallpaper, Remove Disconnect Option from Shut Down Dialog Box, Remove Windows Security Item from Start Menu, Set Compression Algorithm for RDP Data, Start a Program on Connection, and Always Show Desktop on Connection.

▶ **Security:** The Security node contains the following policies: Server Authentication Certificate Template, Set Client Connection Encryption Level, Always Prompt for Password Upon Connection, Require Secure RPC Communication, Require Use of Specific Security Layer for Remote (RDP) Connections, Do Not Allow Local Administrators to Customize Permissions, and Require User Authentication for Remote Connections by Using Network Level Authentication.

▶ **Session Time Limits:** You can find the following policies in the Session Time Limits node: Set Time Limit for Disconnected Sessions, Set Time Limit for Active but Idle Remote Desktop Services Sessions, Set Time Limit for Active Remote Desktop Services Sessions, Terminate Session When Time Limits Are Reached, and Set Time Limit for Logoff of RemoteApp Sessions.

▶ **Temporary Folders:** The Temporary Folders node contains the following policies: Do Not Delete Temp Folder Upon Exit, and Do Not Use Temporary Folders Per Session.

> **NOTE** The most useful policy groups are in the Connections and Session Time Limits nodes. These contain policies that control how many clients are connected to each RD Session Host server and how long they remain connected, affecting the RD Session Host server's capacity.

Using Windows System Resource Manager

Windows System Resource Manager (WSRM) is an operating system feature that allows you to apply policies that control how the server allocates resources, such as processor capacity and RAM. WSRM can be used with many different types of roles on a server running Windows Server 2008 R2 but is especially useful when it comes to managing resources for servers running Remote Desktop Session Host. The idea behind WSRM is that you can ensure that no single user of a Remote Desktop Session Host server consumes a disproportionate amount of system resources. Through the WSRM console, shown in Figure 17-3, you can apply one of the following policies to RD Session Host sessions:

▶ **Equal_Per_User:** This policy ensures that the operating system assigns each user equal resources, even if a single user has more than one session on the RD Session Host server.

▶ **Weighted_Remote_Sessions:** This policy allows you to assign priorities to different groups of users. For example, you can ensure that members of the IT department are always given better access to resources than members of the Accounting department.

▶ **Equal_Per_Session:** This policy distributes resources equally to each session. If a user has multiple sessions, he may end up consuming a disproportionate amount of resources.

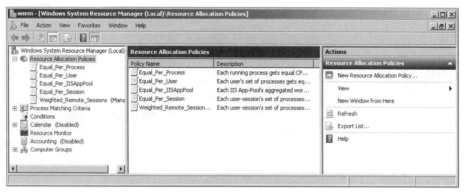

FIGURE 17-3: WSRM console

If you don't install the WSRM feature, resources on an RD Session Host server are allocated on an as-needed basis. This means that one user can end up running a process that pegs the processor at near 100% utilization, making the Remote Desktop experience problematic for all other users of the server.

Running Windows Thin PC

Windows Thin PC (WinTPC) is a version of the Windows 7 operating system that has lower system requirements than standard editions of Windows 7. This means that you can install WinTPC on older computers that would otherwise be retired or on newer computers with less powerful hardware. WinTPC differs from other thin client solutions in that you can still manage it using tools such as System Center Configuration Manager. For example, you can use Group Policy to block users from writing data to a disk or USB devices. WinTPC also works well as a kiosk operating system. It can be more difficult to accomplish this aim if you are using other operating systems, such as Linux, to host the thin client application.

WinTPC allows you to leverage Windows 7 features such as AppLocker, BitLocker, and DirectAccess. WinTPC also supports Microsoft's RemoteFX technology, which allows thin clients to access applications that have complex graphic requirements, such as games, over a Remote Desktop Connection. With DirectAccess support, you can install WinTPC on a laptop, allowing a user remote thin client access to Remote Desktop servers. WinTPC is included with Microsoft's Software Assurance licensing.

▶ Another advantage of WinTPC is that, unlike buying dedicated thin client hardware, you can always revert back to running a full-fledged operating system if it turns out that the thin client model isn't appropriate for your organization.

RUNNING REMOTEAPP

Rather than open a full session, including a desktop, Start menu, and a task bar, *RemoteApp* allows a user to run one or more applications off an RD Session Host server directly. The application runs in such a way that it appears as if it is executing on the local computer. When a client invokes multiple applications from the same host server, the RD Session Host server transmits the applications to the client using the same session.

RemoteApp includes the following benefits:

▶ Any application that can be run on the RD Session Host server can be run as a RemoteApp application.

▶ You can associate RemoteApp applications with local file extensions. This means that the RemoteApp application starts when the user attempts to open an associated document.

▶ Users are often unaware that an application is running remotely.

▶ RemoteApp applications can be used with RD Gateway, allowing access to clients on remote networks such as the Internet.

You can use three methods to deploy RemoteApp applications to the clients in your organization. These methods include:

▶ Creating an RDP shortcut file and distributing this file to clients

▶ Creating and distributing a Windows Installer package. Doing this allows you to associate the RemoteApp with a particular file extension. When a user attempts to open the file, the RemoteApp application executes automatically.

▶ To use RemoteApp, users still need to be members of the Remote Desktop Users group on the RD Session Host server.

You configure RemoteApp server using the RemoteApp Deployment Settings dialog box. Configuring the RemoteApp server allows you to include settings, such as the address of an RD Gateway Server, in RemoteApp applications. You can access this dialog box by opening the RemoteApp Manager console from the Remote Desktop Services folder in the Administrative Tools menu and then clicking on RD Session Host Server Settings in the Actions pane. This dialog box has the following tabs:

▶ **RD Session Host Server:** This tab allows you to direct a RemoteApp session to a particular server. You can enter the address of an RD Connection Broker farm, if one is being used.

▶ **RD Gateway:** Allows you to configure the address of an RD Gateway server for clients accessing RemoteApp applications from external networks.

▶ **Digital Signature:** Allows you to configure RemoteApp RDP shortcuts with digital signatures. This requires that you have access to a signing certificate.

▶ **Common RDP Settings:** Allows you to configure font smoothing as well as whether the RemoteApp application can use Clipboard settings, disk drives, or printers.

▶ **Custom RDP Settings:** Allows you to specify custom RDP settings not included in the Common RDP Settings.

To create a RemoteApp application, perform the following general steps:

1. Open the RemoteApp Manager console from the Remote Desktop Services folder in the Administrative Tools menu.

2. In the Actions menu, click Add RemoteApp Programs. This launches the RemoteApp Wizard.

3. The Choose Programs to Add to the RemoteApp Programs List page displays all applications currently installed on the RemoteApp server. This dialog box is shown in Figure 17-4.

▶ You can configure an RDP file with these settings using Remote Desktop Connection. Edit the RDP file using Notepad and then paste the settings into the Custom RDP Settings textbox.

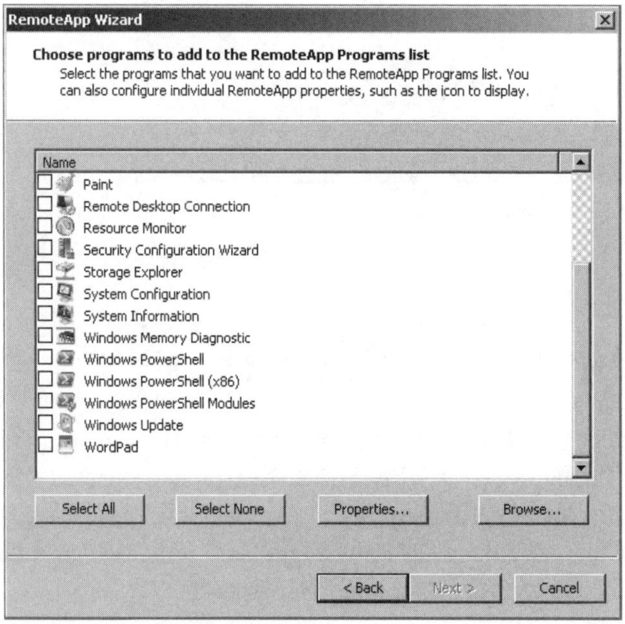

FIGURE 17-4: RemoteApp Programs List

4. Select the program that you want to make available as a RemoteApp, click Next, and then click Finish.

5. To limit the RemoteApp program so that it is available only to a specific group of users, right-click on the RemoteApp program, and click Properties.

6. On the User Assignment tab, as shown in Figure 17-5, specify which groups have access to the program.

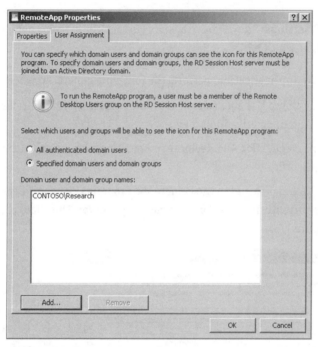

FIGURE 17-5: RemoteApp User Assignment

► RemoteApp isn't directly compatible with third-party operating systems such as Mac OS, IOS, or Linux.

USING REMOTE DESKTOP WEB ACCESS

► As it leverages the Remote Desktop Connection client, RD Web Access isn't directly compatible with third-party operating systems such as Mac OS, IOS, or Linux.

You can use *Remote Desktop (RD) Web Access* to allow clients to connect to an RD Session Host server through a web page link rather than through Remote Desktop Connection client software or by running a RemoteApp application. To use RD Web Access, clients need to run Windows XP SP2, Windows Vista, Windows 7, Windows Server 2003 SP1, Windows Server 2008, or Windows Server 2008 R2.

To deploy RD Web Access, you must install the RD Web Access server role, the Web Server (IIS) role, and a feature called Windows Process Activation Service.

You can use Remote Desktop Web Access to publish RemoteApp applications from multiple Remote Desktop Session Host servers. You use the Remote Desktop Web Access Configuration item, located in the Remote Desktop Services node of the Administrative Tools menu, to configure the list of source RemoteApp servers. You must add the Remote Desktop Web Access server to the local TS Web Access Computers security group on all Remote Desktop Session Host servers from which you want to publish RemoteApp applications.

UTILIZING REMOTE DESKTOP CONNECTION BROKER

If your organization decides to use the thin-client model, it won't be long before you find that a single RD Session Host server can support only a limited number of clients before it begins to run out of resources. Eventually, as the number of thin client connections grows, you need to add another RD Session Host server to your environment to reduce the load on the existing RD Session Host servers. The *RD Connection Broker* role service simplifies the process of adding capacity, allowing you to load balance RD Session Host servers. RD Connection Broker ensures that clients are reconnected to existing sessions if they suffer a disruption.

You can use RD Connection Broker with DNS Round Robin or with Network Load Balancing to distribute clients to RD Session Host servers. When you configure RD Connection Broker with load balancing, the RD Connection Broker service monitors all RD Session Host servers in the group and allocates new clients to the RD Session Host servers that are under the least resource pressure. When used with DNS Round Robin, clients are still distributed evenly, but not on the basis of server load.

The main benefit of using RD Connection Broker is that the service remembers which RD Session Host server hosts a client session. In the event that a client is disconnected from a session unexpectedly, the session will be reconnected if it attempts to reestablish it. You can use the RD Connection Broker service only with RD Session Host servers running Windows Server 2008 R2 or Terminal Services servers running Windows Server 2008.

Prior to joining a farm, you must add the RD Session Host server's Active Directory computer account to the Session Directory Computers local group on the computer hosting the RD Connection Broker service. After you complete these tasks, you then need to configure the Network Load Balancing feature on each of the computers in the farm.

Joining a farm is a matter of specifying the address of an RD Connection Broker server, a farm name, and the condition that the server should participate in session broker load balancing, and the relative weight of the server—based on its capacity—in the farm. You should configure more powerful servers with higher-weight values than those that you configure for less powerful servers. You configure these settings on the RD Connection Broker tab of the RD Session Host server's Properties, as shown in Figure 17-6.

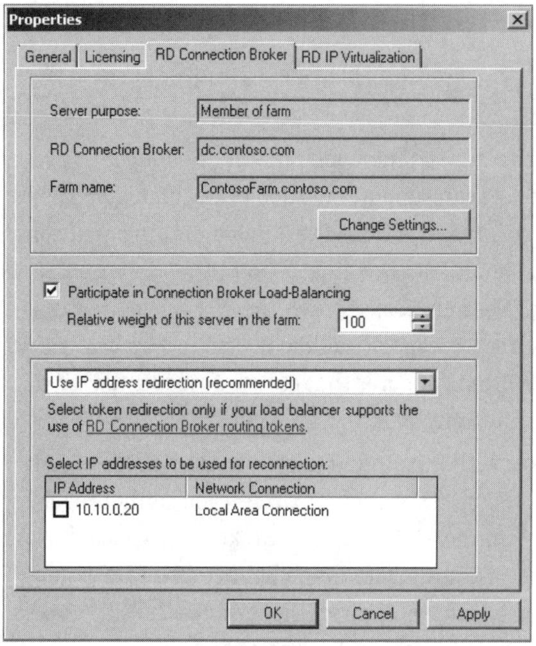

FIGURE 17-6: RD Connection Broker

CONNECTING VIA REMOTE DESKTOP GATEWAY

A *Remote Desktop Gateway (RD Gateway) server* allows clients on remote networks to make Remote Desktop Protocol (RDP) over HTTPS connections to RDP servers located on protected internal networks. An advantage of RD Gateway is that you do not need to set up a VPN or DirectAccess to grant access to RD Session Host servers. Clients only need to add the address of the RD Gateway server on their Remote Desktop Connection client, as shown in Figure 17-7.

FIGURE 17-7: RD Gateway

> **NOTE** You can also use RD Gateway servers to allow people that use their own computers at work access to RD Session Host servers. This allows you to keep these users on a separate network, due to the insecure nature of unmanaged computers, while allowing them limited access to internal network resources through RD Session Host servers.

To install and configure an RD Gateway server, perform the following general steps:

1. Install the RD Gateway role service on a computer running Windows Server 2008 R2 that is located on a perimeter network accessible to the Internet. You should configure the perimeter firewall so that the RD Gateway server is accessible on port 443.

2. Obtain an SSL certificate. The certificate name must match the name that clients use to connect to the server. Install the certificate on the server and then use the RD Gateway Manager console to map the server certificate.

3. Configure RD Connection Authorization Policies and RD Resource Authorization Policies.

It is important that you use only the RD Gateway Manager to map the SSL certificate. If you use another method, the RD Gateway server will not function properly.

Configuring RD Connection Authorization Policies

An *RD Connection Authorization Policy (RD-CAP)* allows you to specify which users can connect through the RD Gateway server to resources located on your organization's internal network. For example, you can configure an RD-CAP that includes all laptop computers in your organization or all user accounts that are members of a special security group. You can also use RD-CAPs to specify acceptable authentication methods, such as whether clients are required to use password or smartcard-based authentication to access internal network resources through the RD Gateway server.

RD-CAPs in conjunction with Network Access Protection (NAP) to ensure that client computers meet a minimum health benchmark before they can successfully establish a connection. The only drawback to using NAP with RD Gateway is that not all client operating systems support NAP. If you've got users connecting from computers running Mac OS, IOS, or Linux, you'll need to get those users to install and configure a NAP client from a third-party vendor.

Configuring RD Resource Authorization Policies

You use an *RD Resource Authorization Policy (RD-RAP)* to control the hosts on your organization's internal network that an incoming RD Gateway client can connect to. When you create an RD-RAP, you specify a group of computers that you want to grant access to and the group of users that you allow this access to. For example, you can create a group of computers called ManagersComputers that will be accessible to members of the Managers user group. To be granted access to internal resources, a remote user must meet the conditions of at least one RD-CAP and at least one RD-RAP.

REMOTE DESKTOP LICENSING

Each client or user that accesses a Remote Desktop server, either through an RD Session Host session, a RemoteApp application, or an RD Web Access application needs to have a license. This special type of license is not included with the licenses you get when you purchase Windows Server 2008 R2 or Windows 7. This license is called a *Remote Desktop Services Client Access License (RDS CAL)*. You install RDS CALs on an *RD license server*. When a user, computer, or thin client initiates a session to a Remote Desktop Services server, the server performs a check to verify that a valid license has been issued or is available.

Installing RDS CALs

You can install two types of license on an RD license server. These licenses cost the same, so you should choose the license type that best reflects the way that your organization uses Remote Desktop. The two different license types are as follows:

▶ **RDS Per User CAL:** An RDS Per User CAL gives a specific user account the ability to access any RD Session Host server in an organization from any computer or device. This type of CAL is a good idea when you have the same person accessing Remote Desktop from different devices, such as a Windows Thin PC at the office and through RD Gateway when connecting from home.

▶ **RDS Per Device CAL:** The RDS Per Device CAL licenses a specific device, such as a normal computer or thin client, the ability to connect to an RD Session Host server. RDS Per Device CALs are reset automatically by the RD license server after a random period between 52 and 89 days. This means that if a computer or thin client is decommissioned, the license assigned to it is reclaimed automatically and can be used again. If you are decommissioning a large number of computers, you can revoke 20% of the RDS Per Device CALs.

Deploying an RD License Server

When you deploy an RD license server, you need to configure its *discovery scope*, as shown in Figure 17-8. License server discovery scope determines which RD Session Host servers and clients can detect the location of the license server automatically. You can change the license server scope at any time after installation. Three scopes are available:

▶ **This Workgroup:** RD Session Host servers and clients that are members of the same workgroup are able to discover this server and acquire licenses automatically. This scope is available only if the computer is not a member of the domain.

▶ **This Domain:** RD Session Host servers and clients that are members of the same domain as the RD license server are able to discover this server and acquire licenses automatically. Appropriate if your organization needs to provide licenses on a per-domain rather than a per-forest basis.

▶ **This Forest:** RD Session Host servers and clients that are members of the same Active Directory forest are able to discover this server and acquire licenses automatically. Appropriate if your organization needs to provide licenses on a per-forest basis, rather than on a per-domain basis.

▶ Unlike previous versions of Windows, client operating systems such as Windows 7 do not include a RDS CAL.

▶ RDS Per User CALs are not enforced by RD Licensing. You can have more client connections occur in an organization than actual RDS Per User CALs installed on the license server. Be careful to ensure that you have an RDS Per User CAL for each user that connects.

▶ RDS Per Device CALs are most useful for organizations like call centers, where multiple users use the same computer.

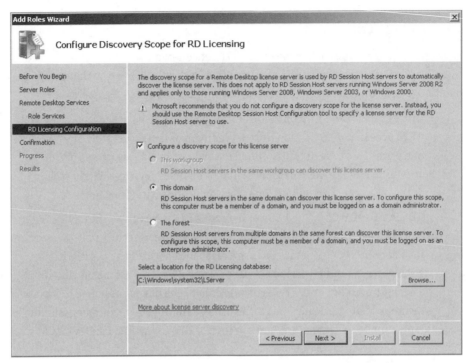

FIGURE 17-8: License server scope

Activating a License Server

You must activate an RD license server before it is able to issue CALs. The activation process is reasonably similar to the one that you need to go through when you perform product activation for a Windows operating system or for an application such as Microsoft Office. The method you use depends on whether the RD license server has a connection to the Internet. If the server does have a connection to the Internet, you can perform automatic activation. If the server does not have a direct connection to the Internet, you can perform an activation using a telephone, or you can navigate to a website on a computer or mobile device that does have a connection to the Internet and perform activation by filling out a form and entering the activation code on the RD license server.

UNDERSTANDING REMOTE DESKTOP VIRTUALIZATION HOST

The *Remote Desktop Virtualization Host* allows you to configure Remote Desktop technologies to support Virtual Desktop Infrastructure (VDI). You can use RD Virtualization Host to allow clients to connect using Remote Desktop to personal virtual machines running on Hyper-V hosts on Windows Server 2008 R2. You can configure RD Virtualization Host to assign users to a unique virtual machine or you can configure RD Virtualization Host to direct users to a pool of shared virtual machines. The RD Virtualization Host role service needs to be installed on a computer that hosts the Hyper-V role and the client virtual machines.

This type of virtualization takes substantially more resources than RD Session Host sessions but also allows greater customization of the user experience. Virtual machines can be treated just like desktop machines, with users using a thin client, such as WinTPC, to access the RD Virtualization Host virtual machines. RD Virtualization Host integrates with RD Session Broker to ensure that users are redirected to their existing virtual machine in the event that their session is disconnected.

▶ With Windows Server 2008 SP1, you can add RemoteFX graphics adapters to virtual machines running Windows 7. RemoteFX allows RD Virtualization Host clients to enjoy complex multimedia that isn't possible on virtual machines that do not have RemoteFX adapters.

VIRTUALIZING APPLICATIONS WITH APP-V

App-V (Application Virtualization) is a component of the Microsoft Desktop Optimization Pack (MDOP) that allows you to virtualize applications. Application virtualization allows you to configure applications to run locally on computers without being installed locally on those computers.

App-V works by creating a separate partitioned space, called a *silo,* for each application, and the application executes within this silo. As each application is walled off from the operating system, App-V allows applications that might not be able to execute on the computer, because of compatibility problems, to execute. This means that, not only can you use App-V to run programs that might be incompatible with Windows 7 on Windows 7 computers, you can also run applications that might be incompatible with each other on the same computer. This means that you can deploy applications that are not compatible with the RD Session Host role.

App-V minimizes network traffic by streaming only the parts of the application that the client needs across the network. When the client needs other parts of the application, it will request those parts from the App-V server. You can deploy App-V applications as Windows Installer packages.

SUMMARY

RD Session Host servers in Windows Server 2008 R2 are the new name for what was called Terminal Services servers in Windows Server 2008 and Windows Server 2003. An RD Session Host server provides users with a complete Remote Desktop from which they can launch applications. RemoteApp provides users with independent applications that run on the RD Session Host server but are displayed on the client computer. RD Web Access allows users to launch RD Session Host sessions and RemoteApp applications from a Web application. RD Connection Broker allows you to use network load balancing technology with RD Session Host and RemoteApp applications. RD Connection Broker ensures that disrupted connections reconnect appropriately. RD Gateway allows clients on remote networks, such as the Internet, to make RD Session Host and RemoteApp connections without having to use a VPN or DirectAccess. RD Session Host and RemoteApp sessions need a separate license issued by an RD Licensing server. RDS Per User CALs are appropriate if a single user needs access from multiple devices. RDS Per Device CALs are appropriate if multiple users need access from single devices. RD Virtualization Host is a VDI technology that allows thin clients access to virtual machines hosted on Hyper-V servers. App-V is an application virtualization technology that allows applications to run in partitioned spaces. This allows applications that are incompatible with an operating system to be streamed to and run on that operating system.

Additional Sources

Application Virtualization TechCenter

http://technet.microsoft.com/en-us/appvirtualization/default.aspx

Monitor an RD Session Host Server with Windows System Resource Manager

http://technet.microsoft.com/en-us/library/cc742814.aspx

Overview of RemoteApp

http://technet.microsoft.com/en-us/library/cc755055.aspx

Remote Desktop Connection Broker

http://technet.microsoft.com/en-us/library/dd560675(WS.10).aspx

Remote Desktop Services

http://technet.microsoft.com/en-us/library/cc770412.aspx

Remote Desktop Services Client Access License

http://technet.microsoft.com/en-us/library/cc753650.aspx

Remote Desktop Services Guide

http://technet.microsoft.com/en-us/library/ee817089.aspx

Remote Desktop Virtualization Host

http://technet.microsoft.com/en-us/library/dd759193.aspx

Windows Thin PC

www.microsoft.com/windows/enterprise/solutions/virtualization/products/
thinpc.aspx

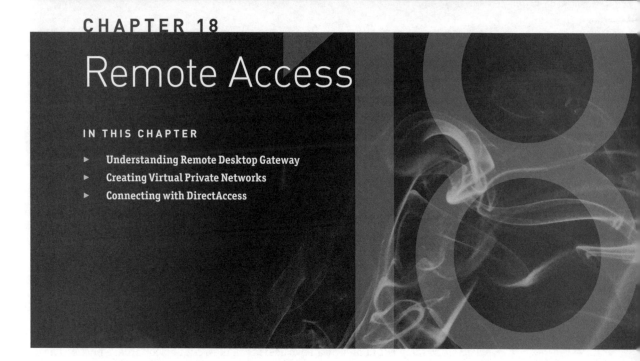

Remote Access

Remote access is constantly changing. Back in the 1990s when I started working in IT, remote access was achieved by dialing into a bank of 14.4Kbps modems connected to my workplace's remote access server. This was enough to launch a Serial Line Internet Protocol (SLIP) or Point-to-Point Protocol (PPP) session that would allow me to interact with workplace fileservers.

As wireless access points and home broadband became more prevalent, workplaces moved away from offering dedicated dial-up access to the network and instead configured virtual private network (VPN) servers. As a greater number of people transition from desktop computers to laptop computers, and those laptop computers increasingly are connected to high-speed cellular networks, organizational computer usage patterns will change. Not only will users be more mobile, they are also almost permanently connected to the Internet. Even airplane flights, the final bastion of disconnected computing, are being increasingly provisioned with Wi-Fi hotspots, allowing people to connect to the workplace from miles above the earth's surface. The trend towards permanent remote connectivity is changing how organizations provide access to internal network resources for external clients. As an experienced systems adminis- trator, it is often up to you to make choices on your organization's strategies in these matters, so it is essential that you know what Windows Server 2008 R2 is capable of.

In this chapter, you learn about Windows Server 2008 R2 remote access technolo- gies and how you can leverage them to enable remote access to your organization's internal network. You learn how each technology is appropriate for a specific usage case and why you might want to use several technologies to support all of the clients in your organization.

SETTING UP REMOTE DESKTOP GATEWAY

Remote Desktop (RD) Gateway allows users to make a connection from a host on the Internet to a host on the local area network using the Remote Desktop Connection (RDC) Client software. Remote Desktop Client software is included in all currently supported versions of Windows XP, Vista, and 7. Though RD Gateway is typically used for connecting to Remote Desktop Session Host servers, it can also be used to connect to desktop workstations. This means that a person can use an RD Gateway server to connect to his work PC from his home PC without having to connect through a VPN.

> ▶ Remote Desktop Gateway allows people to connect very simply through a client. It doesn't involve substantial configuration of certificate services, and it is supported by computers running Windows XP, Windows Vista, Windows 7, and Remote Desktop clients on Mac OSX.

> NOTE Although a computer running Server Core would, at first glance, ap- pear to be an excellent item to place on a perimeter network for the purpose of allowing remote access, the version of Server Core that ships with Windows Server 2008 R2 doesn't support the Network Policy and Access Services role. This means that it cannot function as a remote access server.

RD Gateway servers, like any other remote access servers, need to be placed on perimeter networks and have at least one public IP address. Connections to RD Gateway servers occur using the Remote Desktop Protocol (RDP) over HTTPS protocol. When configuring the external firewall, network administrators need to allow access on port 443 from hosts on the Internet to the RD Gateway server. Connections from the RD Gateway server to RDP hosts on the internal network occur on port 3389.

Installing RD Gateway

You can install RD Gateway as a role service using the Add Roles Wizard or by running the following PowerShell commands:

```
Import-Module ServerManager
Add-WindowsFeature RDS-Gateway
```

When you install RD Gateway on a computer running Windows Server 2008 R2, the following components are automatically installed:

▶ Web Server (IIS)

▶ RPC over HTTP Proxy

▶ Network Policy and Access Services

▶ While you can install RD Gateway on a Web server, it is probably a better idea not to collocate these services.

When you use the GUI to install RD Gateway, you'll be prompted to run the wizard to set up access policies. If you don't use the GUI, you'll need to configure RD Gateway policies manually. You can do this using the RD Gateway Manager console, which is found in the Remote Desktop Services folder of the Administrative Tools menu.

> **NOTE** RD Gateway servers don't need to be members of an Active Directory domain, but it is substantially more difficult to configure the RD Resource Authorization Policy (RAP) to limit connections to specific hosts without such membership. You can accomplish something similar through firewall rules. The drawback to domain membership is the risks involved in placing a domain-joined computer on a perimeter network and configuring the internal firewall to support the configuration.

DEFINING RD GATEWAY CONNECTION AND RESOURCE POLICIES

RD Gateway connection and resource policies allow you to specify the conditions under which users are able to connect to an RD Gateway server. *RD Connection Authorization Policies (CAPs)* can be stored on the RD Gateway server or in a *Central RD CAP Store*. The benefits of using a Central CAP Store is that the same CAPs can apply to multiple RD Gateway servers without having to reproduce them on each server. They can also be updated centrally as necessary. If your organization only has a single RD Gateway server, there is no need to use a central RD CAP Store.

To create an RD Gateway CAP, perform the following general steps:

1. Open the RD Gateway Manager console from the Remote Desktop Services folder of the Administrative Tools menu.

2. Right-click Connection Authorization Policies, click Create New Policy, and then click Custom.

3. On the New RD CAP dialog box, enter a policy name on the General tab.

4. On the Requirements tab, shown in Figure 18-1, select Password or, if your organization supports it, Smart Card. Then click Add Group to specify the User Group to which you wish to grant access to RD servers through the RD Gateway server. You should create a separate security group for users to whom you wish to grant this access to; that way granting and revoking access will just be a matter of removing the user's account from this group. If the people who are connecting using RD Gateway are doing so using computers that are members of the domain, you can also restrict membership based on computer account.

FIGURE 18-1: RD CAP requirements

5. On the Device Redirection tab, choose whether you want to enable device redirection for all client devices, disable it for specific types, such as volumes, clipboard, and plug-and-play devices. You also have the ability to restrict connections to only clients that enforce RD Gateway device redirection policies.

6. On the Timeouts tab shown in Figure 18-2, you can enable an idle timeout, which disconnects users who aren't interacting with their session, and a session timeout, which limits even active sessions. Click OK to finish creating the policy.

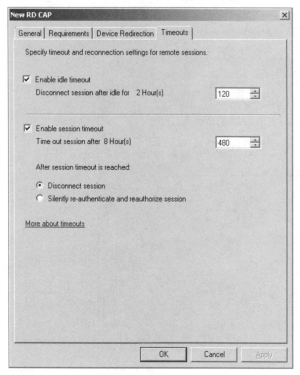

FIGURE 18-2: RD CAP timeouts

After you have configured an RD CAP, you need to configure an *RD Resource Authorization Policy (RAP)*. An incoming connection must meet the conditions specified in one RD CAP and one RD RAP before it can be successfully established. To create an RD RAP, perform the following steps:

1. Open the RD Gateway Manager console from the Remote Desktop Services folder of the Administrative Tools menu.

2. Right-click Resource Authorization Policies, click Create New Policy, and then click Custom.

3. On the New RD RAP page, enter the policy name.

4. On the User Groups page, click Add to add the user groups to which the policy will apply.

▶ Even when you allow users to connect to any resource, they still have to authenticate to the computer to which they are connecting. If they don't have the right to do this, they won't be able to connect.

5. On the Network Resource page, shown in Figure 18-3, choose between Select an Active Directory Domain Services group, Select an existing RD Gateway-managed group, and Allow users to connect to any network resource.

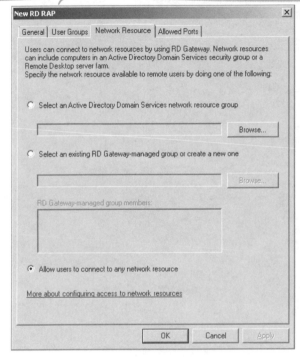

FIGURE 18-3: RAP network resources

6. On the Allowed Ports page, choose between restricting connections from the RD Gateway server to port 3389 (the default), specific ports, or through any ports. Unless the RD servers use alternate ports, the default is appropriate.

▶ If you use a self-signed certificate on your organization's RD Gateway server, you can use the Certificates console to export that self-signed certificate so that it can be transmitted to other computers.

CONFIGURING SERVER SETTINGS

RD Gateway servers need an SSL certificate to encrypt and authenticate the RDP over an HTTPS connection. As is always the case with SSL certificates, obtaining a certificate from a trusted, third-party certification authority (CA) will cost you money, but will mean that any client can use the RD Gateway without problems. Using an internal certificate will be cheaper in that it will not be necessary to purchase a certificate but will require you to configure RD Gateway clients to trust the issuing authority. Given the cost to an organization of supporting the distribution of an internal or self-signed certificate, it is usually just easier to go with one obtained from a trusted, third-party CA.

To configure the certificate for the RD Gateway server, perform the following steps:

1. Open the RD Gateway Manager console from the Remote Desktop Services folder of the Administrative Tools menu.

2. Right-click on the RD Gateway server, and then click Properties.

3. On the SSL Certificate tab, as shown in Figure 18-4, click Create and Import Certificate.

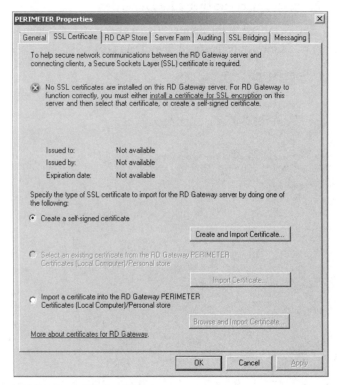

FIGURE 18-4: SSL Certificate

4. In the Create Self-Signed Certificate dialog, verify the certificate name and specify the location where you want the certificate to be saved. Placing this in a shared folder that is accessible to clients makes the distribution of this certificate simpler. Click OK twice.

INTEGRATING NETWORK ACCESS PROTECTION

After you have RD Gateway functioning properly, you can consider integrating *Network Access Protection (NAP)* to ensure that users are both authenticated and are using computers that reach a minimum health standard. To configure an existing RD Gateway server to also use NAP to perform client health checks before allowing a connection to an RD Session Host server on the internal network, perform the following general steps:

1. On the RD Gateway server, open the Remote Desktop Gateway Manager console.

2. Right-click the server name, and then click Properties.

3. On the RD CAP Store tab, click the Request clients to send a statement of health checkbox, as shown in Figure 18-5, and then click OK.

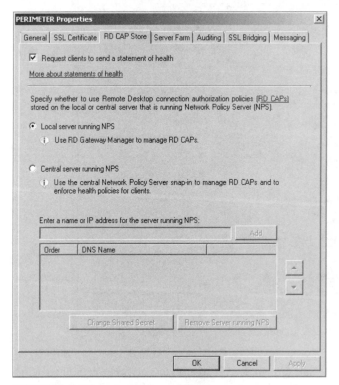

FIGURE 18-5: RD send statement of health

4. In the Remote Desktop Gateway Manager console, expand the Policies\ Connection Authorization Policies node, and then delete any existing RD CAPs.

5. Open the Network Policy Server console from the Administrative Tools menu.

6. Click the Network Access Protection node, and then click Configure System Health Validators.

7. Click Windows Security Health Validator, and then click Settings.

8. Right-click Default Configuration, and then click Properties.

9. Configure the policy settings appropriate for your organization's requirements, and then click OK.

10. In the Network Policy Server console, click NPS (Local), and then click Configure NAP.

11. On the Select Network Connection Method For Use with NAP page, set the drop-down menu to Remote Desktop Gateway (RD Gateway), as shown in Figure 18-6, and then click Next.

12. On the Specify NAP Enforcement Servers Running RD Gateway page, click Next.

▶ It is necessary to add only servers here if you are not running this wizard on the RD Gateway server.

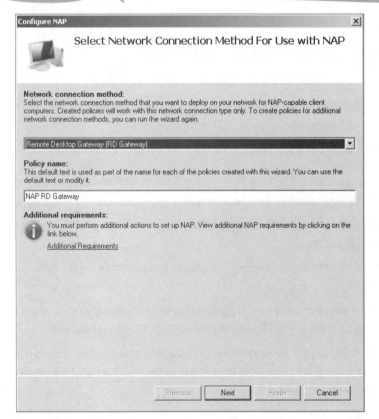

FIGURE 18-6: RD NAP method

13. On the Device Redirection page, review the settings that you will configure for device redirection, and then click Next.

14. On the Configure Idle Timeout and Session Timeout Actions page, configure the appropriate timeout settings for your environment, and then click Next.

15. On the Configure User Groups and Machine Groups page, add the user groups to which this new NAP RAP will apply, and then click Next.

16. On the Define NAP Health Policy page, choose whether you want to allow or deny access to NAP-ineligible client computers. Click Next, and then click Finish.

▶ Depending on the setting, this allows clients running alternate operating systems, or RDP clients, access. Generally, it is a good idea to deny access here to non-supported clients.

> **NOTE** As RD Gateway is a good way of allowing people to use their personal machines to access the internal network, NAP might be more trouble than it is worth. While you want to ensure that people aren't connecting to your internal network with computers infected with malware, turning on NAP is going to substantially limit the number of clients who can actually connect.

Configuring Clients to Use RD Gateway

You can configure clients to use an RD Gateway server either by:

▶ Manually configuring the address of the RD Gateway server by editing the advanced properties of Remote Desktop Connection

▶ Configuring the address of the RD Gateway server through Group Policy

To manually configure Remote Desktop Connection to connect to an RD Gateway server, perform the following general steps:

1. Open Remote Desktop Connection and, on the Advanced tab, click the Settings button.

2. On the RD Gateway Server Settings dialog box shown in Figure 18-7, you can enter the address of the RD Gateway server.

   ▷ The Automatically detect RD Gateway server settings option is used when the address of the RD Gateway server is configured through Group Policy.

   ▷ The Bypass RD Gateway server for local addresses option is used if you want the client computer to automatically detect when the RD Gateway server is required.

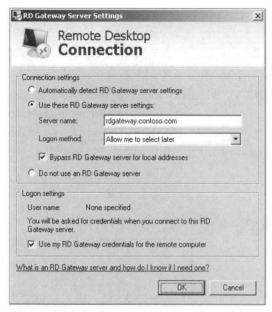

FIGURE 18-7: Enter RD Gateway address.

There are three RD Gateway-related Group Policy items that can be configured to simplify the process of ensuring that clients connect to the correct server. These policy items are located in the User Configuration\Policies\Administrative Templates\ Windows Components\Remote Desktop Services\RD Gateway node of a standard Windows Server 2008 R2 or higher GPO. These policies can be used to configure the following:

- ▶ **Set RD Gateway Authentication Method:** This policy allows you to force a user to use a particular authentication method or to set a default authentication method that the user can override. The options are:

  - ▷ Ask For Credentials; Use NTLM Protocol.

  - ▷ Ask For Credentials; Use Basic Protocol.

  - ▷ Use Locally Logged-In Credentials.

  - ▷ Use Smart Card.

- ▶ **Enable Connection through RD Gateway:** When this policy is enabled, the client attempts to connect through the configured RD Gateway server in the event that it is unable to establish a connection to the specified target of the RD Connection. Set this policy and the RD Gateway Address Policy to ensure

▶ One of the best things that you can do with any remote access solution is reduce the complexity involved in using it. Users hate jumping through hoops.

▶ If you are going to allow people to use their home computers to connect through RD Gateway, you need to come up with some documentation or perhaps a screencast that explains how to manually configure RD Gateway settings.

that domain clients connect through RD Gateway when not connected to the internal network.

▶ **Set RD Gateway Server Address:** This policy allows you to configure the RD Gateway server address, either on the basis of IP address or fully qualified domain name (FQDN). This policy should be set in conjunction with the enable connection through RD Gateway policy to ensure that remote domain clients transparently connect through the RD Gateway server without having to configure anything themselves.

DEPLOYING VIRTUAL PRIVATE NETWORKS

> **NOTE** The VPN technology that you deploy depends on the client computers that you support. If you have to support Windows XP clients, then you need to use either L2TP/IPsec or PPTP. If the minimum client operating system you need to support is Windows Vista, you can use everything except IKEv2. If all the client computers run Windows 7, you can use any of the protocols listed here.

Windows Server 2008 R2 supports four separate *virtual private network (VPN)* technologies: *PPTP, L2TP/IPsec, SSTP,* and *IKEv2.* The simplest of these to set up is PPTP, as it does not require integration with certificate services. The drawback of PPTP is that it is an older protocol and is not as secure as the other VPN protocols available on Windows Server 2008 R2. If you're just interested in providing VPN access, PPTP is a good bet. If you're looking for greater features and security, you'll need to investigate L2TP/IPsec, SSTP, or IKEv2.

> **NOTE** When using VPN protocols that rely on certificates generated by an internal enterprise CA, ensure that a Certificate Revocation List (CRL) Distribution Point (CDP) or Online Responder is accessible to clients on the Internet. Remember that clients need to be able to check the revocation status of certificates, and this is difficult if the CDP is accessible only to clients on the internal network.

Reconnecting with IKEv2 Protocol

> **NOTE** If your clients can use IKEv2, they can probably also use DirectAccess. The only reason to choose IKEv2 over DirectAccess is if the clients in your organization are running Windows 7 Professional or Home Premium editions rather than the Enterprise or Ultimate editions required for DirectAccess, or if your organization has not configured IPv6 on the internal network.

IKEv2 (IPsec Tunnel Mode with Internet Key Exchange version 2) VPN protocol was introduced with the release of the Windows Server 2008 R2 and Windows 7 operating systems. The main benefit of IKEv2 is its capability to allow automatic reconnection when the connection is disrupted without requiring re-authentication. This automatic reconnection can occur even if the client's connection address changes and is possible for up to eight hours. For example, a user might be connected to the internal network through an IKEv2 connection through a laptop computer's cellular modem. He or she boards an airplane and connects to the airplane's Wi-Fi. Under an IKEv2 scenario, the connection would automatically be reestablished without requiring the user to manually re-authenticate even though the connection method, from cellular network to airplane Wi-Fi, has changed. Connections have to be reestablished only when a user puts his or her computer into hibernation.

To configure IKEv2 as an access protocol on a VPN server running Windows Server 2008 R2, you need to do the following:

- ▶ Deploy an enterprise CA.
- ▶ Create a new certificate template based on the IPsec template. It is necessary to modify the application policies of this template to ensure that it supports the IP security IKE intermediate policy and Server Authentication certificate.
- ▶ Install a certificate generated from this template on the VPN server.
- ▶ Ensure that at least one Certificate Revocation List Distribution Point is accessible to clients on the Internet.
- ▶ Ensure that all clients trust the enterprise CA that issued the VPN server's certificate.

Windows 7 clients will attempt to establish an IKEv2 session before they will try SSTP or L2TP/IPsec, and then fall back to PPTP.

Traversing Obstacles with SSTP Protocol

The *SSTP VPN protocol* is only supported on client computers running the Windows Vista SP1 or Windows 7 or later client operating systems. The advantage of the SSTP VPN protocol is that it allows computers that might not normally be able to establish a remote access connection through TCP port 443, which is usually used for SSL connections to websites, to do so. SSTP will almost always work, even if it has to traverse NAT, firewalls and proxy servers.

The typical reason to use SSTP is for employees that travel regularly and use hotel Internet connections from behind restrictive firewalls that block the ports used by L2TP/IPSec and PPTP. The disadvantage of SSTP is that it generally has poorer performance than the other VPN protocols supported on Windows Server 2008 R2.

SSTP has the following requirements:

- ▶ You need to install an SSL certificate on the VPN server.
- ▶ All clients need to trust the CA that issued the SSL certificate.
- ▶ The Certificate Revocation List (CRL) Distribution Point (CDP) of the CA that issued the SSL certificate needs to be accessible to clients on the Internet.

Connecting via L2TP/IPsec and PPTP Protocols

▶ PPTP requires no additional configuration beyond setting up the VPN server and ensuring that port 1723 is open for clients from the Internet.

L2TP/IPsec (Layer Two Tunneling Protocol with IPsec) and *PPTP (Point-to-Point Tunneling Protocol)* are VPN protocols that have been used with Windows Server operating systems, and clients in the case of L2TP/IPsec, since the release of Windows 2000 and with PPTP since the release of Windows NT 4.0. If your organization provides VPN access to computers running the Windows XP operating system, more than likely this access will be through L2TP/IPsec or PPTP.

When configuring L2TP/IPsec you need to ensure that you have configured a CA that is able to issue certificates automatically to connecting clients. As is the case with other VPN protocols, this CA needs to be trusted by the client and the CDP must be accessible to clients making connections from the Internet. You would primarily deploy L2TP/IPsec as a way of providing secure access to Windows XP clients that would not be able to leverage the simpler to implement SSTP (Secure Socket Tunneling Protocol) VPN protocol.

CONFIGURING A WINDOWS SERVER 2008 R2 VPN SERVER

To configure a Windows Server 2008 R2 server that has one network card connected to the perimeter network and which is accessible to clients on the Internet and a second network card that is connected to the internal network to support VPNs, perform the following general steps:

1. Ensure that the prospective VPN server is connected to the Active Directory domain and login with an account that is a member of the Domain Admins group.

2. Open an elevated PowerShell prompt and enter the following commands:

   ```
   Import-module servermanager
   Add-WindowsFeature NPAS-RRAS-Services
   ```

   ▶ This procedure assumes that the server has not been previously configured for routing and remote access. If it has been, remove the role, reboot, and then reinstall.

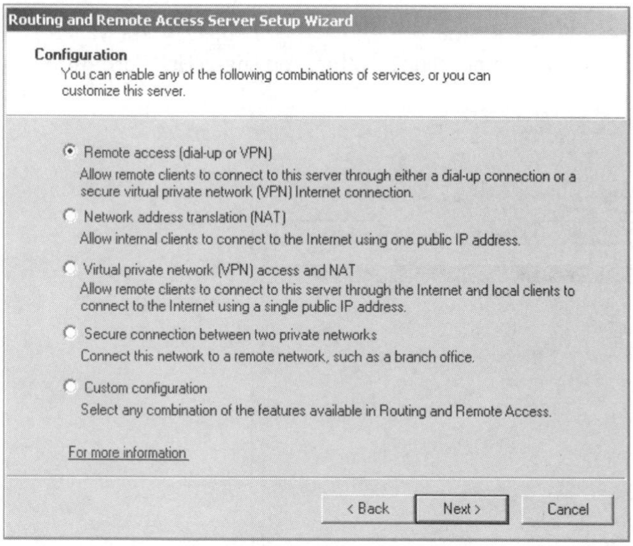

3. Open the Routing and Remote Access console from the Administrative Tools menu.

4. Right-click the server name, and click Configure and Enable Routing and Remote Access. This opens the Routing and Remote Access Server Setup Wizard. Click Next.

5. On the Configuration page, shown in Figure 18-8, select Remote access (dial-up or VPN), and then click Next.

FIGURE 18-8: Remote access setup configuration

6. On the Remote Access page, select VPN, and then click Next.

7. On the VPN Connection page, select the network connection that is connected to the Internet, and then click Next.

8. On the IP Address Assignment page, choose between assigning IP addresses automatically from an existing scope or from a specified range of addresses.

▶ Choose a DHCP scope in deployments where there are more than 50 clients, otherwise create an IP address range.

9. On the Manage Multiple Remote Access Servers page, select No, Use Routing and Remote Access to Authenticate Connection Requests, click Next, and then click Finish.

DISABLING SPECIFIC VPN PROTOCOLS

The default Windows Server 2008 R2 VPN server supports SSTP, PPTP, L2TP and IKEv2 remote access connections. If you want to limit incoming connections to a specific protocol or disable an existing protocol, you need to edit the port properties related to that protocol. If you don't disable a specific protocol, clients may use that protocol to connect to the VPN server. If you've gone to the effort of configuring IKEv2, you don't want to find out a few weeks later that all your clients are still falling back to using PPTP! To configure which VPN protocols are available, perform the following general steps:

1. On the VPN server, open the Routing and Remote Access console from the Administrative Tools menu.

2. Right-click the Ports node under the VPN server, and then click on Properties.

3. On the Ports Properties dialog box shown in Figure 18-9, select the VPN protocol that you wish to limit connections for, and then click Configure.

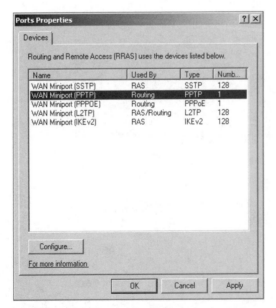

FIGURE 18-9: VPN Ports Properties

4. On the Configure Device dialog, set the Maximum Ports to 1 and ensure that the Remote Access Connections (inbound only) item is not selected. Click OK.

GRANTING ACCESS TO A VPN SERVER

If you only have a small number of users, you can grant access to those users on an individual basis by editing the properties of their user accounts in Active Directory Users and Computers. This is done by choosing Allow access under Network Access Permission on the Dial-in tab of the user's account properties, as shown in Figure 18-10.

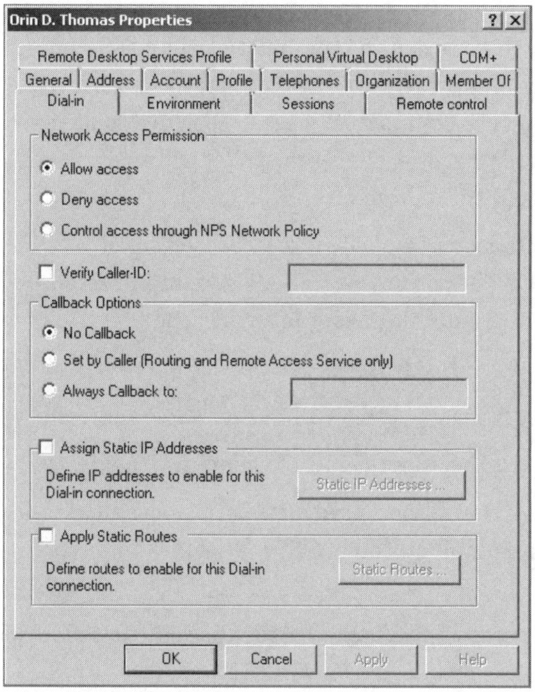

FIGURE 18-10: Remote access user properties

The default setting for network access is for it to be controlled through a Network Policy Server (NPS) network policy. To be granted access, a user must meet the conditions of a *connection request policy* and a *network policy*. A connection request policy includes type of access, time of access and which authentication protocols are available. A network policy can be as simple as specifying that a particular user group has access.

▶ Often, when you are new to configuring remote access policies, it is better to edit an existing policy rather than to fathom the creation of a new one.

When you install a VPN server, a default connection request policy, called Microsoft Routing and Remote Access Service Policy, will be created. You can view the properties of this policy under the Policies\Connection Request Policies node of the Network Policy Server console on the VPN server. To configure this policy, perform the following steps:

1. Open the Network Policy Server console on the VPN server.

2. Expand the Policies\Connection Request Policies node. Right-click the Microsoft Routing and Remote Access Service Policy, and then click Properties.

3. On the Conditions tab, verify that the day and time restrictions match those that you want to have enforced for the remote access policy. You can use this tab to add conditions to the policy. Clients must meet all specified conditions; so the more conditions you add, the fewer clients the policy will apply to. Conditions that you can add include the following:

   ▷ **Location Groups:** Restricts access to members of a *Host Credential Authorization Protocol (HCAP)* location group. HCAP is an interoperability protocol for use between NPS and third-party networking devices.

   ▷ **User Name:** Specifies a specific HCAP user name.

   ▷ **Access Client IPv4 Address:** Specifies the RADIUS client IPv4 address

   ▷ **Access Client IPv6 Address:** Specifies the RADIUS client IPv6 address

   ▷ **Framed Protocol:** Specifies the protocol used for framing incoming packets, such as PPP (Point-to-Point Protocol) or SLIP (Serial Line Internet Protocol)

   ▷ **Service Type:** Limits clients to a specific service such as Point-to-Point protocols

   ▷ **Tunnel Type:** Restricts clients to a specific tunnel type, such as PPTP, L2TP, and SSTP

   ▷ **Day and Time Restrictions:** Specifies when connections can be active

   ▷ **Identity Type:** Allows specific identity types, such as NAP statements of health

   ▷ **Calling Station ID:** Specifies the Network Access Server telephone number

   ▷ **Client Friendly Name:** Specifies the RADIUS client name

   ▷ **Client IPv4 Address:** Specifies the RADIUS client IPv4 address

▶ A RADIUS client is an access device, such as a hardware device on the perimeter network that forwards authentication traffic. It isn't the connecting user or computer.

▷ **Client IPv6 Address:** Specifies the RADIUS client IPv6 address

▷ **Client Vendor:** Specifies the RADIUS client vendor

▷ **Called Station ID:** Specifies the NAS identification string or telephone number

▷ **NAS Identifier:** Specifies the NAS identification string

▷ **NAS IPv4 Address:** Specifies the IPv4 address of NAS

▷ **NAS IPv6 Address:** Specifies the IPv6 address of NAS

▷ **NAS Port Type:** Specifies the RADIUS client access type (ISDN, VPN, IEEE 802.11 wireless, etc)

4. Settings, shown in Figure 18-11, are a set of categories that are required. They include the following:

▷ **Authentication Methods:** Enables you to specify which protocols clients can use to connect to the VPN server. The VPN server attempts to use the most secure protocol first and then attempts less secure protocols, in order, down to least secure protocol supported by the policy.

▷ **Authentication:** This setting determines whether the VPN server performs authentication or whether authentication credentials are passed to another server.

▷ **Accounting:** This enables you to record authentication information to a log file or SQL server database. Doing this gives you a record of which people have gained access through VPN connections.

▷ **Attribute, RADIUS Attributes Standard & Vendor Specific:** These settings are necessary only if you are placing the VPN server into an existing RADIUS infrastructure.

NOTE In most situations, the default conditions and settings are likely to be adequate. Most administrators are just worried about ensuring that clients have remote access and are less concerned about whether a client is coming from a particular IPv6 address. Many of the available conditions are really only appropriate for site-to-site links rather than client VPN links. As most organizations use dedicated hardware devices for site-to-site VPN links, the topic is not covered in this book.

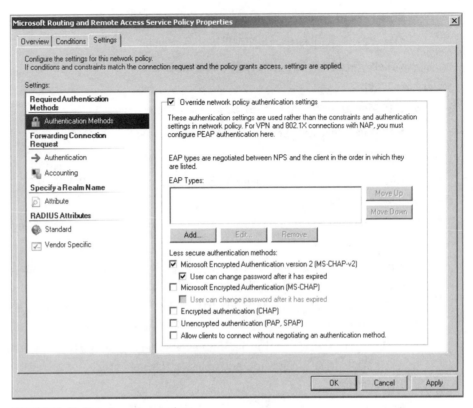

FIGURE 18-11: Remote access settings

After you have ensured that the details of the connection request policies meet your needs, you can configure a network policy. Network policies are useful when you want to give a large number of users remote access but do not want to configure access on a per-account basis. To create a new network policy that allows this access, perform the following general steps:

1. Open the Network Policy Server console. Right-click on the Policies\Network Policies node, and then click New. This will open the Specify Network Policy Name and Connection Type.

2. Enter a name for the policy and set the Type of Network Access Server drop-down menu to Remote Access Server (VPN-Dial Up), and then click Next.

3. On the Conditions page, click Add and add conditions. The conditions that you can add are as follows:

> ▶ The Windows Group condition allows you to use either user or computer groups as a basis for granting remote access. This is the most commonly used remote access condition.

   Windows Groups: Limits access to user or computer groups.

   ▷ **Machine Groups:** Limits access to members of the specified computer group.

▷ **User Groups:** Limits access to members of the specified user group

▷ **Location Groups:** Limits access to members of a HCAP location group. HCAP is an interoperability protocol for use between NPS and third-party networking devices.

▷ **HCAP User Groups:** Limits access to members of an HCAP user group

▷ **Day and Time Restrictions:** Restricts when the policy can be used for access

▷ **Identity Type:** Allows specific identity types, such as NAP statements of health

▷ **MS-Service Class:** Specifies the group of DHCP scopes that should supply an IP address

▷ **Health Policies:** Defines NAP health policies to which the client must comply

▷ **NAP-Capable Computers:** Specifies whether the client can assess NAP health policies

▷ **Operating System:** Restricts access based on the client operating system

▷ **Policy Expiration:** Defines when the network policy expires

▷ **Access Client IPv4 Address:** Specifies the network address of the client

▷ **Access Client IPv6 Address:** Specifies the network address of the client

▷ **Authentication Type:** Defines acceptable authentication protocols

▷ **Allowed EAP Types:** Defines allowed EAP authentication protocols

▷ **Framed Protocol:** Specifies the protocol used for framing incoming packets, such as PPP (Point-to-Point Protocol) or SLIP (Serial Line Internet Protocol)

▷ **Service Type:** Limits clients to a specific service such as Point-to-Point protocols

▷ **Tunnel Type:** Restricts clients to a specific tunnel type, such as PPTP, L2TP and SSTP

▷ **Calling Station ID:** Specifies the Network Access Server telephone number

▷ **Client Friendly Name:** Specifies the RADIUS client name

▷ **Client IPv4 Address:** Specifies the RADIUS client IPv4 address

▶ You should generally disable VPN protocols on the server level rather than through a network policy.

> ▷ **Client IPv6 Address:** Specifies the RADIUS client IPv6 address
>
> ▷ **Client Vendor:** Specifies the RADIUS client vendor
>
> ▷ **MS-RAS Vendor:** Specifies the Network Access Server (NAS) vendor
>
> ▷ **Called Station ID:** Specifies the NAS identification string or telephone number
>
> ▷ **NAS Identifier:** Specifies the NAS identification string
>
> ▷ **NAS IPv4 Address:** Specifies the IPv4 address of NAS
>
> ▷ **NAS IPv6 Address:** Specifies the IPv6 address of NAS
>
> ▷ **NAS Port Type:** Specifies RADIUS client access type (ISDN, VPN, IEEE 802.11 wireless, etc.)

Once you have configured the network policy, it should be possible for VPN connections to be established.

CONNECTING VIA DIRECTACCESS

DirectAccess is an always-on remote access solution. What this means is that if a client computer configured with DirectAccess is connected to the Internet, a persistent connection will be established between that computer and the organization's internal network. The big advantage of DirectAccess is that it does not require users to directly authenticate. The client computer determines that it is connected to the Internet by attempting to connect to a website that is only accessible from the internal network. If the client determines itself to be on a network other than the internal network, it automatically initiates a connection.

When doing this, the client first attempts to determine whether it is connected to a native IPv6 network. If the client has been assigned a public IPv6 address, a direct connection is made to the organization's internal DirectAccess servers. If the client determines that it is not connected to a native IPv6 network, it will attempt to create an IPv6 over IPv4 tunnel using the 6to4 and then Teredo technologies. If connections cannot be established using these technologies, an attempt will be made to use IP-HTTPS, which is similar to the SSTP protocol discussed earlier, except that it encapsulates IPv6 traffic within the HTTPS protocol.

When a connection is established, authentication occurs using computer certificates. These computer certificates must be pre-installed on the client. The benefit of this is that user intervention is not required.

▶ If your organization supports the required infrastructure, DirectAccess is the best remote access option for clients. When set up, DirectAccess is a minimal-fuss solution and users will have access to all necessary internal resources. The drawback of DirectAccess is that your organization needs to have switched to IPv6 internally.

The drawback of DirectAccess is that it is only available to client computers running the Enterprise and Ultimate editions of Windows 7 or higher operating systems that are members of an Active Directory domain. If your organization has Windows XP or Windows Vista client computers, or clients running Windows 7 Professional edition, these clients will be unable to leverage DirectAccess.

> **NOTE** DirectAccess is very much a future remote access solution. Most organizations won't have all clients running the minimum necessary operating systems for some years. This is something that should be on your radar, but probably isn't something that you are going to be able to directly implement.

Understanding DirectAccess Requirements

DirectAccess is a technology that is deeply rooted in Windows Server 2008 R2, though, of course, it is likely to be supported by future versions of the Windows Server and Windows Client operating systems. Like IKEv2 VPNs, DirectAccess is only supported when Windows Server 2008 R2 servers interact with Windows 7 clients.

DirectAccess has the benefit of being *bi-directional*. This means that servers and other clients on the internal network are able to interact with DirectAccess clients on the Internet. This makes scenarios such as software deployment to remote clients far more feasible. It also allows organizations to exercise tighter control over the configuration of remote clients through functionality such as System Center Configuration Manager's Desired Configuration Management, which can detect unauthorized software, such as games and file sharing programs, and trigger remediation, such as removing these items.

To deploy DirectAccess, you must ensure that the following requirements are met:

▶ The DirectAccess server must be running Windows Server 2008 R2 or higher. This feature is not supported on previous versions of the Windows operating system such as Windows Server 2003 or Windows Server 2008.

▶ The DirectAccess server must have two network adapters. One of these adapters must be directly connected to the Internet.

▶ The Internet-connected adapter must be configured with two, consecutive, public IPv4 addresses.

▶ The internal network interface must be configured with a connection-specific DNS suffix.

▶ While the DirectAccess setup wizard requires these two addresses, in reality they are only needed to support the Teredo transition technology.

▶ It is possible to use a non-enterprise CA, but enrolling large numbers of client computers that are members of a domain in the appropriate certificates is better accomplished through certificate autoenrollment.

▶ Placing a server on the perimeter network that is also a member of a domain will present some challenges to administrators that have a no-domain members on the screened subnet policy.

▶ A domain controller and DNS server in the domain must be running the Windows Server 2008 with SP2 operating system or later.

▶ An Active Directory CA, preferably an enterprise CA, must be present to issue computer certificates.

▶ All clients accessing the server must be running the Enterprise or Ultimate editions of Windows 7 or higher and also must be members of the same AD DS forest as the DirectAccess server.

▶ The DirectAccess server must be a member of an AD DS domain.

▶ You must configure DirectAccess with a user account that has permissions to create and apply GPOs in the domain.

Configuring DirectAccess

To configure DirectAccess, perform the following general steps:

1. Create an Active Directory security group. This group contains the computer accounts of the DirectAccess client computers.

2. Ensure that the server that you use as the DirectAccess server has two consecutive public IPv4 addresses assigned to a network adapter accessible to hosts on the Internet.

3. Ensure that the computer is enrolled in a computer certificate from an enterprise CA.

4. Configure Windows Firewall to allow incoming traffic by allowing the ICMPv6-ECHO Request-In rule on the public network interface.

5. Install DirectAccess by running the following commands from an elevated PowerShell prompt:

```
Import-Module ServerManager
Add-WindowsFeature DAMC
```

6. Open the DirectAccess Management console from the Administrative Tools menu. This console is shown in Figure 18-12.

7. In the Remote Clients area, click Configure. Add the names of the security groups that contain the computer accounts of DirectAccess clients.

8. Click Configure in the DirectAccess Server Setup item to specify which network interfaces are connected to the perimeter and internal networks. Click Next.

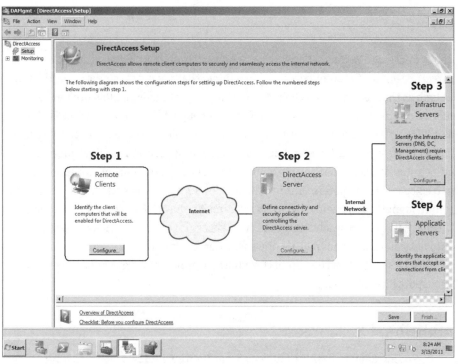

FIGURE 18-12: DirectAccess console

9. On the Certificate Components page, specify the root certificate of the CA that is at the top of the hierarchy of the CA issuing the client certificates. Also specify the computer certificate that will be used to secure HTTPS communication. Click Finish.

10. In the Infrastructure Servers item, click Configure. Specify the location of the internal website that is used to perform the check to determine whether the client is on the internal or on an external network. This website must be configured with an SSL certificate.

11. Specify the DNS servers and domain controllers used by the DirectAccess clients. Specify the client computers on the internal network that you will use to manage DirectAccess clients, for example servers running System Center Configuration Manager.

12. When you finish this wizard, DirectAccess creates two Group Policy Objects in the domain. The first of these applies to the security group you specified in step 6. The second GPO configures the DirectAccess server.

SUMMARY

Remote access to Windows networks is achieved through RD Gateway, VPN, or DirectAccess. RD Gateway works well for clients that are not members of the domain, as long as there are hosts on the network that support incoming Remote Desktop requests. Windows Server 2008 R2 VPN servers support the IKEv2, SSTP, L2TP/IPsec, and PPTP VPN protocols. The PPTP protocol is the easiest to support, because it does not require a certificate server, but it is also the least secure. The IKEv2 protocol supports automatic reconnection without requiring user intervention, but is only supported by client computers running the Windows 7 operating system. DirectAccess is only supported by client computers running Windows 7 Enterprise and Windows 7 Ultimate editions. The advantage of DirectAccess is that connections are established automatically and do not require any user intervention. The disadvantage is that it requires more effort on the part of the administrator to properly configure a network to support DirectAccess.

Additional Resources

Deploying Remote Desktop Gateway Step-By-Step Guide

http://technet.microsoft.com/en-us/library/dd983941(WS.10).aspx

DirectAccess Requirements

http://technet.microsoft.com/en-us/library/dd637797(WS.10).aspx

Remote Access Step-By-Step Guide: Deploying Remote Access with VPN Reconnect

http://technet.microsoft.com/en-us/library/dd637783(WS.10).aspx

Troubleshooting IKEv2 VPN Connections

http://technet.microsoft.com/en-us/library/dd941612(WS.10).aspx

VPN tunneling protocols

http://technet.microsoft.com/en-us/library/dd469817(WS.10).aspx

Remote Desktop Gateway

http://technet.microsoft.com/en-us/library/dd560672(WS.10).aspx

PART VI

MAINTENANCE AND MONITORING SECRETS

Getting the Most Out of Event Logs and Auditing

Administrators bother with event logs only when something goes wrong or they ignore them entirely. Event logs are both voluminous and cryptic. You can spend a long time looking for an event related to something that you are interested in, and, even if you do find an event that sort of describes what you are looking for, the message you are rewarded with often provides little in the way of illumination.

Auditing is the process through which you ensure that events related to certain activities, such as changing passwords and accessing certain files and folders, are recorded in the event log. Auditing is primarily a security concern. It doesn't stop someone from performing an action, but it does provide a record that he or she has performed that action.

In this chapter, you learn some of the secrets to using auditing and event logs on computers running Windows Server 2008 R2. This includes learning how to enable the advanced auditing categories, how to configure event log subscriptions, and setting up Event Viewer tasks.

AUDITING WINDOWS SERVER 2008 R2

▶ Determining what to audit is difficult. It really comes down to "what do you need to know?" Once you figure out what you need to know, you can figure out what you need to audit.

Auditing is the process of recording in the event log things that have happened on the server. Something happens, such as a user logs on, and, if auditing is configured appropriately, an item detailing that occurrence is written to the event log. A common problem that new administrators have is the tendency to turn everything on and assume that they'll be able to dig the interesting things out of the resulting torrent of information. Although this sounds fine in principle, at some stage, you'll need to go through all the events and ask yourself, "Do I need to know this?" It doesn't help that event log items themselves can be rather opaque; it might not be clear from reviewing an item whether it contains information that is important or abstruse.

When configuring auditing policies, set out objectives for what you want to monitor, rather than taking the approach of monitoring everything and hoping that you can dig through the resulting haystack of information to find the proverbial needle. When you start auditing, you're probably mostly interested in finding out such things as if people are constantly attempting to log on with incorrect passwords or whether members of the helpdesk team are changing the password on the CEO's user account. You probably aren't interested in process tracking or policy changes, unless you are working in an environment where a lot of time is spent worrying about security.

Understanding Common Audit Categories

Windows Server 2008 R2 ships with two sets of audit categories: *simple audit categories* and *complex audit categories*. The simple audit categories have been available on Windows Server operating systems for more than a decade. The more complex audit categories are a recent addition, only becoming available with and able to be used on computers running Windows Server 2008, Windows Server 2008 R2, Windows Vista, and Windows 7.

A big problem with the simple audit categories is that they are general. This means that when you enable one of the nine category policies, you end up populating the Security log with a flood of events, most of which you probably aren't interested in. For example, when you audit account logon events, you end up with information about a lot more events than just the authentication of Bob logging on to the domain from his workstation, including events related to Kerberos and IPsec. If you only want to know about Bob logging on to the domain from his workstation, all these extra events can be a bit annoying. You need to know about these simple audit policies if your environment still has computers running Windows Server 2003 or Windows XP. The nine simple auditing policies are shown in Figure 19-1.

▶ One solution to this problem is to structure your Group Policy application so that you apply general auditing policies against the Windows Server 2003 and Windows XP systems and the specific policies against the newer operating systems.

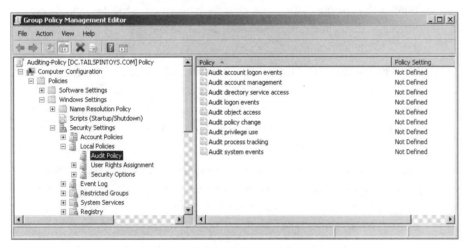

FIGURE 19-1: Basic audit policies

These policies are used to audit events related to the following:

▶ **Audit Account Logon Events:** This policy enables you to audit when a specific machine authenticates a logon. Turn this on for domain controllers, and you'll be able to audit when people authenticate against the domain controller.

▶ **Audit Account Management:** This auditing type enables you to track when accounts are modified, including name changes, password resets, user group modifications, or account unlocks. It is important to audit this type of activity to ensure that accounts aren't being mismanaged or compromised. If a lot of account passwords are changed at 3 in the morning, you probably want to conduct more investigations.

▶ **Audit Directory Service Access:** This policy enables you to see if someone has accessed an object in Active Directory that has its own system access control list (SACL). This policy tends to only be used in high-security environments where you might want to monitor whether someone has changed the delegation privileges on an object such as an Organizational Unit.

▶ **Audit Logon Events:** This audit category determines whether a local logon has occurred. Use this on Remote Desktop Services servers to audit logons; but, as most logon events occur on workstations and workstation logs are rarely checked, you should take care with the scope of this policy.

▶ **Audit Object Access:** This policy enables you to check whether particular items such as printers, files, or folders have been accessed. You should only perform auditing on sensitive objects, as there is no real reason to audit access to common objects.

▶ **Audit Policy Change:** When enabled, this policy records modifications to user rights assignments, auditing policies, or trust policies. This policy is generally only useful in high-security environments, where you are reasonably concerned about the possibility of Group Policy being compromised in such a way that privileges are being altered.

▶ **Audit Privilege Use:** When enabled, this policy allows you to track when privileges are being used. As there are uncountable privileges that are regularly used, auditing this category can end up clogging the Security log with uninteresting events.

▶ **Audit Process Tracking:** This category allows you to track applications and processes. Unless you have a need to track when specific applications or processes are run, auditing against this category can also end up clogging the Security log with uninteresting events.

▶ **Audit System Events:** This category allows you to track computer shutdown or startup but also allows you to track whether programs have attempted to change system settings without permission. While this sounds interesting, it is better to have an anti-malware program monitoring whether applications are doing anything unusual related to security than it is to find out about it by trawling event logs.

▶ Consider using a technology such as Active Directory Rights Management Services to control access to special objects rather than relying on permissions and auditing to keep them secure.

Auditing for Success and Failure

When you configure an audit policy, you enable the audit policy and then choose audit for success or failure. Generally it is a good idea to audit for failure, as you want to know when a user fails to log on or access a file. Auditing for failure can tell you interesting things about what is happening on your network, such as a user continually entering an incorrect password. Auditing for success can be less interesting, such as when a user correctly enters his password and logs on to the network.

> **NOTE** Auditing account authentication failures can give you an idea about how often people incorrectly enter their password and can allow you to fine tune your password lockout policy. If you check the event logs and find that when people mistype their password, they only do it once or twice, you can configure your password lockout policy to lock them out if they do it three times in a row without worrying about it causing a massive spike in calls to the helpdesk.

Figure 19-2 shows that the Audit Account Logon Event policy is configured to audit only for failure. When you enable this policy in a GPO that applies to domain controllers, it will record authentication failures that occur in the domain controller's Security log.

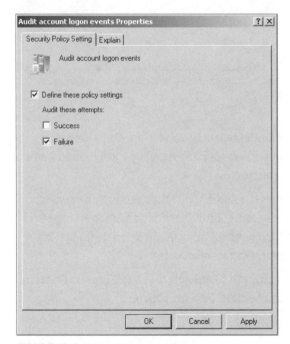

FIGURE 19-2: Audit success and failure

Utilizing Advanced Audit Policies

Instead of providing nine general categories, the advanced audit policies provide you with 55 different auditing categories. Rather than auditing all account logon events, you can audit granular events, such as credential validation. When you use specific audit policies, you won't fill up your security event log with minutiae that you have no interest in following up on. A good rule for auditing is that if you aren't going to follow up on something, you shouldn't bother auditing it in the first place.

As you can see in Figure 19-3, the advanced audit policies are broken up into ten different nodes. Generally speaking, there is broad mapping between the nine general categories and the ten categories listed here. The policies that you can find in each node are as follows:

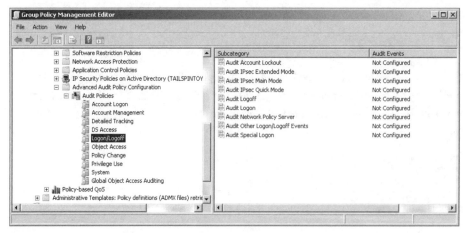

FIGURE 19-3: Advanced audit policies

- ▶ **Account Logon:** Includes the Audit Credential Validation, Audit Kerberos Authentication Service, Audit Kerberos Service Ticket Operations, and Audit Other Account Logon Events policies

- ▶ **Account Management:** Includes the Audit Application Group Management, Audit Computer Account Management, Audit Distribution Group Management, Audit Other Account Management Events, Audit Security Group Management, and Audit User Account Management policies

- ▶ **Detailed Tracking:** Includes the Audit DPAPI Activity, Audit Process Creation, Audit Process Termination, and Audit RPC Events policies

- ▶ **DS Access:** Includes the Audit Detailed Directory Service Replication, Audit Directory Service Access, Audit Directory Service Changes, and Audit Directory Service Replication policies

- ▶ **Logon/Logoff:** Includes the Audit Account Lockout, Audit IPsec Extended Mode, Audit IPsec Main Mode, Audit IPsec Quick Mode, Audit Logoff, Audit Logon, Audit Network Policy Server, Audit Other Logon/Logoff Events, and Audit Special Logon policies

- ▶ **Object Access:** Includes the Audit Application Generated, Audit Certification Services, Audit Detailed File Share, Audit File Share, Audit File System, Audit Filtering Platform Connection, Audit Filtering Platform Packet Drop, Audit Handle Manipulation, Audit Kernel Object, Audit Other Object Access Events, Audit Registry, and Audit SAM policies

- ▶ **Policy Change:** Includes the Audit Policy Change, Audit Authentication Policy Change, Audit Authorization Policy Change, Audit Filtering Platform Policy Change, Audit MPSSVC Rule-Level Policy Change, and Audit Other Policy Change Events policies

- ▶ **Privilege Use:** Includes the Audit Non Sensitive Privilege Use, Audit Other Privilege Use Events, and Audit Sensitive Privilege Use policies

- ▶ **System:** Includes the Audit IPsec Drive, Audit Other System Events, Audit Security State Change, Audit Security System Extension, and Audit System Integrity policies

- ▶ **Global Object Access Auditing:** Includes the File System and Registry policies

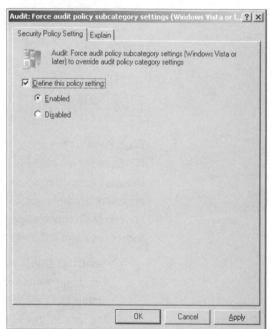

To use the audit subcategories rather than the more general simple categories, you must enable the Force Audit Subcategory Settings policy, shown in Figure 19-4. This policy is located in the Computer Configuration\Policies\Windows Settings\Local Policies\Security Options node of a GPO. When you apply this policy against computers running Windows Vista, Windows 7, Windows Server 2008, or Windows Server 2008 R2, any of the general policies that are enabled will be ignored, and these specific policies will come into effect.

FIGURE 19-4: Force audit subcategory settings

You can learn what specific policies do by right-clicking on the policy in the Group Policy editor, selecting Properties, and then clicking the Explain tab. Figure 19-5 shows the Explain tab for the Audit Credential Validation policy. This provides guidance about where to apply the policy and also provides information on the volume of events that applying the policy will generate.

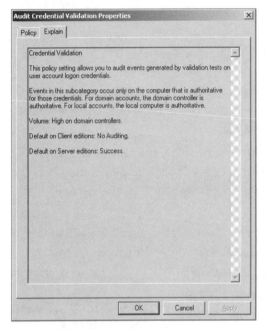

FIGURE 19-5: Audit properties

FILTERING AND VIEWING EVENT LOGS

Event Viewer is the primary way that people manage event logs on computers running Windows Server 2008 R2. It is possible to use PowerShell to view event log information, but even on computers running the Server Core installation option, this is probably more trouble than it is worth. The key logs are located in Event Viewer's Windows Logs node. Except for one, these logs were present on computers running Windows Server 2003 and Windows 2000 Server. These logs include the following:

▶ **Security:** This log stores all security events and is the container that holds all events generated through auditing. This is one of the two most important logs visible in Event Viewer but will only be useful to you if you've enabled auditing for the type of event that you want to know about.

▶ **System:** This log records all interesting system-related events, such as failure of services and components. This is the second of the two most important logs visible in Event Viewer, as the System log will provide you with information about a server's health including critical, error, or warning events.

▶ **Application:** This log records application events. Increasingly, applications have separate logs located in the Application and Service Logs area; for example, the DNS Server writes events to the DNS Server Logs. Any applications that don't have their own logs tend to dump their events in this log.

▶ **Setup:** This log records events related to application, feature, and role setup. As most server applications, such as Exchange and SQL, also write their own separate installation logs, most administrators don't spend much time examining this log.

▶ **Forwarded events:** This log collects events forwarded from other servers. Forwarded events are covered in more detail later in this chapter, and this log category is new to Windows Server 2008 and Windows Server 2008 R2.

You can quickly determine how many error, warning, alert, and caution events you have in a log by clicking on the Level column in Event Viewer. This sorts the logs according to level, as shown in Figure 19-6. You can then expand each level and review the events that are listed there.

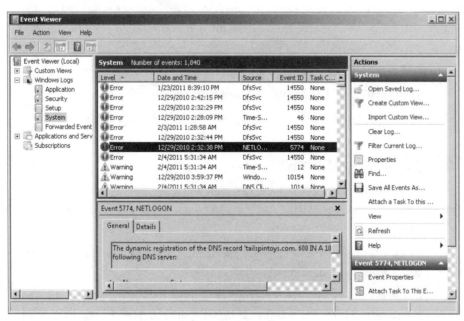

FIGURE 19-6: Sort by level

The Administrative Events custom view, which is available under the Custom Views node, also displays the "warning," "error," and "critical events" located in all of the logs on your server. These custom views are important, because it is extremely unlikely that you will open the event log and see the precise event that you are looking for on the first screen. Where Windows Server 2003 was restricted to logs that were 4 GB in size, the theoretical limit for a Windows Server 2008 R2 event log exceeds a petabyte. Even if you read an event log entry every second, you'd need a couple of million years to read every event that could be stored in an event log of that size!

> **NOTE** You shouldn't approach event logs as something you simply scroll through until you notice something interesting. This random approach can distract you—you spend time looking at red markers that indicate that a service is functioning erratically, and you miss the multiple success audits that indicate that the CEO seems to be logging in an awful lot at 2:00am, when you know she's actually scuba diving off the Great Barrier Reef.

Grouping by Task Category

You can determine which audit category caused an event to be written to the Security log by grouping events by task category. This allows you to determine whether enabling a specific task category has led to a flood of useless events written to the log, or whether it has only generated a small number of interesting events. Grouping by task category is shown in Figure 19-7.

To do this, perform the following general steps:

1. Open Event Viewer and select the Windows Logs\Security log.

2. From the View menu, click Group By, and then click on Task Category.

Using Filters and Views

Although the Administrative Event custom view does provide useful information, you are likely to get more out of using Filters and Custom Views. The difference between these is as follows:

▶ A *filter* is a one-off way of sorting a specific log. You lose any filters that you create when you close Event Viewer.

▶ A *custom view* is a persistent way of locating events across multiple logs. You can convert filters to views. You can also export and import custom views so that you can use them across multiple computers.

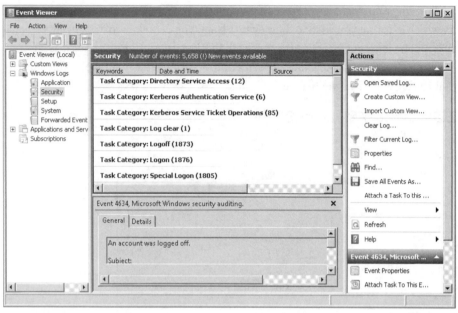

FIGURE 19-7: Group by Task Category.

To create a filter, perform the following general steps:

1. In Event Viewer, open the specific event log that you wish to filter.

2. From the Actions menu, click Filter Current Log. This opens the Filter Current Log dialog box, shown in Figure 19-8.

3. On the Logged section, determine whether you want the filter to apply to the log in its entirety, the last hour, last 12 hours, last day, last 7 days, last 30 days, or a custom range.

4. Select which event levels you want shown.

5. On the Event Source drop-down menu, select all event sources that you wish to include in the filter.

6. On the rest of the dialog, specify the event IDs, task categories, keywords, users, and computers for which you want to filter the log.

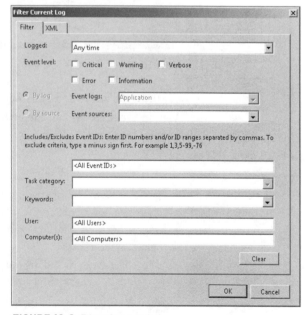

FIGURE 19-8: Filter Current Log.

Creating a custom view involves a very similar process, except that you can specify which logs that you wish to draw events from. The default is to draw events from all Windows logs, but you can also check all Application and Services Logs, as shown in Figure 19-9. The only drawback of selecting a custom view that involves all logs is that the log will be slower to load.

▶ It's better to create a number of specific views than super views that trawl through all logs. This follows the theory that you should approach event logs with a purpose in mind rather than browse for interesting nuggets.

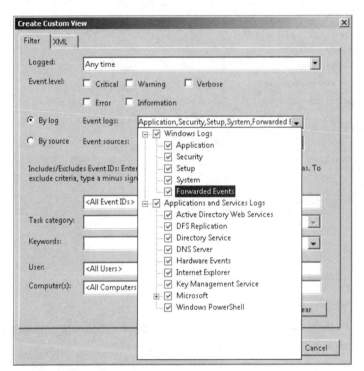

FIGURE 19-9: Create custom view.

Once you've created a custom view, you can export it by selecting the Custom View in Event Viewer and then clicking on Export Custom View. This will allow you to export the view definition in XML format. You can then import the custom view on other servers.

> **NOTE**   One of the most annoying things about event log entries is that many of them are downright cryptic. A lot of administrators avoid reading event messages, because they find them so uninformative. One of the ways that you can make sense of cryptic events is to use search engines. Usually, you should search by event ID and the name of the log. There are also several sites devoted specifically to explaining what event logs mean. One or two event-related sites are listed in the Further Links section at the end of this chapter.

EVENT LOG FORWARDING

Event log forwarding is a technology that became available in Windows Server 2008 that allows you to configure events generated on one or more computers to be transferred to another computer. The benefit of event log forwarding is that it allows you to centralize your important events. Rather than connecting to each computer in your organization to check the event logs, you can have all important logs forwarded to a central location.

There are two methods through which you can configure event log forwarding. These are as follows:

▶ **Collector Initiated Subscription:** In this configuration, a central computer queries source computers and retrieves event logs that meet the subscription criteria.

▶ **Source Computer Initiated Subscription:** In this configuration, each source computer forwards events that meet the subscription criteria to the central collecting computer.

Prior to setting up event log forwarding, you need to perform the following steps:

1. Run the following command on both the source and collector computers:

    Winrm quickconfig

2. Run this additional command on the collector computer:

    Wecutil qc

3. Add the computer account of the collector computer to the local Administrators group on each source computer.

Once you have performed these steps, you can configure event log forwarding. To do this, navigate to the Subscriptions tab of the Event Viewer, and then click on Create Subscription in the Actions menu. This will open the Subscription Properties dialog box, shown in Figure 19-10.

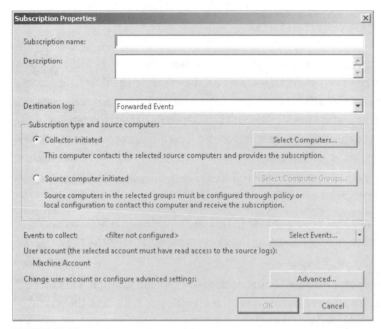

FIGURE 19-10: Subscription Properties

On the Subscription Properties dialog, configure the following:

▶ Provide a subscription name and description, and then choose the log on which events collected from the source computer should be stored.

▶ Choose the Collector Initiated Subscription type if you want to specify which computers to retrieve event logs from. Choose Source Computer Initiated if you want to have source computers forward events.

▶ Click Select Computers to specify the source computers. Click Test when adding computers to verify that connectivity has been established.

▶ Click Select Events to create a view for the collection of events.

▶ Use the Advanced Subscription Settings dialog shown in Figure 19-11 to specify advanced settings. If you are retrieving events from the Security log, you must provide credentials of an account that has local Administrator privileges on the source computer.

▶ You configure Source Computer Initiated Subscription properties by editing the policies located in the Computer Configuration\ Administrative Templates\ Windows Components\ Event Forwarding node of a standard Windows Server 2008 GPO.

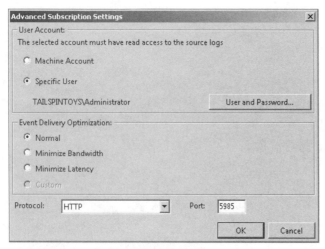

FIGURE 19-11: Advanced Subscription Settings

CREATING EVENT VIEWER TASKS

You can use Event Viewer to create tasks that are triggered when a pre-defined event is written to the event log. For example, you could create a task that triggers an e-mail message to be sent any time the membership of a sensitive group, such as the Domain Admins or Enterprise Admins group, is modified.

The trick with creating tasks is that you need to have an example of the event that you want to create a task from sitting in the event log. When you have located the example event, you build the Event Viewer task by performing the following steps:

1. In Event Viewer, select the event that you want to use as the basis for the task.

2. In the Actions pane, click Attach Task to This Event. This launches the Create Basic Task Wizard. Add a meaningful name and description to the task, and then click Next.

3. On the When an Event Is Logged page, verify that the event details match the specifics of the event that you wish to build the task around, and then click Next.

4. On the Action page, shown in Figure 19-12, choose between Start a program, Send an e-mail, or Display a message.

> ► You can use the Start a program option to run a script. Do this if automating a resolution to the event is straightforward. You shouldn't choose the Display a message option, as these notifications tend to be ignored unless someone is logged on directly and paying attention.

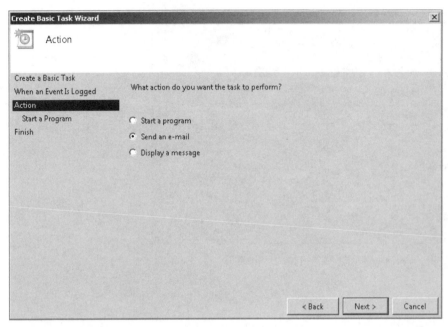

FIGURE 19-12: Start a program or send an e-mail.

> When you create an Event Viewer task using this method, you won't be able to configure settings such as which account the program is executed under. You must do this by editing the task later in Task Scheduler.

5. If you choose to start a program, you will need to specify the path to the program and any command-line arguments that are necessary. If you choose to send an e-mail, you need to specify a From address, a To address, a Subject for the e-mail, the text to include in the e-mail, and the SMTP server that will be used to route the message to your mail server. When you have provided the necessary details, click Next. Click Finish if you have finished with the task, or select Open the Properties Dialog for This Task When I Click Finish to edit the advanced properties for the task. You will learn more about editing the properties of tasks later in this chapter.

NOTE If you are in a situation where you want to create an Event Viewer task, and you don't have an event sitting in your event log to use as a basis for the task, you can use the **EVENTCREATE** command to create an event with the same ID in the appropriate log and use it to create the task.

Once you have created your event-driven task, you can test that it works by using the eventcreate.exe command-line utility to create a dummy event to populate the event log. The key to this is knowing the event ID and log that you want to target.

For example, to create a warning event with ID 777 in the Application log, issue the following command from an elevated command prompt:

```
EVENTCREATE /T WARNING /ID 777 /L APPLICATION /D "My custom error"
```

Creating Alerts for Everything

A mistake that inexperienced administrators make once they learn how to create Event Viewer tasks is then going on to create tasks to send them an e-mail message for every possible event that they can think of. The problem with this is that even the most sedulous administrator gets to the point where he creates an e-mail filter to move incoming event-related-emails into a folder. This folder eventually ends up being ignored, because there are simply too many events to go through to sort the interesting from the truly important.

The lesson here is that you should only create e-mail alerts for events to which you are going to actually respond. For example, there are services that allow you to send text messages to mobile phones if you send an e-mail to a specific address. You would only set this up to happen to your own mobile phone if you really needed to know that something happened. You certainly would be reluctant to configure such an alert to notify you at 2:00am via text message that a backup has failed. While a failed backup is an important event, it probably isn't something that you need to know about instantly.

Rather than sending e-mail alerts to a mailbox that is checked by you or other systems administrators, there are products, such as Microsoft's System Center Service Manager, that can use e-mail messages as a way to automatically create jobs in a service desk job tracking system. Service Manager also integrates directly to create jobs based on alerts generated by System Center Operations Manager, though you should only consider this approach in large enterprise environments because of the complexity involved in getting it all to work.

Creating Meaningful Alerts

If you do decide to have e-mail messages sent, provide yourself with a reasonable description of why the e-mail message has been sent. This means six months later, when you have forgotten the precise reason why you created the event alert, and you receive an e-mail message generated by it, you'll be able to quickly figure out:

 ▸ What the message is trying to tell you

 ▸ What you should do about it

Figure 19-13 provides an example of a message that provides information. Remember, there is no need to be cryptic when creating these messages, as the whole point of sending yourself a message is to ensure that you are aware of a specific problem. You might even want to provide a link to an internal knowledge base article that deals with how to address that problem.

FIGURE 19-13: Task message

Managing Event Viewer Tasks

Although you create Event Viewer tasks in Event Viewer, you manage those tasks using Task Scheduler. Task Scheduler, located in the Administrative Tools menu, allows you to manage both Event Viewer tasks and all other automatic operating system-related tasks. The Event Viewer Tasks node of Task Scheduler is shown in Figure 19-14.

> **NOTE** Most administrators aren't even aware that there are a lot of automatic operating system tasks that they can modify. These scheduled tasks include all the little things that administrators don't need to think about, such as performing an automatic volume defragmentation at 1:00am every Wednesday, as well as performing automatic diagnostics on RAM when certain event IDs are written to the event log. Although you probably don't need to know the minutiae of what goes on in scheduled tasks, having a look at what is scheduled to go on under the hood can be rather enlightening.

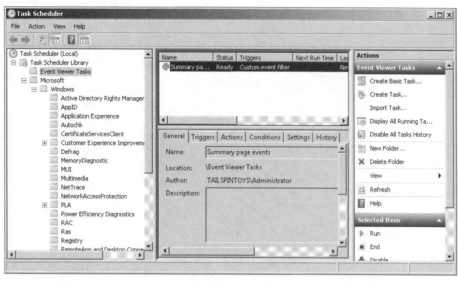

FIGURE 19-14: Event Viewer tasks

You can use the Task Scheduler to perform the following functions on Event Viewer tasks:

> **NOTE** The default settings for an Event Viewer task have it running only when the user that created the task is logged on to the server. You need to modify this by modifying the task properties to ensure that the task runs independently of whether a user is logged in or not. If you don't do this, you'll have to keep an account logged on at all times to ensure that you get your alerts!

▶ **Modify an existing event-driven task:** This allows you to modify the properties of an existing Event Viewer task. You can modify which account is used to run the task, configure whether the task is hidden, configure whether the task runs only when a specific user is logged on or runs at all times as shown in Figure 19-15, configure the task to run again if it fails, and configure termination conditions for the task if it runs longer than a certain amount of time. If you configure an Event Viewer task to run a program, you will want to modify the account the task runs under.

▶ **Disable an event-driven task:** There may be some circumstances where you want to disable, but not completely remove, an event-driven task. You might do this if you have to perform maintenance on a server and don't want it to trigger a lot of Event Viewer tasks that are designed to tell you that something has gone awry.

▶ When disabling tasks during maintenance cycles, the key is to ensure that you enable them again when you finish!

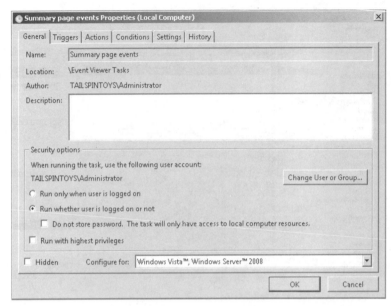

FIGURE 19-15: Run when logged off.

> ▶ **Delete an event-driven task:** Use Task Scheduler to delete an event-driven task if it is no longer useful or has become unnecessary.

> ▶ **Run a task:** This allows you to execute an Event Viewer task even if the conditions that generated the task haven't occurred. This is a good way of testing that the task works without having to use `eventcreate.exe`.

> ▶ **End:** Doing this allows you to forcibly terminate the task.

> ▶ **Export:** Rather than recreate the same tasks on all of the servers that you manage, you can use the export functionality to export the task definition to a shared storage location.

> ▶ **Import:** You can then use the Import function to import the pre-configured task.

▶ Administrators who use Event Viewer tasks often spend a lot of time hunting around Event Viewer to delete the tasks, because they forget that they can only delete these tasks using the completely separate Task Manager tool.

▶ Exporting and importing tasks is the simplest way of both ensuring that the same Event Viewer tasks are running on all of the servers in your organization and of backing up the Event Viewer tasks themselves.

GOING FURTHER WITH OPERATIONS MANAGER

System Center Operations Manager is designed specifically to assist administrators with the laborious task of dealing with events across hundreds, if not thousands of servers. If you only need to manage ten or so servers, you'll be able to use the techniques outlined in this chapter to stay on top of important events. If you need to manage 100 or 500 servers, you'll want to consider a product like Operations Manager, primarily because it will cost your organization more money in terms of your time to effectively manage a large number of servers using the techniques described than it will to purchase the appropriate Operations Manager licenses. That isn't to say that the techniques described in this chapter are ineffective, just that techniques that work well for managing less than 20 servers rarely work well if you need to manage several hundred.

When you deploy Operations Manager, you deploy special agent software to each computer that you want to manage. You also install special management packs on the Operations Manager server. Management packs are usually written or approved by a specific product team or third party organization to make note of those events generated by the product that are worthy of an administrator's attention. Put another way, Operations Manager contains a set of really good product-specific filters that trawl the event logs and forward the important ones to a central console so that you don't have to.

Operations Manager also allows you to set up remediation actions so that if certain events, like a service failure, occur, Operations Manager can connect to the monitored machine and attempt to automatically restart the service without requiring direct administrator intervention. Orchestrator, another product in Microsoft's System Center stable, can go even further than this; it uses event alerts generated in Operations Manager to trigger a chain of complex events, such as deploying an entirely new virtual machine infrastructure or altering a specific registry key.

SUMMARY

Windows Server 2008, Windows Vista, Windows 7, and Windows Server 2008 R2 all support advanced auditing policies. These 55 policies replace the nine general policies that were available in previous versions of the Windows operating system. The benefit of using one or more of these 55 policies is that you can be more specific about what events generate event log entries than you can be with one of the nine general categories. Event log filters allow you to view a selection of events in a particular log and are not persistent. Custom event log views allow you to view a selection of events across multiple logs. Custom event log views can be exported from one computer and imported on another. Event log subscriptions allow you to retrieve specific events from one or more separate computers as a method of centralizing those events for easy review. Event Viewer tasks allow you to execute a task when a specific event is written to an event log, which can include running a program or sending an e-mail message. System Center Operations Manager is an appropriate solution for managing event logs when you have to manage a large number of servers.

Further Links

Advanced Security Audit Policy Step-by-Step Guide

http://technet.microsoft.com/en-us/library/dd408940(WS.10).aspx

Advanced Security Auditing FAQ

http://technet.microsoft.com/en-us/library/ff182311(WS.10).aspx

Configure Computers to Forward and Collect Events

http://technet.microsoft.com/en-us/library/cc748890.aspx

Event ID

www.eventid.net/

Event Logs

http://technet.microsoft.com/en-us/library/cc722404.aspx

Performance and Resource Management

Chances are the first time that you become aware of a problem is not the first time the problem has occurred. This can make diagnosing the problem difficult, as cause can be a challenge to trace when you aren't precisely sure when the first "effect" occurred. For example, you might have updated a driver a couple of months ago but only noticed today that the hardware it controls is suffering intermittent failures. There are tools built into Windows Server 2008 R2 that can help with this, but if you are like most administrators, you probably aren't aware of their existence.

In this chapter, you learn some tricks to assist you with monitoring the performance and reliability of computers running the Windows Server 2008 R2 operating system. You learn not only how to determine whether a specific process causes the performance problem, but also how you can set up Windows Server 2008 R2 to take regular performance measurements, so you can view basic performance trends over time. You also learn how to correlate a particular system event, such as the installation of a driver or update with a decrease in system stability.

MONITORING POINT-IN-TIME PERFORMANCE

Sometimes you know a server is running slowly, but you don't know why. If you have been a systems administrator for a while, perhaps the first thing you do is log onto the server and run Task Manager. Right-clicking on the task bar and running Task Manager is an almost automatic response for anyone experiencing performance difficulties and has been using a Windows-based operating system in the last decade. The reason that Task Manager, shown in Figure 20-1, is often the first port of call is that it enables you to see the status of a particular server's CPU, how much memory is being used, what the status of running processes are, networking data, which users are currently logged on to the server, and which applications are currently open.

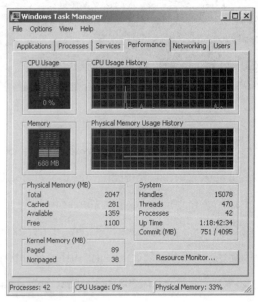

FIGURE 20-1: Task Manager

The drawback of Task Manager is that it is fairly basic in its functionality. Task Manager works great in terms of diagnosing the problem if a server runs slowly because an application is consuming all of the processor's capacity. Task Manager isn't great at determining whether a server is running slowly because of memory utilization problems, disk access problems, or network problems.

When you encounter an errant process, you can attempt to use Task Manager to reduce the priority of that process, or, if that doesn't work, you can sometimes, but not always, use it to forcibly terminate a task. To reduce the priority of a task, perform the following general steps:

1. Open Task Manager and navigate to the Processes tab.

2. Right-click the process, click Set Priority, and then click the priority that you wish to configure for the task, as shown in Figure 20-2.

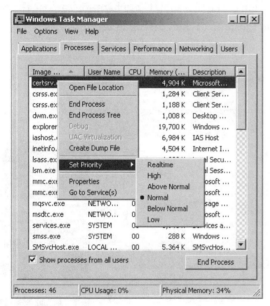

FIGURE 20-2: Task priority

The most reliable way to kill an errant task is with the taskkill.exe command-line utility. Taskkill.exe is more effective at terminating tasks than Task Manager. To use taskkill.exe, issue the tasklist.exe from an elevated command prompt to determine the name of the process that you want to terminate. You might have to use the command `tasklist.exe | more` if the list of tasks requires more than one screen to display all the tasks that are running on the server.

After you've determined the name of the task, you can use the taskkill.exe with the /f /im option to kill the task using its image name. Although you can kill based on process ID (PID), this can sometimes mean that you terminate a child process that is capable of respawning itself. Using the /im: option allows you to specify all instances of a task. The /f option forces the task to be terminated. For example, to kill all instances of the task iexplore.exe, issue the command:

```
Taskkill.exe /f /im:iexplore.exe
```

Using Resource Monitor

You can think of *Resource Monitor* as an extended version of Task Manager. Whereas Task Manager provides only basic reporting on tasks and processor utilization, Resource Monitor provides detailed information that allows you to break down CPU, disk, network, and memory utilization on the basis of process. For example, Figure 20-3 shows the Disk section of the Overview tab, where you can use the columns to sort process images on the basis of their disk read activity, disk write activity, or total activity.

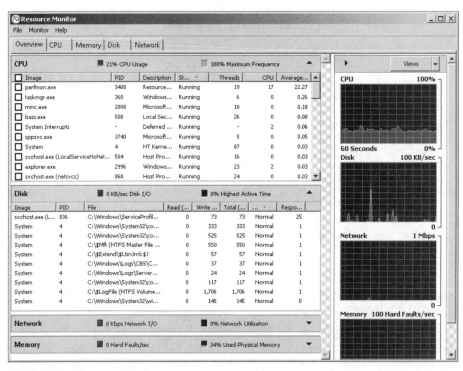

FIGURE 20-3: Resource Monitor

▶ This display is much more useful than Task Manager, because it allows you to see at a glance which server resource is the most congested.

The Overview tab allows you to view summarized CPU, Disk, Network, and Memory utilization information, and constantly updated displays that show utilization of each of these resources on a second-by-second basis. On the Overview tab, you can sort each of these categories by the following:

▶ **CPU:** Image, PID, Description Status, Threads, CPU, and Average CPU

▶ **Disk:** Image, PID, File, Read, Write, Total, I/O Priority, and Response Time

- **Network:** Image, PID, Address, Send, Receive, and Total
- **Memory:** Image, PID, Hard Faults, Commit (virtual memory), and Working (physical memory)

Once you've determined which of the resources on the server that you are investigating is under the most pressure, you can select the tab related to that resource for more information. These tabs provide the following information:

- **CPU:** From this tab, you can view Process, Services, Associated Handles, and Associated Modules information about tasks running on the CPU. You can use this tab to end a specific process, end the process tree, analyze the wait chain, and suspend or resume a process. Suspending and resuming processes can be more effective than terminating processes in some circumstances and should be tried before terminating a process.

- **Memory:** The Memory tab provides a bar graph displaying how memory is being used. This graph is shown in Figure 20-4. You can also select a process on this tab and perform the standard functions of ending it, ending the process tree, analyzing the wait chain, suspending the process, and resuming the process.

▶ Suspending and resuming a process is like giving it a good thump. A surprising number of things start working after you thump them. If the thump doesn't work, you can always kill the process.

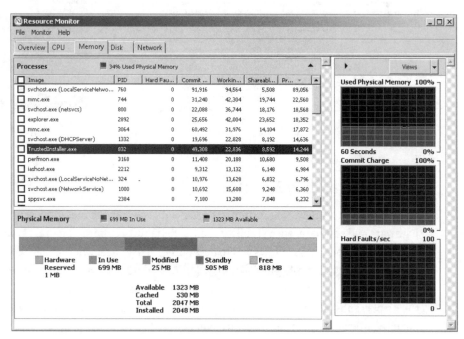

FIGURE 20-4: Memory tab

▶ **Disk:** The Disk tab gives you the ability to view the disk activity of specific processes. You can also view the disk activity of specific files to determine which ones are being read and written to the most. You can also associate these files with a specific process.

▶ **Network:** This tab allows you to diagnose network information. The first category allows you to view sent and received bytes against specific processes. On the Network Activity category, you can view the remote address of specific connections. On the TCP Connections tab, you can view local address and port, and remote address and port traffic. On the Listening Ports tab, shown in Figure 20-5, you can view information based on process, port, and firewall status.

A specific process might consume a disproportionate amount of processor resources, but the Network tab might show that process serves an unusual number of network connections. This can mean the problem is external to the server you are monitoring.

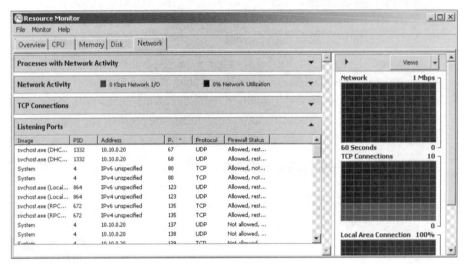

FIGURE 20-5: Listening Ports

Using Reliability Monitor

Reliability
Monitor is a great
tool for mapping
cause to effect.

Reliability Monitor allows you to map system events, such as the installation of new hardware and software, with stability events. Reliability Monitor is a great troubleshooting tool, because it allows you to determine, at a glance, whether a computer configuration change has led to a drop in system stability. For example, you might install a new graphics card driver on a server but not really notice that it is causing the display subsystem to restart regularly, because you log onto the server using Remote Desktop. Each of these restart events would be recorded in Reliability Monitor and an examination would indicate that the restarts began after the new graphics card driver was installed.

Reliability Monitor makes a calculation of the current system stability by looking at past stability events. If no problems have occurred in the last 28 days, the reliability index is set at 10, as shown in Figure 20-6. The less reliable the system is, the closer the reliability index drops toward a reading of zero. You can tell when a change has caused a problem with system reliability, because that's when the graph drops from a straight line at 10 to a jagged line as it charts problems.

▶ You can use Reliability Monitor as a quick way to assess system health. Rather than going through the event log looking for red X icons, if the Reliability Monitor event log isn't a straight line, you know the server has some problematic issues.

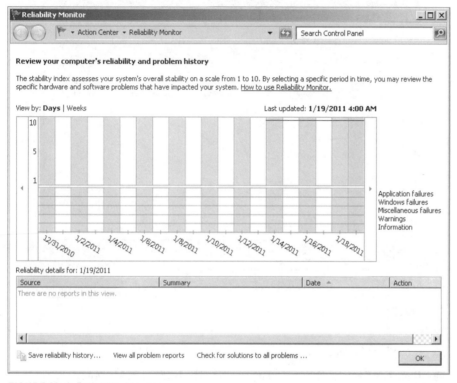

FIGURE 20-6: Reliability Monitor

When you install Windows Server 2008 R2, Reliability Monitor is available, but not enabled. You can enable Reliability Monitor on a computer running Windows Server 2008 R2 by performing the following steps:

1. Open the Task Scheduler and navigate to the Microsoft\Windows\RAC node.

2. Right-click the RAC node and, under View, ensure that Show Hidden Tasks is enabled.

3. Double-click RacTask in the Details pane.

4. Click the Triggers tab. Select the One Time Trigger, and then click Edit. This brings up the Edit Trigger dialog.

5. In the Edit Trigger dialog, check the Enabled box, and then click OK.

6. Verify that the RacTask Properties dialog box matches what is shown in Figure 20-7, and then click OK.

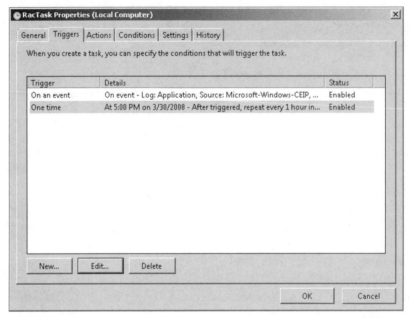

FIGURE 20-7: RacTask Properties

7. Close Task Scheduler.

8. Open the Registry Editor and navigate to the HKEY_LOCAL_MACHINE\ SOFTWARE\Microsoft\Reliability Analysis\WMI node. Set the WMIEnable key to 1.

9. Restart the server.

UNDERSTANDING DATA COLLECTOR SETS

Data Collector Sets allow you to collect and record performance information over a specific period of time, usually a minute. One of the advantages of the built-in Data Collector Sets is the "traffic light" approach. A big problem in performance monitoring is determining not only which performance counters to use—and there are hundreds of them—but also what the numbers reported by the performance counters actually mean. Depending on the performance counter, a reading that may indicate that there is a performance problem on one server might turn out to be unproblematic on another computer. By giving a "traffic light" green, yellow, or red indicator for a critical component such as CPU, Network, Disk, or Memory utilization, you can quickly determine whether a component is under resource pressure. You can access Data Collector Sets through the Performance Monitoring Console, shown in Figure 20-8.

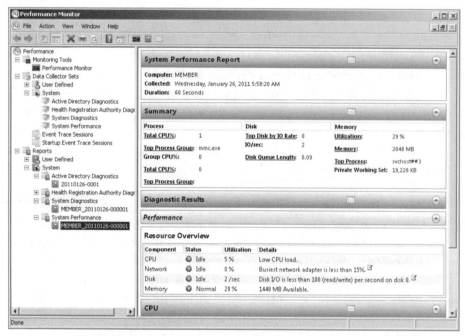

FIGURE 20-8: Performance Monitor

There are two general categories of Data Collector Sets: the user-defined Data Collector Sets, which are user-created sets that are usually based on an existing template; and the system Data Collector Sets, which are automatically installed when certain roles or applications are installed. These are covered in the next section.

Understanding System Data Collector Sets

Depending on which roles you have installed, there are up to four system Data Collector Sets that are available on computers running the Windows Server 2008 R2 operating system. When you install some applications, such as SQL Server 2008 R2, additional system Data Collector Sets are added. After you run a Data Collector Set, the output of those sets is written to the Reports node of the Performance Monitor console. These reports are stored in separate folders, and you can review them or back them up as necessary.

The system Data Collector Sets are as follows:

- **Active Directory Diagnostics:** This Data Collector Set provides you with information on Active Directory. Primarily useful on a domain controller, you can use this report to access how many requests the domain controller is responsible for handling over a period of 300 seconds. You should run this Data Collector Set if you want to determine whether your organization needs to deploy additional domain controllers for performance reasons.

- **Health Registration Authority Diagnostics:** This Data Collector Set provides diagnostics for the Health Registration Authority (HRA) role service. This role service is installed when you use the Network Access Protection (NAP) with IPsec enforcement technology. Running this Data Collector Set allows you to determine how well the HRA is performing and whether it is causing delays in providing certificates needed for network access.

> The drawback to this particular Data Collector Set is that it can often be difficult to determine whether a particular counter's value is noteworthy.

- **System Diagnostics:** This Data Collector Set monitors performance counters across a broad spectrum of the system to provide information about areas of the system that might be performing poorly. Rather than having to select individual performance counters, almost all the important ones are included in this Data Collector Set. When you review the output, you can filter out information that you are not interested in. Running this Data Collector Set is much faster than manually adding performance monitor counters, which involves a fair amount of mucking about, especially if you aren't certain which counters to add!

- **System Performance:** This Data Collector Set is the most useful, because the reports it generates display information in a simple-to-understand, traffic light format, as shown in Figure 20-9. Running this report on a regular basis allows you to create an ongoing set of measurements that you can use as a basic form of trend measurement. This Data Collector Set is covered in more detail in the next section.

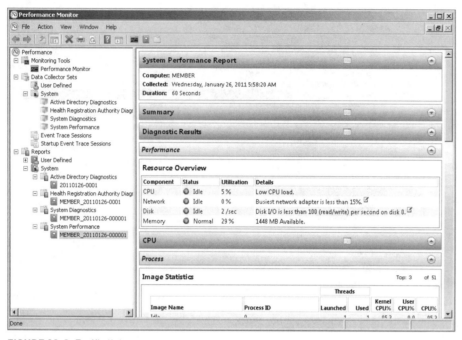

FIGURE 20-9: Traffic light report

GENERATING A SYSTEM PERFORMANCE REPORT

The System Performance report is by far the most useful of the included Data Collector Sets. This is because it contains detailed information about what processes are currently running on the server and how those processes influence CPU usage, memory consumption, disk access, and network utilization.

By right-clicking on the report and then clicking on View and then clicking on Folder, you can see the files that were generated by the report. This is useful, because the displayed report is stored in HTML format. This means that you can forward the report to the appropriate people when you need to argue that the server is under resource pressure.

The report also stores the performance counter readings over that period of time, so you can go back and look at the performance monitor readout over that period. You can also view the rules that were used to generate the report, which are stored in text format. The Folder View is shown in Figure 20-10.

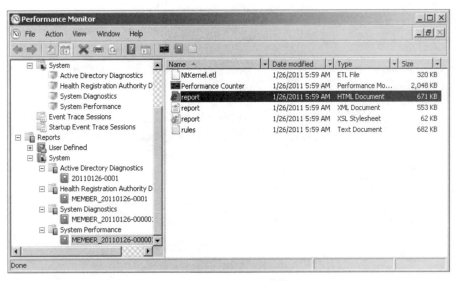

FIGURE 20-10: Folder view

The Systems Performance report contains the following information:

▶ **Summary:** Provides summary information, including the top process consuming the CPU, disk queue length, average memory utilization, and the process that consumed the most memory.

▶ **Diagnostic Result:** Gives an overview, in traffic light format, of the CPU, Network, Disk, and Memory with utilization information, as well as summary information specifying whether the CPU load is low, medium, or high; how busy the network adapters are; the average Disk I/O; and how much memory remains available.

▶ **CPU:** Allows you to drill down and view utilization information on the basis of Process, Service, Services and System.

▶ **Network:** Allows you to drill down and view information on the basis of Interface, IP, TCP, and UDP information.

▶ **Disk:** Allows you to view hot files, disk breakdown, and physical disk information.

▶ **Memory:** Allows you to drill down into process and counters information.

▶ **Report Statistics:** Provides you with general information about the report, such as when it started, duration, and the number of events that were processed.

SCHEDULING DATA COLLECTOR SETS

Although you can manually run a Data Collector Set, if you need the information right now, you might as well just open Resource Monitor and get the information directly. The only point in manually running a Data Collector Set is if you want a record of the information to study later. To manually run a Data Collector Set, right-click it in Performance Monitor, and then click Start. The Data Collector Set runs for a period of about a minute, and the information gathered is available in the reports section.

Data Collector Sets are most useful when you schedule them to be taken on a regular basis. To schedule a system Data Collector Set to be run on a periodic basis, you need to first create a custom Data Collector Set and then edit its properties to create a schedule. To create a schedule for the Systems Performance Data Collector Set, perform the following general steps:

1. Open Performance Monitor.

2. Right-click the Data Collector Sets\User Defined node, click New, and then click Data Collector Set. This launches the Create New Data Collector Set Wizard. Enter the name **System_Performance_ Custom** and ensure that Create from a Template is selected. Click Next.

3. On the Which Template Would You Like to Use page, click System Performance, and then click Finish.

4. Right-click the new System_Performance_Custom Data Collector Set, and then click Properties.

5. On the Schedule tab, shown in Figure 20-11, click Add.

6. On the Folder Action page, enter a beginning date, an expiration date, a start time and then select which days of the week you want the Data Collector Set to run.

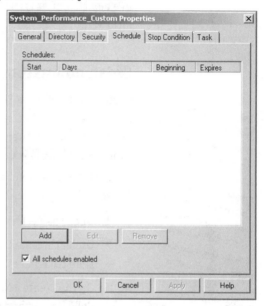

FIGURE 20-11: Schedule Data Collector

▶ If you want to have the Data Collector Set run at multiple times during the day, simply add additional schedules.

DETERMINING PEAK USAGE

You should be most interested in the performance of your server when it is under peak load. It doesn't really matter if the server that you are responsible for managing performs well during off-peak times if it becomes unresponsive to client requests during peak times. Of course, if you don't know when peak load is, performance monitoring through Data Collector Sets can allow you to determine when your server is under peak load. Generally, you'll have a suspicion about when this occurs, but unless you have hard data, you probably won't be sure.

To determine when your server is under peak load, create a temporary schedule where you run a Data Collector Set every 15 minutes during business hours in a normal working week. Check back and determine what times the server is under peak load. You may need to run this over the course of a month, as some servers, such as those used by Accounting, might be under extreme resource pressure only two days in a month; but, it is those two days of the month that the server really needs to perform well.

Creating Custom Data Collector Sets

Custom Data Collector Sets allow you to either customize the properties of an existing Data Collector Set, such as creating a schedule, or make a brand new collection of performance counters. The key to creating a new Data Collector Set is knowing which performance counters you want to record.

To create a custom Data Collector Set that is not based on one of the existing Data Collector Sets, perform the following tasks:

1. Open the Performance Monitor console.

2. Under the Data Collector Sets node, right-click User Defined, click New, and then click Data Collector Set.

3. On the Create a New Data Collector Set Wizard, enter a new name for the Data Collector Set and select the Create Manually option. Click Next.

4. On the What Type of Data Do You Want to Include page, shown in Figure 20-12, select the type of data that you wish to include. If you want to include only performance counter data, select that option. You can also include event trace information or system configuration information. Event trace information allows you to track a specific process. You can also configure a performance counter alert. A performance counter alert allows you to trigger a task when a performance counter reaches a particular threshold. For example, the system sends you an e-mail when the disk queue length exceeds a particular value.

▶ The drawback to creating custom Data Collector Sets is that you need to make sense of the counters, as your Data Collector Set won't tell whether a specific reading indicates that a resource is under a problematic amount of pressure or underutilized.

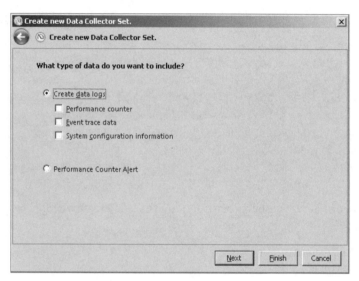

FIGURE 20-12: Schedule Data Collector

5. If you have chosen to record performance counter data, then add each performance counter to the Data Collector Set as appropriate. Choose a sample interval, and then click Next.

6. Specify the location where you want to have the Data Collector Set information saved, and then click Finish.

7. Once the Data Collector Set is created, you can then edit the properties of the Data Collector Set to configure an appropriate schedule.

USING WINDOWS SERVER RESOURCE MANAGER

Windows Server Resource Manager (WSRM) is a Windows Server 2008 R2 feature that allows you to allocate how resources on a server are distributed between sessions, processes, or users. You can think of them as "quotas for processors" rather than quotas for disk space. You can use WSRM to balance RD Session Host sessions, grant one specific user greater resources than other users, and configure which time resource policies come into effect. You can also use WSRM to perform process accounting, which allows you to audit which resources a particular process uses.

> **NOTE** I used to work with an accountant who performed sophisticated business calculations on a Terminal Services server every Thursday afternoon using a program that hooked into Excel. The calculations he performed were so intensive that they would peg the processor at near 100 percent utilization for almost two hours. The problem with this was that no one else in the office could use the server during those hours. His calculations and their results were so important to the business that everyone had to put up with him hogging the server every Thursday. If WSRM had been around when I was working with that guy, I could have used it to limit his level of processor utilization.

To install Windows Server Resource Manager, run the following PowerShell commands:

```
Import-Module ServerManager
Add-WindowsFeature WSRM
```

When installed, WSRM is available from the Administrative Tools menu. The key to understanding WSRM is the Resource Allocation Policies, which are shown in Figure 20-13.

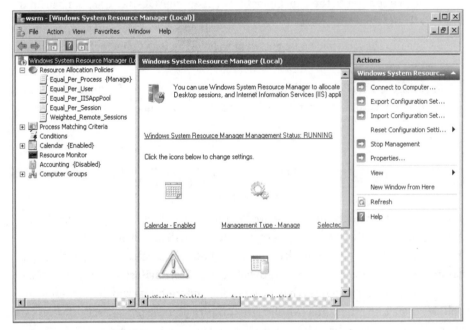

FIGURE 20-13: WSRM policies

WSRM ships with the following resource allocation policies:

▶ **Equal_Per_Process:** All processes that can be managed are given an equal share of the CPU.

▶ **Equal_Per_User:** Each user is allocated an equal amount of available CPU resources.

▶ **Equal_Per_IISAppPool:** Each IIS application pool is allocated an equal share of 99 percent of the available CPU resources. You can add and remove Web applications from application pools as a way of manipulating how load is distributed. For example, your server might have four Web applications.

▶ **Equal_Per_Session:** This policy works best on an RD Session Host Server where you can ensure that each session connected to the server is allocated an equal share of the available CPU resources. If a single user has multiple sessions, then each session is allocated an equal share of available resources.

▶ **Weighted_Remote_Sessions:** This policy allows you to assign weight to RD Session Host sessions based on which user account is connecting to the session. As Figure 20-14 shows, the priorities that you can allocate are Premium, Standard, and Basic.

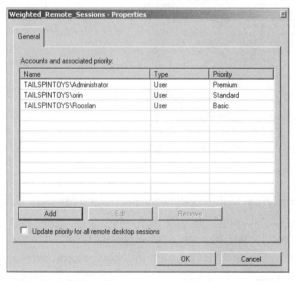

FIGURE 20-14: Weighted remote sessions

Policies only come into force when there is resource contention. For example, if you have the Equal_Per_Process policy in place, and there are five processes, but four of the processes only need 5 percent of available CPU capacity, the remaining process can utilize up to 80 percent of CPU capacity. If each of those five processes wants to use as much of the processor as possible, each is pegged at 20 percent capacity.

The following list describes how to perform some basic tasks with WSRM:

▶ **Apply a specific policy:** Right-click the policy that you want to apply, and then click Set As Managing Policy. You may have to restart the server to have the policy start to manage the server.

▶ **Exclude a specific application:** To exclude a particular application from being managed by WSRM, right-click the top node, titled Windows System Resource Manager (Local), and then click Properties. Click the Exclusion List tab, shown in Figure 20-15, and then click Add. Browse to the application that you want to add and then click OK.

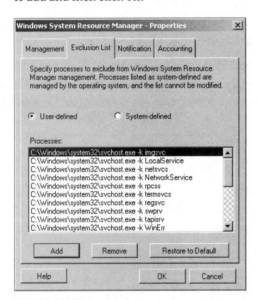

FIGURE 20-15: Application exclusion

▶ **To stop policies applying:** Right-click the top node titled Windows System Resource Manager (Local), and then click Stop Management. You cannot stop management if the Weighted_Remote_Sessions policy is set as the managing policy. You need to change policies before being able to stop policies applying.

▶ **To configure the calendar:** To configure the calendar to apply policies at different times, right-click the Calendar node and then click Enable. In the Actions pane, click New Schedule. This opens the New Schedule dialog. Enter a name for the schedule and then double-click to set a time and policy as shown in Figure 20-16.

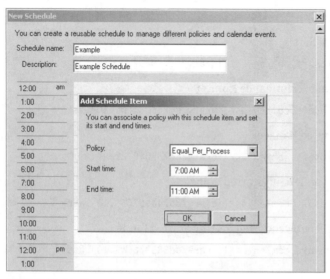

FIGURE 20-16: Example schedule

SUMMARY

Resource Monitor is like an extended version of Task Manager, except that it provides detailed information about current processor, memory, hard disk, and network utilization. You can use Resource Manager to determine the processes that consume the greatest resources, which can help you determine if one specific process is causing performance problems.

Reliability Monitor allows you to view a system stability ranking against system events, such as when applications and drivers are installed. This allows you to determine if the installation of a particular application or driver is related to an increase in the number of errors or problems.

Data Collector Sets allow you to collect performance data over an extended period of time. You can configure Data Collector Sets to record performance data at a certain time every day. This allows you to perform a basic sort of trend analysis, where you can then view how performance characteristics have changed over an extended period of time.

You can use Windows Server Resource Manager to manage how processor resources are allocated on a server. If you are running a Web server, you can use the Equal_Per_ IISAppPool to ensure that no single Web app pool dominates your resources.

Additional Sources

Creating Data Collector Sets

http://technet.microsoft.com/en-us/library/cc749337.aspx

Windows Reliability and Performance Monitor

http://technet.microsoft.com/en-us/library/cc755081(WS.10).aspx

Windows System Resource Manager

http://technet.microsoft.com/en-us/library/cc755056.aspx

Performance Monitoring Getting Started Guide

http://technet.microsoft.com/en-us/library/dd744567(WS.10).aspx

Resource Availability Troubleshooting Getting Started Guide

http://technet.microsoft.com/en-us/library/dd883276(WS.10).aspx

Index

allow rules, IP address and domain name filtering, 344

anonymous authentication, 340

answer files, for automating installation process, 24–26

anycast addresses, IPv6, 206

AppCmd.exe

  adding virtual directories, 335–336

  adding web site to existing server, 334

  adding/disabling default document, 343

  configuring site authentication, 341

  creating URL authorization rule, 346

  creating web applications, 337

  enabling directory browsing, 343

application pools

  adding web site to existing server, 333

  configuring recycling, 349–350

  creating, 348–349

  overview of, 348

  WSRM policies, 523

Application Virtualization (App-V), 436, 453

applications

  backing up, 310

  creating web applications, 336–337

  event logs, 493

  failover clustering and, 422–423

  recovering, 318–319

approver role, AGPM (Advanced Group Policy Management), 121

App-V (Application Virtualization), 436, 453

ASP.NET impersonation, 340

attack surface, reducing by use of Server Core, 52

audio files, FSRM file groups, 260–261

Audit Credential Validation policy, 492

auditing

  advanced policies, 490–492

  common categories, 486–489

  online resources for, 506

  overview of, 485–486

  for success and failure, 489

  summary, 505

authentication

  auditing account authentication failures, 489

  BitLocker features, 290

configuring for web sites, 339–341

creating exceptions, 230–231

creating server-to-server rules, 233–234

FTP and, 352, 354

inbound rules and, 226

IPSec settings and, 228–229

isolation rules and, 232–233

network access policies and, 475

Network Level Authentication, 40

RD Gateway clients, 467

RD Gateway servers, 462–463

tunnel rules and, 235

authoritative restore process, Active Directory, 104–107

Authority Information Access (AIA), 169

Authority Restore Wizard, 185

authorization

  of DHCP servers, 196–198

  of FTP, 353–354

  RD policies for, 450

  URL authorization rules, 345–346

autoconfiguration, of IPv6 addresses, 208

autoenrollment, in CAs, 181–182

automatic approvals, of updates, 388

automatic updates

  configuring, 392–393

  enabling, 60

  factors in, 394

availability. *See* high availability

B

backup catalog, recovering, 321

backup files, FSRM groups, 260

backups. *See also* recovery

  of applications, 310

  of certificate services, 184–185

  enabling shadow copies of shared folders, 313–316

  of GPOs, 129–131

  installing AD from, 101–102

  optimizing performance of, 312–313

  overview of, 303–304

  performing one-time backup, 305–308